The Middle East Military Balance
2000–2001

The BCSIA Studies in International Security book series is edited at the Belfer Center for Science and International Affairs at Harvard University's John F. Kennedy School of Government and published by The MIT Press. The series publishes books on contemporary issues in international security policy, as well as their conceptual and historical foundations. Topics of particular interest to the series include the spread of weapons of mass destruction, internal conflict, the international effects of democracy and democratization, and U.S. defense policy.

A complete list of BCSIA Studies appears at the back of this volume.

The Middle East Military Balance 2000–2001

Shai Feldman and Yiftah Shapir
Editors

BCSIA Studies in International Security

Jaffee Center for Strategic Studies
Tel Aviv University

The MIT Press
Cambridge, Massachusetts
London, England

Second printing, 2001

© 2001 by the Belfer Center for Science and International Affairs
John F. Kennedy School of Government, Harvard University
Cambridge, Massachusetts 02138
(617) 495-1400

All rights reserved. No part of this book may be reproduced, stored in a retrieval system, or transmitted in any form or by any means—electronic, electrostatic, magnetic tape, mechanical, photocopying, recording, or otherwise—without permission in writing from the Belfer Center for Science and International Affairs, 79 John F. Kennedy Street, Cambridge, MA 02138.

Library of Congress Control Number: 2001090018
ISBN: 0-262-06219-4

Jaffee Center for Strategic Studies
The purposes of the Jaffee Center are: first, to conduct basic research that meets the highest academic standards on matters relating to Israel's national security as well as to Middle East regional and international security affairs; and second, to contribute to the public debate and governmental deliberation of issues that are—or should be—at the top of Israel's national security agenda. The Jaffee Center seeks to address the community of scholars in the field of security studies in Israel and abroad, as well as Israel's policy-making and opinion-making elite and its public at large. The Center relates to the concept of strategy in its broadest sense, namely, the complex of processes involved in the identification, mobilization, and application of resources in peace and war, in order to solidify and strengthen national and international security.

This book was typeset in Isreal by Kedem Ltd., Tel Aviv, and was printed and bound in the United States of America.

Cover photo: Development Options for Cooperation: The Middle East/East Mediterranean Region 1996. Government of Israel, Jerusalem: August 1995.

Contents

Preface	9
Part I: Middle East Strategic Assessment / *Shai Feldman*	
Introduction	15
Chapter One: **General Trends in the Middle East 1990–2000**	17
Chapter Two: **Strategic Crossroads — The Peace Process**	27
Negotiating Peace	27
Palestinian-Israeli Negotiations	27
Syrian-Israeli Talks	34
The Status of Peace	38
Egyptian-Israeli Relations	38
Jordanian-Israeli Relations	41
Israel-Lebanon Relations: A New Era	43
Chapter Three: **Regional Issues and Global Interests**	47
Security in the Persian Gulf	47
Iraq: A Power Contained	47
Iran: Unresolved Struggle	51
Extra-Regional Players	56
US Policy: Engagement and Containment	56
Russian Policy: Defiance	59
Chapter Four: **Strategic Balances in the Middle East**	63
Toward an Arab-Israeli Net Assessment	63
The Strategic Balance in the Gulf	72
Summary	77

Contents *(continued)*

Part II: Military Forces / *Yiftah Shapir*

Introductory Note	83
1. Algeria	87
2. Bahrain	99
3. Egypt	109
4. Iran	129
5. Iraq	149
6. Israel	163
7. Jordan	185
8. Kuwait	195
9. Lebanon	205
10. Libya	213
11. Morocco	225
12. Oman	237
13. Palestinian Authority	249
14. Qatar	253
15. Saudi Arabia	263
16. Sudan	279
17. Syria	289
18. Tunisia	301
19. Turkey	309
20. United Arab Emirates (UAE)	329
21. Yemen	343

Contents *(continued)*

Tables and Charts

The Middle East Military Balance at a Glance	354
The Eastern Mediterranean Military Forces	356
The Persian Gulf Military Forces	360
The North African Military Forces	364

Glossary of Weapons Systems

Land Forces Equipment	371
Air Defense Equipment	394
Air Force Equipment	398
Navy Equipment	420

Abbreviations 422

Contributors 425

Preface

By late 2000, the Middle East once again witnessed bloodshed and peril. Until late 1999, peacemaking efforts in the region focused on Israeli-Syrian negotiations, with two US-sponsored negotiating sessions being held on December 15, 1999 in Washington and January 3–11, 2000 in Shepherdstown, West Virginia. Both failed, however, to bridge the gaps between the parties. President Clinton's attempt to mediate directly in a summit held with President Hafez al-Assad in Geneva in April 2000 proved similarly fruitless. Soon thereafter, in May 2000, Assad died and was replaced by his son Bashar.

Having failed to secure a withdrawal of its forces from south Lebanon within the context of an agreement with Syria, Israel decided on May 25, 2000 to withdraw unilaterally. The withdrawal was accompanied by considerable drama: the South Lebanese Army collapsed, allowing the de-facto takeover of south Lebanon by the Iranian-backed Hizbullah. The scenes of Israel's hurried withdrawal — with some equipment left behind — were not complimentary to the IDF, and concern was expressed over potential damage to Israel's credibility and deterrence capability. At the same time, Israel went from defying international institutions to obtaining UN approval and cooperation by conducting its withdrawal within the context of United Nations' Security Council Resolution 425.

Following the withdrawal, attention and energy were refocused on the Palestinian track. On July 5, 2000, President Bill Clinton agreed to Prime Minister Ehud Barak's repeated requests and invited Barak and Chairman Yasser Arafat to a fourteen-day summit at Camp David. There could have been no more poignant symbol of America's commitment to peace in the Middle East: not since President Jimmy Carter convened the first Camp David summit in 1978 has any president of the United States personally devoted as much time and energy to resolving an international conflict. While the meeting contributed greatly to narrowing the two parties' differences and helped break long-standing taboos, it did not end in a document defining the principles for an Israeli-Palestinian final status agreement.

During this period, US-Israeli relations, though essentially stable, went through an extremely rocky period, but improved dramatically later in the year. Beginning in late 1999, Israel experienced a two-pronged attack from the Clinton administration and Congress aimed at persuading the Barak government to cancel the sale of the "Phalcon"

Airborne Warning and Command System to China. In July 2000, Barak finally cancelled the sale, but not before Israel suffered scathing criticism, even from some of its closest allies in the US. Following Camp David II, relations between the two countries improved dramatically and reached a new high when Clinton praised Barak for the courage he displayed at the summit and hinted that Arafat was largely to blame for the failure to reach agreement.

In the Persian Gulf, Iraq continued to defy the UN Security Council's attempts to implement Resolution 687 and, with Russia's help, succeeded in blocking effective monitoring or inspections by a follow-on to the UNSCOM teams — the proposed UNMOVIC. Iraq also continued to test short-range ballistic missiles — a reminder that it had not lost interest in the ability to deliver weapons of mass destruction.

But more interesting developments took place in Iran where, in February, the reformists registered an impressive success in the elections to the Majlis. The magnitude of this victory triggered the conservatives to into action, leading them to curtail freedom of expression by closing some twenty pro-reform newspapers. While the internal struggle over the character of Iran continued, its defense community scored the first successful test of the Shahab-3, a 1300-kilometer range ballistic missile.

Finally, by the end of 2000, attention in the Middle East shifted once again to the Palestinian-Israeli conflict. Beginning in late September, Palestinian protests over Israel's continued control of large parts of the West Bank and the Gaza Strip evolved into large-scale violence. These protests included Palestinian use of terrorism against Israeli civilians and military personnel and the implementation of tough measures by the Israel Defense Forces in an effort to stem the violence. With negotiations between the parties near collapse, the danger of further escalation loomed higher than at any previous period since the signing of the 1993 Oslo Accords.

Thus, the Middle East at the end of the decade continued to be characterized by dynamic and dramatic political and military developments. These developments re-emphasized the importance of understanding the various facets and implications of the military balance in the region: standing armed forces, paramilitary organizations, weapons of mass destruction and ballistic missiles.

This volume of The Middle East Military Balance comprises two parts. The first provides the strategic context within which the inventories of the weapons possessed by the region's armed forces should be viewed. It analyzes the general trends characterizing developments in the region over the past ten years, revealing that most of these trends favored enhanced peace and security in the region. It then addresses the present strategic crossroads, explaining the open questions about the region's future in key realms — from the Arab-Israeli peace process to developments in the Persian Gulf. Finally, it attempts to provide a "net assessment" of the distribution of power in the Middle East.

The writing of Chapter Four took place in the wake of an important debate in Israel that followed the publication of last year's edition of The Middle East Military Balance. The debate focused on the measurement of military threat, contrasting the intelligence approach that emphasizes the potential capabilities of the sides, and a "net" approach that compares these capabilities with the means available to addressing the threats they pose.

The second part of this volume, compiled by Yiftah Shapir, provides the most detailed data available in open literature regarding the composition of the region's military forces. It is updated until early 2000. Since changes in the region's military balance rarely develop overnight, we expect the balance to remain accurate for most of 2001.

The Jaffee Center launched its study of military forces in the Middle East in the early 1980s. The first volume analyzing these forces was published in 1983 and, beginning in 1985, the volume was produced on an annual basis.

The Middle East Military Balance 2000–2001 is the second to be published by MIT Press in the framework of the BCSIA Studies in International Security. Previously they had been published in conjunction with the Jerusalem Post and Columbia University Press. The publication is yet another facet of the growing relationship between Tel Aviv University's Jaffee Center for Strategic Studies and the Belfer Center for Science and International Affairs at Harvard University's John F. Kennedy School of Government. We are grateful to Graham Allison, Director of the Belfer Center, and to Steven Miller, Director of the International Security Program at the Center, for having initiated the relationship that resulted in the production of this volume.

Finally, we would like to express our gratitude to those who made the preparation of this volume possible. Moshe Grundman, assistant to the Head of the JCSS, coordinated every aspect of completing this volume and bringing it to press; Hirsh Goodman, Jacqueline Hahn-Efrati, and Daniel Levine made an invaluable contribution in editing the text. Yoel Kozak and Tamir Magal performed the difficult task of compiling, updating and setting the data on the region's military forces; helpful assistance and comments were provided by JCSS researchers, research assistants and documentation managers, especially Orna Zeltzer, Tamar Malz and Avi Mor.

We are also deeply indebted to Karen Motley, Executive Editor at the Belfer Center, for the time and energy she invested in supervising the entire production process and for the extreme care and patience she demonstrated during the months that resulted in the publication of this volume.

Prof. Shai Feldman
Head of Jaffee Center for Strategic Studies

Tel Aviv
December 2000

PART I

MIDDLE EAST STRATEGIC ASSESSMENT

Shai Feldman

Introduction

The Middle East strategic balance continues to be tilted toward the forces favoring stability in the region. Most factors affecting the overall regional balance seem to have developed in recent years in ways that support accommodation among Middle East states. At the same time, as evidenced by the eruption of Palestinian-Israeli violence in late 2000, some important question marks remain regarding the region's future, and factors that threaten to disturb recent positive developments are gathering potency. Hence, while the prospects for near- and medium-term stability appear very promising at present, the danger of this being reversed is not trivial.

This section is divided into four chapters. The first analyzes the basic developments in the region and its international environment in the 1990s that account for the current outlook for the Middle East. It also notes some negative developments that have affected the region's stability. The second and third chapters describe the current crossroads. They elaborate the remaining question marks about the region's future and highlight the factors and considerations that may endanger stability in the Middle East over the next few years. The fourth chapter attempts to provide "net assessments" of Middle East strategic balances in the Arab-Israeli arena and the Persian Gulf. The chapter is designed to provide the reader with an Israeli perspective on the distribution of power in the Middle East, taking into account the overall military balance as well as other factors and developments, some of which are described in the first two chapters.

Chapter One
General Trends in the Middle East 1990–2000

Over the past ten years, the Middle East has witnessed a number of trends that encourage stability in the region. There are also good prospects that over the next few years these and other factors will play a dominant role in maintaining these trends. As the escalation of Palestinian-Israeli violence in late 2000 illustrated, this does not make the Middle East immune to bloodshed and war. However, it implies that many factors are currently operating to reduce the likelihood that such violence would escalate to a regional confrontation.

The most important positive developments that have affected the Middle East during the past ten years are the end of the Cold War and the dissolution of the Soviet Union. They eliminated at least one important source fueling the arms race in the region: the superpowers' desire to gain influence with the region's states, primarily through arms supplies. This was particularly true for the Soviet Union, which had few other means to compete with the economic and technological power of the United States. Moscow, therefore, was engaged in massive arms transfers to some Middle East states at extremely favorable financial terms.

The growing financial problems encountered by the Soviet Union in the mid-1980s had already forced Moscow to insist that the weapons it supplied be paid for in cash, bringing the era of discounted arms transfers to the Middle East to an end. This diminished the capacity of cash-poor countries like Syria to modernize their armed forces with continued procurement from Russia.

Furthermore, radical Arab leaders could no longer assume that the USSR would come to their assistance should the stability of their regimes come under threat. In the early 1970s, Moscow gave ample reasons for some Arab regimes to make this assumption: when Israel bombed strategic targets in Egypt during the War of Attrition, the USSR stationed an air defense division there. Also, during the later stages of the 1973 Yom Kippur War, the USSR signaled its willingness to intervene militarily on behalf of Syria, by ordering seven Soviet paratroop and airborne infantry divisions stationed in Poland and East Germany to prepare for their possible deployment in Syria.

Assessing that Moscow would intervene on his behalf if Damascus were threatened, President Hafez al-Assad could assume that if Syria attacked Israel and the results on the battlefield turned sour, his regime would survive the expected counterattack. This affected his calculations of the risks of war at the time, thus keeping the military option open. With the Soviet factor eliminated, Syria's assessment changed. Pursuing the peace process thus became a more sensible path, especially if limited aims — regaining territory conquered by Israel in 1967 rather than the elimination of the Jewish state — were to be pursued.

The second element in altering the strategic equation was the acceleration of the Arab-Israeli peace process in the aftermath of the Gulf War. In late 1991, the first comprehensive Middle East peace conference was convened in Madrid, launching bilateral negotiations between Israel and Jordan, the Palestinians, Syria and Lebanon. In early 1992, these were supplemented by multilateral discussions among Israel, the Palestinians, and thirteen Arab countries addressing regional, multilateral problems. The biggest advances were the historic breakthroughs reached between Israel and the Palestinians with the signing of the Oslo Accords in September 1993 and the peace treaty signed between Jordan and Israel in November 1994.

The cumulative strategic impact of these negotiations and agreements was to gradually diminish the number of states in the region that could be considered candidates for joining a war coalition against Israel. By the early 1990s the Egyptian-Israeli peace treaty had endured for over ten years; the Palestinians and Jordan were concluding peace agreements with Israel; and the Syrians (and as a by-product, the Lebanese) had entered into extensive negotiations with the Jewish state. Under these circumstances it became much less likely that the kind of war coalition that attacked Israel in 1973 could again be formed. The peace process has had another effect: the 1994 Jordanian-Israeli peace treaty contains a clause that bans the introduction of foreign forces into Jordan. This, in effect, transformed Jordan into a buffer between Israel and Iraq. At the very least, it made it clear that the entrance of such forces would comprise a serious violation of the peace treaty and would legitimize a strong Israeli military response.

The likelihood that Arab states would unite to launch an attack on Israel was further lessened by yet another factor: disunity in the Arab world. In August 1990, for the first time, one Arab state (Iraq) conquered another (Kuwait). In response, in early 1991, a coalition that included Egypt, Syria and Saudi Arabia was formed to confront Iraq, supported in various degrees by Jordan, the PLO, Yemen and Sudan. Currently, rivalry continues between Syria and the PLO, as does the competition for influence among Syria, Egypt, and Iraq. Thus, for all practical purposes, "the Arab world" as a unifying concept has became largely meaningless.

The relatively low price of oil for most of the 1990s also had a profound impact on the region, primarily in limiting the ability of oil producing states to pursue the arms race. The drop in oil prices during the second half of the 1980s and most of the 1990s was due to a surplus of energy reserves. Between 1992–1998, the average price of oil was $18.1 a barrel. This contrasted sharply with the $31.5 a barrel that oil producers charged on average between 1974–1980. The consequence of these lower oil prices was that surplus funds were not available to fuel another arms race in the region. For example, these prices limited Syria's oil revenues and prevented Saudi Arabia and the Gulf States from subsidizing Syria's arms acquisitions.

The abundant availability of oil had another effect: Arab states could no longer use it as a political weapon. Put simply, the existence of an oil surplus, much of it held by non-Arab members of OPEC (and some by states which were not even OPEC members), diminished the possibility of using the threat of withholding oil supplies as leverage. The combined effect of the expanding peace process and the oil glut meant that an oil embargo against Israel was no longer relevant.

The arms race in the Middle East during the 1990s was further slowed by the effective arms embargo and economic sanctions exercised by the international community against Iraq. As a result, since the end of the Gulf War, Saddam Hussein has been prevented from restoring his conventional forces, which suffered serious attrition during the war. Sanctions have been particularly detrimental to the backbone of Saddam's regime, the Republican Guard and the Iraqi air force.

Similarly, the combined effect of low oil prices and the embargo exercised against Iran prevented significant modernization of its armed forces after the end of the Iran-Iraq War. As a result, the two countries most committed to changing the strategic landscape of the Middle East lacked the means to acquire the military capacity required for implementing such changes throughout the 1990s.

The improvement in economic conditions toward the end of the decade in some of the region's states played a role in increasing domestic stability. Almost without exception, states reduced their defense expenditures and at the same time diverted resources from security to social issues. Even with the steep rise in oil prices at the end of the 1990s, the hard currency earned by some of the Arab states and Iran was funneled into domestic priorities.

The consequence of these developments has been an improvement in the economies of some of the Arab states and Iran in recent years. This upturn was especially apparent in countries directly affected by oil revenues such as Iran, Iraq and Saudi Arabia, as well as smaller exporters and countries heavily dependent on remittances transferred home by their citizens employed in the oil producing states. For example, Egyptians employed abroad transfer home some $3 billion annually. Such remittances also constitute the main source of foreign currency for Syria and Jordan.

In addition, a number of states in the Middle East have succeeded in effecting a decline in birth rates, although they remain high by Western standards. The best example is Egypt, where birth rates fell from 3.2 percent in the 1980s to about 2 percent in 1999. This created some hope that economic development might outpace population growth in the Arab world.

Another element contributing to regional stability in the 1990s has been the slower than anticipated pace with which Arab states and Iran have acquired weapons of mass destruction (WMDs) and the means of delivering them. In that vein, the monitoring regime applied against Iraq throughout most of the 1990s by the United Nations Special Commission (UNSCOM) effectively prevented it from rebuilding its chemical weapons industry and its sensitive nuclear facilities.

Iran's development of WMDs was also somewhat slower than analysts had predicted in the mid-1990s. In January 1995, Iran signed a framework agreement with Russia regarding the completion of its nuclear complex in Bushehr and a specific contract for the completion of a 1000 Mw pressurized water power reactor there. But the implications for a military nuclear program remain uncertain because this type of reactor is particularly unsuitable for the production of weapons-grade material. There is little doubt that Iran is continuing its efforts to develop a military nuclear option, a goal supported by both reformist and conservative elements within the regime. However, intelligence agencies that follow developments in Iran closely have not located a uranium enrichment plant or a plutonium-reprocessing plant that would enable Iran to produce fissile material.

There were also no dramatic changes during most of the 1990s in the realm of ballistic missile proliferation. The end of the Gulf War left Iraq with only a small number of surface-to-surface missiles and missile launchers hidden in different locations. While far from perfect, the United Nations' weapons monitoring program, coupled with the sanctions applied against Baghdad, prohibited it from constructing and testing rockets and ballistic missiles with ranges that exceed 150 kilometers, thus severely hampering its efforts to rebuild its ballistic missile force. By contrast, the Iranian ballistic missile program showed some progress. In mid-1998, the first flight test of the 1300-km range Shahab-3 missile took place, but it was considered a failure. Two years later, on July 15 and on September 21, 2000, two additional tests were conducted, this time with somewhat better results.

Syria possesses a ballistic missile force that includes twenty-six launchers for Scud B and Scud C missiles, and another eighteen launchers for more accurate short-range SS-21s. It should be noted that the number of launchers it possesses has remained constant since 1993. In the year 2000 there may have been some development in the Syrian ballistic missile force structure with the reported acquisition of a number of 700-kilometer range Scud D missiles. There is no evidence, however, that this has increased the total number of launchers in the Syrian inventory. (Scud B, C, and D missiles use the same launcher.)

The more dramatic change in this realm has taken place in Egypt's ballistic missile order-of-battle. During the 1990s, the number of Scud B launchers has increased from nine to twenty-four. Unconfirmed reports claim that Egypt also acquired technology from North Korea for assembling ballistic missiles indigenously.

Throughout the decade, the United States remained fully engaged in Middle East affairs, contributing greatly to regional stability. America has been involved in peacemaking in the Near East since the 1960s, with different administrations manifesting different styles. During this decade, involvement in the Arab-Israeli sphere has been continuous from the Madrid Conference in 1991 to the Camp David II summit in July 2000.

In the Persian Gulf, the US continued implementing its policy of "Dual Containment," articulated at the beginning of the decade. This doctrine calls for achieving stability in the Gulf not by balancing Iraq and Iran against one another, but by containing each of them separately and preventing them from expanding their control and influence in the Persian Gulf and beyond.

Although not widely perceived as such, dual containment has proven successful. Iraq's power has been checked. It cannot rebuild its conventional forces or unconventional capabilities. As a result it neither poses a real threat to its neighbors, thus making another invasion of Kuwait inconceivable, nor can it reassert its sovereignty over the northern territories controlled by the Kurds.

The policy equally contained Iran. Indeed, with the exception of the growing influence of the Hizbullah in Lebanon, the export of the Iranian revolution scored no successes. At home, the economic sanctions applied against Iran may have had a visible impact. If the electoral victory of the reformists was derived to some extent from general discontent over the poor state of Iran's economy, sanctions that exacerbated the situation may have played a role in the successes of Khatami and of the reformist candidates to the Majlis, the Iranian parliament.

The success of America's policy of dual containment and an array of domestic and regional factors combined to have an important effect on the stability of the Middle East by arresting extremism in the region. If the 1980s were characterized by a general fear that Iran's revolution was "a sign of things to come," in the 1990s it became increasingly clear that Islamic extremism had been largely contained and failed to topple secular Arab regimes. The influence of political Islam as a global movement seemed also to have been stymied. The regimes of Iran, Afghanistan, and Sudan apparently failed to set an example worth emulating.

The government of Algeria survived, despite the prevailing assessment in the West a decade ago that its days were numbered. Also, despite the success of the extremists in carrying out spectacular acts of terrorism that caused grave damage to Egypt's economy, especially to foreign tourism, they failed to mount a serious challenge to the Mubarak regime. Using different methods and approaches, Jordan, Morocco, Tunisia, and the Palestinian Authority have also been successful in checking their respective Islamic movements.

One consequence of the above was that by the end of the 1990s, the Middle East experienced a significant decline in international terrorism. There was no repeat of the spectacular airplane hijackings of the early 1970s or other acts of international terror of the 1980s, although attacks by Hamas and Islamic Jihad groups against Israeli civilians succeeded in causing a temporary suspension of the Israeli-Palestinian peace process in 1996. This was seen as a major threat to Middle East stability and to US interests in the region. As a result, the Sharm el-Sheikh summit was convened in March 1996, with President Bill Clinton presiding over the most important international gathering ever assembled for the specific task of combating terrorism.

At that time, fear grew that the veterans of the war in Afghanistan — the so-called "Afghan Alumni" — would cause havoc in the Middle East. The bombings of the Khobar Towers in Saudi Arabia in June 1996, and of US embassies in Nairobi and Dar es-Salaam in August 1998, exacerbated fears that determined and well-financed terrorists, lead by extremists like Osama bin-Laden, would spread death and destruction throughout the region.

By the beginning of the millennium, however, this threat had not materialized and terrorism in the Middle East seemed to have been contained. This can be accounted for by a number of factors in the aftermath of the summit: cooperation among the intelligence agencies of the region's different states; cooperation between some of these states and the intelligence agencies of Western countries — primarily the US; internal security measures taken by some countries of the Middle East; and clear indications provided by the US that it would not tolerate terrorist attacks against its citizens.

For example, the Palestinian Authority's greater willingness to take severe action against Hamas following the wave of suicide bombings in early 1996 and increased cooperation between the Palestinian and Israeli security services that evolved after these events combined to curtail terrorism conducted by Palestinian extremists against Israel. Similarly, the retaliatory bombings conducted by the US against suspected terror sites in Sudan and Afghanistan — whether or not these facilities were actually connected to terrorist organizations — clearly signaled that the US would be willing to go to considerable lengths to punish perpetrators of terrorist acts. The priority given to combating terrorism by the US was critical to bringing about a sharp decline in state-sponsored terrorism in the Middle East.

This priority was manifested in the US bombing of Libya in April 1986 and the sanctions imposed against Tripoli in the aftermath of the Lockerbie affair. The US also made the support of terrorism a litmus test for improved relations with Washington. Thus, better relations with both Syria and Iran were made contingent on an improvement of their behavior in this realm. The loss of their Soviet patron — following the dissolution of the USSR — also played a role in deterring Syria and Libya from continuing to initiate and support terrorist activities.

As a result, by the end of the 1990s there was considerable evidence that Middle East states had opted out of sponsoring terrorism. The most dramatic example is Libya. In recent years there has been no evidence of Libyan involvement in terrorism abroad. It appears that the price extracted for such sponsorship was now too high and the benefits too low.

In addition to the decline in political extremism and international terrorism, the Middle East has witnessed in recent years yet another important facet of regional stability: smooth successions experienced by a number of the region's states. Israel experienced an orderly transition, following the shock entailed by the murder of Prime Minister Yitzhak Rabin in 1995, its first political assassination. Also at least two Middle East monarchies and one republic have experienced orderly successions: in Jordan, Prince Abdullah assumed the crown following the death of his father King Hussein Ibn Talal in February 1999, with little apparent difficulty. Similarly, in July 1999, Prince Muhammad succeeded King Hassan in Morocco. In Syria, Dr. Bashar al-Assad was approved on July 10, 2000 as the successor to his father, Hafez al-Assad, who had ruled Syria during the previous thirty years. Although the change in Syria has only begun to be felt, all four examples demonstrate that governments in the Middle East have experienced much easier transitions than the region's image as a hotbed of instability could have led one to expect.

Coupled with these positive regional trends, there are a number of factors that threaten Middle East stability, primarily the serious economic difficulties from which most of the region's states suffer and the resulting deep poverty experienced by the large populations of the Middle East. Despite some improvement in some countries, most of the region has yet to embark on a path of stable and rapid economic growth. The development of industries in most of these countries is slow, as are the growth of the private sector and the pace of economic reforms. Birth rates have remained high in most Arab states (an average of 3 percent, with the exception of Egypt), as have the unemployment rates (15 percent in Syria and 25 percent in Jordan).

These factors affect a second source of potential instability in the Middle East: the social conditions of the region's states with widespread poverty provide a constant breeding ground for movements challenging the legitimacy of the ruling regimes. Despite the rise in oil prices, the economic stagnation from which these countries suffer does not give cause to believe that this situation will be alleviated any time soon. Thus, while political Islam has been checked and forces of extremism contained, the underlying economic and social conditions in the region's states continue to have the potential of producing forces and movements that could undermine stability.

Israel has also experienced the rise of movements challenging the legitimacy of its government, particularly its legal system. The Shas party, representing a mainly religious, hawkish Sephardi constituency of Jews of Middle Eastern and North African origin, presents a growing challenge to the largely secular Ashkenazi Jews of European origin, who comprise the country's dovish elite and have enjoyed much of the control of the nation until now.

The rise of Shas was only part of a wider social evolution in Israel. In the late 1990s, Israel experienced increased fragmentation of its political system and social fabric. Electoral reform legislation approved by the Knesset (the Israeli parliament) in 1992 — allowing for separate direct elections of the prime minister and the Knesset — was a hybrid of a parliamentary system based on proportional representation and a semi-presidential system. As it soon turned out, the system produced the worst of both worlds: a highly fragmented legislature and an executive that cannot obtain the requisite support of parliament for any desired program. By mid-2000 this resulted in an almost total paralysis of the government's social and economic reform policies.

At the same time, the Israeli party system has become dramatically weaker, losing any capacity to mediate between the population and its elected leaders. The Knesset has come to amplify, rather than ameliorate, the growing divisions in Israeli society: rich and poor; hawks and doves; religious and secular; Ashkenazi and Sephardi; Jew (majority) and Arab (minority); immigrants and native born. The resulting rifts have increased the difficulty in creating and managing coalitions across these divides and have raised growing doubts as to whether Israel's current political system is tenable. Specifically, these rifts contributed to the rapid deterioration of two Israeli governments: that led by Benjamin Netanyahu in 1999 and that led by Ehud Barak in late 2000.

Israel's amplified social divisions, ironically, have emerged partly as a result of its improved regional posture. Israelis' perception that the existential threat against them has diminished has led to a slackening of national cohesion and increasing national tensions. Issues dating back to the 1950s but not discussed due to the preponderance of outside threats are now being openly aired. The flow of talented Israelis into the private sector, given the reduced importance of defense, has led to a decline in the quality of the public sector which is now less able to deal with the problems, thus generating further frustration among the public.

As the dramatic escalation of Palestinian-Israeli violence in late 2000 demonstrates, renewed terror could also be a potential source of disruption. While terrorism in the Middle East was contained in the late 1990s, it was by no means eradicated. In the mid-1990s, two developments set the stage for future efforts by extremists. The assassination of Prime Minister Rabin in 1995 created a precedent in Israel: for the first time a senior leader fell victim to domestic terrorism. The assassination resulted in a strategic change, since Rabin's successor, Shimon Peres, was unable to continue the peace process they jointly launched in 1993. In addition, the wave of suicide bombings conducted by the Islamic fundamentalist Hamas organization in early 1996 were widely interpreted as contributing to Peres' subsequent electoral defeat. The policies pursued by his successor, Benjamin Netanyahu, resulted in a considerable slowdown in the peace process. Thus, terrorism served the strategic goal of its perpetrators: to stop the peacemaking efforts.

In the next few years the Middle East may also witness instability resulting from the reemergence of issues kept dormant by the long period of conflict and war. For example, Israel's withdrawal from Lebanon and parts of Gaza and the West Bank — and in the future, possibly from the Golan Heights as well — may result in a reinvigorated Lebanese demand for the withdrawal of Syrian forces from Lebanon. At that point, resistance by Damascus may breed wider tension as the Arab states and Iran would have to decide between supporting Syria's or Lebanon's demands.

In summary, as the Middle East entered the new millennium, it seemed that the region was more stable than ever. The superpower that was once willing to underwrite some of the region's more radical regimes had disappeared; the Arab-Israeli peace process had added more and more states to the list of countries opposing conflict and war; the degree of disunity in the region had reduced the likelihood that a new anti-Israel war coalition would emerge; oil revenues were no longer used to fuel the Middle East arms race; America's dual containment policy toward Iraq and Iran proved effective; no country in the region matched Iraq's previous achievement in obtaining weapons of mass destruction; and Islamic fundamentalists did not succeed in toppling governments. Moreover, the US has remained engaged in combating extremism and terrorism in the Middle East and the none of region's states seem to continue to view the sponsorship of violence as rewarding.

A related effect of these developments is growing recognition among the states of the Middle East that conflicts and disputes must be resolved through peaceful means. This increased awareness is primarily the result of recognition by the Arab states that Israel cannot be defeated militarily; that the cumulative costs of the continuation of the conflict are considerable; and that the damage caused by the wars in the Gulf over the past two decades was immense. Israel, for its part, recognized that it could not control civilian populations — Palestinian and Lebanese — by force.

A number of long-term problems in the region, however, continue to fester, derailing progress toward greater stability and peace. Dire economic conditions continue to create the conditions for social movements that challenge the legitimacy of existing regimes. Political and social developments encouraged movements and organizations to revert to acts of terror that, in turn, undermined the prospects for future cooperation among the security services — the same cooperation that accounted for limiting terror in the late 1990s. Finally, further progress in peace and reconciliation between Israelis and Arabs — if achieved — may reopen other issues that lie dormant as long as the Arab-Israeli conflict remains center stage.

Chapter Two
Strategic Crossroads — The Peace Process

By late 2000 it has become evident that the trends elaborated in the first chapter do not guarantee a more stable strategic environment in the future. This is because it is far from certain that the developments described earlier will continue to unfold in a linear fashion, and because other factors may be coming into play to undermine whatever semblance of stability was achieved at the end of the 1990s.

While at the moment the factors favoring regional stability seem stronger than the challenges facing it, it should be recognized that the Middle East is approaching a number of strategic crossroads that will determine the region's fate. Together they will comprise the strategic landscape of the Middle East in the next decade. It is within the context of this new contour that the balance of military forces portrayed in the second section of this volume and assessed in the fourth chapter of this section should be viewed.

Negotiating Peace
The most challenging task is to assess the opportunities and risks associated with the Middle East peace process. This is because no other realm has experienced as many breakthroughs and setbacks, so many hopes and disappointments. It is also because it is extraordinarily difficult to predict how the leaders of the different countries and parties involved will assess the potential costs and benefits they face. This is compounded by the fact we do not fully understand all the factors and considerations that have previously hindered efforts to bring negotiations to a successful conclusion, let alone their relative importance in causing the failure of negotiations thus far.

Palestinian-Israeli Negotiations
In early summer of 2000, Israeli Prime Minister Ehud Barak persuaded US President Bill Clinton to make a major effort to bridge the gap between Israeli and Palestinian

positions regarding the principles for reaching a final status agreement. Both Barak and Palestinian Authority Chairman Yasser Arafat entered the Camp David II summit in July 2000 with considerable uncertainty regarding the possible outcome. Indeed, in the weeks prior to the meeting both parties invested as much energy in preparing their respective publics, government officials and security forces for a probable failure of Clinton's efforts as they did in planning how a positive breakthrough could be achieved.

Barak has noted on a number of occasions why, in his view, there was no reason to wait a few more years before attempting to reach an Israeli-Palestinian final status agreement, having argued that there was little, if anything, about this dispute that was not already known. Israelis and Palestinians have lived alongside one another since the inception of Zionism, and their interactions were intensified after the Six Day War. Over the years, the two leaderships have studied each other's domestic political environment, this being especially true for the Palestinians who have become keen observers of the Israeli domestic scene.

The gaps between the parties were also quite clear on the eve of the Camp David II summit. During the months and weeks leading up to the summit, considerable efforts were made to map out and define positions on all key issues to be negotiated. The magnitude of the concessions that both leaders were required to make if an agreement was to be reached was also clear. There was little doubt that these concessions would be monumental and that the task of obtaining domestic support for them would be the most difficult challenge ever faced by either Barak or Arafat.

It also appeared that support for far-reaching concessions was greater among the people of the two sides than among their respective policy elites. While there was great division within Israeli and Palestinian governing circles, the public on both sides displayed cumulative fatigue over the possible continuation of the conflict. In Israel this was reflected in wide public support for a grand bargain — provided it would truly result in an end to the conflict. Among the Palestinians there was a strong desire to see an end to the daily humiliation caused by Israel's continued occupation and to focus on their economic well-being.

The importance that both parties attached to symbols was also clear. Some issues — notably border demarcation, security arrangements and the distribution and control of water resources — were extremely difficult, yet subject to practical compromise. Other issues, for example the Palestinian "Right of Return" and sovereignty over Jerusalem, presented obstacles that far exceeded the practical matters involved. Whatever solution would be found for Jerusalem needed to accord with the Israelis' claim that the city must remain undivided and with the Palestinians' demand for sovereignty in the city. Equally, whatever answer would be found for the Palestinian refugees, Barak needed Arafat to declare it as exercising the

Palestinians' "Right of Return", while at the same time ensuring that Arafat was not accused of betraying the Palestinian Diaspora. Without resolution on these issues, neither party was likely to consider the file as closed.

It was also clear that Israeli and Palestinian negotiators would be approaching one another from fundamentally different philosophical perspectives. For Israelis who take their pre–1967 state for granted, the negotiations were about the fate of the West Bank and Gaza. Hence, from their standpoint, accepting that over 90 percent of these territories would be returned to form the Palestinian State seemed a huge concession. By contrast, for the Palestinians to accept the State of Israel within its pre–1967 territory was considered already a monumental concession, implying that they had already conceded some 78 percent of Palestine. Consequently, to them every square kilometer of the area that remained subject to negotiation seemed "essential". This philosophical gap made compromise — especially regarding the crucial territorial issue — extremely difficult.

On the eve of Camp David II, at issue was not whether the two parties' able negotiators could find practical compromises to the various dimensions of the dispute, but rather whether the two leaders — Barak and Arafat — could master the political will needed to make the historic compromises necessary to end conflict. Thus, what remained highly uncertain was whether the two were prepared to face their respective publics and present not only the hopes and aspirations associated with Israeli-Palestinian peace but also the very painful concessions that such an agreement would entail.

On the eve of the Camp David II summit, both Barak and Arafat were yet to make up their minds as to whether they were prepared to take the final step. For Barak the alternatives seemed clear: should Camp David fail to produce an agreement he could market to the Israeli public, he at least would have demonstrated to his domestic constituents, his American supporters and hosts, and the international community that he had made every effort to reach such an agreement. For Arafat the situation also appeared clear: he had given Clinton another chance to achieve an Israeli-Palestinian breakthrough; if it failed he would be able to demonstrate to his constituency that he had managed to defy the combined pressure of Israel and the US and to refuse to surrender Arab historical rights.

An accurate assessment of the present crossroads in Palestinian-Israeli negotiations also requires an appreciation of the long distance that both parties have already traveled toward one another. For decades, Palestinians have rejected any notion that Israel should be considered an acceptable feature of the Middle East. The Palestinian national movement rejected the various proposals advanced for the partition of Palestine, from the Peel Commission plan of 1937 to the UN General Assembly Resolution of November 1947. The Zionist movement initially treated

Palestine as if it were unpopulated. It later changed its position, but even after statehood in 1948, Israel continued to ignore the existence of a Palestinian national movement.

The first breakthrough in Palestinian-Israeli relations did not come until the 1978 Camp David Accords signed between Egypt and Israel. In their framework, Israel recognized for the first time "the legitimate rights of the Palestinian people" and contemplated granting an "autonomy" to the Palestinians residing in the West Bank and Gaza. Yet until 1988 Israel and the PLO continued to reject one another's legitimacy. Only then did the Palestinian National Council, striving to be recognized by the US, adopt a "Two State Solution" to the Palestinian-Israeli conflict, calling for the establishment of an independent Palestinian State alongside Israel. But Israel, regarding the establishment of such a state as a mortal danger, offered the Palestinians autonomy, which they refused to accept unless predicated on a commitment (by Israel, the US, or both) that it would be a short step on the road to independent statehood.

The first intifada (the Palestinian popular uprising), which began in 1987, altered Israeli perceptions. The costs entailed in controlling the uprising caused many Israelis to recognize that ruling a large Palestinian population indefinitely against its will was not a feasible long-term proposition. Indeed, by the early 1990s, left-wing Israelis who sought an accommodation with the Palestinians were joined by many constituents of right-wing parties who supported a solution that promised to separate Israel from its Palestinian neighbors.

The Oslo Accords negotiated in 1993 codified the first major narrowing of Palestinian-Israeli differences. For the first time, the Palestinians accepted a phased solution that was not predicated on a formal commitment that the end product of the process would be an independent Palestinian state. The PLO also undertook to end all forms of violence against the Jewish state. Israel agreed to transfer control over parts of the West Bank and Gaza to Palestinian control. It also recognized the PLO as representing the Palestinians and, as such, its partner in Palestinian-Israeli peacemaking.

The implementation of the Oslo Accords did not result in the expected development of mutual confidence and trust between Israelis and Palestinians. Moreover, the accords stipulated that the most sensitive issues at dispute between the two peoples — borders, Jerusalem, the settlements, and refugees — were left to be resolved later. Nonetheless, by the end of the 1990s the implementation of the Oslo Accords and various interim agreements resulted in a considerable narrowing of the gaps dividing the two parties. With the creation of the Palestinian Authority, it became increasingly clear that the establishment of independent statehood was only a matter of time.

The progress gradually made toward narrowing Israeli and Palestinian differences received a further dramatic boost at Camp David II. For the first time, Israel accepted the creation of an independent Palestinian state. It also agreed that some Israeli settlements in the West Bank and Gaza would have to be abandoned, dismantled or left under Palestinian sovereignty. Reportedly, Israel also indicated that it was willing to contemplate a very limited return of Palestinian refugees to Israel, in the framework of "family reunification," and to contribute to an international fund that would be set up to help settle Palestinian refugees and to compensate them for lost land. The Palestinians for the first time accepted that Israeli withdrawal would be to a line short of the pre–1967 borders, provided that they obtain, in the framework of a "swap," land in pre–1967 Israel equal in size and quality. With this, they also acknowledged that the most populous Israeli settlements in the West Bank would be annexed by Israel. Considerable progress was also made on the future economic relations between the two entities.

Differences over Jerusalem were also narrowed. The Palestinians accepted permanent Israeli sovereignty over the Jewish Quarter and the Wailing Wall in the Old City. Israel, on its part, agreed to Palestinian sovereignty over sections of Jerusalem proper, including a large part of the Old City, and conceded that the Palestinians could have institutions of state in Jerusalem.

Yet the gaps between the two parties' positions remained wide. On Jerusalem, the Palestinians rejected an American proposal that sovereignty of the Old City be divided, with Israel retaining sovereignty over the Jewish and Armenian Quarters, including the Western Wall, as well as "formal sovereignty" over Temple Mount. On the territorial issue, there remained considerable gaps as well, pertaining to the land that Israel would retain, primarily the Jerusalem environs and the Jordan Valley. The Palestinians refused to regard the settlement of refugees in the prospective Palestinian state and the Israeli offer for a very limited return of refugees to pre–1967 Israel as a one-time exercise of "the right of return."

At the same time, Arafat found himself equally pressured in Arab quarters. There, he was criticized for his willingness to concede parts of Jerusalem to Israeli sovereignty and control. Jerusalem is an all-Arab and all-Muslim issue, he was told by many in the Arab world, and the Palestinian leadership was not authorized to negotiate parts of it away. If this were not enough, Lebanese leaders told him that any solution to the refugees issue must entail the repatriation of Palestinian refugees from Lebanon.

Thus, in the immediate aftermath of Camp David II, Arafat found himself cornered from two directions. Barak succeeded in persuading the Clinton administration and the governments of most European states that he was willing to break every Israeli taboo in an effort to reach an agreement with the Palestinians. At the same time, Arafat was criticized in the Arab world for even contemplating concessions in Jerusalem.

In order to avoid a complete rupture with the Clinton administration in the weeks following Camp David II, Arafat continued to engage Israel and the U.S. in discussions. Indeed, on September 25 he even paid an unprecedented visit to Barak's private residence. The discussions seemed to have been aimed at further narrowing the remaining gaps between the two sides' positions.

In late September, however, the parameters of the Palestinian-Israeli discourse changed dramatically. Palestinian protests on September 29 over a visit to Jerusalem's Temple Mount a day earlier by Israeli opposition leader Ariel Sharon, and Israeli police efforts to stem those demonstrations, resulted in seven Palestinians dead and several score wounded. Violence soon escalated, with rock-throwing Palestinian youth marching against Israeli checkpoints near the large population centers of the West Bank and Gaza. On their part Israeli troops responded with plastic bullets that at close range turned out to be lethal.

In contrast to previous cases of deadly incidents when after a few days of clashes the Palestinian Authority quelled the violence, this time Arafat permitted the deadly incidents to continue escalating. A cycle soon developed: Mounting casualties incurred at Palestinian-Israeli friction points resulted in funerals that were often transformed into mass demonstrations that headed toward the nearest IDF checkpoints, ending with more clashes and resulting in additional casualties.

The violence, and the casualties induced by Israeli measures to stem it — photographed and aired by the international mass media — served Arafat's need to escape the predicament in which he found himself in August-September. Thus, he managed to change the playing field of Palestinian-Israeli interactions: from the diplomatic front in which he suffered a tactical defeat in the aftermath of Camp David II, to the electronic media that portrayed Israel as using excessive force against unarmed Palestinian youth.

In late October, President Clinton attempted to break the cycle of violence by convening — together with President Mubarak of Egypt and King Abdullah of Jordan — a summit at Sharm el-Shiek. But Barak and Arafat could not reach an agreement there, and a statement made by President Clinton, committing Israelis and Palestinians to take various "step down" measures, was soon ignored. In the process, all remnants of cooperation that developed over the years between the Palestinian and Israeli security services broke down. As a result, whatever remained of the confidence each side had developed regarding the other's intentions was also shattered. Rather, by late November, the conflict turned ever more violent as the Palestinians shifted their emphasis from demonstrations to terrorism — from rock throwing to bullets, explosives and suicide bombings — all in an effort to redress the imbalance in the casualties incurred.

Meanwhile, a number of Arab leaders — notably President Mubarak and King

Abdullah — moved to stem any attempt to export unrest to their countries and to escalate Palestinian-Israeli violence into a region-wide confrontation. Thus, while tolerating some public expression of solidarity with the Palestinians, both leaders took tough measures to insure that the demonstrations do not rally the masses in broader protests against other government policies and that they do not damage U.S. and Israeli embassies in Cairo and Amman. Equally important, President Mubarak made clear that he would not tolerate calls for escalation to a regional war, publicly mocking Arab leaders who generously proposed that such a war would be waged "until the last Egyptian soldier."

Although initially Israelis and Palestinians both insisted that they would not resume peace negotiations under conditions of continued violence, on December 19 Barak and Arafat sent their negotiators to Bollings Airforce Base outside Washington. Despite active involvement in the talks by President Clinton and Secretary of State Albright, the two sides again failed to reach an understanding on the various dimensions of a possible "permanent status" agreement. Instead, on the eve of their departure, President Clinton presented both sides' negotiators with a set of understandings that could serve as a basis for further intensive talks on a framework agreement. Arafat and Barak were asked to inform Clinton within a matter of days whether they accept his proposal as a basis for such talks.

Earlier, Barak had announced his resignation and the Israeli Knesset decided that the resulting early elections would be held on February 6. With President Clinton due to hand over the presidency to George W. Bush on January 20, Palestinian-Israeli interactions were now operating under double jeopardy: a breakdown of legitimacy for negotiations among Israelis and Palestinians and political timetables in the U.S. and Israel that left little time for closure.

While the Israeli Cabinet quickly responded positively to Clinton's proposal, when in early January Arafat provided the Palestinians' "yes" it seemed too late to negotiate a framework agreement. By then, Israel asked that Arafat first fulfill his commitment to lower the level of violence, thus making it even less likely that any agreement could be reached before Clinton left office.

Meanwhile, personalities close to president-elect Bush indicated that he would avoid the heavy personal involvement that characterized Clinton's engagement in Israeli-Palestinian peacemaking. At about the same time, Israeli opposition leader Ariel Sharon — enjoying a 20-point lead in public opinion polls — committed himself to use whatever measures would be necessary to put an end to Palestinian violence. Sharon and his associates also made clear that they had no intention of offering the Palestinians terms that are even remotely close to the generous proposals made by Barak and his negotiators.

Thus, as George Bush was to be sworn in and the Israeli elections neared, the Israeli-Palestinian peace process seemed to have reached a major crossroad. Given the expected priorities of the Bush administration and the post-election Israeli government, the prospects of a negotiated resolution of the conflict appeared even less promising than in the Clinton-Barak era. Moreover, in the absence of a viable negotiation process, it was not clear how a major escalation of the violence could be avoided.

Most important, it was not clear that the authority of the Palestinians' present leadership could survive under conditions of escalated violence. Such violence was bound to be associated with a further deterioration of economic conditions in the West Bank and Gaza, making it impossible for the Palestinian governmental organs to meet the population's basic needs. In addition, a continuation of the violence may yet lead to Israeli countermeasures that would make ties between the West Bank and Gaza and between the various areas that are under Palestinian control within the West Bank more difficult. This, in turn, may result in a further rise in the stature of local Fatah leaders, thereby threatening the Palestinian Authority's future control. Thus, by late 2000, the danger that the Palestinian state-in-formation might deteriorate to an anarchic realm could not be ruled out. The ability to protect Jordan from the possible demographic consequences of such chaos seemed was also not assured.

In the immediate aftermath of Camp David II, Clinton praised Barak's courage and flexibility at the summit, placing a larger part of the responsibility for the failure to reach an agreement at Arafat's doorstep. He also made clear that the US would react strongly — to the point of reassessing its support of the Palestinian Authority — if Arafat were to declare independence unilaterally. Thus, the principle strategic gain of the Palestinians in the 1990s — close ties with the US — was now threatened. At the same time, European leaders also made clear their opposition to a Palestinian unilateral decleration of independence.

Syrian-Israeli Talks
The death of President Hafez al-Assad on June 10, 2000, led to a widely-shared expectation that the efforts to negotiate peace between the two countries would now remain stalled, at least until his son, Dr. Bashar al-Assad, fortified his position as his father's successor. According to this view, Bashar's priority would be to ensure his power base, and until this was achieved he would not venture into the uncertain waters of negotiations with Israel.

Predictions regarding the future prospects of Israeli-Syrian negotiations rest on shaky grounds. This is because our understanding of the logic propelling Syria's behavior in the peace process is limited. The Barak government was surprised by Assad's decision to renew negotiations in December 1999. It was equally mystified by his decision to have Syria quit these talks after the January 2000 trilateral meeting in Shepherdstown, West Virginia.

Ascertaining the causes of the stalemate could help the prospect that the obstacles could be overcome, allowing a resumption of the talks and their positive conclusion. Yet identifying these causes and assessing their relative weight is not easy. Primarily, three sets of causes may explain Syria's behavior: the first is that the talks were broken off due to the wide gap between the parties' positions. At issue are five main subjects: the extent of Israel's withdrawal from the Golan; the security arrangements to be implemented following Israel's withdrawal; the 'depth' of peace to be established (i.e., the scope of various normalization measures to be applied); arrangements for ensuring Israel's water supply; and finally, the synchronization of the various measures that would be taken in the first four areas.

Accordingly, the first explanation for the Syrian refusal to resume the talks is that the elder Assad had decided that there were few prospects for bridging the gaps in the parties' positions. Yet a review of the non-paper that the US formulated following the January 2000 meeting in Shepherdstown to define the points of agreements and disagreements between the two parties does not rule out the possibility that these gaps could have been bridged.

Thus, the variance between the parties' positions cannot easily explain Syrian behavior during and after the Assad-Clinton summit in Geneva. In the meeting, Assad is said to have rejected Israel's offer to relinquish all of the territory it now occupied, except for a few dozen meters of the lakeshore along the northeastern shores of the Sea of Galilee. Syria's position — that it be given access to the northeastern shores of the Sea of Galilee — can explain why the summit did not produce a Syrian-Israeli agreement. However, it does not explain why Assad did not permit a resumption of the talks.

A second possibility is that the stalemate in Syrian-Israeli negotiations had little to do with the gaps between the parties' positions and everything to do with President Assad's unease regarding the possible impact of peace with Israel for the security and survival of his regime. According to this explanation, while Assad had a strategic interest in *pursuing* peace negotiations — the talks allowed continued contact with America's top leaders, thus diminishing Syria's isolation — he feared that his regime would not survive the degree of openness that the actual *implementation* of peace would entail.

According to this view, Hafez al-Assad was much more comfortable with the status quo — a known quantity — than with the uncharted waters of peace. A reclusive leader who rarely traveled abroad, he was not sure what new tribulations openness to the West would bring. If this was the case, Assad was not truly prepared to accept "yes" for an answer in Geneva. If it were not the northwestern shores of the Sea of Galilee, Syria's president would have found another topic on which to allow the deal to falter.

A third explanation for the failure of the Syrian-Israeli talks focuses of the health of Assad during the year that preceded his death in June 2000. According to this view, while going through the motions of negotiating with Israel for the reasons enumerated above, Assad was no longer fit for the task of building a domestic consensus for the compromises required. Instead, aware of his illness, he was compelled to give priority to arranging a smooth succession for his son Bashar. These different explanations for the failure of Israeli-Syrian negotiations — although not mutually exclusive — have different implications for the chances of resuming the talks. Clearly, if the latter two explanations played a major role in inducing Hafez al-Assad to stall the talks after Shepherdstown and to reject their resumption after Geneva, chances are that his son Bashar will renew the talks. The death of the elder Assad eliminates the third explanation for the stalemate — provided that Bashar proves successful in fortifying his position as his father's successor. Moreover, having studied in England, Bashar may be more comfortable with opening Syria to the West. Consequently, his assessment of the costs and benefits of the status quo versus peace may well be very different than his father's. To him, peace may seem much less frightening. At the same time, his confidence in the ability to manage the hazards of the status quo while avoiding inadvertent escalation may be somewhat lower than that of the elder Assad.

If this general analysis is correct, Bashar Assad may not only allow a resumption of the Syrian-Israeli talks, he may even be more amenable than his father to solving the issues that still divide the two parties. Thus, while even under the best of circumstances Bashar cannot be expected to abandon Syria's long-standing demand that Israel return to the 1967 lines, he may be more open to creative interpretations regarding the precise translation of this principle into facts on the ground.

The chances that this more hopeful scenario will materialize is likely to be affected by the manner in which Bashar al-Assad views the key to addressing Syria's problems and to securing his regime. If his years in the West have instilled in him the desire to see Syria emerge from its isolation and economic stagnation, the odds are that he will place considerable emphasis on opening Syria to foreign trade and investments. While the response of European states to the new Assad government will be important, a change in Washington's relations with Syria will be essential to changing the approach of multilateral lending institutions, primarily the World Bank and the International Monetary Fund. Yet without Syrian-Israeli peace, America's attitude toward Syria is unlikely to alter. Peace is an absolute prerequisite — although not necessarily a sufficient condition — to transforming the attitude toward Syria on Capitol Hill.

It should be noted that while an analysis of Syria's predicaments and the requirements of addressing them may lead to the expectation that the new president would reengage Syria in the peace process, initial signs of his priorities indicate otherwise. The fact that Bashar has surrounded himself with "old hands" such as Vice President 'Abd al-Halim Khaddam, Foreign Minister Farouk al-Sharaa', and

Defense Minister Mustafa al-Tlass indicates that he does not plan to break with his father's hard-line policies any time soon. Alternatively, these re-appointments may mean that although the son may prefer to reopen negotiations, he remains a captive of the Ba'ath old guard.

Even if the more optimistic analysis of Bashar al-Assad's possible priorities and their probable implications for Syria's approach to the peace process is accurate, this does not imply that an agreement with Israel would be easy to reach. By late 2000, at least two developments may have adversely affected the climate of negotiations for the Israeli side, making it more difficult to match the flexibility it demonstrated up to the Clinton-Assad summit in Geneva.

The first of these is Israel's withdrawal from Lebanon in late May 2000. Previously, the cumulative costs of Israel's presence in southern Lebanon and the widespread belief that a withdrawal from the area could not be conducted safely except in the context of an agreement with Syria motivated a significant number of Israelis to support far reaching concessions to Syria. Following the withdrawal, Israel no longer experienced the regular tally of casualties. The relative tranquility experienced in Israel's north following the withdrawal seemed to further reduce the Israeli public's propensity to view peace with Syria as an urgent matter. Hence, obtaining the requisite public support for the concessions was now likely to prove much more difficult.

Second, since the Geneva summit and particularly in the aftermath of Camp David II, the Barak government has experienced growing internal problems, in part generated by the Israeli-Palestinian negotiations, leading to a breakdown of his coalition and to new elections. This made it unlikely that Israel would reengage in talks with Syria, at least until political stability is restored.

The success or failure of Syrian-Israeli negotiations would each affect the Middle East strategic landscape very differently. Given the likelihood that an Israeli-Syrian peace would quickly lead to an agreement between Israel and Lebanon, the outcome of the more optimistic scenario would be a complete transformation of the strategic landscape of the Near East. Under such new circumstances, the odds that the large conventional forces of Israel and Syria would be used again would diminish considerably, as well as weaken part of the rationale behind Iran's hostility toward Israel. While other issues — primarily the management of Egyptian-Israeli relations (see below) — could be strained by a broader Arab-Israeli peace, the likelihood of major war in the Middle East would reach an all time low.

Conversely, if the pessimistic view materializes and the parties fail to reengage in productive talks, the odds of Syrian-Israeli escalation may prove higher than under the late Assad. This because Bashar's ability to control such crises with the same talent as his late father is untested and unclear.

The Status of Peace

Egyptian-Israeli Relations

Egyptian-Israeli relations are an important pillar of the Arab-Israeli peace process. Without Egypt's pioneering role, Arab-Israeli peacemaking is unlikely to have advanced to its present point. Yet, as the process to which it has given birth has developed, Egypt seems to have become more nervous about the child it has helped rear.

Egyptian-Israeli relations did not improve despite the change in government in Israel in mid-1999. And, in late 2000, in reaction to escalating Israeli-Palestinian violence, Egypt decided to recall its ambassador to Israel. Yet there is no evidence of any intention on Egypt's part to withdraw from the basic commitments it undertook in the framework of the 1979 Israel-Egypt peace treaty. Egypt continues to comply with all the security clauses of the agreement and there are no indications that it plans to alter its behavior in this realm. Indeed, the slogan of the late President Anwar Sadat — "no more war" — appears to enjoy a national consensus in Egypt.

Tension between Egypt and Israel seems to result from the manner in which the two countries perceive one another as powerful players in the Middle Eastern arena. Egypt is the largest and most populous of the Arab states, while Israel is the most technologically advanced country in the region and its economy the most robust. For Egypt, Israel's success is a constant reminder of its own failure in the economic realm. For Israel, its rejection by Egypt's intellectual elite and the mass media underscores the extent to which it continues to be perceived as a foreign entity in the region.

Israel remains worried about the military buildup that has been taking place in Egypt in recent years. In the absence of potent enemies that can provide a clear justification for such buildup — Libya and Sudan hardly qualify — Israel is concerned that the buildup is intended to provide Egypt with the capabilities to confront Israel militarily. That peace between the two countries lacks support beyond the governing elite, that the intellectual community and the mass media have attached a highly negative connotation to the term "normalization," practically equating it with betrayal, and that business transactions with, and travel to, Israel are blocked by the requirements of debriefing by Egypt's security services and other governmental authorities, all add up to an Israeli perception that peace with its neighbor to the south is precarious.

Israel, however, continues to refrain from regarding Egypt as a threat and assesses that its growing capabilities are not coupled with any observable intention to violate the peace agreement. Yet the negative attitude expressed toward Israel in Egypt's mass media and among the intellectual and religious communities has led to an Israeli assessment that support for peace with Israel within Egyptian society remains thin. In turn, this feeds on Israeli concerns that if the attitude of Egyptians regarding

Israel does not change soon, its government may be pressured to further curtail relations with Israel and, ultimately, to break them off.

Egypt, conversely, seems to be concerned that Israel's power is growing steadily — in the military, economic and technological spheres — with no corresponding improvement in relations with its Arab neighbors. Egypt views Israel as committed to maintaining every dimension of its unconventional arsenal. Israel's refusal to sign the 1968 Nuclear Nonproliferation Treaty (NPT) and the 1975 Biological Weapons Convention (BWC) are seen as conclusive evidence to that effect. Moreover, Israel's commitment to prevent other states in the region from obtaining a nuclear capacity is seen as proof that it intends to ensure its regional nuclear monopoly.

In the realm of conventional arms, Israel's efforts to maintain its "qualitative edge" — particularly its capacity to enhance advanced platforms with its own state-of-the-art technologies — is viewed as determination by Israel to continue enjoying military superiority over the entire neighborhood. In this context, Washington's declared commitment to maintain Israel's qualitative edge — while limiting technology transfers to its Arab allies, including Egypt — only reinforces Cairo's sense of being discriminated against.

Israel's new role in the global marketplace and its robust economy provide additional fuel to Egyptian fears that Israel intends to dominate the region, thus achieving economically what it has failed to achieve militarily. Furthermore, Egypt perceives globalization as a new threat to its traditional value system, which is rooted in both Egyptian and Islamic culture. Israeli pleas of innocence, pointing out that Israeli businessmen have no interest in dominating Middle East economies and are, instead, interested in markets located far beyond the region, are viewed in Egypt as merely another manifestation of Israeli arrogance.

The slow pace of the Israeli-Palestinian peace process has had three effects on Egyptian perceptions regarding Israel. First, Egyptians regard this as reflecting Israel's reluctance to relinquish control over the Palestinians. A milder interpretation is an image of Israel as having failed to internalize the full meaning of peace and as stubbornly adhering to old thinking. Second, they argue that this pace keeps the Egyptians exposed to the claim that in signing the peace treaty with Israel in 1979, they abandoned the Palestinians. Not surprisingly, therefore, Egypt is the first to support every Palestinian demand. Finally, as long as their television sets show Israeli troops battling Palestinian civilians on a daily basis, an atmosphere conducive to closer Egyptian-Israeli ties cannot develop.

The combination of realities and perceptions described here is open to two possible interpretations of the Egyptian scene, yielding distinct expectations regarding the future of Egyptian-Israeli relations. The first views the Egyptian commitment to peace as limited to a very narrow strata that include the top echelons of the Egyptian government, as well as a small number of businessmen and defense and foreign policy experts, who view peace with Israel as serving Egypt's strategic and economic interests. For them, peace with Israel is a prerequisite to Egypt's strategic relations with the United States, a hedge against unpredictable Israeli behavior, and a "must" if Egypt is to devote its resources to economic growth, since a return to confrontation would require that precious resources be shifted to military spending.

According to this view, beneath the thin strata that support peace, most of Egypt's society is opposed to peace on national and religious grounds. Thus, references to Israel in the mass media — which range from highly negative reporting to expressions of conspiracy theories and anti-Semitic diatribes — are seen as reflecting popular sentiments. The government has responded by prohibiting the development of any ties with Israel that do not directly serve Egypt's strategic interests. Hence Israeli assistance in the agricultural sector is accepted, as are ties with Israeli experts in the arms control realm — the former is intended to assist the most critical sector of Egypt's economy and the latter is aimed at persuading Israelis that they should abandon their nuclear deterrent. All other contacts, particularly in the cultural field, are highly discouraged, if not prohibited.

This can lead to the conclusion that the Egyptian-Israeli peace is unstable and that its durability is questionable. While analysts who adhere to this assessment do not necessarily regard Egypt as a threat, they do regard it as a potential risk that requires close monitoring.

The second evaluation of the Egyptian scene is quite different from the first. It views Egyptian society as a spectrum: at one end is the governmental elite, admittedly a thin stratum that continues to adhere to all stipulations and requirements of the peace treaty with Israel. Very close to this stratum is the Egyptian business community that is largely interested in improving economic ties with Israel, and particularly with the West. It is a potential proponent of peace not because it has high expectations for economic transactions with Israel, but rather because it views Israel as a potential bridge to other Western economies and because peace is essential to a positive investment climate.

At the other end of the spectrum are the intellectual community, mass media, and religious extremists — the bastions of anti-Israeli sentiments. While this elite may be thinner than the governmental backers of peace, they enjoy open access to Egypt's media, leading them to be cited as evidence of Egyptian sentiment, thus producing distorted analyses.

According to this view, the bulk of Egypt's population lies somewhere between the two extremes. And, while the population is influenced by what it reads in the newspapers, the long years of "mobilized" media have made the masses skeptical, if not cynical, of what they read. Thus, the Egyptian public's image of Israel is affected less by the diatribes in print and more by the pictures it sees on television. According to this view, once peace is concluded between Israel and the Palestinians and pictures of Israeli soldiers battling Palestinian youth disappear from the television screens, the Egyptian population's attitude towards Israel will change.

Finally, this assessment of the Egyptian scene places its bets on the Egyptian business community. With time, this community is expected to gain strength, while the relative power and influence of the Nasserite and Islamic intellectuals are expected to diminish. As a result, rational thinking will overcome ideological commitments, and as the political atmosphere improves with the implementation of Israeli-Palestinian peace, Egypt's business leaders will be better able to press their case regarding the potential economic utility of closer Egyptian-Israeli ties.

It is difficult to tell which of these perspectives on Egypt's attitude toward Israel is closer to reality, since there is plenty of evidence to support both. It is even more difficult to attach probabilities to the very different expectations regarding the future of Egyptian-Israeli relations. At the same time, it should be noted that even if reality is closer to the more pessimistic assessment of the Egyptian scene, vital national interests — primarily related to Egypt's relations with the US — will prod Cairo to continue to maintain its commitments to the 1979 Egyptian-Israeli peace treaty. A revolution in Egypt's domestic political scene or a sea of change in its strategic environment would be required for Egypt to return to the warpath.

Jordanian-Israeli Relations
The relations between Jordan and Israel comprise another important pillar of Middle East peace. For Israel, these relations involve at least two vital strategic interests: first, the commitment undertaken by Jordan in the framework of the peace treaty with Israel to prohibit the entrance of foreign forces creates a land buffer between Israel and Iraq. This not only makes Israel safer, it also allows Israel greater flexibility in negotiations with the Palestinians. In particular, the greater the extent to which Jordan can be regarded as a buffer from the east, the less important is Israel's control over territory in the Jordan valley.

Israel's second strategic interest in peace with Jordan is concerned with its desire to limit the security risks involved in independent Palestinian statehood. With large Palestinian populations residing in Israel as well as in Jordan, the two countries have a common interest in limiting the prospective Palestinian state's capacity to intervene in their respective domestic affairs.

Jordan also has a strong interest in close defense ties with Israel. For many years these ties have been an important component of Jordanian deterrence against external threats, even prior to the signing of the peace treaty in 1994. Thus, close contacts are maintained between the leaders of both countries' armed forces. The transfer of power from the late King Hussein to his son, King Abdullah, has made no difference in this realm. These defense ties survived even the considerable tensions that arose in the two country's relations in September 1997, following the attempted assassination of Khaled Mashaal, a political officer of the Palestinian Islamic fundamentalist organization, Hamas, by Mossad agents in Amman.

While on a different scale, Jordanian-Israeli peace is experiencing some of the same problems inherent in Egyptian-Israeli ties. Support for interacting with Israel is somewhat wider than in Egypt, but it is still limited to the relatively narrow strata of government officials, military officers, and businessmen. In addition to opposition to closer relations with Israel by intellectuals and religious extremists, there has been a deep disappointment among the Jordanian population with regard to "peace dividends" — the economic benefits of peace. While there has been a general expectation that peace with Israel would result in rapid economic growth, Jordan's economy has registered no meaningful change.

In large part, the disappointment of Jordan's population with the fruits of peace resulted from the tendency of its Hashemite leaders to oversell the anticipated benefits of the agreement. To an even larger extent, the disappointing economic consequences of peace resulted from the failure of Israeli leaders to make Jordan's economy a priority. Thus, bureaucratic considerations and special interests were allowed to present numerous obstacles to trade between Jordan and Israel and, especially, between Jordan and the Palestinian Authority. Only in early 2000 was a serious effort made to begin to rectify the situation.

On the whole, the succession from King Hussein to King Abdullah seems to have been managed successfully. The new king is said to have gained popularity by working to reduce government red tape, inefficiency and corruption. But three points should be remembered: the new monarch has yet to be tested in managing major crises. While the escalating Israeli-Palestinian violence comprised a source of serious concern, until late 2000 it had not presented king Abdullah with a serious challenge. Secondly, Jordan's economy remains its weakest dimension. Without significant economic progress, the Hashemite kingdom will be increasingly exposed to expressions of public dissatisfaction, such as the "Bread Riots" experienced in the 1980s and 90s. Third, during the next few years Jordan may face a formidable challenge: dealing with the ramifications of the establishment of an independent Palestinian state. Given Jordan's large Palestinian population, the repercussions are likely to be considerable.

Whether or not Jordan will be able to continue to fulfill its vital strategic role in the future will largely depend on two factors: first, the state of its economy. Given its financial and managerial resources, the US can do much to ensure Jordan's prosperity. Israel, with the strength of its own economy and its access to Western markets, can also do more to assist its eastern neighbor. Hence, the prospects of Jordan's stability depend heavily on whether or not the US and Israel will do what they can to ensure Jordan's prosperity. Second, the future relations between Israel and the Palestinians: should efforts to resolve the Israeli-Palestinian conflict fail and violence escalate further, Jordan's stability — given that over half of its population is Palestinian — may be threatened.

Israel-Lebanon Relations: A New Era
Lebanon witnessed a dramatic development in mid-2000: Israel's decision to withdraw unilaterally from southern Lebanon, in the framework of UN Security Council Resolution 425. The implementation of the decision, completed on May 24, brought about the collapse of the Security Zone and the elimination of the South Lebanese Army (SLA).

The debate regarding the best manner of ensuring the security of Israel's north began in the mid-1970s and, again, in the aftermath of the 1982 war in Lebanon. Since then, Israeli opinion was divided between those favoring a defense along the international border and those advocating forward deployment. The latter entailed the creation of a Security Zone in which the SLA and a small number of Israeli troops would be deployed.

Until the 1982 invasion, Israel was confronted along its northern border primarily by Palestinian terrorists. The war resulted in the expulsion from Lebanon of the most significant force responsible for attacks against Israel — the Palestine Liberation Organization (PLO). But Israel's presence in Lebanon in the immediate wake of the invasion and the change in the internal balance in Lebanon caused by the PLO's departure resulted in the rise of the Shi'ite movement Hizbullah.

While primarily aimed at ridding Lebanon of Israel's presence in the south and gaining influence in the Lebanese domestic arena, Hizbullah was ambiguous regarding its intentions vis-à-vis Israel. Its leaders at times argued that their sole purpose was to compel Israel to withdraw from southern Lebanon. On other occasions they indicated that their Islamic movement was committed to liberating Jerusalem. This led the Israeli intelligence community to assess that Hizbullah was determined to engage in violence across the border and to warn that a withdrawal from the south would expose Israel's north to untold dangers.

Strategically, Hizbullah was the only success that Iran could register in its effort to export its revolution abroad. It seemed unlikely that the clerics in Tehran would be willing to forgo this success, and it was not clear whether in their view such success could be sustained without the movement's continued struggle against Israel. For Syria, following the PLO's departure, Hizbullah terrorism seemed the only channel through which Israel could be inflicted with low levels of constant pain. It was not clear that Damascus could afford to be deprived of the only effective means at its disposal for pressuring Israel.

Therefore Syria and Iran were viewed as likely to encourage Hizbullah to continue exercising violence against Israel. Moreover, since after the Soviet Union's collapse Iran remained as Syria's only backer, the Assad regime was seen as unlikely to block Tehran from supplying Hizbullah with weapons and ammunition through Damascus International Airport and the Syrian-controlled territory in the Beka'.

For all these reasons it was feared that if an Israeli-Syrian agreement was not reached — thereby changing Syria's calculations — and Israel was to withdraw unilaterally from southern Lebanon, Hizbullah would harass Israel's northern towns and settlements following Israel's withdrawal. Under such conditions Israel would be compelled to react with considerable force, thereby risking general escalation.

Militarily, the view favoring Israel's continued presence in southern Lebanon argued that the combined effect of the presence of the SLA, Israel's technological edge, and the stationing of Israeli troops in fortified strongholds allowed the Security Zone to be maintained at a relatively low level of casualties. Indeed, it seemed that the very presence of SLA and IDF strongholds in the Security Zone attracted Hizbullah attacks, thus diverting its attention from the Israeli towns and settlements south of the international border.

Israelis who favored withdrawal rejected the analysis presented above. They argued that Hizbullah was primarily a Lebanese indigenous movement, not a puppet of Syria and Iran. Hence, if its calculations would warrant an end to the fight against Israel, the movement would refrain from cross-border harassment. According to this view, Hizbullah had already transformed itself into a Lebanese mass social movement and it no longer needed to prove itself successful on the battleground to support its claim for power and influence in Beirut.

Militarily, those supporting a pullback argued that the IDF's deployment in southern Lebanon compelled it to adopt defensive tactics and operations, thus destroying its offensive ethos. Consequently, the military analysts favoring withdrawal argued that Israel should withdraw to the international border and employ offensive tactics and operations if its civilian population in the north came under attack.

Sensing the growing popular discontent with the cumulative costs associated with the IDF's continued deployment in southern Lebanon, in March 1999 then-candidate Barak committed himself to "bringing the boys home" if elected. Initially, due to opposition to unilateral withdrawal by the IDF Chief of Staff, Lt. Gen. Shaul Mofaz, and the Chief of the Intelligence Branch, Maj. Gen. Amos Malka, once in office Prime Minister Barak instructed the IDF to prepare for a withdrawal "within the context of an agreement with Syria." Only when the Clinton-Assad summit in Geneva in March 2000 failed were these instructions altered, and the IDF was told to prepare for a truly unilateral withdrawal. By early 2000, news of the IDF's pending withdrawal had already weakened the SLA, causing significant defections among its ranks. When on May 22, it became clear that the IDF's unilateral withdrawal was imminent, the SLA deteriorated rapidly and the Security Zone collapsed. On May

24, the IDF pullback was completed, without Israeli casualties. Thousands of members of the militia and their family members sought refuge in Israel, while others surrendered and were placed on trial in Beirut, some receiving long sentences.

In order to guarantee the security of its civilian population in the north after the withdrawal, Israel's top leaders issued stern warnings that they would hold Syria responsible for any violence directed at Israel's northern towns and settlements. Specifically, Barak and Mofaz made it clear that Israel would respond to such violence by attacking "Syrian interests" in Lebanon. In this way, Israel has attempted to transform southern Lebanon from an arena of guerrilla war with Hizbullah to an offspring of its over-all deterrence relationship with Syria.

To strengthen the credibility of its new deterrence posture, Israel sought to accompany its withdrawal by steps that would bestow international legitimacy upon its moves. Thus, it placed the withdrawal within the context of UN Security Council Resolution 425, made every effort to coordinate the IDF's withdrawal with the UN secretary general, and sought the Security Council's acknowledgement that it had complied fully with the stipulations of the UN resolution.

In the initial period following Israel's withdrawal, Hizbullah refrained from carrying the fight across the international border. While this accorded with the expectations of those who favored the withdrawal, it may have also been, at least in part, the result of the succession that meanwhile took place in Syria. Most probably Bashar al-Assad was not about to allow Hizbullah and the opposition Palestinian groups that maintain a presence in Lebanon to drag Syria into a new crisis before his power was fully entrenched.

The future stability of the Israeli-Lebanese border depends, however, on the future of the Syrian-Israeli peace process. If negotiations between Syria and Israel are to be renewed and to lead to an agreement, the result is likely to be the resumption of talks between Israel and Lebanon and an agreement between the two countries that would establish peace along their common border. Under such circumstances, tranquility along the border will be maintained by both the Lebanese and Syrian governments not only because the agreement reached will commit them to do so, but also because this will serve to create a stable environment for economic growth.

Conversely, if Syria gives up on the hope of regaining its sovereignty over the Golan through negotiations, it may actively encourage Lebanese factions to increase tension along Israel's northern border. In this case, even if the mainstream of Hizbullah prefers to concentrate its efforts on affecting social and economic conditions in Lebanon, it would be pressed by Damascus to renew hostilities against Israel. Should Hizbullah resist such pressures, Syria could encourage some of the currently dormant Palestinian rejectionist groups that maintain a presence in the refugee camps in southern Lebanon to renew the fighting.

Whether or not Syria is likely to adopt such a policy remains an open question.

Even if a complete Israeli withdrawal to the Sea of Galilee proves impossible to obtain through diplomacy, Syria will have to consider its options very carefully before reverting to violence along Israel's border with Lebanon. This is because Israel's new deterrence policy commits the government to retaliate heavily against Syrian targets in Lebanon. Under such circumstances, violence exercised against Israel may quickly escalate. As the current balance of forces between Israel and Syria, in the narrow military sense as well as in the broader strategic context, favors Israel dramatically (see below), escalation may expose Damascus to great peril with no Soviet-style guarantors in sight. Thus, even in the worst case scenario, the likelihood that southern Lebanon would become a combat zone once again does not seem very high.

By late 2000, the situation in southern Lebanon and Syria's policy regarding this matter remained unresolved. On one hand, a number of incidents along the Israeli-Lebanese border — most notably the abduction of three Israeli soldiers by the Hizbullah in October — made clear that the Shi'ite movement had no intention of abandoning the violent dimension of its activities. There were also important indications that this continued engagement took place with Syria's blessing — not only did President Bashar Assad refrain from taking steps to prevent these Hizbullah activities, he permitted Iran to continue to supply the Shi'ite movement with arms and ammunition through Damascus airport. Thus, it appeared that Syria was willing to have Hizbullah test Israel's new deterrence posture.

Yet Assad seemed careful in limiting the risks that he was willing to assume in testing Israeli deterrence. First, most of the aforementioned incidents took place as Israel was simultaneously engaged in attempting to stem Palestinian violence in the West Bank and Gaza. Israel's reluctance to open "a second front" under such conditions seemed to assure that testing its deterrence would be conducted under favorable conditions.

Second, Hizbullah — probably under directives from Damascus — limited its activities to a very narrow area of the border, where Israel's withdrawal to the international border was less than complete. Hizbullah seemed to feel that it could legitimately continue military activity if limited to that area, despite Israel's argument that it conquered that area from Syria and not from Lebanon and notwithstanding UN announcements that Israel was in full compliance with UNSC Resolution 425. Thus, while by late 2000 the stability of the new reality along the Lebanese-Israeli border was already challenged, these tests were of limited nature and did not provide a clear indication regarding the direction of future developments along that front.

Chapter Three
Regional Issues and Global Interests

Security in the Persian Gulf
Security in the Persian Gulf has implications that extend far beyond the Gulf region. Instability in the Gulf poses a threat to vital Western interests: the unhindered supply of oil at reasonable prices and the sustainability of Gulf regimes with which the US maintains close ties. It also affects the economic security of non-Gulf Arab countries. For example, remittances of Palestinian and Egyptian laborers comprise an important component of both parties' macroeconomies. Thus, when Iraq expelled close to a million Egyptian workers in October–November 1989, the latter's economic security was directly threatened.

Gulf security issues affect other states in the region militarily. Extended range ballistic missiles fired from Iraq and, in the future, from Iran can reach the Mediterranean Sea. The Iraqi Scud attacks on Israel during the 1991 Gulf War demonstrated that no state in the region could remain indifferent to the stability and security of the Persian Gulf states.

Iraq: A Power Contained
As noted earlier, Iraq remains weak, militarily as well as economically. In the military sphere, the sanctions applied against Iraq since the Gulf War prevent the rebuilding of its armed forces. Some leakage of spare parts and large-scale cannibalization of platforms enable Iraq to maintain the bulk of its Republican Guard divisions, but its combat-ready order-of-battle was much reduced in comparison to its size on the eve of the Gulf War. It can prevent the Shi'ites in the south from tearing themselves away from Baghdad's control, but it cannot project a threat beyond Iraq's borders.

Iraq's air force and navy have been practically wiped out, partly due to bombing by the US-led coalition and partly due to a move by Saddam during the Gulf War to transfer some of these forces for safekeeping to other countries, notably Iran. Some components of Iraq's air defense system remain intact, but they are in no position to pose a threat to an advanced air force. Hence, US aircraft operate unhindered above

Iraqi territory, in the framework of Operation Northern Watch and Operation Southern Watch.

Iraq's ballistic missile force has also been largely destroyed, and at most, only a few launchers and missiles are believed to have escaped the eyes of UNSCOM inspectors. As long as Iraq is prevented from rebuilding its long-range ballistic missile production lines, countries located far from Iraq's borders will continue to be immune to attack. Iraq's nuclear and chemical weapons facilities were also destroyed through a combination of coalition bombings during the Gulf War and UNSCOM activities in the war's aftermath. Until Iraq ended UNSCOM inspections unilaterally in late 1998, it could have safely been said that Iraq was incapable of posing a nuclear or chemical threat to its neighbors.

Since inspections ended, the Iraqi unconventional capabilities include new components, as well as long-standing ones. It had been clear since the end of the Gulf War that Saddam Hussein remains determined to make every effort to rebuild his unconventional weapons capability. If this was not so, Saddam would have complied fully with UN Security Council Resolution 687, thus saving his country years of sanctions and losses in oil revenues in the order of some $200 billion It should, therefore, be assumed that if the sanctions are lifted and the US eases the constant military pressure it exercises through operations Northern Watch and Southern Watch, Saddam will move to restore his unconventional weapons program. Moreover, Iraq has the potential financial means to rebuild its facilities for the production of weapons of mass destruction. As long as the sanctions regime remains in place — thus limiting its oil revenues — and Iraq continues to be compelled to devote a large part of its oil revenues to the compensation fund, it does not have the surplus funds with which to rebuild such expensive programs. But Iraq's oil reserves are sufficiently large to generate the income to allow it to pursue these programs, if sanctions are lifted.

Third, the human infrastructure of Iraq's unconventional weapons programs remains intact. There have been very few defections among the ranks of thousands of Iraqi nuclear scientists and engineers and their counterparts in the chemical and biological realms. In the absence of facilities where practice and experience can be gained, there has probably been some degradation in the quality of Iraq's professional personnel, particularly in the nuclear sphere. But work on weapons design has most probably continued throughout the past ten years. Similarly, in the ballistic missile realm, Iraq is exploring (but not testing) ways of extending the range of the missiles that it is permitted to develop, test and possess under UN Security Council Resolution 687 — that is, missiles with a range of up to 150 kilometers. Iran's testing of its Shahab-3 missile in July and September 2000 will probably further encourage Iraq to pursue such explorations.

Fourth, Iraq has most likely continued its research, development and production of biological weapons. Saddam's government admitted in 1995 that it had developed biological agents, but claimed it had destroyed all such weapons and the facilities to manufacture them. However, Iraq refused to reveal the location of these facilities, let alone to permit UNSCOM inspectors to visit them. Thus, it should be assumed that Iraq already possesses biological weapons, although not necessarily the means for delivering them to long distances and dispersing them effectively.

For all these reasons, the task of containing Iraq will continue to be formidable, at least as long as Saddam Hussein continues to rule the country. At present there are no signs that his grip on power is weakening. He continues to rule with an iron fist. Opposition forces remain small, divided and weak, while the Shi'ites in the south and the Kurds in the north are in no position to affect the fate of the government in Baghdad.

Iraq thus continues to be a potential threat to stability in the Gulf region and beyond. Saddam's intentions are clear: if given an opportunity he would rebuild the Iraqi armed forces and an unconventional weapons arsenal, and would use these forces in an attempt to threaten his neighbors once again. Until late 1998, it was clear that his ability to restore Iraq's power was limited by UN-imposed sanctions and by constant and intrusive UNSCOM inspections. Now the picture is less clear.

Since August 1998, when the last UNSCOM inspection of Iraqi sites was conducted, the state of Iraq's activities in the unconventional weapons realm cannot be ascertained. All efforts to construct an alternative international inspection and monitoring regime for Iraq following Desert Fox in 1998 have failed, and Saddam has refused to allow any more inspections of Iraqi facilities. By late 2000, Saddam continued to reject any compromise that would allow some further lifting of sanctions in exchange for his willingness to allow the reinstatement of UN inspections and monitoring in the form of the proposed United Nations' Monitoring, Verification and Inspection Commission (UNMOVIC).

It should be emphasized that the end of UNSCOM inspections in late 1998 does not mean that Iraq is now free to do as it pleases in the unconventional realm. Developments in Iraq in this area are followed closely by the technical means of the US and other intelligence communities. These agencies have learned enough about Iraq's modus operandi over the past ten years to know what to look for. Other interested parties that possess greater capabilities in other realms of intelligence collection (primarily human intelligence) also follow the Iraqi scene closely. It should be noted that the production of nuclear fissile material and chemical weapons need to be conducted at industrial scales in order to be meaningful, thus making detection easier.

For these reasons, it is doubtful that under conditions of ongoing US engagement (see below) and continued — even if scaled back — UN sanctions it would be possible for Iraq to revert to pre–Gulf War-type grand-scale production of WMDs. Most probably, Iraq is continuing its efforts in the undetectable research and development of biological weapons. It probably has also tried to renew its production of chemical weapons, but in much smaller quantities than before. It is most certainly attempting to perfect its nuclear bomb design. And it is making every effort to extrapolate from permitted tests of short-range ballistic missiles knowledge that would be applicable to the production of long-range missiles.

The limitations enumerated, however, indicate that Iraq's potential remains seriously curtailed in the critical realms of fissile material production, the industrial scale production of chemical weapons and the manufacture of long-range ballistic

Range of Iraq's Ballistic Missiles

missiles and missile launchers. Its ability to pose a new threat at a scale similar to that on the eve of the Gulf War would require that two developments take place: a complete collapse of the UN sanctions and a decision by the US to cease its close monitoring of Iraq and to end operations Northern Watch and Southern Watch. Even under such circumstances, Iraq is unlikely to rebuild its WMD production capability overnight. The damage it sustained in this field has been considerable; a reconstruction of this capability would require an inordinate, albeit not an impossible, effort.

Iran: Unresolved Struggle
Militarily, Iran remains weak. It has been unable to restore the military capabilities it possessed until it lost US assistance and sales in the aftermath of the 1979 revolution and has been unable to compensate itself for the heavy losses it suffered during the 1980–88 Iran-Iraq War. It is also economically weak and overwhelmed by domestic problems. Consequently, its ability to pose a conventional military threat to its immediate neighbors is now quite limited. Its ability to project conventional threats to more distant parts of the Middle East is currently negligible.

Unable to project a credible conventional military threat, Iran has sought to address its security concerns and to meet its objectives of expanding its influence in the region wherever and whenever this can be done at acceptable costs by building capacities in two realms: terrorism and weapons of mass destruction. In both areas, however, Iran's activities have been somewhat tentative and equivocal.

Recent years have seen important changes in the Iranian domestic scene as reformers have gained ground. This was reflected clearly in the election of Mohammed Khatami as president in May 1997, and in the reformers' success in the February 2000 elections to the Majlis. However, the struggle between the reformers and the conservatives continues. The latter are attempting to regroup after the defeat they suffered in the parliamentary elections. Since then they have banned the publication of some twenty reform-oriented newspapers. Earlier, they arrested Abdollah Nuri, the reformist publisher of the *Hurdad* newspaper, who had previously served as Iran's Minister of the Interior and was a close associate of Khatami. Nuri was sentenced to five years in prison. The conservatives also played a role in the arrest of thirteen Jews in early 1999 on suspicion of espionage and who were subsequently sentenced to substantial prison terms in June 2000.

Thus, while the reformers' main focus is domestic — they are primarily seeking to increase personal freedom and choice within the Islamic system — their positions on foreign policy issues also differ from those held by the conservatives. During the late 1990s and early 2000, Khatami and his associates made clear that he was interested in improving ties with the US. In January 1998, Khatami signaled his interest in such improvement by recognizing that "American civilization is worthy of respect." Further, during a visit to Germany in early July 2000, he expressed very clearly his hopes that Iran's ties with the US would improve.

In assessing Iran's contribution to Gulf security and, conversely, the threat it may pose to its neighbors, as well as to other countries in the Middle East, the following factors need to be taken into account: first, it is difficult to assess the relative influence of the reformers and conservatives in the foreign and defense policy making process. For example, while some of Iran's government officials indicate their interest in improved ties with the US, other branches of the ruling elite (notably the country's

Supreme Leader, the Revolutionary Guards and the judiciary) act in ways that undermine the prospects of such improvement. The best example of this is Iran's assistance to Hizbullah in southern Lebanon, a move that the US Congress, if not always the administration, interprets as support of terrorism. The source of this confusion is that while reformers won the presidency and the Majlis, the conservatives continue to control many of the most sensitive government institutions, including the security and intelligence services.

Not surprisingly, Israel's withdrawal from Lebanon encouraged these institutions to instruct Hizbullah to prepare to conduct terrorism against Israel. During 1999–2000, Iran also armed its Revolutionary Guard units stationed in Lebanon with 43-kilometer range Fajr-3 and 70-kilometer range Fajr-5 rockets. In the aftermath of Israel's withdrawal, Iran assisted Hizbullah in building a regular military presence in the south, including the conducting of routine training and exercises.

There is also clear evidence that Iran is constructing an infrastructure for the production of weapons of mass destruction and their delivery systems, with ranges of up to 1300 kilometers. Iran is apparently already producing chemical weapons and probably some biological agents as well. It commissioned North Korea to manufacture a derivative of the NoDong II missile — the Shahab-3 — and upgraded it with Russian-made navigation technology. As noted earlier, the missile system was first tested in July 1998, but the test was widely considered a failure. Only two years later, in mid-July and late September 2000, did two additional, more successful, tests take place.

In January 1995, Iran signed a framework agreement with Russia regarding the completion of its nuclear complex in Bushehr, the construction of which was stopped by the Ayatollah Khomeini immediately after the 1979 revolution. Russia and Iran also signed a contract for the completion of a 1000 Mw power reactor, one of two reactors that comprise the backbone of the Bushehr project.

The implications of Bushehr for a military nuclear program remain uncertain. pressurized water power reactors are particularly unsuitable for the production of weapons-grade material. In addition, Iran is an NPT signatory and the complex is under full-scope International Atomic Energy Agency (IAEA) safeguards. Although Iran has not signed the special protocols that allow the implementation of the added 93+2 safeguards, to date no country — including Iraq — has been successful in diverting significant amounts of nuclear material from declared facilities monitored by IAEA without being detected. Hence, the potential of Bushehr to play a direct role in providing Iran with a military nuclear capability remains limited.

Nonetheless, at the same time, according to information not available from non-open sources, Iran is apparently making efforts to develop a military nuclear option. A number of intelligence agencies claim that Iran is attempting — with mixed results but with increasing vigor — to purchase some of the same materials that Iraq had

Regional Issues

Range of Iran's Ballistic Missiles

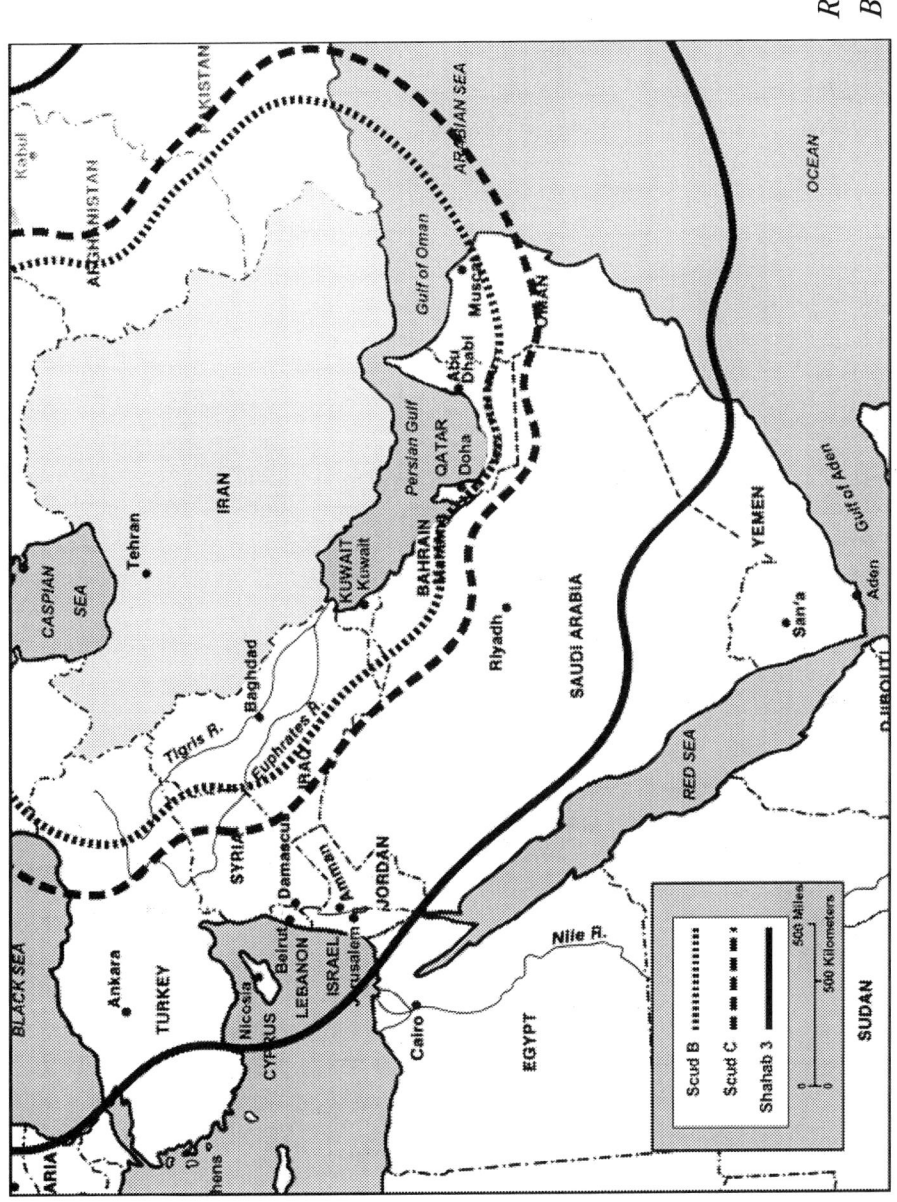

acquired in the late 1980s in order to construct its sensitive nuclear facilities. Clearly it is in a position to hide sensitive materials needed to construct enrichment facilities within the large shipments of materials it is purchasing for the Bushehr project. Iran is also able to exploit the knowledge of Russian nuclear engineers at Bushehr, who are present for legal and legitimate purposes but could be persuaded to contribute to the military nuclear program.

However, even intelligence agencies that follow developments in Iran closely have not located a uranium enrichment plant or a plutonium-reprocessing plan there. That they have good intelligence on Iran was made clear by their prediction of the second Shahab-3 missile test flight two weeks before it took place in July 2000. The Israeli intelligence community also seems to have a good track record in identifying technology transfers from Russia to Iran.

It should also be noted that a reprocessing plant would be relevant only if Iran possessed a plutonium-producing power or research reactor. As noted earlier, the reactor being completed at Bushehr does not meet this requirement. Currently, there is no evidence that Iran will be acquiring either a power reactor or a large-scale research reactor that will provide it with significant quantities of plutonium. If the US intelligence community locates a fissile material production plant in Iran, Washington will surely demand an IAEA inspection of the facility. This could trigger a crisis similar to the one that followed the sighting of the North Korean reprocessing facility. That such a demand has not yet been made is another indication that, to date, the construction of a uranium enrichment plant has not been spotted in Iran.

It should be admitted that from Iran's standpoint, obtaining weapons of mass destruction makes perfect strategic sense. It should be recalled that in early 1991 Iran was as surprised as other governments to discover the extent of Iraqi efforts to produce WMDs. It was also alarmed at how close Iraq was to obtaining operational nuclear capability. In the light of these revelations, it would have been surprising if Iran had not sought a hedge against the possibility that at some point in the future Iraq would be able to rebuild its WMD capabilities and its ballistic missile force. Iran also cannot be expected to be completely indifferent to the nuclear test conducted by Pakistan — a country with whom its relations have often been strained.

Clearly, Iranian leaders are unlikely to gamble their nation's security on the possibility that UN sanctions against Iraq will continue indefinitely or on the US continuing operations Northern Watch and Southern Watch. Their willingness to take such a gamble is probably also reduced by pronouncements from former UNSCOM senior officials regarding Iraq's residual WMD capabilities and mounting evidence of Saddam's determination to rebuild these capabilities without regard to the heavy costs entailed.

Fourth, Iran has been surprisingly cooperative within the global nonproliferation regime. Contrary to widespread expectations, in 1995, it refrained from presenting serious obstacles to the indefinite extension of the Nuclear Nonproliferation Treaty (NPT). In January 1993, it became an original signatory to the Chemical Weapons Convention (CWC) and in November 1997, it ratified the treaty, despite the inclusion of the most intrusive verification measures ever attached to a global nonproliferation regime. In 1998, it complied with the treaty by submitting a statement in which it admitted to having produced chemical weapons, thus committing itself to destroying these weapons and to verifying that it had done so.

Iranian behavior toward global nonproliferation regimes has been very different from the defiant behavior exhibited by countries like Iraq and North Korea. It has also been less militant than Egypt in tying its adherence to global nonproliferation treaties to the issue of Israel's signing the NPT. For example, while Egypt continues to refuse to sign and ratify the CWC as long as Israel does not sign the NPT, Iran signed and ratified the CWC nonetheless.

Fifth, the Iranian government demonstrates an impressive degree of cost-sensitive pragmatism in its conduct of foreign affairs. Surprisingly enough, such pragmatism was exercised even during the more militant phases of the Iranian revolution when Ayatollah Khomeini ruled the country. While efforts were made to export the revolution abroad, this was done where costs were limited. This is the case with the limited financial support that Iran provides Hamas, and it is also true regarding the much greater financial, political and operational support given to Hizbullah.

Other examples of Iran's pragmatism involve its relations with the Gulf States. While Iran initially made some efforts to destabilize Saudi Arabia and smaller GCC states, once the potential costs of this policy became clear, it curtailed its efforts, seeking instead to engage these very same governments. In recent years, Iran has improved its ties with Saudi Arabia dramatically; it has signed an agreement stipulating maritime boundaries with Kuwait; and it maintains excellent relations with Qatar and Oman. Only its relations with the UAE, related to the control of Abu Musa and two other small islands in the Gulf, remain tense.

Iranian pragmatism is best reflected in its policy toward Central Asia. In the immediate aftermath of the disintegration of the Soviet Union, it was widely assumed and feared that the Khomeini regime would attempt to spread its militant version of Islam to the Muslim populations of the Caucasus and the former Soviet Central Asian republics. It soon became clear that this would generate a harsh Russian reaction. Consequently, the Iranian government worked out a very detailed tacit understanding with Moscow that defined the boundaries of acceptable Iranian involvement in the affairs of these districts and states. This understanding explains Iran's silence on the harsh measures taken by the Russian Army against the Muslim Chechens — including the destruction of Grozny — in 1999–2000. In this case, Tehran clearly sacrificed its commitment to the Islamic cause in favor of realpolitik.

Taking all five considerations into account, an over-all assessment of Iran's impact on the stability of the Gulf region and on the Middle East yields uncertain results. On the one hand, the country remains a bastion of Islamic rule — the debate between the reformers and the conservatives continue to be conducted within a system of government in which the religious establishment imposes its rule, values and preferences on the general population. Despite considerable gains by the reformers in recent years, the conservatives continue to control many of the more sensitive institutions, including those fostering terrorism abroad. The struggle between reformers and conservatives does not appear to have influenced Iran's plans to develop weapons of mass destruction, the program appearing to enjoy bipartisan support.

That being said, the depth of Iran's commitment to developing WMDs is not clear. While its government works toward obtaining non-conventional arms, particularly in the chemical and nuclear spheres, it simultaneously supports global arms control initiatives that may undermine its ability to obtain such weapons. And, even if Iran were to obtain such weapons and their means of delivery, it is unlikely to use them except for deterrence purposes. The Iranian government is pragmatic and cost-sensitive. In contrast to Iraq, Iranian past behavior provides no indications of a chronic propensity to miscalculate. Hence, it is unlikely to ignore counter-deterrence threats. If during the Gulf War, Iraq's fear of reprisals led it to refrain from attacking Israeli, Saudi Arabian and US forces with the unconventional weapons that it possessed, the likelihood that Iran would use such weapons are much lower still.

Extra-Regional Players
With the end of the Cold War and the dissolution of the Soviet Union, the Middle East ceased being an arena of superpower competition and conflict. But the US has a wide array of interests in the region, and Russia's interests in the Middle East and the Persian Gulf date back to Czarist times. These interests do not always coincide. Indeed, after a short respite immediately following the Soviet Union's dissolution, Washington and Moscow now find themselves again operating at cross-purposes in the Middle East.

US Policy: Engagement and Containment
US policy in the Middle East has demonstrated considerable consistency. Since the end of the Cold War, when the goal of containing Soviet influence in the region became irrelevant, US interests in the region have remained unchanged: securing the free flow of oil at acceptable prices, insuring Israel's security and survival, assisting the Arab-Israeli peace process, supporting America's allies in the region — particularly in the Persian Gulf — and preventing the proliferation of weapons of mass destruction in the Middle East.

The means employed by Washington to meet its goals in the Middle East have also remained fairly constant in recent years: its "dual containment" policy is aimed at insuring the stability of the Gulf by deterring both Iran and Iraq; its continuous presence in the Gulf is designed to ensure the free flow of oil from the Straits of Hormuz; its active involvement in Israeli-Syrian and Israeli-Palestinian negotiations is aimed at facilitating Arab-Israeli peace; its military assistance to, and defense ties with, Israel are designed to sustain the latter's qualitative edge, thus insuring Israel's security and survival.

The constant US presence and involvement in the Middle East became the most important dimension of the region's external environment. Since then, the balance of political and military forces in the region has been tamed by what Washington considered acceptable behavior. Thus, when Iraq invaded Kuwait and threatened Saudi Arabia and some of the smaller Gulf states in 1990, the US reacted effectively as the region's policeman, judge and executioner. Without its leadership, the coalition that checked Iraq's ambitions and capabilities would not have been created.

It is within this context that US policy in the region has evolved in recent years. In the framework of Arab-Israeli peacemaking, the US increased its support of the Palestinian cause. When President Clinton visited the Gaza Strip in 1998, Washington seemed to have become the de facto guarantor of Palestinian statehood. However, after the Camp David II summit this ceased to be the case, as Clinton laid much of the responsibility for the failure of the summit at the Palestinians' doorstep and warned Chairman Arafat that the consequences of a unilateral declaration of statehood would be considerable.

In early 2000, the US had become much more assertive in its relations with Israel, primarily regarding the issue of technology transfers. Major tension between Washington and Jerusalem had developed regarding Israel's planned sale of the "Phalcon" Airborne Warning and Command System (AWACS) to China. Following unprecedented pressure exerted by the US in May and June, Israel cancelled the sale in mid-July.

By the end of the 1990s, the US policy of dual containment had also evolved. With respect to Iraq, the Clinton administration and the US Congress made it clear that they would no longer be content with mere "containment," and that they would, henceforth, attempt to bring about Saddam Hussein's downfall. This was based on the premise that Saddam's personality is a source of instability, and that as long as he stays in power, Iraq will continue to endanger Gulf stability. American policy toward Iraq that was previously intended strictly to contain Iraqi ambitions and capabilities, now included the declared aim of removing Saddam Hussein from power and ending his regime.

Yet the magnitude of the change in the Clinton administration's policy toward Iraq should not be exaggerated. It is not clear whether the policy change reflected an assessment by US government officials that bringing about Saddam's downfall was a realistic objective. Most administration officials seem to believe that Saddam is extraordinarily well-protected against assassination attempts, and that opposition to him is too weak to mount a real challenge to his regime. Thus, the putative change in administration policy on this issue seems to have been made largely in response to pressures from Capitol Hill, which themselves hardly reflected a real commitment to Saddam's downfall. The appropriation of $90 million for the purpose leads to the suspicion that the decision reflected lip service rather than realistic operational planning to remove Saddam.

With regard to Iran, US policy of dual containment evolved by the end of the decade in the opposite direction. Although the reformists' progress proved far from linear and every two steps forward seemed to be followed by a step backward, their achievements were nonetheless clear — especially in the elections to the parliament in February 2000. This gain, in addition to the indications that President Mohammed Khatami was interested in improving relations with the US, brought Washington to couple containment of Iran with an effort to engage Tehran positively as well, and to relax some of the economic measures applied against it. Accordingly, on March 17, 2000, Secretary of State Madeline Albright announced that the US would lift its 1987 ban on the import of "traditional goods" from Iran. Dual containment, therefore, has evolved in two different directions: "containment plus rollback" in the case of Iraq and "containment plus engagement" in the case of Iran.

US interests in the region are unlikely to change in the next few years. Nevertheless, a number of factors may affect the manner in which these interests will be pursued after January 2001: the importance attached to the Middle East, relative to other regions by the new administration; developments outside the region that will affect Washington's ability to devote the time, energy and resources to addressing the problems of the Middle East; the results of the next administration's expected reevaluation of the extent to which US policies in the region are optimized to achieve its purposes; and finally, developments in the region that may necessitate Washington to respond, thus affecting its agenda and priorities.

The next administration may give relatively greater weight to addressing US relations with Russia and to the security of northeast Asia than to the Middle East. Dramatic developments in the Pacific basin may induce Washington to concentrate all of its efforts there, as could a major crisis between China and Taiwan. These events would preclude Washington from devoting as much time and energy to Middle East peacemaking.

US Middle East policy will also be affected by the results of the next administration's review of current policy. For example, it may judge operations Northern Watch and Southern Watch as failing to help remove Saddam Hussein from power or compelling him to accept a reinstatement of UN monitoring and inspections. Similarly, such a review may lead the administration to engage Iran unconditionally, making Washington's current preconditions to improved ties with Iran — that it stop its involvement in international terrorism, that it cease its efforts to obtain weapons of mass destruction, and that it drop its opposition to the Arab-Israeli peace process — a subject of engagement rather than a prerequisite to such talks.

Finally, US policy in the Middle East will be affected by developments in the region itself. Thus, a further escalation of violence between Israelis and Palestinians, for example, is unlikely to leave Washington indifferent. Also, developments in the Persian Gulf may require the US to take military action in the sub-region once again. Among these possible developments are another Iraqi attempt to threaten Kuwait or to restore sovereignty over the Kurdish-held territories of northern Iraq. Similarly, if the US discovers an Iranian fissile material production plant, it would have to decide whether its counter-proliferation policy requires that military action be taken to destroy the facility.

In summary, it should be reiterated that while such developments may affect the specifics of US policy in the Middle East, the general contours of America's involvement in the region are unlikely to be altered, as they are determined by US vital interests and basic purposes in the region. There is no reason to believe that these vital interests will change or that the manner in which Washington defines its goals in the region will be altered. Thus, to the extent that US presence and involvement in the Middle East comprise an important context within which the region's strategic balance should be viewed, no major change in this context is anticipated.

Russian Policy: Defiance
Russia's policy in the Middle East has evolved over the past few years. In the immediate aftermath of the dissolution of the Soviet Union, Moscow adopted a low profile in the region. Facing an economic catastrophe at home, Russia attempted to gain repayment of at least part of the enormous sums that various Arab states owed the Soviet Union. These debts are said to have reached $11 billion in the case of Syria, $9 billion for Iraq, and $2 billion for Libya. Russia's efforts thus far, have been in vain — Syria and Iraq were in no position to repay these outstanding amounts.

In the mid-1990s, Moscow attempted to reassert itself in the Middle East by playing a more active role in the peace process. This was particularly the case under the tenure of Yevgeniy Primakov as foreign minister and, later, as premier of the Russian Federation. However, neither the US nor the local protagonists in the region were willing to accord Russia a role in the process that would match its formal position as co-chair of the 1991 Madrid Conference.

Meanwhile, other developments have led Russia to adopt a more defiant position vis-à-vis the US. In the mid-1990s, Moscow was antagonized by Washington's expansion of NATO, despite Russian concerns. Toward the end of the decade, it was equally angered by America's plan to construct and deploy a National Missile Defense (NMD) system, even if this risked a collapse of the ABM Treaty. In light of what it regarded as clear manifestations of US insensitivity, Moscow saw no reason to cooperate with the US on other matters, including the Middle East.

In 1993, Russia ignored US nuclear non-proliferation concerns and concluded a framework agreement on nuclear research cooperation with Iran. In 1995, it signed a specific contract for the completion of the 1000 Mw power reactor in Bushehr. Indeed, Russia claimed that Washington's objection to the deal comprised a violation of Article IV of the NPT, which assures treaty signatories access to peaceful nuclear technology. Moscow did refuse Iran's request that it also be supplied with a uranium enrichment plant — a request that made Iran's ultimate objectives quite transparent — but it ignored Washington's argument that the Bushehr project would help train hundreds of Iranian nuclear engineers who would, in turn, be able to build facilities for Iran's nuclear bomb program. It also rejected concerns that Iran would be able to hide transfers of prohibited nuclear materials within the large stream of nuclear material purchases made for the Bushehr project.

Moscow has taken an equally non-cooperative position with regard to the transfer of ballistic missile technology to Iran. It has stonewalled Israeli and US pleas that it prevent such transfers, arguing that the Russian government is not involved and has no knowledge of these transfers. When US and Israeli intelligence officials provided their Russian counterparts with hard facts on such transactions, the information was often conveyed to the firms and individuals involved, in order to alert them that they should be more careful.

The Russian leadership and later the Duma adopted regulations and legislation that outlawed the transfer of sensitive technologies, but made no effort to implement them. Ballistic missile technology related to navigation systems therefore continue to be transferred from Russia to Iran.

Russian defiance was also reflected in its policy toward Iraq. In 1996, Moscow made it clear that its support for the extension of UN sanctions against Iraq should not be taken for granted. In 1997, it emphasized its refusal to support the application of military punitive measures against Saddam. In the summer of 1998, when Iraq defied UNSCOM and rejected any further cooperation with UN inspectors and monitors, Russia made clear that it would not support the use of harsh measures to compel Iraqi compliance. It threatened the use of its veto in the UN Security Council to prevent the application of such measures, thus guaranteeing Iraqi obstructionism. Ever since, Moscow has repeatedly made clear that it would not support the resumption of UN inspections and monitoring of Iraq, except under conditions acceptable to Baghdad.

The issues that comprise the essence of Russia's current interaction with the Middle East — nuclear and ballistic missile technology transfers to Iran and the inspection of Iraq's WMD programs — are central to determining the region's strategic landscape. Thus, Russia's future conduct in the region will have a direct impact on peace and stability in the Middle East.

Four sets of factors are likely to affect Moscow's future behavior toward the region: Russia's long-standing interest in maintaining political influence in the Middle East; the opportunities that the region may present to Russia; the challenges that Russia may confront in other areas, to which it may react in the Middle East; and, finally, developments in Russia's domestic arena.

Russia regards itself as a power with traditional interests in the Middle East, resulting from complex historical, geographic, and demographic considerations. Consequently, it views its claims to a prominent status in peacemaking and peace enforcement in the region as perfectly understandable. Eliciting more responsible Russian behavior in the Middle East — for example, one that does not encourage the possession of weapons of mass destruction by autocratic and revolutionary regimes — requires that Moscow's quest for a legitimate role in the Arab-Israeli peace process be recognized and accommodated.

The second factor that will determine Russia's future involvement in the region concerns the opportunities that may present themselves. For example, if Syria were to gain the required financial resources, Moscow would surely be prepared to step in and supply Damascus once again with its best weaponry. The same applies to other countries — notably Iraq and Iran.

Third, Russia's behavior will be affected by developments in other spheres of its foreign and defense affairs. Thus, if in the next few years tensions with the US will grow over issues ranging from NMD deployment and a possible collapse of the Anti-Ballistic Missile Treaty to Western involvement in the Baltic States, Russia may react by posing the US with even greater challenges in the Middle East. Under such conditions, Russian may become even bolder in taking steps that undermine US interests in the region, particularly in the realm of weapons proliferation.

Finally, Russia's interaction with the Middle East will be affected by developments within the Russian Federation. A further deterioration of economic conditions may increase Moscow's interest in arms sales. This may lead it to ignore US concerns by making more aggressive efforts to market its weapons in the region. Even more important, such possible deterioration may result in what so far has been averted: the leakage of fissile material from the Russian nuclear complex to one of the Middle East states that is seeking to obtain a nuclear capability, primarily Iraq and Iran. Needless to say, such a development would change the region's strategic landscape overnight.

Chapter Four
Strategic Balances in the Middle East

The second section of this volume provides a detailed account of the weapons inventories possessed by the armed forces of Middle Eastern states. Charts allow some comparisons between the region's armed forces and a sense of military balances can be obtained. Once this data is supplemented by information regarding the activities of the region's states in other military realms — primarily, the efforts to acquire ballistic missiles and WMDs — an initial assessment of the threats faced by the region's states can be made.

Toward An Arab-Israeli Net Assessment
The threat Israel faces comprises a number of central features of its strategic environment. First, a number of Israel's neighbors possess large conventional forces. For example, with some 380,000 troops, 3700 tanks, 5000 armored personnel carriers, 2600 artillery pieces, 520 combat aircraft and 295 helicopters, the threat posed to Israeli security by the Syrian armed forces cannot be ignored. Moreover, resting on a much larger population base, the Syrian order-of-battle consists almost entirely of regular forces. By contrast, the majority of Israel's order-of-battle is comprised of reserve forces, which take time to deploy. As was the case in 1973, this difference exposes the IDF to a surprise attack — before its forces are fully mobilized.

Despite twenty-one years of Egyptian-Israeli peace, Israel also pays attention to the growth in Egypt's military power. In particular, it places emphasis on Egypt's access to Western military technology. This is manifested by the integration of advanced US platforms into its air and ground forces, notably some 250 M1A1 tanks (of a total of 555 in its inventory), 190 F-16 aircraft, and 36 attack helicopters.

Israel also faces a growing threat from surface-tō-surface ballistic missiles. While the overall magnitude of this threat has diminished as a consequence of the 1991 Gulf War and the destruction of most of Iraq's remaining missiles and launchers by UNSCOM inspectors, the total number of ballistic missile launchers and missiles facing Israel is considerable. Currently, Israel's neighbors possess sixty-five launchers capable of sending missiles that would reach Israel's industrial and population centers. In addition, Syria possesses eighteen launchers for accurate missiles (SS-21s) capable of reaching military targets in Israel's north. In the future, the number of missiles and launchers that could potentially threaten Israel's strategic assets will increase, as Iran's 1300-kilometer range Shahab-3 becomes operational.

A number of Israel's neighbors are also developing the infrastructure for the production of weapons of mass destruction. Syria is producing chemical agents, including sarin, mustard and VX; Iraq is suspected of hiding a significant quantity of biological weapons (anthrax, aphlatoxin, botulinum and possibly a limited quantity of chemical weapons as well). Egypt reportedly possesses mustard and nerve gases, and Iran has admitted that it has produced significant quantities of mustard and other chemical agents. In addition, Iran continues to develop a nuclear infrastructure, the military significance of which has been assessed earlier.

Finally, Israel's geographical confines make it particularly vulnerable to both conventional and unconventional attack. Its narrow topography deprives it of any strategic and operational depth. Paradoxically, this problem has been exacerbated by the expanding Arab-Israeli peace process and Israel's withdrawal from Lebanon. As the peace process results in Israel's withdrawal to borders that will be close to the lines it held until June 1967, the IDF will no longer have room for maneuver. Likewise, in the aftermath of Israel's withdrawal from Lebanon, Hizbullah has positioned its fighters along the international border, depriving the IDF of tactical depth. A similar situation will arise between Israel and the future Palestinian state when their armed forces will be positioned adjacent to one another.

Israel's narrow confines and the concentration of its small population and industrial infrastructure in a narrow strip of land make it particularly vulnerable to unconventional attack. Its dense population means that an adversary's ballistic missiles armed with chemical and biological munitions — and the ability to spread these munitions effectively — need not be accurate to cause considerable damage. Naturally, Israel is especially vulnerable in the nuclear realm: a single Hiroshima-type bomb that penetrated its defenses would be devastating.

Despite these sources of weakness and vulnerability, a net assessment of the Arab-Israeli strategic balance yields that by late 2000 Israel was stronger than ever. A number of factors combine to produce this conclusion: while it faces large conventional forces, Israel's armed forces are far from small. Thus, against Syria's inventory listed above, Israel can field 3930 tanks, 8040 armored personnel carriers, 1348 artillery pieces, 628 combat aircraft, and 287 helicopters. This places the threat presented by Syria's sizable armed forces in perspective.

Second, while a quantitative analysis of the military balance shows Israel at rough parity with Syria, the balance is decidedly in Israel's favor when the qualitative dimension of the weapons systems is taken into account. For example, while the

Syrian and Israeli air forces are of roughly equal size, the Syrian air force possesses only twenty air-superiority aircraft (MiG-29s) capable of confronting an Israeli air force that possesses over 345 such aircraft (of the F-15 and F-16 variety).

This example of Israel's qualitative edge represents a wider phenomenon. During the 1990s, Israel's remaining Arab adversaries and Iran were prevented from modernizing their armed forces. This was caused by developments elaborated earlier: the end of massive Soviet arms transfers to some Arab states; the absence of alternative suppliers willing to sell arms at discounted rates; the acute shortage of hard currency experienced by some of these states, caused partly by low oil prices; and the sanctions and embargoes applied against Iran and Iraq.

Consequently Syria has not purchased any advanced aircraft since 1987, when it received the twenty MiG-29s mentioned above, and it has not received new combat helicopters since the late 1980s, when it received the last of the fifty-five MI-25 helicopters in its inventory. Syria's air defense system is also aging: no new surface-to- air missiles have been acquired since 1985. As for its ground forces, Syria's only acquisition during the 1990s were some 400 T-72 tanks purchased from Russia and the Czech Republic and some 300 2S1 self-propelled artillery platforms acquired from Bulgaria. The Syrian navy has not received a single new combat vessel since 1982, and its submarine force is rotting.

As noted earlier, Iraq has been able to maintain its Republican Guard divisions through cannibalization and some smuggling of spare parts. However, it has not been able to purchase new platforms for its ground, naval and air forces since 1990. As long as this situation continues, and until the Iraqi armed forces are restored — a process that is likely to take years even after sanctions are lifted and the embargo is removed — Iraq will not be in a position to contribute significant forces to a war effort against Israel. While the obstacles to the modernization of Iran's armed forces are somewhat less severe, its distance from the Arab-Israeli arena makes its conventional forces largely irrelevant to an Israeli-Arab net assessment.

In contrast, Israel steadily continued to modernize all branches of its armed forces during the 1990s. Its air force acquired F-16 Cs and F-16 Ds (in addition to F-16 As and F-16 Bs obtained from US surplus stockpiles), extended range F-15 Is, and Apache and Cobra combat helicopters. In March 2000, the Israel Air Force decided to purchase fifty additional combat aircraft — the F-16 I. Its ground forces continued to integrate the Merkava Mk III tanks and MLRS systems. Its navy absorbed three Dolphin-class submarines and three Sa'ar-5 corvettes. Meanwhile, state-of-the-art subsystems and software integrated into new and older platforms allowed the IDF not only to maintain, but also to expand its qualitative edge. Particular emphasis was placed during the 1990s on the development of cutting-edge technologies in the areas of battle management, intelligence, and missile defense.

Finally, the US commitment to maintain this edge makes it very likely that the qualitative gap between the IDF and the Arab armed forces will be maintained in the future. An important example of this was the US-Israeli cooperation in developing the Arrow Anti-Tactical Ballistic Missile (ATBM) system. In March 2000, the first battery of Arrow missiles was delivered to the IDF. Another example is the Nautilus project — developing the capacity to kill Katyusha rockets with a high-energy laser beam. The system was successfully tested in the US on June 8, 2000.

The Arab states could not match Israel's achievements in these realms. In software development, none of the region's states were able to build an industry that even remotely resembled Israel's. In the military realm, this implied that even when purchasing advanced Western platforms, Arab states could not upgrade these weapons with the level of self-made technologies that Israel had. As a result, not only has Israel been able to maintain its qualitative edge, but this edge continued to expand throughout the 1990s.

Range of Syria's Ballistic Missiles

Israel's net advantage over its neighbors is even greater when the qualitative comparison focuses on the totality of the complex military systems. This comparison takes into account a variety of unit-level and system-level factors: the quality and training of manpower; force multipliers in the realm of command, control, communications and intelligence; and the successful integration of advanced weapons in force structure and doctrine.

This multi-dimensional analysis is especially pertinent when a particular threat faced by Israel is compared with the array of measures available to address the threat. For example, Israel's response to the threat presented by Syrian Scud missiles carrying chemical weapons comprises the following elements: the means by which Israel can deliver painful retaliation against Syria's high value assets; active defense measures designed to kill incoming ballistic missiles (i.e. the Patriot PAC-3 and the Arrow ATBM system); the offensive means available to destroy the missile launchers through the use of aircraft and, in the future, to destroy launchers or missiles immediately after their launch through use of Boost Phase Interception (BPI) or Boost Phase and Launcher Interception (BPLI) systems; and an array of passive defense measures ranging from sealed rooms to gas masks. This range of responses promises to reduce considerably the total damage that Israel might incur because of Syrian employment of ballistic missiles, even if armed with chemical or biological weapons.

The asymmetry described earlier as favoring Israel in the conventional sphere is at least as dramatic in the realm of WMDs. The chemical and biological capabilities of Syria, Iraq and Iran are matched, according to foreign sources, by Israel's possession of a wide range of such weapons. And while Iraq and Iran are interested in rebuilding (in the case of Iraq) and constructing (in the case of Iran) a nuclear option, Israel remains the only country in the region widely perceived as possessing a large inventory of nuclear warheads. This perception has been reinforced in recent years as foreign publications named the specific units of Israel's alleged nuclear strike force and the locations where these weapons are stationed. Foreign sources also report that Israel enjoys superiority in the realm of ballistic missiles. In this area Israel is widely regarded as possessing the most advanced capability in the region. According to foreign reports, its inventory includes a considerable number of Jericho-I and Jericho-II launchers and missiles, with ranges of up to 1500 kilometers.

Israel's growing edge in the military sphere is compounded by non-military factors that affect the net Arab-Israeli balance. The most important of these are the expanded Middle East peace process and the disunity in the Arab world — which the peace process has exacerbated. During the 1990s, these two factors combined to reduce the number of states that are candidates for joining a war coalition against Israel. Most importantly, these developments diminish the likelihood that the IDF would have to fight on more than one front and the danger that it would have to face quantitatively superior forces. Consequently, they have increased the chance that if a military confrontation does develop, the full force of the IDF could be brought to bear against one adversary (at most supported by some expeditionary forces contributed by more distant states) along a single front.

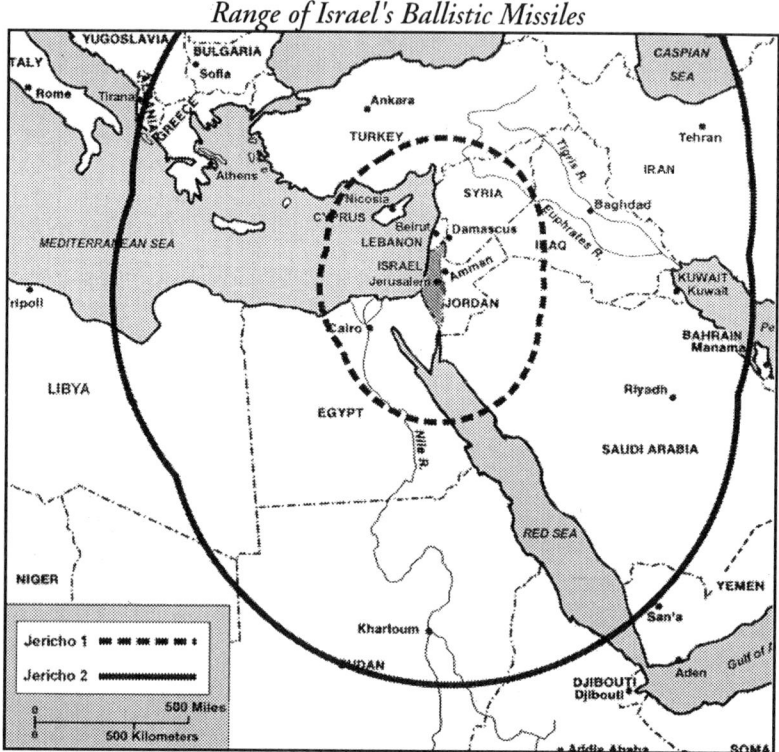

Range of Israel's Ballistic Missiles

* According to foreign sources

Israel's edge in the military technologies described earlier is backed by a huge technological gap in the civilian sphere. Israel is now considered as a second Silicon Valley and a larger part of its economy has become an integral part of the global village. In 1999, its high-tech exports rose by some 40 percent and exports of "traditional goods" increased by some 12 percent. In high-tech investments, Israel — a country of six million people — is now ranked fifth in the world in absolute terms and first in investments per capita.

The combination of advanced technologies in the military and civilian sectors has made Israel a global player and a significant exporter of high-tech weapons. This is because the sale of force multipliers — in the realm of intelligence and battle management — can, potentially, alter regional balances. The planned sale of the "Phalcon" AWACS to China — cancelled in July 2000 — is a case in point.

These developments, as well as other factors that included the fiscal and monetary policies pursued during the 1990s, have strengthened Israel's economy significantly. With its advanced technological infrastructure and highly skilled labor force, Israel's economy has progressed in recent years differently from that of its neighbors. Having developed very rapidly in the early 1990s due to the immigration from Russia, economic growth slowed in 1996–99 (on the average only 2.2 percent annually). But by 1999 Israel's economy picked up again, driven primarily by the high-tech sector. Its GDP per capita reached $16,160 (in contrast to Egypt's $1,306 and Syria's $1,097 GDP per capita). By the late 1990s, Israel's inflation rate had been brought down to European levels and was expected to be no higher than 2 percent in 2000. Foreign currency reserves climbed from an average of four to five billion dollars in the 1980s, to over $24 billion in 1999.

Also, by early 2000 it seemed that for the first time Israel has taken a significant step towards greater independence in the energy sector. This was due to a series of successful offshore natural gas explorations. The reserves discovered are currently assessed as being able to provide Israel with the ability to meet its natural gas requirements until the year 2015.

In addition to building the physical, technological and economic attributes of its national power, Israel has gained increasing international legitimacy in recent years. This resulted partially from the manner in which it has conducted its withdrawal from southern Lebanon. While in earlier years Israel was quite critical of international institutions, in mid-2000 the government decided to depart from past habits and to coordinate its moves fully with the UN. Not only did it place its decision to withdraw from southern Lebanon within the context of UN Security Council Resolution 425, it decided to comply with a strict definition of the resolution: to coordinate its moves with the UN Secretary General's Office and to insist on obtaining the approval of the UN Security Council that it had complied fully with all stipulations of the resolution.

These diplomatic moves enabled Israel to gain the international legitimacy it required in case it needed to react militarily to attacks on its northern towns and settlements in the aftermath of its withdrawal from southern Lebanon. While in the past the Israeli government insisted on taking unilateral measures — based on the right of self-defense — it now sought to acquire a priori international legitimacy for such actions.

The withdrawal from Lebanon was only one manifestation of the improvement in Israeli-UN relations. Although Israel was founded on the basis of a UN General Assembly resolution and became a UN member immediately after the state's establishment in 1948, it remained an "outsider," being refused membership in the Middle East group, despite the expanding Arab-Israeli peace process. In early 2000, however, after years of diplomatic effort, Israel was made a member of the European group.

The change in Israeli-UN relations is the latest development in a much more fundamental transformation of Israel's international standing. In the 1970s and throughout most of the 1980s, Israel suffered relative isolation in the international community. It did not have diplomatic relations with the Soviet Union, any of the East European countries except Romania, any African country except South Africa, or with the giants of the north and south Asia: China and India.

Following the fall of the Soviet empire, the 1991 Gulf War and the 1993 Oslo Accords, Israel's international standing underwent a complete reversal. During the second half of the 1980s and the start of the 1990s, some thirty countries moved to restore or establish diplomatic relations with Israel, including the Soviet Union, all the countries of Eastern Europe, China and India. Since the signing of the Oslo Accords, thirty-five more have followed suit, including almost all countries of the African continent.

In addition, during the 1990s other forms of relations were expanded with countries with which Israel did not have formal diplomatic ties, including those from the Persian Gulf and North Africa, and Indonesia. Israel's ties with countries with which it did have diplomatic relations — notably Japan and the states of Western Europe — were improved considerably during this period. In stark contrast to the relative isolation it suffered in the 1970s, by the mid-1990s Israel had become completely integrated into the international community.

Many of these countries chose to improve relations with Israel for a combination of reasons: the expanded peace process meant that states outside the region could improve their relations with Israel without damaging their ties with Arab states; the advanced state of Israeli technology provided expanded business opportunities; and the international oil glut deprived Arab states from using oil as leverage, which implied that even states that imported a very large percent of their energy from the Middle East — most notably, Japan — could, for the first time, separate their Middle East and oil policies.

A final significant dimension of Israel's strength is the alliances it has built up over the years with key strategic players. The most important of these are the close defense ties developed between Israel and the US. These ties are based on shared values, common strategic concerns and an active American Jewish community that has made Israel part of the US domestic agenda.

Strategic cooperation between the US and Israel has been codified in a large number of bilateral Memoranda of Understanding (MOUs) and Memoranda of Agreement (MOAs). These documents have affected Israel's deterrent profile significantly by formalizing America's commitment to Israel's qualitative edge and deterrence requirements and stipulating an array of activities: joint exercises between IDF and US military units; the pre-positioning of US weapons and ammunition in Israel; and cooperation between the two countries in developing advanced weapon systems like the Arrow ATBM and the Nautilus laser anti-rocket system.

Another part of this alliance network is the close defense ties which developed during the 1990s between Israel and Turkey and, to a lesser degree, between Israel and Jordan. These ties affect not only Israel's overall deterrence profile, but also the specific Israeli-Syrian net assessment. While Syria experiences strained relations with Turkey and tension with Iraq and Jordan, Israel has developed strategic and defense-industrial cooperation with Turkey and a degree of military cooperation with Jordan, all backed by close defense ties with the US.

At the turn of the new millennium, Israel continues to face security threats. The most worrisome elements of its strategic environment are the large conventional forces possessed by some of its neighbors — notably Syria and Egypt — and the efforts of many of the region's states to acquire WMDs and the ability to deliver these weapons. Israel's robust capabilities, however, more than offset these sources of danger. In the military sphere, Israel's qualitative edge has expanded at a rapid pace. In the unconventional realm, Israel's alleged capabilities are the most advanced in the region. And, importantly, Israel's capacities in both areas are backed by a robust economy, the most technology-intensive industry in the region and close defense ties with the US. Consequently, a net assessment of the Arab-Israeli strategic balance indicates that Israel has never been stronger.

Two reservations are nevertheless in order. First, the net assessment presented above would be significantly altered if one of the Arab states or Iran were to acquire nuclear weapons. Due to reasons elaborated earlier, none of these states is likely to obtain such weapons in the near future through indigenous means. However, if Iraq or Iran were able to acquire fissile materials smuggled from the former Soviet Union or elsewhere, the Arab-Israeli strategic balance would be affected overnight. This development would once again pose an existential threat to Israel. More generally, it is likely to encourage the states possessing these weapons to exercise greater boldness in conducting their external affairs. It may also affect the will of the US to continue its efforts to contain these regimes, as the risks associated with US involvement will rise exponentially. Thus, while by mid-2000 Israel seemed stronger than ever and the Middle East appeared more stable than before, this positive assessment remains vulnerable to a sudden proliferation of nuclear weapons in the region.

The second reservation is that while Israel's current overwhelming advantage significantly reduces the likelihood that it will be attacked, it does not eliminate the possibility altogether. This is because even vast military superiority does not automatically translate into effective deterrence, as other factors affecting deterrence may negate expectations derived from a net assessment of military capabilities. For example, an asymmetry between two parties' determination may affect deterrence, offsetting one side's favorable capabilities. A retroactive net assessment of the Arab-Israeli balance yields that Israel enjoyed a considerable advantage on the eve of the Yom Kippur War. This is clearly evidenced by the outcome of the military confrontation. Yet, the determination of Egypt and Syria to regain the territories they lost in 1967 led them to challenge the IDF despite its proven superiority.

Hence, even a net assessment that yields a very dramatic disparity between the military forces of the two sides does not necessarily imply that the weaker party lacks a military option altogether. Rather, it forces the weaker party to be very creative in attempting to find an asymmetric response to the stronger side's superiority — one that prevents the stronger party from being able to utilize the full strength of its military means. This was well demonstrated when Hizbullah confronted the IDF in southern Lebanon and during the two Palestinian uprisings, in 1988-90 and in late 2000. However, when a serious threat to national security is presented, limitations on the use of force are usually dropped, allowing countries to bring the full power of their armed forces to bear. In such cases, net assessment should provide an accurate prediction of the outcome.

The Strategic Balance in the Gulf

The strategic equation in the Persian Gulf includes four primary elements: Iraq, Iran, the Gulf Cooperation Council (GCC) states and US involvement in the region. Since the end of the 1991 Gulf War, stability in this region has been largely maintained by a delicate balance among these elements.

As noted earlier, Iraq and Iran have both been weakened significantly by war. As long as Iraq remains constrained by sanctions, embargoes and the resulting lack of hard currency, it will not be able to rebuild its forces to their pre–Gulf War levels. Moreover, its forces will continue to deteriorate as Iraq cannibalizes platforms in order to maintain its remaining weapons. Thus, these forces have diminished from their initial post–Gulf War level. Since 1994, the Iraqi operational tank force has shrunk by an additional 10 percent (from 2200 to 2000); its inventory of armored personnel carriers and other armored fighting vehicles diminished by some 40 percent (from 3500 to 2000); and the number of its combat aircraft was reduced by half (from 400 to 210).

Despite the fact that the constraints implemented against Iran are far less stringent than those imposed on Iraq, and although its population base is three times larger than Iraq's, the Iranian armed forces suffer endemic weaknesses. For example, its tank forces are smaller than Iraq's by a quarter (1460 versus 2000) and its inventory of operational armored personnel carriers is about 40 percent less (1240 versus 2000). This is somewhat balanced by the fact that the two countries' air forces are of roughly equal size (each possess about 200 combat aircraft) and Iran enjoys some advantage in artillery — 2650 versus 2130 pieces in Iraq's inventory.

The main constraint on Iran's capacity to build up its forces is financial. It managed to implement only a small part of a major arms buildup program widely reported in the early 1990s. In the absence of the requisite hard currency, Iran could not fund most of the program.

As long as Iran and Iraq remain constrained by existing sanctions and embargoes, and as long as they lack sufficient financial resources, both countries' armed forces will remain weak. Moreover, since the two armed forces are currently of roughly equal size, and since they suffer different but equally important weakness, militarily they seem to balance one another. As long as they continue to experience their present financial constraints, their inability to fund another military confrontation — similar to the 1980–88 war — makes it highly unlikely that such an adventure would be attempted again any time soon. Militarily weak and financially bankrupt, neither state is likely to threaten the stability of the Gulf region by challenging the other.

The inability of either Iran or Iraq to launch a challenge to Saudi Arabia and the smaller members of the GCC results from the combined military capacity of these states, as well as from the US military presence that backs its commitment to prevent such a challenge. Yet assessing the military capabilities of the GCC states is not easy. On one hand, these states' oil revenues have allowed them to purchase modern weapons systems during the 1990s, despite low oil prices. For example, Saudi Arabia acquired M1A2 tanks and F-15 aircraft; Kuwait has purchased M1A1 tanks and F-18 aircraft; and the UAE acquired Leclerc 2 tanks, Mirage 2000 aircraft and Apache helicopters. Even when totaled, however, these inventories are inferior in quantity to those of Iran and Iraq.

Moreover, serious problems are associated with any effort to add up the GCC states' weapons inventories. First, the degree of military cooperation among these states is limited; their armies do not exercise together regularly in a fashion permitting them to prepare adequately for joint operations. Second, their limited population base places a major constraint on their ability to absorb larger quantities of advanced weapons systems. Third, the manpower shortage also limits the ability of the GCC states to operate their forces independently, since they rely on foreign technicians to maintain their weapons systems.

Thus, while possessing some self-defense capabilities, the GCC states rely on the US to provide the requisite responses to the challenges presented by the military capacities of Iran and Iraq. In turn, America's ability to maintain strategic stability in the Gulf rests on five elements: US military forces stationed in the GCC states; the pre-positioning of US arms and ammunition in these states and in nearby locations; the access that US forces enjoy to military facilities in the Gulf; America's ability to transfer troops to the region at short notice; and US forces stationed in Turkey.

On the average, the US maintains some 11,500 troops (of which some 2400 are naval personnel) in the GCC states, mostly in Saudi Arabia, Kuwait and Bahrain. It also pre-positions equipment in Saudi Arabia, Bahrain, Kuwait, Oman, Qatar and the UAE. In addition, the US enjoys access to naval facilities in Bahrain, Oman and the UAE, and to airbases in Kuwait, Oman and Saudi Arabia, from which Operation Southern Watch is being conducted. These forces and pre-positioned stocks are commanded from the Mina Salman base in Bahrain.

In addition to these land and shore facilities, the US 5th Fleet maintains a permanent naval presence in the Persian Gulf. In mid-2000, these forces comprised some fourteen ships, sixty-six aircraft and some 7300 sailors and marines. They include: an aircraft carrier, a guided missile cruiser, three destroyers and guided missile destroyers, a guided missile frigate, an attack submarine, two mine countermeasure ships and other auxiliary vessels.

The forces that the US would be able to deploy in case of a major military confrontation in the Persian Gulf would not be as large as those deployed during Desert Storm. This is the result of the major downsizing of US forces in the 1990s in the aftermath of the end of the Cold War. Many of the units deployed in the Persian Gulf in late 1990 and early 1991 no longer exist. However, the continuous modernization of US forces makes their smaller order-of-battle extremely effective. This is especially true in the case of the Persian Gulf, where topography and weather conditions are particularly conducive to the effective use of precision-guided munitions.

The final element allowing US operations in the Persian Gulf is the access it enjoys to facilities — particularly airbases — in Turkey. It is from these bases that the US employed its air power in most post–Gulf War operations — notably Desert Fox — and from which Operation Northern Watch has been conducted since 1996. Clearly, close US-Turkey defense ties will continue to be a key to America's ability to employ forces in Gulf contingencies.

The present distribution of power in the Persian Gulf allows the effective checking of Iraqi and Iranian ambitions. Obviously, despite the considerable downsizing of the Iraqi and Iranian forces, these remain significant in size. Nevertheless, they are contained by two elements: the first are the military forces of the GCC states. While small, uncoordinated and dependent on foreign elements for their maintenance, these forces are much more modern than those possessed by Iraq and Iran. The second and stronger element is the significant US military presence in the region. America's forces have a double role in checking the military power of Iran and Iraq. Militarily, their capabilities are considerable, and politically, they increase the confidence of the GCC states and increase the likelihood that they would cooperate with the US in future military operations.

In the final analysis, the key to the stability of the strategic balance in the Gulf seems to be the future of the sanctions and embargoes applied against Iraq. Once these sanctions and embargoes are lifted and Iraq is allowed to rebuild its military capabilities, Iran will be compelled to shift much more of its limited resources to defense spending in conventional, as well as non-conventional, spheres. In turn, the combined effect of a new Iran-Iraq arms race will surely increase the nervousness of Saudi Arabia and the smaller GCC states. With limited capacity to increase the size of their armed forces, these states will put added pressure on the US to sustain its dual containment policy.

Even if sanctions and embargoes are lifted, Iraq's capacity to disrupt the Gulf balance in the short run is uncertain. On one hand, Iraq is bankrupt and has enormous debts to repay. On the other hand, Saddam Hussein has already demonstrated his willingness to completely ignore the welfare of the Iraqi people by allowing them to suffer, while devoting huge resources to weapons build-up. If the price of oil remains high, by the early 2000s Iraq will be able to gain considerable oil revenues. By summer 2000, its oil production had already reached the pre–Gulf War level of three million barrels a day.

A reassertion of Iraqi power will have repercussions beyond the Gulf region, threatening instability in the region at large. Jordan is likely to feel directly threatened; Israel will fear a replay of the challenges it faced during the Gulf War; and Egypt will be concerned that its leadership in the Arab world is being challenged once again by Saddam Hussein. While these developments are unlikely in the short-term, their possible materialization in the mid-2000s cannot be ruled out.

Summary

The Middle East has become a more stable environment in the 1990s. The end of the Cold War and the dissolution of the Soviet Union eliminated a major source of the arms race in the region; the lower price of oil further dampened any new arms buildup; the acceleration of the Arab-Israeli peace process reflected a growing appreciation that conflicts and disputes should be resolved through diplomacy, not war; the race to acquire weapons of mass destruction was at least temporarily halted by Iraq's defeat during the Gulf War; political Islam has failed to topple the secular Arab regimes; and there has been a general decline in international terrorism and, particularly, in state-sponsored terrorism exported from the Middle East.

These general trends appear remarkably positive especially when the 1990s are compared to the tumultuous preceding three decades when the region experienced the War in Yemen (1962–67), the Six Day War (1967), the War of Attrition (1969–1970), the Yom Kippur War (1973), the Lebanon War (1982–85), the Iraq-Iran War (1980–88), and, finally, the Gulf War (1990–91). Indeed, the nine-year period between mid-1991 and mid-2000 has been the longest period to be free of any major military confrontation in recent history.

In late-2000, however, the region once again seems to be poised at a strategic crossroads. The future of the peace process remains in question, it being unlikely that Israel, Syria, and the Palestinian Authority are in a position to walk the extra mile needed to conclude negotiations for peace and a final status agreement. Egypt, for its part, seems to have become increasingly ambivalent about the peace that it concluded with Israel in 1979 — wishing to be recognized as the initiator of Arab-Israeli peacemaking while at the same time unsure about its role in a future post-peace Middle East.

The Persian Gulf remains an area of considerable uncertainty. It appears possible that the pursuit of weapons of mass destruction in the Middle East could again be accelerated, specifically by Iran and Iraq. It is not clear if some form of monitoring of Iraq will be reinstated, or if the remaining sanctions and embargoes applied against Baghdad remain in place. Consequently, it is uncertain how long Iraq can be prevented from reconstructing its capacity to produce WMDs.

Different questions surround developments in Iran, where the struggle between the reformists and the conservatives continues. Having won the elections to the presidency in 1998 and to the Majlis in February 2000, the reformists lost ground immediately thereafter when the conservatives reacted by suppressing freedom of the press and put several leading reformists on trial. The reformists have signaled their interest in improving relations with the US, while at the same time, Iran continues its efforts to develop weapons of mass destruction and long-range missile delivery systems.

With regard to the US and Russia, they seem to work increasingly at cross-purposes in the Middle East. Washington continues its engagement in Arab-Israeli peacemaking and in maintaining close defense ties with Israel, Egypt, Jordan and the GCC states. Having succeeded in preventing Iraq and Iran from threatening the region's stability in the early 1990s, by the end of the decade American policy of "dual containment" has evolved in two different directions: "containment plus rollback" in the case of Iraq and "containment plus engagement" in the case of Iran.

Russia, on the other hand, has played an increasingly non-constructive role in the late 1990s. In the UN Security Council, it has prevented any forceful moves to compel Iraq to accept an effective successor to the monitoring and supervisions previously conducted by UNSCOM, and it refrained from taking effective measures against the transfer of ballistic missile and nuclear technologies to Iran.

Dark clouds also surround the region's social-economic front. Despite the progress made by some of the Middle East economies during the 1990s, most of the region's states continue to suffer serious economic difficulties, resulting in deep poverty. In turn, such poverty creates the breeding ground for movements challenging the legitimacy of ruling regimes. While terrorism has been contained, it has not been abandoned or eradicated. Political developments could encourage socio-political movements and organizations to escalate violence and terrorism.

A "net assessment" of the Arab-Israeli military balance yields that by late-2000 the distribution of power in the Middle East favored Israel. Despite its quantitative inferiority, its inherent vulnerability to ballistic missiles and WMDs, and the influx of Western technology to a number of its neighboring Arab states, Israel's qualitative edge has grown consistently during the 1990s, as has its array of countermeasures against strategic threats. Furthermore, the number of Arab states considered as potential members of a war coalition against Israel has diminished. Indeed, Israel's edge is even more dramatic when non-military factors are added to the equation: the advanced state of its technology, a robust, globally linked economy and its increased international legitimacy.

Strategic stability in the Gulf rests on a different set of factors. Iraq and Iran were both weakened significantly by their long war from 1980–88, and — in the case of Iraq — by the 1991 Gulf War. As long as the two countries remain constrained by existing sanctions and embargoes and lack sufficient financial resources, both countries' armed forces will remain weak. And, as long as their present weaknesses persist, they can continue to be held in check primarily by the formidable deterrent power of the US, spearheaded by its military forces deployed in, and proximate to, the Persian Gulf theater.

The stability of the Arab-Israeli and Gulf arena remains, however, vulnerable to the same possible development: the acquisition of nuclear weapons by Iraq or Iran. While this is unlikely to be achieved in the next few years through indigenous means, a massive influx of technology or the leakage of fissile material may result in the possession of atomic weapons by either of these states within a short period. While in the 1990s this danger did not materialize, there is no guarantee that it will not happen in the next decade.

As in the case of the Indo-Pakistan subcontinent, nuclear proliferation in the Gulf does not mean that nuclear war in the Middle East becomes imminent. Moreover, if such proliferation develops gradually, the region's governments are likely to adjust themselves to the resulting limitations and threats. Yet such a development — especially if abrupt — would introduce considerable uncertainties into the region's affairs. Arab-Israeli peacemaking may be further hampered as the parties assess the impact of this development on their relative bargaining power. Israel may react by altering its own nuclear posture, propelling various chain reactions in Arab capitals. The power struggle in the Gulf would accelerate, as would the competition between the Nile and Mesopotamia for influence in the Arab world. And the US would be likely to reassess the imperatives and potential costs of sustaining dual containment in a nuclear regional environment. These developments — while still preventable — threaten to negate the relative stability experienced in the Middle East in the past decade.

PART II

MILITARY FORCES
Yiftah Shapir

Introductory Note

This part of the *Middle East Military Balance* contains data on the arsenals and the orders-of-battle of 20 states and the Palestinian Authority. It also contains information on other security activities of these states — arms procurement, military production and security cooperation.

Appendices providing a glossary, technical data on weapon systems, a list of abbreviations, a comparative table, and charts, appear at the end of this part of the book.

Definitions and Criteria

Data on military acquisitions and sales as well as on security assistance are limited to information pertaining to the past five years. The year in parentheses in these sections always refer to the most recent information on an entry.

Armor

Tanks are divided into two main categories: light tanks (under 25 tons) and main battle tanks (MBTs). High quality MBTs and other MBTs are also differentiated.
The criteria for "high quality" are any three of the following attributes:
- A 120mm (or higher) caliber gun
- A power plant of more than 900 hp and/or power-to-weight ratio of 19 hp/t or better
- Reactive or modular armor
- A capability to fire barrel launched anti-tank missiles
- An advanced fire control system, with tracking capability

Under this categorization some versions of the T-72 MBT are categorized as "high quality," although they are not necessarily on par with tanks like the M1A1 or the Merkava Mk III.

Armored Fighting Vehicles (AFVs)

AFVs are divided into three categories:
- Armored personnel carriers — armored vehicles designed to carry several infantrymen, armed with light weapons only
- Infantry fighting vehicles — armored vehicles built to carry several infantrymen, armed with heavier weapons, such as guns or missiles
- Reconnaissance vehicles — armored vehicles of various sizes and armament, designed to carry a small crew of weapons operators, but not intended for dismounted infantry fighting

It should be noted that the dividing line between the categories are not well-defined, and sometimes it is difficult to decide how a certain vehicle should be categorized. For example, heavier reconnaissance vehicles can be categorized as light tanks, especially when they use tracks rather than wheels.

Air Defense

Some militaries in the region have a separate Air Defense arm. In other countries, air defense equipment is divided between the Air Force and the Ground Forces. In this volume all air defense weapon systems are aggregated into one sub-section in each chapter, regardless of the organizational distribution of the weapons systems.

Air defense equipment is categorized as follows:
- Shoulder-launched missiles
- Light SAMs — with a range up to 12 km, self-propelled or towed.
- Mobile medium SAMs — self-propelled, with a range of 12 – 30 km.
- Medium to heavy SAMs — stationary or towed systems with a range of 12 – 30 km, or any system with a range of more than 30 km.
- Other systems — AA guns and combined systems.

Numbers are given according to the number of independent fire units. Thus, for example, the number of SA-2 (Guideline) will represent the number of batteries, but for SA-8 (Gecko) the number of launchers is given. However, an exception is made in the "Order-of-Battle" table at the beginning of the "Armed Forces" section for each country where only the number of batteries is calculated for the sake of brevity.

Combat Aircraft

Combat aircraft are divided into the following categories:
- Interceptors
- Multi-role (high quality and others)
- Ground attack
- Obsolete

Navy

Size and armament for each vessel appear in the tables for each country.

Non-Governmental Forces

Listed are only major non-governmental forces that might have military significance. There are two types of non-governmental forces. First, there are those opposing the government of the country in which they act. Second, there are those which are based in — and sometimes financed by — another country. These organizations are listed according to the host country.

Note on Symbols

In this volume several symbols are used to denote instances where accurate data is not available:

- NA   Data not available. This symbol is used in the economic data tables only.
- ~   The tilde is used in front of a number to denote approximate number.
- +   The weapon system is known to be in use, but the quantity is not known.
- ∗   There is doubt whether the weapon system exists in the order-of-battle.
- 0   The weapon system exists but known to be not in use.

Economic Data

The tables on economic data include data on GDP (in current US dollars). Per capita GDP is derived from a simple division of the GDP by the size of the population.

Data on military expenditures in the Middle East are notoriously elusive. Hence such data should be regarded, at best, as indicators of trends.

Acknowledgments

The hard work of compiling, updating and setting the data was done by Yoel Kozak and Tamir Magal, to whom I owe a great debt of gratitude. Jacqueline Hahn-Efrati worked on the editing and proofreading. I alone, however, bear responsibility for any inaccuracies.

Yiftah S. Shapir
December 2000

1. ALGERIA

General Data

Official Name of the State: Democratic and Popular Republic of Algeria
Head of State: President of the High State Council Abd al-Aziz Buteflika
Prime Minister: Hammed Ben-Bitur
Minister of Defense: Nureddin Zarhouni
Chief of General Staff: Major General Muhammad Lamari
Commander of the Ground Forces: Major General Salih Ahmad Jaid
Commander of the Air Force: Brigadier General Muhammad Ibn Suleiman
Commander of Air Defense Force: Brigadier General Achour Laoudi
Commander of the Navy: Admiral Brahim Dadci

Area: 2,460,500 sq. km.
Population: 29,800,000

Demography

Ethnic groups		
Arabs	23,393,000	78.5%
Berbers	5,781,200	19.4%
Europeans	298,000	1.0%
Others	327,800	1.1%
Religious groups		
Sunni Muslims	29,502,000	99.0%
Christians and Jews	298,000	1.0%

Economic Data

		1994	1995	1996	1997	1998
GDP (current prices)	$ bn	41.97	41.16	45.56	47.08	50.77
GDP per capita	$	1,526	1,465	1,593	1,617	1,704
Real GDP growth	%	-1.0	3.9	3.8	1.3	5.1
Consumer price index	%	29.0	32.1	21.7	3.8	4.5
External debt	$ bn	29.9	32.8	33.4	30.9	30.3
Balance of payments						
• Exports fob	$ bn	8.89	10.26	13.21	13.82	10.14
• Imports fob	$ bn	9.15	10.10	9.09	8.13	8.63
• Current account balance (including services and income)	$ bn	-0.55	-2.24	1.25	3.46	-0.91

Economic Data *(continued)*

		1994	1995	1996	1997	1998
Government expenditure						
• Total expenditure	$ bn	13.17	12.36	13.23	14.65	14.9
• Defense expenditure	$ bn	1.3	1.23	1.37	1.65	1.73
• Real change in defense expenditure	%	21.5	-5.4	11.4	20.4	4.8
• Defense expenditure/GDP	%	3.1	3.0	3.0	3.5	3.4
Population	m	27.5	28.1	28.6	29.1	29.8
Official exchange rate	AD: $1	35.06	47.66	54.75	57.70	58.74

Sources: EIU Quarterly Report, EIU Country Profile, IMF International Financial Statistical Yearbook, SIPRI Yearbook

Arms Procurement and Security Assistance Received

Country	Type	Details
Belarus	• Arms transfers	MiG-29 aircraft (2000)
France	• Arms transfers	Ecureuil helicopters (1995)
Russia	• Arms transfers	Mi-17 helicopters (1995), Kh-35 missiles (1998)
South Africa	• Arms transfers	UAV systems (1998)
UK	• Arms transfers	Naval vessels (1997)
US	• Arms transfers	C^3I system (1999)
	• Assistance	$ 125,000 for training program (1998)

Foreign Military Cooperation

Type	Details
• Joint maneuvers	US maritime SAR exercise (2000)
• Security agreement	Russia

Defense Production

	M	P	A
Army equipment			
• Trucks (in collaboration with France)		√	
• Small arms		√	
Naval craft			
• Tugs	√		
• Kebir class PBs		√	√

Note: M - manufacture (indigenously developed)
P - production under license
A - assembly

Weapons of Mass Destruction

NBC Capabilities
Nuclear capability
- A nuclear reactor of 15 Mw, probably upgraded to 40 Mw (from PRC); a 1 Mw nuclear research reactor (from Argentina); basic R&D; signatory to the NPT. Safeguards agreement with the IAEA in force. Signed and ratified the African Nuclear Weapons Free Zone Treaty (Treaty of Pelindaba).

Chemical weapons and protective equipment
- No data on CW activities available. Signed and ratified the CWC.

Biological weapons
- No data on BW activities available. Not a party to the BWC.

Armed Forces

Major Changes: No major change was recorded in the Algerian order-of-battle. There was no updated information about implementing a deal to acquire MiG-29 fighters from Belarus.

Order-of-Battle

Year	1995	1996	1997	1999	2000
General data					
• Personnel (regular)	152,500	152,500	124,000*	127,000	127,000
• SSM launchers	35	35	*		
Ground Forces					
• Divisions	5	5	5	5	5
• Total number of brigades	37	37	26*	26	26
• Tanks	1,100	1,100	930* (1,060)	860 (1,060)	860 (1,060)
• APCs/AFVs	1,780	1,780	1,930	1,930	1,930
• Artillery (including MRLs)	980	980	985	900 (985)	900 (985)
Air Force					
• Combat aircraft	205	205	205	187* (205)	187 (205)
• Transport aircraft	76	76	48*	39 (45)	39 (45)
• Helicopters	108	108	116	114	114
Air Defense Forces					
• Heavy SAM batteries	30	30	11*	11	11
• Medium SAM batteries	23	23	18*	18	18
• Light SAM launchers	+	+	40*	78*	78

Order-of-Battle *(continued)*

Year	1995	1996	1997	1999	2000
Navy					
• Combat vessels	32	32	29	29	26
• Patrol crafts	28	28	21*	21	21
• Submarines	2	2	2	2	2

Note: Beginning with 1997, data refers to quantities in active service. The number in parentheses refers to the total inventory.
* Due to change in estimate.

Personnel

	Regular	Reserves	Total
Ground Forces	107,000	150,000	257,000
Air Force	14,000		14,000
Navy	6,000		6,000
Total	**127,000**	**150,000**	**277,000**
Paramilitary			
• National Security Force	16,000		16,000
• Republican Guards Brigade	1,200		1,200
• Gendarmerie	24,000		24,000

Ground Forces

Formations

	Divisions	Independent brigades/ groups	Independent battalions	Brigades in divisions
Armored	2	1		3 armd., 1 mech. each
Mechanized/Infantry	2			1 armd., 3 mech. each
Motorized/Infantry		5		
Special forces/ Airborne	1			
Artillery			7	
Air defense			5	
Engineers			4	
Total	**5**	**6**	**16**	

Algeria

Tanks

Model	Quantity	In service	Since	Notes
MBTs				
High quality				
• T-72	300	285	1980	
Medium and low quality				
• T-62	330	300	1978	
• T-55/T-54	310	275	1964	
Subtotal	640	575		
Light tanks				
• AMX-13	50	0	1962	Possibly phased out
• PT-76	70	0	1985	Possibly phased out
Subtotal	120	0		
Total	**1,060**	**860**		

APCs/AFVs

Model	Quantity	In service	Since	Notes
APCs				
• BTR-50/60	445	445	1975	
• BTR-152	100	100	1965	
• Fahd	200	200	1992	
• M-3 (Panhard)	50	50	1983	
Subtotal	795	795		
IFVs				
• BMP-2	230	230	1989	
• BMP-1	685	685	1981	
Subtotal	915	915		
Reconnaissance				
• Engesa EE-9	50	50	1981	
• AML-60	55	55	1963	
• BRDM-2	115	115	1980	
Subtotal	220	220		
Total	**1,930**	**1,930**		
Future procurement				
• Akrep	700		1995	

Artillery

Model	Quantity	In service	Since	Notes
Self-propelled guns and howitzers				
• 152mm 2S3	35	+	1966	
• 122mm 2S1	150	+	1977	
Subtotal	185	~100		

Artillery *(continued)*

Model	Quantity	In service	Since	Notes
Towed guns and howitzers				
• 152mm ML-20	20	20	1966	
• 130mm M-46/Type-59	10	10	1991	
• 122mm D-74			1966	
• 122mm M-1931/37	~190	~190	1984	Refers to all types
• 122mm M-30 (M-1938)			1983	
• 122mm D-30	190	190	1984	
• 85 mm M-1945/ D-44 field/AT	80	80	1976	
Subtotal	~490	~490		
Mortars, over 160mm				
• 160mm M-43	60	60	1978	
Mortars, under 160mm				
• 120mm M-43	120	120	1974	
MRLs				
• 240mm BM-24	30	30	1962	
• 140mm BM-14-16	50	50	1962	
• 122mm BM-21	50	50	1980	
Subtotal	130	130		
Total	~985	~900		

Anti-Tank Weapons

Model	Quantity	In service	Since	Notes
Missiles				
• AT-3 (Sagger)	+	+	1975	Some mounted on BRDM-2 APCs
• AT-4 (Spigot)	+	+		
• AT-5 (Spandrel)	+	+		Mounted on BMP-2 APCs
• MILAN	~200	~200	1982	
Total	~1,400	~1,400		
Guns				
• 76mm AT gun	50	0		Possibly phased out
• 107mm B-11 recoilless rifle	40	40		Unconfirmed
Total	90	40		

Air Force

Order-of-Battle

Category	Quantity	In service	Notes
• Combat	205	187	
• Transport	45	39	
• Helicopters	114	114	

Combat Aircraft

Model	Quantity	In service	Since	Notes
Interceptors				
• MiG-25 A/B/U (Foxbat)	20	12	1979	
• MiG-23MF/MS (Flogger G)	30	30	1978	
Subtotal	50	42		
Ground attack				
• Su-24 (Fencer C)	10	10	1991	
• MiG-23BN (Flogger B/D)	40	40	1978	
• Su-20/22 (Fitter C)	15	15	1978	
Subtotal	65	65		
Obsolete				
• MiG-21 MF/bis/U (Fishbed)	90	80	1970	
Total	205	187		
Future procurement				
• MiG-29	36			

Transport Aircraft

Model	Quantity	In service	Since	Notes
• An-12 (Cub)	4	0		
• Beechcraft Queen Air/ Beechcraft King Air/ Beechcraft Super King Air B-200T	12	12	1977	2 employed in maritime patrol role
• C-130H/ L-100-30 Hercules	17	17	1981	
• Fokker F-27 Mk 400/ Mk 600	3	1	1973	Employed in maritime patrol role
• Gulfstream III	3	3	1983	
• IL-76 (Candid)	4	4	1994	
• Mystère-Falcon 900	2	2	1990	Unconfirmed
Total	45	39		

Training and Liaison Aircraft

Model	Quantity	In service	Since	Notes
Jet trainers				
• CM-170 Fouga Magister	20	20	1971	
• L-39 Albatross	30	24	1987	
Subtotal	50	44		
Piston/Turbo-prop				
• Beechcraft Sierra 200	18	18	1976	
• Zlin 142	30	30	1990	
• Beechcraft T-34C (Turbine Mentor)	6	0	1978	Possibly phased out
Subtotal	54	48		
Total	**104**	**92**		

Helicopters

Model	Quantity	In service	Since	Notes
Attack helicopters				
• Mi-24/Mi-25 (Hind)	36	36	1978	Number unconfirmed
Medium transport				
• Mi-8/Mi-17 (Hip)	56	56	1975	
• SA-330 Puma	5	5	1971	
Subtotal	61	61		
Light transport				
• Alouette II/III	6	6	1983	
• Bell 206	3	3	1988	
• AS-350 Ecureuil	8	8	1995	
Subtotal	17	17		
Total	**114**	**114**		
Future procurement				
• Rooivalk				Under negotiation
• Mi-8/17	47			

Miscellaneous Aircraft

Model	Quantity	In service	Since	Notes
Reconnaissance				
• MiG-25R	4	4	1979	Also listed under Combat Aircraft
Maritime surveillance				
• Fokker F-27 Mk 400/ Mk 600	3	1	1973	Also listed under Transport Aircraft

Miscellaneous Aircraft *(continued)*

Model	Quantity	In service	Since	Notes
• Super King Air B-200T	2	2	1986	Also listed under Transport Aircraft

UAVs and Mini-UAVs

• Seeker	4-8		1998	

Advanced Armament

Air-to-air-missiles
AA-2 (Atoll), AA-6 (Acrid), AA-7 (Apex), AA-11 (Archer)

Air-to-ground-missiles
AT-2 (Swatter), AT-6 (Spiral), AS-10 (Karen), AS-14 (Kedge)

Air Force Infrastructure

Military airfields: 13
Ain Ousira, Algiers, Amanas, Balida, Bechar, Biskra, Boufarik, Bousfear, Laghuat, Oran, Ouargla, Tafa Aoui, Tindouf

Air Defense Forces

Surface-to-Air Missiles

Model	Batteries	Launchers	Since	Notes
Heavy missiles				
• SA-2 (Guideline)	6		1970	
• SA-3 (Goa)	5		1982	
Total	11			
Medium missiles				
• SA-6 (Gainful)	10		1979	
• SA-8 (Gecko)		24	1986	
Total	10	24		
Light missiles				
• SA-9 (Gaskin)		46	1980	
• SA-13 (Gopher)		32		Unconfirmed
Total		78		
Shoulder-launched missiles				
• SA-7 (Grail)		180	1978	
Total		180		

Other Air Defense Systems

Model	Quantity	In service	Since	Notes
Short-range guns				
• 57mm ZSU 57x2 SP	+	+	1980	
• 57mm S-60	50	50	1974	
• 23mm ZSU 23x4 SP (Gun Dish)	30	30	1980	
• 23mm ZU 23x2	50	50	1986	
• 37mm M-1939	145	145	1986	
• 20mm	100	100	1987	
Total	~375	~375		

Navy

Submarines

Type	Original class name	Quantity	Length (m.)/ displacement (t.)	Notes/ armament
• K class	Kilo		273.8/3,076 (dived)	6x533mm torpedoes or 24 mines

Combat Vessels

Type	Original class name	Quantity	Length (m.)/ displacement (t.)	Notes/ armament
Missile corvette				
• Nanuchka II		3	59.3/660	4xSS-N-2B (Styx) 2xSA-N-4 (Gecko)
MFPBs				
• Ossa II		5	38.6/171	4xSS-N-2B (Styx) 4 possibly non-operational
ASW frigate				
• Mourad rais	Koni	3	96.4/1,440	RBU 6000 a/s mortars 2xSA-N-4 (Gecko)
Gun corvette				
• Djebel chinoise (C-58)	Type 802	2	58.4/496	76mm guns 40mm guns
Mine warfare vessel				
• T 43		1	58.0/500	2 ASW mortars 16 mines 2x45mm guns

Combat Vessels *(continued)*

Type	Original class name	Quantity	Length (m.)/ displacement (t.)	Notes/ armament
Gunboats				
• Kebir class	Brooke Marine	12	37.5/166	1x76mm gun 4x25mm guns
Total		26		
Future procurement				
• Kebir class		3		Total order of 15
• Kh-35 missiles		48		

Patrol Craft

Type	Original class name	Quantity	Length (m.)/ displacement (t.)	Notes/ armament
• El mouderrib	Chui-E	7	58.8/388	2xtwin 14.5mm MG
• Baglietto mangusta		5	30/91	1x40mm gun 1x20mm gun
• Baglietto 20 GC		5	20.4/44	1x20mm gun
• El Munkid		4		SAR ships
Total		21		

Landing Craft

Type	Original class name	Quantity	Length (m.)/ displacement (t.)	Notes/ armament
• Polnochny class		1	75/760	2x140mm MRLs 2x30mm guns
• Kalaat Beni Hammad	Brooke Marine	2	93/2,450	2x40mm guns 2x25mm guns
Total		3		

Auxiliary Vessels

Type	Original class name	Quantity	Length (m.)/ displacement (t.)	Notes/ armament
• Poluchat I		1	29.6/70	

Coastal Defense

Type	Quantity	Notes
• SS-N-2 Styx	4	

Naval Infrastructure

Naval bases: 5
Algiers, Annaba, Mers al-Kebir, Oran, Skikda
Ship maintenance and repair facilities: 8
Three slipways belonging to Chantier Naval de Mers al-Kebir at Oran; 4,000-ton dry docks at Algiers; 3 small graving docks at Annaba; a small dry dock at Beni Saf.

Major Non-Governmental Paramilitary Forces

Personnel

	Active	Reserves
• Islamic Salvation Army (AIS)	+	+
• Armed Islamic Group (GIA)	+	+
Total	1,000 - 1,500	1,000 - 1,500

2. BAHRAIN

General Data

Official Name of the State: State of Bahrain
Head of State: Amir Shaykh Hamad bin Isa al-Khalifa
Prime Minister: Khalifa ibn Salman al-Khalifa
Minister of Defense: Lieutenant General Khalifa ibn Ahmad al-Khalifa
Commander in Chief of the Armed Forces: Salman bin Hamad al-Khalifa
Chief of Staff of the Bahraini Defense Forces: Major General Abdallah ibn Salman al-Khalifa
Commander of the Air Force: Hamad ibn Abdallah al-Khalifa
Commander of the Navy: Lieutenant Commander Yusuf al-Maluallah

Area: 620 sq. km.
Population: 630,000

Demography

Ethnic groups		
Arabs	460,000	73.0%
Southeast Asians	82,000	13.0%
Persians	50,000	8.0%
Others	38,000	6.0%
Religious groups		
Shi'ite Muslims	472,500	75.0%
Sunni Muslims	157,500	25.0%
National groups		
Bahrainis	397,000	63.0%
Southeast Asians	82,000	13.0%
Alien other Arabs	63,000	10.0%
Iranians	50,000	8.0%
Others	38,000	6.0%

Economic Data

		1994	1995	1996	1997	1998
GDP (current price)	$ bn	5.3	5.5	6.1	6.3	6.2
GDP per capita	$	8,833	9,166	10,166	10,500	10,333
Real GDP growth	%	-0.5	4.0	3.9	3.1	4.8
Consumer price index	%	0.8	2.8	-0.2	0.2	-0.4
External debt	$ bn	2.8	2.9	2.4	2.4	2.8

Economic Data *(continued)*

		1994	1995	1996	1997	1998
Balance of payments						
• Exports fob	$ bn	3.617	4.112	4.700	4.383	3.270
• Imports fob	$ bn	3.373	3.344	3.847	3.624	3.299
• Current account balance (including services and income)	$ bn	-0.327	0.236	0.260	-0.024	-0.731
Government expenditure						
• Total expenditures	$ bn	1.792	1.630	1.832	1.872	1.875
• Defense expenditure	$ bn	0.255	0.273	0.281	0.359	NA
• Real change in defense expenditure	%	2.0	7.05	2.93	27.75	NA
• Defense expenditure/GDP	%	4.81	4.96	4.60	5.69	NA
Population	m	0.6	0.6	0.6	0.6	0.6
Official exchange rate	BD: $1	0.376	0.376	0.376	0.376	0.376

Sources: EIU Quarterly Report, EIU Country Profile, IMF International Financial Statistical Yearbook, SIPRI Yearbook

Arms Procurement and Security Assistance Received

Country	Type	Details
Netherlands	• Arms transfers	203mm SP howitzers (1994), AIFVs (1996) armored CPs, ARVs (1996)
	• Military training	Foreign advisers
Saudi Arabia	• Military training	Trainees abroad
Sweden	• Arms transfers	Early warning system (1997)
UK	• Military training	A number of retired British officers hold senior positions in Bahraini force, training the new National Guard
US	• Arms transfers	F-16 combat aircraft (2000), Black Hawk helicopters (1996), AIM-120 AAMs (2000), AGM-65G/F (2000), MLRS (1997), a missile frigate (1997)
	• Military training	Foreign advisers/instructors; trainees abroad
	• Maintenance	Foreign technicians

Arms Sales and Security Assistance Extended

Country	Type	Details
UK	• Facilities	Air force facilities
US	• Facilities	Naval facilities, storage facilities, pre-positioning of army equipment and intelligence installations, HQ facilities for the US forces in the Gulf at Mina Salman

Foreign Military Cooperation

Type	Details
• Foreign forces	About 1,000 US soldiers
• Forces deployed abroad	Saudi Arabia (part of GCC "Desert Shield" Rapid Deployment Force)
• Joint maneuvers	US air force, navy and special forces exercises
• Security agreements	US, Britain, GCC countries

Weapons of Mass Destruction

NBC Capabilities

Nuclear capability
No known nuclear activity. Signatory to the NPT.

Chemical weapons and protective equipment
No known CW activities. Party to the CWC.

Biological weapons
No known BW activities. Party to the BWC.

Armed Forces

Major Changes: The Bahraini Air Force received its first F-16, out of a contract for 10 aircraft.

Order-of-Battle

Year	1995	1996	1997	1999	2000
General data					
• Personnel (regular)	7,100	7,400	7,400	7,400	7,400
Ground Forces					
• Total number of brigades	3	3	3	3	3
• Number of battalions	6	6	7	7	7
• Tanks	81	81	110*	180	180
• APCs/AFVs	192	192	217 (237)	277* (297)	277 (297)
• Artillery (including MRLs)	44	44	44 (50)	48 (50)	48 (50)

Order-of-Battle (continued)

Year	1995	1996	1997	1999	2000
Air Force					
• Combat aircraft	24	24	24	24	24
• Transport aircraft	3 – 4	3 – 4	2	2	2
• Helicopters	23	23	41*	41	41
Air Defense Forces					
• Heavy SAM batteries	1	1	1	1	1
• Medium SAM batteries	7	7	2*	2	2
• Light SAM launchers	160	160	40*	40	40
Navy					
• Combat vessels	8	11	11	11	11
• Patrol boats	26	19	19	19	22

Note: Beginning with 1997, data refers to quantities in active service. The number in parentheses refers to the total inventory.
* Due to change in estimate.

Personnel

	Regular	Reserves	Total
Ground Forces	6,000		6,000
Air Force	700		700
Navy	700		700
Total	7,400		7,400
Paramilitary			
• Coast Guard and National Guard	2,000		2,000

Ground Forces

Formations

	Brigades	Independent battalions	Battalions in brigade
Armored	1		2 armd., 1 reconn.
Infantry	1		2 mech., 1 inf.
Artillery	1		6 batt.
Air Defense		1	
Special Forces		1	
Total	3	2	

Tanks

Model	Quantity	In service	Since	Notes
MBTs				
Medium and low quality				
• M60 A3	180	180	1987	
Total	180	180		

APCs/AFVs

Model	Quantity	In service	Since	Notes
APCs				
• M113	110	110	1990	
• M-3 (Panhard)	110	110	1979	
• AT-105 Saxon	10	10	1981	
Subtotal	230	230		
IFVs				
• YPR-765	25	25	1996	
Reconnaissance				
• AML-90	22	22	1979	
• Ferret	10	0	1972	Possibly phased out
• Saladin	10	0	1973	Possibly phased out
Subtotal	42	22		
Total	297	277		

Artillery

Model	Quantity	In service	Since	Notes
Self-propelled guns and howitzers				
• 203mm M110	13	13	1994	
Towed guns and howitzers				
• 155mm M198 A1	20	18	1984	
• 105mm L-118	8	8		
Subtotal	28	26		
MRLs				
• 227mm MLRS	9	9	1992	
Total	50	48		

Anti-Tank Weapons

Model	Launchers	Missiles	Since	Notes
Missile launchers				
• BGM-71C Improved TOW	15	+		
• BGM-71E (TOW 2A)	*	*		

Air Force

Order-of-Battle

Category	Quantity	In service	Notes
• Combat	24	24	
• Transport	2	2	
• Helicopters	41	41	

Combat Aircraft

Model	Quantity	In service	Since	Notes
Advanced multi-role				
• F-16C/D	12	12	1990	
Multi-role				
• F-5E/F	12	12	1985	
Total	**24**	**24**		
Future procurement				
• F-16 C/D	10			Delivery scheduled to begin in year 2000

Transport Aircraft

Model	Quantity	In service	Since	Notes
• Gulfstream II	2	2	1977	

Helicopters

Model	Quantity	In service	Since	Notes
Ground attack				
• AH-1E	14	14	1996	
• 500MD	2	2	1981	
• BO-105	5	5	1976	
Subtotal	21	21		
Medium transport				
• UH-60A Black Hawk	2	2	1996	Executive a/c
• S-70L	1	1		
• AB-212	12	12	1980	
• Bell 412	3	3	1982	With police
Subtotal	18	18		
Naval combat				
• SA-365 Dauphin	2	2	1988	
Total	**41**	**41**		

Advanced Armament

Air-to-air-missiles
AIM-9P/L Sidewinder (150), AIM-7M Sparrow (48), AGM-65D Maverick (24)

Air-to-ground missiles
AS-15TT anti-ship missile

Future procurement
Lantirn (for F-16 a/c); AIM-120 AMRAAM (26), AGM-65G/F

Note: Numbers in parentheses refer to number of units purchased.

Air Force Infrastructure

Military airfields:	1
Shaykh Isa	

Air Defense Forces

Surface-to-Air Missiles

Model	Batteries	Launchers	Since	Notes
Heavy missiles				
• MIM-23B Improved HAWK	1		1994	
Medium missiles				
• Crotale	2		1995	Number unconfirmed
Light missiles				
• RBS-70		40	1980	
Shoulder launched missiles				
• FIM-92A Stinger		18	1987	400 missiles (number unconfirmed)

Other Air Defense Systems

Model	Quantity	In service	Since	Notes
Short range guns				
• 35mm Oerlikon	12	12		Possibly with Skyguard FCS

Navy

Combat Vessels

Type	Original class name	Quantity	Length (m.)/ displacement (t.)	Notes/ armament
Missile frigates				
• Sabha	Oliver Hazard Perry class	1	135.6/3,638	1xSH-2G helicopter 4xHarpoon SSM 36xStandard SM-1 6x324mm torpedoes 1x76mm gun 1xVulcan Phalanx 20mm gun
Missile corvettes				
• al-Manama	Lürssen MGB-62	2	63.0/632	4xExocet MM-40 1x76mm gun 1xtwin 40mm gun
MFPBs				
• Ahmad al-Fateh	Lürssen TNC-45	4	44.9/259	4xExocet MM-40 1x76mm gun 1xtwin 40mm gun
Gunboats				
• al-Riffa	Lürssen FPB-38	2	38.5/205	2xtwin 40mm guns 1x57mm rocket launcher
• al-Jarim	Swift FPB-20	2	19.2/33	1x20mm gun
Subtotal		4		
Total		11		

Patrol Craft

Type	Original class name	Quantity	Length (m.)/ displacement (t.)	Notes/ armament
• al-Muharraq	Wasp 30	1	30/90	1x30mm gun
• Dera'a	Tracker	2	19.5/31	
• Dera'a	Halmatic	4	20.1/31.5	
• Dera'a	Wasp	2	20/36.3	
• Saham 1	Wasp	3	11/7	
• Saif	Halmatic	6	14.4/17	
• Saif	Fairey Marine Sword	4	13.7/15	
Total		22		

Landing Craft

Type	Original class name	Quantity	Length (m.)/ displacement (t.)	Notes/ armament
• LCU 1466		1	36.3/360	176-ton cargo
• Safra LCM	Fairey Marine	1	22.5/150	
Total		2		

Auxiliary Vessels

Type	Original class name	Quantity	Length (m.)/ displacement (t.)	Notes/ armament
• Ajeera class		1	39.6/420	200-ton fuel/water
• Safra		1	25.9/165	

Naval Infrastructure

Naval bases: 1
Mina Salman

Ship maintenance and repair facilities
Arab Shipbuilding and Repair Yard (ASRY), a 500,000 dwt dry-dock engaged in repairs and construction (mainly supertankers; jointly owned by Bahrain, Kuwait, Qatar, Saudi Arabia, UAE-each 18.84%;Iraq-4.7%; and Libya-1.1%)

3. EGYPT

General Data

Official Name of the State: The Arab Republic of Egypt
Head of State: President Muhammad Husni Mubarak
Prime Minister: Atef Muhammad Ebeid
Minister of Defense and Military Production: Field Marshal Muhammad Hussayn Tantawi
Chief of General Staff: General Magdi Hatata
Commander of the Air Force: Lieutenant General Ahmad Muhammad Shafik
Commander of the Navy: Vice Admiral Ahmad Saber Salim

Area: 1,000,258 sq. km.
Population: 63,250,000

Demography

Ethnic groups		
Arabs	62,238,000	98.4%
Greeks, Italians, Armenians	632,500	1.0%
Nubians	63,250	0.1%
Others	316,250	0.5%
Religious groups		
Sunni Muslims	59,455,000	94.0%
Copts, other Christians	3,795,000	6.0%

Economic Data

		1994	1995	1996	1997	1998
GDP (current price)	$ bn	51.622	60.471	67.345	75.604	82.654
GDP per capita	$	892	1,020	1,111	1,219	1,306
Real GDP growth	%	3.9	4.7	5.0	5.5	5.6
Consumer price index	%	8.1	15.7	7.2	4.6	4.2
External debt	$ bn	32.3	33.3	31.3	29.9	30.4
Balance of payments						
• Exports fob	$ bn	4.04	4.67	4.78	5.53	4.40
• Imports fob	$ bn	10.00	12.27	13.17	14.16	14.62
• Current account balance (including services and income)	$ bn	0.03	-0.25	-0.19	-0.71	-2.57

Economic Data (continued)

		1994	1995	1996	1997	1998
Government expenditure						
• Total expenditure	$ bn	17.184	18.846	19.712	20.879	21.805
• Defense expenditure	$ bn	1.81	1.97	2.11	2.22	2.36
• Real change in defense expenditure	%	7.73	8.83	7.1	5.21	6.30
• Defense expenditure/GDP	%	3.50	3.25	3.13	2.93	2.85
Population	m	57.85	59.23	60.60	62.01	63.25
Official exchange rate	E£: $1	3.39	3.39	3.39	3.39	3.39

Sources: EIU Quarterly Report, EIU Country Profile, IMF International Financial Statistical Yearbook, SIPRI Yearbook

Arms Procurement and Security Assistance Received

Country	Type	Details
Czech Republic	• Arms transfers	L-59 jet trainer aircraft
Finland	• Cooperation in arms production, assembly, R&D	Transfer of technology and production license of 155mm gun (1999)
France	• Military training	Trainees abroad
	• Cooperation in arms production, assembly, R&D	Electronics, components of SP AA systems
Germany	• Military training	Trainees abroad
	• Maintenance of equipment	Transport aircraft, anti-mine equipment (1998)
India	• Arms transfers	Spare parts for Soviet-made aircraft (1998)
Italy	• Arms transfers	Terminally-guided aerial bombs
Netherlands	• Arms transfers	AIFVs (1997)
North Korea	• Arms transfers	Assistance to Egyptian production of SSMs (2000-alleged)
PRC	• Arms transfers	Spare parts for F-7 combat aircraft (1995), K-8 training aircraft (1999)
Russia	• Arms transfers	Upgrading of SA-3 SAMs (1999)
Turkey	• Arms transfers	US-designed F-16 fighter a/c, assembled in Turkey
UK	• Military training	Trainees abroad
	• Arms transfers	Naval radars (1996), mortar-locating radar upgrade (1997)

Egypt

Arms Procurement and Security Assistance Received *(continued)*

Country	Type	Details
US	• Assistance	$1.3 billion grant (2000), and a few items from US drawdown, worth several hundred million dollars
	• Military training	Foreign advisers/instructors, trainees abroad (1998)
	• Arms transfers	F-16 C/D a/c (1999), helicopters including AH-64 (1995), SH-2G (1997), CH-47D (1999), AAMs, Patriot PAC-3 SAMs (1999), F-16 simulators (1998), artillery (1997), TOW ATGMs (1996), missile frigates (1998), Harpoon anti-ship missiles (1998), torpedoes, fire control systems for submarines, sonars, communication and ECCM equipment, upgrading kits for SAMs and tanks (1999), upgrading of AEW a/c (1999), upgrading of TPS-59 radars (1999)
	• Cooperation in arms production, assembly, R&D	Assembly of M1A1 tanks and M-88 recovery vehicle (1999), upgrading M113 APCs, AIFVs (1997), ammunition, electronics including radars and radio transceivers
	• Construction aid	Upgrading of airfields and dry docks
	• Maintenance aid	Aircraft

Arms Sales and Security Assistance Extended

Country	Type	Details
Algeria	• Arms transfers	Fahd APCs (1995)
Bosnia	• Arms transfers	10 T-55 tanks and spare parts (1997), artillery
Congo	• Military training	Advisers in country
Greece	• Military training	Foreign trainees (1997)
Lebanon	• Military training	Foreign trainees (1995)
Mali	• Arms transfers	Fahd APCs (1995)
Oman	• Military training	Advisers in country
Palestinian Authority	• Military training	Police trainees (1995)
Saudi Arabia	• Military training	Advisers in country
US	• Facilities	Use of airfields at Cairo West, Qena, Inshas, Hurghada

The Middle East Military Balance 2000-2001

Foreign Military Cooperation

Type	Details
• Foreign forces	US forces as of June 1999 includes some 1,400 soldiers
• Forces deployed abroad	Troops with MINURCA forces in Central African Republic
• Joint maneuvers	France, Germany, Greece, Italy, Jordan, Kuwait, Netherlands, UAE, UK, US

Defense Production

	M	P	A
Weapons of mass destruction			
• Upgraded Scud B SSMs (with North Korean cooperation)	√		
• Chemical agents (unconfirmed)	√		
Army equipment			
• M1A1 tanks, with cooperation from US (some parts will be produced in Egypt)			√
• 155mm GH 52 APU towed field gun (with assistance from Finland)		√	
• Conversion of 122mm D-30 howitzers to 122mm AR SP howitzers	√		
• 130mm artillery pieces		√	
• 122mm Saqr 18/30/36 MRLs	√		
• Short-range SAMs (Saqr eye)			√
• M88 Armored Recovery Vehicles			√
• Fahd APCs (with FRG components and assistance)		√	
• Trucks and jeeps (with US)		√	
• British tank guns		√	
• Mortars		√	
• Upgrading of Russian tanks (with British assistance)		√	
• Conversion of 23mm AAGs to Sinai 23 SP AA systems (with French assistance)	√		
• Add-on armor to M113 APCs	√		
• Tank tracks		√	
• Soviet-design AAGs and small arms		√	
• Minefield crossing systems (similar to Viper)		√	
• Mines, including scatterable	√	√	
• Ammunition for artillery, tanks, and small arms	√		
Air Force equipment			
• CBUs (US design)		√	
• Anti-runway bombs		√	
• Parts for F-16		√	
• Parts for Mirage 2000		√	

Defense Production *(continued)*

	M	P	A
• Parts for Mystère-Falcon 50 executive aircraft		√	
• Aircraft fuel pods		√	
• Aerial bombs		√	
Navy equipment			
• Timsah patrol boats	√		
• Type 83 patrol boats	√		
Electronics			
• SAM electronics (in collaboration with UK)		√	
• Fire control system		√	
• Bassal artillery fire control system	√		
• Simulators for rifle firing	√		
Optronics			
• Night vision devices		√	

Note: M - manufacture (indigenously developed)
P - production under license
A - assembly

Weapons of Mass Destruction

NBC Capabilities

Nuclear capability
22 Mw research reactor from Argentina, completed 1997; 2 Mw research reactor from the USSR in operation since 1961. Party to the NPT. Safeguards agreement with the IAEA in force. Signed, but not ratified the African Nuclear Weapon Free Zone Treaty (Treaty of Pelindaba).

Chemical weapons and protective equipment
Alleged continued research and possible production of chemical warfare agents. Alleged stockpile of chemical agents (mustard and nerve agents); personal protective equipment; Soviet type decontamination units; Fuchs (Fox) NBC detection vehicle (12); SPW-40 P2Ch NBC detection vehicle (small numbers). Refused to sign the CWC.

Biological weapons
Suspected biological warfare program; no details available. Not a party to the BWC.

Ballistic Missiles

Model	Launchers	Missiles	Since	Notes
• SS-1 (Scud B/Scud C)	24	100	1973	Possibly some upgraded
Future procurement				
• Scud C/Project-T		90		Locally produced
• Vector				Unconfirmed

Note: See also under Rockets

Armed Forces

Major Changes: Egypt will produce 100 additional M1A1 Abrams MBTs. These will be added to the 555 tanks already produced. The Egyptian artillery will receive, by the end of 2000, 24 additional SP122 self-propelled cannons. The Air Force received 21 F-16C, fighter aircraft and ordered 24 be supplied in 2001. The Air Defense Forces will upgrade 50 SA-3 launchers and its TPS-59 surveillance radars.

Order-of-Battle

Year	1995	1996	1997	1999	2000
General data					
• Personnel (regular)	426,000	424,000	421,000	455,000	450,000
• SSM launchers	9	9	9	24*	24
Ground Forces					
• Divisions	12	12	12	12	12
• Total number of brigades	50	50	53	49	49
• Tanks	2,800	2,900	2,662 (3,162)	~2,750 (3,462)	~2,750 (3,505)
• APCs/AFVs	4,400	5,180	3,025 (4,995)	~3,185 (~5,055)	~3,400 (~5,300)
• Artillery (including MRLs)	2,213	3,060	3,158	3,510	~3,550
Air Force					
• Combat aircraft	497	497	505	498 (505)	481 (494)
• Transport aircraft	47	43	35*	38	44
• Helicopters	211	211	223	224 (234)	~225
Air Defense Forces					
• Heavy SAM batteries	122	122	105*	105	109
• Medium SAM batteries	48	48	48	44	44
• Light SAM launchers	50	50	50	50	50

Order-of-Battle *(continued)*

Year	1995	1996	1997	1999	2000
Navy					
• Submarines	8	8	6	6	4
• Combat vessels	58	59	64	66	65
• Patrol crafts	69	70	83	83	104

Note: Beginning with 1997, data refers to quantities in active service. The number in parentheses refers to the total inventory.
* Due to change in estimate.

Personnel

	Regular	Reserves	Total
Ground Forces	320,000	150,000	470,000
Air Force	30,000	20,000	50,000
Air Defense	80,000	70,000	150,000
Navy	20,000	14,000	34,000
Total	450,000	254,000	704,000
Paramilitary			
• Coast Guard			2,000
• Frontier Corps			6,000
• Central Security Forces			325,000
• National Guard			60,000
• Border Guard			12,000

Ground Forces

Formations

	Corps/armies	Divisions	Independent brigades/groups	Brigades in divisions
All Arms	2			
Armored		4	4	2 armd., 1 mech., 1 aty. each
Mechanized		7	4	2 mech., 1 armd., 1 aty. each
Infantry		1	2	
Airborne			1	
Paratroopers			1	

Formations *(continued)*

	Corps/armies	Divisions	Independent brigades/groups	Brigades in divisions
Special Forces			+	
Artillery			15	
SSM			2	
Total	2	12	~30	

Tanks

Model	Quantity	In service	Since	Notes
MBTs				
High quality				
• M1A1	555	250	1992	
Medium and low quality				
• M60 A3	850	835	1981	
• M60 A1	700	600	1990	
• T-62	600	~550	1972	
• T-55	800	~500		Most in storage
Subtotal	2,950	~2,500		
Total	3,505	~2,750		
Future procurement				
• M1A1	100			
• M60 A3	340			Out of US drawdown (under negotiation)
• M60 A1				Upgrading to A3 standard contemplated

APCs/AFVs

Model	Quantity	In service	Since	Notes
APCs				
• M113 A2	1,768	1,000	1980	52 M901 ITV
• BMR-600	250	250	1983	
• Fahd	165	160	1986	
• OT-62/BTR-50	1,100	+		Possibly phased out
Subtotal	3,283	~1,410		
IFVs				
• BMP-1	220	220		
• YPR-765	600	600	1996	200 with TOW under armor

APCs/AFVs *(continued)*

Model	Quantity	In service	Since	Notes
• V-150/V-300 commando	~180	~180		
Subtotal	~1,000	~1,000		
Reconnaissance				
• BRDM-2	300	300	1968	
• BTR-40/152	~675	~675		
Subtotal	~975	~975		
Total	~5,300	~3,400		
Future procurement				
• Fahd				

Artillery

Model	Quantity	In service	Since	Notes
Self-propelled guns and howitzers				
• 155mm M109 A2	200	200	1984	
• 122mm SP122	100	100	1987	
Subtotal	300	300		
Towed guns and howitzers				
• 130mm M-46/Type-59	+	+		
• 122mm D-30	+	+		
Subtotal	~970	~970		
Mortars, over 160mm				
• 240mm	+	+		
• 160mm	60	60		
Subtotal	~60	~60		
Mortars, under 160mm				
• 120mm M-43	1,800	1,800		
• 107mm (4.2") M-30 SP	100	100		On M106 A2 carrier
Subtotal	1,900	1,900		
MRLs				
• 122mm BM-11 }	100	100		
• 122mm BM-21 }				
• 122mm Saqr 18/30/36	200	200		
Subtotal	~300	~300		
Rockets				
• FROG-7	12	12		
• 210mm Saqr 80	*	*		
Subtotal	~12	~12		
Total	~3,550	~3,550		

Artillery (continued)

Model	Quantity	In service	Since	Notes
Future procurement				
• 155mm GH 52 APU	+			To be produced in Egypt
• 122mm SP122	24			To be delivered in December 2000

Ground Radars

Model	Quantity	In service	Since	Notes
Artillery/mortar locating radars				
• AN/TPQ-36	6	6	1999	
• AN/TPQ-37	2	2	1989	
Future procurement				
• AN/TPQ-37	+			

Logistics and Engineering Equipment

Bar mine-laying system, EWK pontoon bridges, GSP self-propelled ferries, M-123 Viper minefield crossing system or Egyptian Viper-like system, designated al-Fatah, MT-55 bridging tanks, MTU-55 bridging tanks, Egyptian bridging tanks (on T-34 chassis), mine-clearing rollers, PMP folding pontoon bridges, PRP motorized bridges, M88 armored recovery vehicles

Anti-Tank Weapons

Model	Launchers	Missiles	Since	Notes
Missiles				
• AT-3 (Sagger)		1,400	1972	
• BGM-71C Improved TOW/ BGM-71D TOW II	~600	+		
• M901 ITV	52	+		Also listed also under APCs
• YPR-765 (TOW under armor)	200	+	1996	Also listed under APCs
• MILAN	250	+	1978	
• Swingfire	200	+	1976	
Total	~1,300	+		
Future procurement				
• Tow IIB	540			

Air Force

Order-of-Battle

Category	Quantity	In service	Notes
• Combat	494	481	
• Transport	44	44	
• Helicopters	~225	~225	

Combat Aircraft

Model	Quantity	In service	Since	Notes
Advanced multi-role				
• F-16A/B	40	34	1982	Will be upgraded to C/D standard
• F-16C/D	153	153	1986	
• Mirage 2000	18	18	1986	
Subtotal	211	205		
Multi-role				
• F-4E Phantom	32	25	1980	
Ground attack				
• Alpha Jet and Alpha Jet MS-2	42	42	1983	Normally an advanced trainer; defined in Egypt as CAS a/c
Obsolete				
• F-7 Shenyang/ MiG-21 MF	150	150	1972	Partly used as strike a/c; 14 additional under reconn.
• Mirage 5	59	59	1974	Including 6 Mirage 5DR
Subtotal	209	209		
Total	**494**	**481**		
Future procurement				
• F-16C/D	24			To be supplied beginning of 2001

Transport Aircraft

Model	Quantity	In service	Since	Notes
• Beechcraft 1900C	6	6	1988	4 in various surveillance roles
• Boeing 707	1	1	1974	
• C-130H/ C-130H-30 Hercules	21	21	1978/1990	2 in various surveillance roles

Transport Aircraft (continued)

Model	Quantity	In service	Since	Notes
• DHC-5D Buffalo	9	9	1982	
• Gulfstream III/V	4	4	1985/1996	
• Mystére-Falcon 20	3	3		
Total	44	44		

Training and Liaison Aircraft

Model	Quantity	In service	Since	Notes
Jet trainers				
• Alpha Jet and Alpha Jet MS-2			1983	Also listed under Combat Aircraft
• L-29 (Delfin)	60	60	1972	
• L-39 (Albatross)	10	10	1990	
• L-59	48	48	1993	
Subtotal	118	118		
Piston/Turbo-prop				
• al-Gumhuriya	36	36	1973	
• Embraer EMB-312 (Tucano)	54	54	1984	
Subtotal	90	90		
Total	208	208		
Future procurement				
• K-8 Karakorum	80			To be delivered in 2000

Helicopters

Model	Quantity	In service	Since	Notes
Attack				
• AH-64A Apache	36	36	1995	
• SA-342 L/M Gazelle	65	65	1983	
Subtotal	101	101		
Heavy transport				
• CH-47C/D Chinook	19	19	1981	
Medium transport				
• Mi-8 (Hip)	~40	~40	1972	Some may be armed
• UH-60A Black Hawk	2	2		VIP service
• Westland Commando Mk 2	25	25	1974	
Subtotal	~65	~65		
Light transport				
• UH-12E Hiller	17	17	1982	

Helicopters *(continued)*

Model	Quantity	In service	Since	Notes
Naval combat				
• Westland Sea King Mk 47	5	5	1976	
• SH-2G Seasprite	10	10	1997	
• SA-342L Gazelle	9	9	1983	
Subtotal	24	24		
Total	~225	~225		
Future procurement				
• CH-47D Chinook	6			Upgrading of existing CH-47C
• UH-60L Black Hawk	2			VIP

Miscellaneous Aircraft

Model	Quantity	In service	Since	Notes
Reconnaissance				
• MiG-21R	14	14		
• Mirage 5DR	6	6	1974	
AEW/AWACS				
• E-2C Hawkeye	5	5	1986	
ELINT/maritime surveillance/ASW				
• Beechcraft 1900C	4	4	1992	Also listed under Transport Aircraft
• C-130H	2	2	1978	Also listed under Transport Aircraft
UAVs and mini-UAVs				
• Kader	+	+		
• R4E-50 Skyeye	48	48		
• 324 Scarab	50	50		
Target drones				
• CT-20	+	+		
• Beech AQM-37A	+	+		
• Beech MQM-107B	+	+		
• TTL BTT-3 Banshee	Several dozen	Several dozen		

Advanced Armament

Air-to-air-missiles
AIM-7F/M Sparrow (550), AIM-9L/P Sidewinder (1,100), R-550 Magic, R-530D Super

Air-to-ground missiles
AGM-65 Maverick (1,100), AS-30L, AGM114 Hellfire (1,000), HOT

Avionics
LANTIRN (30)

Note: Numbers in parentheses refer to number of units purchased.

Air Force Infrastructure

Aircraft shelters
In all operational airfields, for combat aircraft

Military airfields: 28
Abu Hammad, Abu Suweir, Alexandria, Aswan, Beni Suef, Bilbeis, Cairo International, Cairo West, Fayid, Hurghada, Inshas, Janaklis, Jebel al-Basour, Kabrit, Kom Awshim, Luxor, al-Maza, al-Minya, Mansura, Marsah Matruh, Qena, al-Qutamiya, Saqqara, Sidi Barani, Ras Banas, Salahiya, Tanta, al-Zaqaziq

Air Defense Forces

Surface-to-Air Missiles

Model	Batteries	Launchers	Since	Notes
Heavy missiles				
• MIM-23B Improved HAWK	16		1981	
• SA-2 (Guideline)	40		1965	
• SA-3 (Goa)	53		1965	
Total	**109**			
Medium missiles				
• Crotale	12		1977	
• SA-6 (Gainful)	14		1972	
• Sparrow	18			Included in Skyguard AD system
Total	**44**			
Light missiles				
• MIM-72A Chaparral		50		

Surface-to-Air Missiles *(continued)*

Model	Batteries	Launchers	Since	Notes
Shoulder-launched missiles				
• Ain al-Saqr (Saqr Eye)		+		
• SA-7 (Grail)		~2,000	1972	
Future procurement				
• Avenger system		50		With 1,000 missiles
• SA-3 (Goa)		50		Upgrade of launchers and missiles; to be delivered in 2003
• Patriot PAC-3	1+2 optional			With 32 missiles

Other Air Defense Systems

Model	Quantity	In service	Since	Notes
Air defense systems (missiles, radars and guns)				
• Skyguard AD system	18	18		Also listed under SAMs (Egyptian designation: Amoun)
• Sinai 23mm AD system	~45	~45		
Total	~65	~65		
Short-range guns				
• 57mm ZSU 57x2 SP	40	40		
• 35mm Oerlikon-Buhrle 35x2 GDF-002	36	36		Integral part of Skyguard AD systems
• 23mm ZSU 23x4 SP (Gun Dish)	360	360		
• 23mm ZU 23x2	117	117		
Total	553	553		
Radars				
• AN/TPS-59(V)2	5	5		
• AN/TPS-63	42	42		
• P-15 Flat Face	+	+	1973	
• P-12 Spoon Rest	+	+	1973	
• Tiger S (TRS-2100)	15	15		
Future procurement				
• Trackstar L-band acquisition radar	+			
• AN/TPS-59(V)3	5			Upgrading of existing radars
• Skyguard AD systems				

Navy

Submarines

Type	Original class name	Quantity	Length (m.)/ displacement (t.)	Notes/ armament
• R class (Romeo ex-Chinese)		4	76.6/1,830	Ssub-Harpoon SSM 8x533mm torpedoes or 28 mines

Combat Vessels

Type	Original class name	Quantity	Length (m.)/ displacement (t.)	Notes/ armament
Missile frigates				
• Descubierta class		2	88.8/1,233	8xHarpoon SSMs 24xAspide SAMs 6x324mm torpedoes 1x375mm ASW launcher 1x76mm gun 2x40mm guns
• Jianghu class		2	103.2/1,425	4xHai Ying-II SSMs 4x57mm guns 12x37mm guns 2 RBU 1200 ASW mortars
• Knox class		2	134/3,011	1x Seasprite helicopter 8xHarpoon SSMs 1x127mm gun 1x20mm phalanx 4x324mm torpedoes
• Oliver Hazard Perry		4	135.6/2,750	2xSeasprite helicopters 4xHarpoon SSMs 36xStandard SAMs 1x76mm gun 1x20mm Phalanx 6x324mm torpedoes
Subtotal		10		

Combat Vessels *(continued)*

Type	Original class name	Quantity	Length (m.)/ displacement (t.)	Notes/ armament
MFPBs				
• Hegu class		6	27.0/88	2xSY-1 SSMs or 2xSS-N-2 Styx 2x23mm guns 1 non-operational
• October	Komar	6	25.5/82.0	2xOtomat SSMs 4x30mm guns
• Ossa I		4	38.6/171	4x SS-N-2A Styx SA-N-5 Grail 4x30mm guns 1 non-operational
• Ramadan	Vosper Thornycroft	6	52.0/307	4xOtomat SSMs 1x76mm gun 2x40mm guns SA-N-5 portable SAMs
Subtotal		22		
Mine warfare vessels				
• T-43 class minesweeper		6	58.0/580	4x37mm guns 20 mines 2 non-operational
• Swiftships coastal minesweep		3	33.8/203	
• Yurka class minesweeper		4	52.4/540	4x30mm guns 10 mines
• Swiftships route survey		2	27.4/165	
Subtotal		15		
Gunboats				
• Hainan class		8	58.8/375	4x57mm guns 4x23mm guns 3 possibly non-operational
• Shanghai II		4	38.8/113	4x37mm guns 4x23mm guns

Combat Vessels (continued)

Type	Original class name	Quantity	Length (m.)/ displacement (t.)	Notes/ armament
• Shershen class		6	34.7/145	SA-N-5 portable SAM 4x30mm guns 2x122mm MRL
Subtotal		18		
Total		65		

Patrol Craft

Type	Original class name	Quantity	Length (m.)/ displacement (t.)	Notes/ armament
• Spectre		12	13.8/37	
• Peterson		9	13.9/18	
• Peterson		3	15.5/20	
• Crestitalia		6	21.0/36	2x30mm guns 1x20mm gun
• DC 35 type		29	10.7/4	
• Nisr class	de Castro	5	31.0/110	2-4x25mm guns 1x122mm RL
• Swiftships		9	28.4/102	2x23mm guns 1x20mm gun
• Timsah class		22	30.5/106	2x30mm guns or 2x20mm guns
• Type 83		9	25.5/85	2x23mm guns 1x20mm gun
Total		104		

Landing Craft

Type	Original class name	Quantity	Length (m.)/ displacement (t.)	Notes/ armament
• LCM		5		
• Polnochny class LSM		3	73.0/800	2x30mm guns 2x140mm MRL 6 tanks or 350 tons
• Vydra class LCU		9	54.8/425	4x37mm guns 200 troops or 250 tons

Landing Craft *(continued)*

Type	Original class name	Quantity	Length (m.)/ displacement (t.)	Notes/ armament
• Seafox		6	11/11.3	Swimmers' delivery craft
Total		23		

Future procurement
- US-made landing ship

Auxiliary Vessels

Type	Original class name	Quantity	Length (m.)/ displacement (t.)	Notes/ armament
• Black Swan class frigate (training)		1	91.2/1,925	6x102mm guns 4x37mm guns possibly no longer serviceable
• El Fateh	Zenith, Wessex	1	110.6/1,730	2xSA-N-5 SAMs 4x115mm guns 6x37mm guns 2x40mm guns 8x533mm torpedoes used for training
• Niryat diving support		1		
• Okhtensky (tug)		6	47.6/930	
• Poluchat II torpedo recovery		2	29.6/100	
• Toplivo 2 class tanker		8	53.7/1,029	500 tons diesel
• Training		5		1xSekstan, 1x4,650-ton, 1x3,008-ton and 1 other

Coastal Defense

Type	Quantity	Notes
• OTOMAT	3	
• HY-2	+	In coastal defense role
Total	~30 launchers	Unconfirmed

Naval Infrastructure

Naval bases: 8
Abu Qir (naval academy), Alexandria, Hurghada, Marsa Matruh, Port Said, Safaga, Suez, Berenice (Ras Banas)

Ship maintenance and repair facilities
Alexandria (including construction up to 20,000 dwt), Port Said, Ismailiya

4. IRAN

General Data

Official Name of the State: Islamic Republic of Iran
Supreme Religious and Political National Leader (Rahbar): Hojatolislam Ali Hoseini Khamenei
Head of State (formally subordinate to the National Leader): President Hojatolislam Seyyed Mohammed Khatami
Minister of Defense: Rear Admiral Ali Shamkhani
Commander in Chief of the Armed Forces: Hojatolislam Ali Hoseini Khamenei
Chief of the Joint Staff of the Armed Forces (including IRGC): Brigadier General Mustafa Turabipur
Commander of the Army: Major General Mohammad Salimi
Commander of the Air Force: Brigadier General Assad Abadi Habiballah Baqa'i
Commander of the Navy: Rear Admiral Abbas Mohtaj
Commander-in-Chief of the Islamic Revolutionary Guards Corps (IRGC): Major General Yahya Rahim Safavi
Commander of the IRGC Ground Forces: Brigadier General Aziz Ja'afri
Commander of the IRGC Air Wing: Brigadier General Ahmad Kazemi
Commander of the IRGC Naval Wing: General Ali Akbar Ahmadian

Area: 1,647,240 sq. km. (not including Abu Musa Island and two Tunb islands; control disputed)
Population: 62,000,000 est.

Demography

Ethnic groups		
Persians	31,620,000	51.0%
Azeris	14,880,000	24.0%
Gilaki and Mazandarani	4,960,000	8.0%
Kurds	4,340,000	7.0%
Arabs	1,860,000	3.0%
Balouchis	1,240,000	2.0%
Turkmens	1,240,000	2.0%
Lurs	1,240,000	2.0%
Others	620,000	1.0%
Religious groups		
Shi'ite Muslims	55,180,000	89.0%
Sunni Muslims	6,200,000	10.0%
Christians, Zoroastrians, Jews, Baha'is and others	620,000	1.0%

Economic Data

		1994	1995	1996	1997	1998
GDP (current prices)	$ bn	73.45	102.29	134.32	160.12	187.38
GDP per capita	$	1,228	1,666	2,198	2,638	3,022
Real GDP growth	%	0.9	2.8	5.5	3.0	1.8
Consumer price index	%	31.5	49.7	28.9	17.1	19.4
External debt	$ bn	22.63	21.88	16.7	10.3	NA
Balance of payments						
• Exports fob	$ bn	19.43	18.36	22.39	18.37	12.98
• Imports fob	$ bn	12.62	12.77	14.99	14.60	13.61
• Current account balance (including services and income)	$ bn	4.96	3.36	5.23	1.55	-1.90
Government expenditure						
• Total expenditure	$ bn	16.53	23.63	32.44	37.3	40.58
• Defense expenditure	$ bn	3.44	2.55	2.43	2.91	2.98
• Real change in defense expenditure	%	35.4	-25.9	-4.7	19.7	2.4
• Defense expenditure/GDP	%	4.7	2.5	1.8	1.8	1.6
Population	m	59.8	61.4	61.1	60.7	62.0
Official exchange rate	IR: $1	1,748	1,749	1,751	1,753	1,752

Sources: EIU Quarterly Report, EIU Country Profile, IMF International Financial Statistical Yearbook, SIPRI Yearbook

Arms Procurement and Security Assistance Received

Country	Type	Details
France	• Arms transfers	Socata training aircraft (1997)
Germany	• Arms transfers	Aircraft (1997), missile parts (1997), chemical and nuclear technology (1997) (unauthorized by government)
Israel	• Arms transfers	M113 APC parts (1996), optical sights (1992) (unauthorized by government)
North Korea	• Arms transfers	SSM technology (1998)
Poland	• Arms transfers	T-72 tanks (1995)
PRC	• Arms transfers	C-802 naval SSMs (1995), Houdong MFPBs (1995), missile technology (1998) transport aircraft (1997); chemical weapons precursors, alleged (1998)
	• Foreign advisers	Nuclear technicians

Arms Procurement and Security Assistance Received *(continued)*

Country	Type	Details
Russia	• Arms transfers	SSM technology (2000), T-72S tank production under license (1997), Kilo-class submarines (1997), SAMs (1998); satellite technology (1998), transport aircraft (1999)
	• Assistance	Training of nuclear technicians
Singapore	• Arms transfers	Spare parts for American-made weapons
Taiwan	• Arms transfers	Spare parts for American-made a/c
Ukraine	• Arms transfers	Tanks (1996), transport a/c (1999)

Arms Sales and Security Assistance Extended

Country	Type	Details
Bosnia	• Military training	Several hundred IRGC fighters (1997)
	• Arms transfers	Chinese ATGMs, artillery shells (1996)
Congo	• Arms transfers	Scud missiles, alleged (1999)
KUP, KDP	• Arms transfers	Shoulder-launched SAMs (1997)
Lebanon	• Arms transfers	Hizbullah militia: artillery, MRLs, small arms, ATGMs, engineering equipment, SAMs, night vision equipment (1997)
	• Assistance	Hizbullah militia: grant estimated at tens of millions of dollars annually (1999)
	• Military training	Some IRGC instructors with Hizbullah militia in Syrian-held Beka'
Palestinians	• Assistance	$20 million annually for Hamas (1997)
	• Military training	Palestinian Hamas and Islamic Jihad; PFLP-GC
Sudan	• Military training	A few IRGC personnel in the Sudanese Army and with People's Defense Forces (1996)
	• Arms transfers	Tanks (1996), combat a/c (1996), MRL launchers (1999)
	• Assistance	(1998)
Syria	• Cooperation in arms production, R&D	Joint development of Scud C SSMs (1999)

Foreign Military Cooperation

Type	Details
• Forces deployed abroad	300 IRGC troops in Lebanon
• Joint maneuvers	India, Pakistan (naval maneuvers), Kuwait (proposed naval maneuvers), Oman (observers 1999)
• Security agreements	Armenia, Greece (1999), Oman (2000)

Defense Production

	M	P	A
Weapons of mass destruction			
• Assembly and production of Scud C, Shahab 3, Shahab 4, and Kosar SSMs (with North Korea, Russia, and possibly also Pakistan)	√		√
• Chemical agents (mustard, attempts to produce nerve agents)	√		
Army equipment			
• Production of Russian T-72S tanks		√	
• Zulfikar and Towsan tanks	√	√	
• Upgrading of T-55 tanks to Iranian model Type 72Z	√		
• Upgrading of T-54 tanks to Iranian model Safir-74	√		
• Boragh, Cobra and BMT-2 APCs	√		
• Zelzal, Nazeat, Shahin and Fajer rockets	√		
• 122, 160, and 240mm MRLs	√		
• 122 and 155mm SP guns	√		
• 81, 120, and 320mm mortars and artillery ammunition	√		
• 120mm Russian artillery guns		√	
• Laser-guided AT missiles	√		
• RPG-7, Nafez and Saegheh ATRLs	√	√	
• Raad (AT-3) Towsan (AT-5) ATGM	√		
• ERA protection for various tanks	√		
• Gas masks	√		
• Spare parts, trucks	√		
Air Force equipment			
• Azarakhsh and Owaz fighter aircraft	√		
• Tondar and Dorneh training aircraft	√		
• An-140 and An-74 transport aircraft		√	√
• Zafar 300 attack helicopter, Sanjack light helicopter	√		
• Shahbaviz 2-75, Shahbaviz 2061 and Shahed 5 helicopters	√	√	
• Parasto light aircraft (probably still under development)	√		
• Ababil, Tallash, Saeqeh and Muhajer UAVs	√		
• Upgrading of F-4, F-5 and F-14 aircraft	√		
• Conversion of HAWK and Standard missiles to be carried on aircraft	√		
• ZU-23mm anti-aircraft guns		√	
• SAMs (assembly of Chinese HN-5A and HQ-2, unconfirmed)			√
• Reverse engineering of Crotale and Rapier SAMs	√		
• Laser-guided missiles	√		
• ARM missiles	√		
• TV-guided missiles	√		
• Spare parts for aircraft	√		

Defense Production *(continued)*

	M	P	A
Electronics			
• Radio transceivers (copy of US model)	√		
• Night vision systems			
Naval equipment			
• Tareq patrol craft	√		
• MIG-S-1800, MIG-S-1900 and MIG-S-2600 patrol crafts	√		
• MIG-S-3700 LCU (Foque class)	√		
• Darya anti-ship missile	√		
• Hendijan auxiliary vessels	√		
Space			
• Telecommunication satellite under development, to be launched with French cooperation	√		

Note: M - manufacture (indigenously developed)
P - production under license
A - assembly

Some of the weapons systems may be copies of foreign types and not indigenously developed. In addition, some may be only prototypes, which were displayed for propaganda purposes and are not in production.

Weapons of Mass Destruction

NBC Capabilities

Nuclear capability
A 5 Mw research reactor acquired from the US in the 1960s (in Tehran) and a small 27 kw miniature neutron source reactor (in Esfahan). A 1,000 Mw VVER power reactor under construction, under a contract with Russia, in Bushehr.
Party to the NPT. Safeguards agreement with the IAEA in force.

Chemical weapons and protective equipment
Iran admitted in 1999 that it possessed chemical weapons in the past. Party to the CWC, but nevertheless suspected of still producing and stockpiling of Mustard and other chemical agents. PRC and Russian firms and individuals allegedly give assistance in CW technology and precursors. Personal protective equipment and munitions decontamination units for part of the armed forces.

Biological weapons
Suspected biological warfare program; no details available. Party to the BWC.

Ballistic Missiles

Model	Launchers	Missiles	Notes
• SS-1 (Scud B/Scud C)	10 – 20	300 Scud B, 100 Scud C	
• CSS-8	16		
Total	~30		
Future procurement			
• Shahab-3	~5		
• Shahab-4/Kosar			Under development

Note: See also under Rockets

Armed Forces

Major Changes: The Iranian Air Force is acquiring An-74 transport aircraft from the Ukraine, some of which will be assembled in Iran, and will receive Mi-17 helicopters from Russia. The Iranian Army is in a slow process of receiving indigenously built Zulfikar and T-72 S main battle tanks, Boragh APCs and artillery pieces.

Order-of-Battle

Year	1995	1996	1997	1999	2000
General data					
• Personnel (regular)	413,000	410,000	518,000*	518,000	518,000
• SSM launchers	15	15	26 – 36*	~30	~30
Ground Forces					
• Divisions	32	32	32	32	32
• Total number of brigades	87	87	87	87	87
• Tanks	1,500	1,500	1,500	1,520	1,460
• APCs/AFVs	1,000	1,300	1,200	1,235	1,240
• Artillery (including MRLs)	1,500 – 2,000	1,500 – 2,000	2,640* (2,930)	2,640 (2,930)	2,650 (2,950)
Air Force					
• Combat aircraft	214	214	226 (318)	205 (297)	205 (333)
• Transport aircraft	119	119	93 (114)*	91 (112)	92 (111)
• Helicopters	275	275	310 (553)*	293 (555)	300 (560)
Air Defense Forces					
• Heavy SAM batteries	30 – 35	30 – 35	30 – 35	30 – 35	30 – 35
• Medium SAM batteries	+	+	+	+	+
• Light SAM launchers	110	110	95	95	95

Order-of-Battle (continued)

Year	1995	1996	1997	1999	2000
Navy					
• Combat vessels	34	33	33	31	29
• Patrol craft	177	176	136	139	~120
• Submarines	2	2	3	3	3

Note: Beginning with 1997, data refers to quantities in active service. The number in parentheses refers to the total inventory.
* Due to change in estimate.

Personnel

	Regular	Reserves	Total
Ground Forces	~350,000	350,000	~700,000
Air Force	18,000		18,000
Air Defense	12,000		12,000
Navy	~18,000		~18,000
IRGC - Ground Forces	100,000		100,000
IRGC - Navy	20,000		20,000
Total	~520,000	350,000	~870,000
Paramilitary			
• Baseej		2,000,000	

Ground Forces

Formations

	Corps/armies	Divisions	Independent brigades/groups	Brigades in divisions
• All arms	4			
• Armored		4	1	3 armd., 1 mech., 1 aty. each
• Mechanized/Infantry		6	1	4 inf., 1 aty. each
• Airborne			1	
• Special forces		2	5	3 commando each
• Artillery			6	
Total	4	12	14	

IRGC Formations

	Divisions	Independent brigades/groups	Brigades in divisions
Armored	4		
Mechanized/Infantry	16		
Special forces		3	
Artillery		6	
SSM		1 – 2	
Total	20	10 – 11	

Note: The IRGC has possibly reorganized as 26 divisions without independent brigades. IRGC divisions are smaller in size than army divisions, sometimes equivalent to the strength of one brigade.

Tanks

Model	Quantity	In service	Since	Notes
MBTs				
High quality				
• T-72 S/M1	240	240	1990	Indigenously produced tanks. Low production rate estimated
• Zulfikar	~40	~40	1996	Based on estimated production rate of 20 per year
Subtotal	~280	~280		
Medium and low quality				
• Chieftain MK 3/MK 5	~100	~100	1973	
• T-62	150	150	1982	
• T-55 and derivatives	~550	~550	1985/1996	Type 69/Type 59/Type 72Z/Safir 74
• M60 A1	150	150	1972	
• M48/M47	150	150	1958	
Subtotal	~1,100	~1,100		
Light tanks				
• Scorpion	~80	~80	1977	
• Towsan	+	+	1998	
Subtotal	~80	~80		
Total	~1,500	~1,500		
Future procurement				
• Zulfikar				Being produced
• T-72S	500			Being produced

APCs/AFVs

Model	Quantity	In service	Since	Notes
APCs				
• M113	200	200	1968	
• Boragh	100	100	1996	Based on estimated production rate of 20 per year
• BTR-50/60	500	500	1967	
• MT-LB	+	+		
Subtotal	~800	~800		
IFVs				
• BMP-1	300	300	1977	
• BMP-2	100	100	1985	
Subtotal	400	400		
Reconnaissance				
• Engesa EE-9 Cascavel	35	35	1982	
Total	~1,240	~1,240		

Artillery

Model	Quantity	In service	Since	Notes
Self-propelled guns and howitzers				
• 203mm M110	~30	~30	1976	
• 175mm/170mm Koksan M-1978	~20	~20	1994	
• 175mm M107	25	25	1975	
• 155mm M109	440	~150	1978	
• 155mm Thunder 2	+	+	1998	Indigenously developed; low production rate
• 122mm Thunder 1	+	+	1998	Indigenously developed; low production rate
• 122mm 2S1	60	~50	1993	
Subtotal	~600	~300		
Towed guns and howitzers				
• 203mm (8") M-115	30	~30	1974	
• 155mm G-5	30	30	1989	
• 155mm GHN-45	100	100	1988	
• 155mm M114	~100	~100	1970	
• 152mm (PRC)	30	30		
• 130mm M-46/Type 59	~800	~800	1973	
• 122mm D-30	~500	~500	1982	

Artillery *(continued)*

Model	Quantity	In service	Since	Notes
• 122mm Type 54/60	~100	~100	1990	
• 105mm M-101	~200	~200	1966	
Subtotal	~2,000	~2,000		
Mortars, over 160mm				
• 320 mm	+	+		
Mortars, under 160mm				
• 120mm M-65	+	+	1980	
• 107mm (4.2") M-30	+	+	1981	
MRLs				
• 122mm BM-21	~100	~100	1978	
• 122mm Hadid/ Azrash/Nur	50	50	1994	
• 107mm Type 63	100	100	1986	
Subtotal	~250	~250		
Total	~3000	~2,700		

Rockets

Model	Quantity	In service	Since	Notes
• 610mm Zelzal-2	+	+	1998	
• 355mm Nazeat	+	+	1988	
• 333mm Shahin 2	+	+	1989	
• 333mm Fajer-5	+	+	1998	
• 240mm Fajer-3	+	+	1994	
• 230mm Oghab	+	+	1987	

Logistics and Engineering Equipment

Pontoon bridges, light infantry assault boats, self-propelled pontoons, AFV transporters (several hundred)

Anti-Tank Weapons

Missiles
AT-11 (Spandrel), AT-4 (Spigot), AT-3 (Sagger), BGM-71A TOW, SS-11/SS-12

Guns
106mm M-40 A1C recoilless rifle (200)

Air Force

Order-of-Battle

Category	Quantity	In service	Notes
• Combat	333	205	
• Transport	111	92	
• Helicopters	560	300	

Note: About 60% serviceable, not counting most of the 115 combat a/c and the transport and civilian a/c brought from Iraq during the 1991 Gulf War; the only Iraqi a/c integrated into the Iranian force are 24 Su-24s and a few MiG-29s; all figures include a/c with army and navy aviation.

Combat Aircraft

Model	Quantity	In service	Since	Notes
Interceptors				
• F-14A Tomcat	60	25	1972	
• MiG-29	35	35	1990	
Subtotal	95	60		
Multi-role				
• F-4 D/E/RF Phantom	70	40	1968	
• Mirage F1-E	24	12	1991	
Subtotal	94	52		
Ground attack				
• Su-24	24	24	1991	
Obsolete				
• F-7	60	24	1987	
• F-5 A/B/E	60	45	1974	
Subtotal	120	69		
Total	333	205		
Future procurement				
• Su-25				Negotiations with Georgia
• Su-27				Negotiations with Russia

Transport Aircraft

Model	Quantity	In service	Since	Notes
• Aero Commander 690	3	3	1978	
• Boeing 747	9	9	1976	

Transport Aircraft *(continued)*

Model	Quantity	In service	Since	Notes
• Boeing 707 and KC-707 tanker	14 – 15	~14	1973	Including Boeing 707s in electronic surveillance/ECM/ECCM role
• C-130 E/H Hercules	48	~30	1970	Including 2-3 in electronic surveillance role
• Dornier Do-228	4	4		Employed in maritime surveillance role
• Fokker F-27 400M/600	18	18	1972	
• An-74	+	+	1999	
• Mystère-Falcon 20	13	13	1991	
• Jetstar	1	1		
Total	111	~92		
Future procurement				
• An-74	12			Being delivered

Training and Liaison Aircraft

Model	Quantity	In service	Since	Notes
Jet trainers				
• Mushshak (PAC Mushshak)	25	25	1991	
• Embraer EMB-312 (Tucano)	25	25	1989	
• T-33	9	9	1968	
Subtotal	59	59		
Piston/Turbo-prop				
• Beechcraft Bonanza F-33	20 – 25	20 – 25	1974	
• Cessna 185/180/150	45	45	1978	
• Socata TB 21/TB 200 (Trinidad/Tobago)	12	12	1996	
• Pilatus PC-7 Turbo-trainer	45	45	1983	
• Pilatus PC-6	15	15	1982	
Subtotal	142	142		
Total	201	201		
Future procurement				
• EMB-312				

Helicopters

Model	Quantity	In service	Since	Notes
Attack helicopters				
• AH-1J Cobra	100	70	1974	
Naval combat				
• SH-3D	3	+	1977	
Heavy transport				
• CH-47C Chinook	45	35	1973	
• RH-53D/SH-53D	20 – 25	10	1976	
Subtotal	~70	~45		
Medium transport				
• AB-214A	180 – 200	~70	1974	
• AB-205/Shahbaviz 2061	50	50	1969	
• AB-212/Shahbaviz 2-75	28	28	1971	
• Mi-17	5	5	1999	
• SA-330/IAR-330 Puma	+	+		
• AS-61	2	2	1978	
Subtotal	~285	~155		
Light transport				
• AB-206 Jetranger	90	+	1969	
• IAR-316	12	12	1994	
• IAR-317	+	+		
Subtotal	~102	~25		
Total	~560	~300		
Future procurement				
• Mi-17	20			Under negotiation
• Shahbaviz 2-75/Shahed 5				Production of 2 – 4 helicopters annually
• Shahbaviz 2061				Production of 2 – 4 helicopters annually

Miscellaneous Aircraft

Model	Quantity	In service	Since	Notes
Electronic surveillance				
• RC-130	~3	~3		Also listed under Transport
Maritime surveillance				
• Dornier DO-228	4	4		Also listed under Transport
• P-3 Orion	5	2	1974	

Miscellaneous Aircraft *(continued)*

Model	Quantity	In service	Since	Notes
Target drones				
• Tallah I/II	+	+	1996	
• Saeqeh I/II	+	+	1996	
UAVs				
• Ababil-S	*	*	1999	
• Ababil-T	*	*	1999	
• Mohajer III (Dorne)	+	+	1997	
• Mohajer IV (Hodhod)	+	+	1997	

Advanced Armament

Air-to-air-missiles
AA-10 (Alamo), AA-11 (Archer), AIM-54A Phoenix (280), AIM-9L Sidewinder (1,270), AIM-7 Sparrow (430), PL-2 (540), PL-7 (360)

Air-to-ground-missiles
AGM-65 Maverick, AS 10 (Karen), AS-12, C-801 anti-ship missile

Future procurement
AA-11 (Archer AAM), AA-12

Note: Numbers in parentheses refer to quantity of missiles purchased.

Air Force Infrastructure

Aircraft shelters:
In all operational airfields

Military airfields: 13
Bandar Abbas, Birjand, Bushehr, Ghaleh-Marghi, Isfahan, Kerman, Kharg Island, Mehrabad, Mashhad, Qeshm, Shiraz, Tabriz, Tehran.

Air Defense Forces

Surface-to-Air Missiles

Model	Batteries	Launchers	Since	Notes
Heavy missiles				
• HAWK/MIM-23B Improved HAWK	12 – 15		1964	
• SA-2 (Guideline)/ HQ-2J	8 – 10		1986	May be under control of IRGC
• SA-5 (Gammon)			1991	
Total	30 – 35			
Medium missiles				
• SA-6 (Gainful)	+		1974	

Surface-to-Air Missiles (continued)

Model	Batteries	Launchers	Since	Notes
Light missiles				
• Rapier		30	1971	To be upgraded
• RBS-70		50	1984	
• Tigercat		15	1968	
Total		**95**		
Shoulder-launched missiles				
• FIM-92A Stinger		+	1987	With IRGC
• SA-7 (Grail)/ HN-5A/SA-14		+	1974	
Future procurement				
• SA-10/(S-300-P)	6			
• SA-5 (Gammon)				
• SA-6				
• C³I system				Upgrading air defense C³I by Russia (unconfirmed)

Other Air Defense Systems

Model	Quantity	In service	Since	Notes
Air defense systems (missiles, radars and guns)				
• 35mm Contraves Skyguard ADS	100	24		
Short-range guns				
• 57mm ZSU 57x2 SP	100	100	1974	
• 57mm S-60	50	50	1966	
• 40mm L-70	95	95		
• 40mm M1	20	20	1968	
• 23mm ZSU 23x4 SP (Gun Dish)	75	75	1974	
• 23mm ZU 23x2	500	500	1977	
Total	**840**	**840**		
Radars				
• AR-3D	+	+		

Navy

Submarines

Type	Original class name	Quantity	Length (m.)/ displacement (t.)	Notes/ armament
• Kilo class	Type 877	3	73.8/3,076	6x533 torpedoes 24 mines
• Iranian midget submarines		3	9.2/90	
Total		6		

Combat Vessels

Type	Original class name	Quantity	Length (m.)/ displacement (t.)	Notes/ armament
Missile frigates				
• Alvand class	Vosper Mk 5	3	94.5/1,100	4xC-802 SSMs/ 1 Seakiller II SSM 1 MK-10 a/s mortar 1x114mm gun 2x35mm guns 3x20mm guns
MFPBs				
• Kaman class	Combattante II	10	47.0/249	4xC-802/Harpoon SSMs 1x76mm gun 1x40mm gun
• Thondor class	Houdong	10	36.6/171	4xC-802 SSMs 2x30mm guns
Subtotal		20		
Gun corvettes				
• Bayandor class	PF-103	2	84/900	2x76mm guns 2x40mm guns 2x20mm guns
Mine warfare vessels				
• MSC 292 and MSC 268 class		2	44.5/384	Acoustic and magnetic sweep 2x20mm guns

Combat Vessels *(continued)*

Type	Original class name	Quantity	Length (m.)/ displacement (t.)	Notes/ armament
• Cape class		2	33.9/239	Mechanical, acoustic and magnetic sweep 1x12.7mm MG
Subtotal		4		
Total		29		

Patrol Craft

Type	Original class name	Quantity	Length (m.)/ displacement (t.)	Notes/ armament
• Parvin class	PGM-71	3	30.8/98	4 depth charges 1x40mm gun 2x20mm guns 2x12.7mm MGs
• MIG-S-2600		5	26.2/85	1x107mm MRL 2x23mm guns
• PBI	Peterson	40	15.2/20.1	1xTigercat SSM 2x12.7mm MGs
• Peterson Mk IIs		6	15.2/22.9	2x12.7mm MGs
• US Mk III coastal patrol craft		9	19.8/41.6	1x20mm gun 1x12.7mm MG
• MIG-S-1800		6	18.7/60	1x20mm gun 1x12.7mm MG
• MIG-G-1900		10	19.5/30	2x23mm guns
• Boghammar		20	13/6.4	1x107mm MRL 1x106mm RCL 3x12.7mm MGs RPG 7
• Boston Whaler craft type 1		20	6.7/1.3	1x107mm MRL 1x12.7mm MG
• Various other small craft		+	5 - 7 m	Some with 12.7mm MGs
Total		~120		

Landing Craft

Type	Original class name	Quantity	Length (m.)/ displacement (t.)	Notes/ armament
• Wellington class hovercraft	BH-7 class	0	23.9/53.6	6 non-operational
• Hengam class		4	93/2,540	Up to 9 tanks or 227 troops 4x40mm guns 8x23mm guns 2x12.7mm MGs
• Iran Ajr class		2	53.7/2,274	65 tons 2x12.7mm MGs
• Iran Hormuz 24 class		3	73.1/2,014	9 tanks or 140 troops
• Iran Hormuz 21 class		3	65/1,280	600 ton
• Fouque class	MIG-S-3700	3	37/276	140 ton
Total		15		

Auxiliary Vessels

Type	Original class name	Quantity	Length (m.)/ displacement (t.)	Notes/ armament
• Delvar class support ship		7	64/890	765 dwt 2x23mm guns
• Luhring Yard- supply ship		2	108/4,673	3,250 dwt 1 AB 212 helicopter 3x20mm guns
• Kangan class water tanker	Mazagon	4	148/12,000	9,430 dwt 2x23mm guns
• Swan Hunter replenishment ship		1	207.2/33,014	9,367 dwt 3 Seaking helicopter 1x76mm gun
• Hendijan	MIG-S-4700	13	50.8/460	40 ton on deck and 95m^3 liquid
• Damen 1550		10	16/25	

Coastal Defense

Type	Batteries	Missiles	Notes
HY-2 (Silkworm)	~12	300	
C-802	15 – 25	~100	
SS-N-22 (Sunburn)			Alleged. Probably non-existent
Total	25-30	400	

Naval Infrastructure

Naval bases: 9
Bandar Abbas, Bandar Anzelli, Bandar Khomeini, Bandar Lengeh, Bushehr, Chah Bahar, Farsi Island, Jask, Kharg Island.

IRGC naval bases: 10
Abadan oil terminal, Abu Musa Island, al-Fayisiyah Island, Cyrus oilfield, Halul Island platform (unconfirmed), Larak Island, Qeshm Island, Rostam Island oilfield, Sir Abu Nuair, Sirri Island.

Ship maintenance and repair facilities: 1
MAN Nordhaman 28,000-ton floating dock

Major Non-Governmental Paramilitary Forces

Personnel

	Active
• Ismael Khan (Afghans)	1,000 – 2,000
• Supreme Council for Islamic Revolution in Iraq (SCIRI)	10,000
• Democratic Party of Iranian Kurdistan (DPIK)	10,000

5. IRAQ

General Data

Official Name of the State: The Republic of Iraq
Head of State: President Saddam Hussein
Prime Minister: Saddam Hussein
Minister of Defense: Lieutenant General Sultan Hashim Ahmad al-Jabburi Tai
Supreme Commander of the Armed Forces: President Saddam Hussein
Chief of Staff of Ground Forces: General Ibrahim Abd al-Sattar Mohammad al-Takriti
Commander of the Air Force: Lieutenant General Khaldoun Khatab Bakr
Commander of the Navy: Rear Admiral Khalid Baqer Khadar

Area: 432,162 sq. km.
Population: 22,500,000 est.

Demography

Ethnic groups		
Arabs	16,537,500	73.5%
Kurds	4,860,000	21.6%
Turkmens	540,000	2.4%
Assyrians and others	562,500	2.5%
Religious groups		
Shi'ite Muslims	12,375,000	55.0%
Sunni Muslims	9,450,000	42.0%
Christians, Yazidis, and others	675,000	3.0%

Economic Data

		1994	1995	1996	1997	1998
GDP (at 1987 prices)	$ bn	4.5	4.5	4.5	5.62	6.58
GDP per capita	$	226	220	211	255	292
Real GDP growth	%	0.0	0.0	0.0	25.0	17.0
Consumer price index	%	300.0	250.0	225.0	200.0	140.0
External debt	$ bn	101	106	112	118	124
Balance of payments						
• Exports fob	$ bn	0.77	0.85	0.95	5.68	6.45
• Imports fob	$ bn	1.20	1.38	1.73	4.18	4.73
• Current account balance (including services and income)	$ bn	-0.23	-0.4	-0.25	0.2	-0.17

Economic Data (continued)

		1994	1995	1996	1997	1998
Government expenditure						
• Total expenditure	$ bn	NA	NA	NA	NA	NA
• Defense expenditure	$ bn	NA	NA	NA	NA	NA
• Real change in defense expenditure	%	NA	NA	NA	NA	NA
• Defense expenditure/GDP	%	NA	NA	NA	NA	NA
Population	m	19.9	20.5	21.3	22.0	22.5
Official exchange rate	ID: $1	0.311	0.311	0.311	0.311	0.311

Sources: EIU Quarterly Report, EIU Country Profile, IMF International Financial Statistical Yearbook, SIPRI Yearbook

Arms Procurement and Security Assistance Received

Country	Type	Details
Belarus	• Cooperation in arms production	Upgrading of Iraqi AD systems and fighter aircraft (1999) alleged
France	• Cooperation in arms production	AD systems (1999) alleged (unauthorized by government)
Romania	• Arms transfers	Guidance systems for SSMs (1999) alleged
Russia	• Advisers	15 Russian experts (1999) alleged
	• Cooperation in arms production	Upgrading of Iraqi AD systems and fighter aircraft (1999) alleged
Yugoslavia	• Arms transfers	Chemical protection equipment (1999) alleged
	• Cooperation in arms production	Upgrading of Iraqi AD systems and fighter aircraft (1999) alleged

Note: Since the Gulf War data are scarce.

Defense Production

	M	P	A
Weapons of mass destruction			
• SSMs under development	√		
• Chemical agents	√		
• Biological agents	√		
Army equipment			
• Tanks		√	
• Artillery		√	
• MRLs		√	

Defense Production (continued)

	M	P	A
• Small arms and artillery ammunition	√		
• Electronics	√		
• Land mines, including scatterable	√		
• ATRLs			√
Air Force equipment			
• AD systems	√		
• Conversion of aircraft to UAVs	√	√	
• Mini-UAVs	√		
• Aerial bombs	√	√	
Naval equipment			
• Small PBs	√		
• Rubber boats	√		
• Naval mines based on Soviet designs		√	

Note: M - manufacture (indigenously developed)
P - production under license
A - assembly

Weapons of Mass Destruction

NBC Capabilities

Nuclear capability
Since the Gulf War, all known Iraqi facilities have been destroyed by the UN's and IAEA's facility-destruction and monitoring teams. Though inspections were suspended in 1998, renewal of nuclear weapons' activities still unlikely. Party to the NPT.

Chemical weapons and protective equipment
Production of chemical agents could have been renewed due to suspension of UNSCOM inspections in Iraq.
Chemical agents produced in the past included mustard (sulfur mustard and purified mustard), sarin, tabun, soman, VX, hydrogen cyanide (unconfirmed); large quantities of chemical agents were destroyed by UN missions, but some may have remained.
Delivery systems: SSM warheads, artillery shells, mortar bombs, MRL rockets, aerial bombs and land mines.
Personal protective equipment, Soviet-type unit decontamination equipment.
Not a party to the CWC.

NBC Capabilities *(continued)*

Biological weapons
Production and development of biological agents could have been renewed due to suspension of UNSCOM inspections in Iraq.
Biological agents produced in the past included Anthrax, Aphlatoxin, Botulinum and Typhoid. Iraq claims that they were destroyed, but stocks were largely unaffected by UN inspectors' activity. Experiments were also carried out with other agents.
Delivery systems: SSM warheads, aerial bombs, and airborne spraying-tanks for combat aircraft, helicopters and UAVs.
Party to the BWC.

Ballistic Missiles

Model	Launchers	Missiles	Notes
• al-Hussein	up to 5	20 – 30	Concealed
• Soumoud	+	+	
Total	~5	~30	

Armed Forces

Major Changes: No major change was recorded in the Iraqi order-of-battle due to the sanctions on Iraq. International monitoring of Iraq's proscribed activities in developing and producing WMD was suspended in 1998. Production of ballistic missiles, chemical and biological weapons probably resumed.

Order-of-Battle

Year	1995	1996	1997	1999	2000
General data					
• Personnel (regular)	450,000	400,000	391,800	432,500	432,500
• SSM launchers	5	5	5	5	5**
Ground Forces					
• Divisions	26	23	23	23	23
• Tanks	2,100	2,100	2,000	2,000	2,000
				(2,300)	(2,400)
• APCs/AFVs	3,300	3,300	2,000*	2,000	2,000
			(3,300)	(2,900)	(2,900)
• Artillery (including MRLs)	1,800	1,800	2,050*	2,050	2,100
Air Force					
• Combat aircraft	380	380	215*	215	215
			(333)	(333)	(333)
• Transport aircraft	+	+	+	+	+
• Helicopters	400	400	370* (460)	370 (460)	360 (460)

Order-of-Battle (continued)

Year	1995	1996	1997	1999	2000
Air Defense Forces					
• Heavy SAM batteries	NA	NA	60*	60	60
• Medium SAM batteries	NA	NA	NA	NA	NA
• Light SAM launchers	NA	NA	NA	NA	NA
Navy					
• Combat vessels	7	7	5	2	0
• Patrol crafts	9	9	9	0	0

Note: Beginning with 1997, data refers to quantities in active service. The number in parentheses refers to the total inventory.
* Due to change in estimate.
** Number does not include unguided rocket launchers.

Personnel

	Regular	Reserves	Total
Ground Forces	400,000	650,000	1,050,000
Air Force	15,000		15,000
Air Defense	15,000		15,000
Navy	2,500		2,500
Total	**432,500**	**650,000**	**1,082,500**
Paramilitary			
• Border guards	20,000		20,000
• Security forces	25,000 – 45,000		25,000 – 45,000
• Special Republican Guard	26,000		26,000

Ground Forces

Formations

	Corps/ armies	Divisions	Independent brigades/groups	Brigades in divisions
All arms	5+2*			
Armored		6		
Mechanized		4		
Infantry		13		
Special forces			2	
Total	5	23	2	

* 5 corps and 2 corps HQs.

Tanks

Model	Quantity	In service	Since	Notes
MBTs				
High quality				
• T-72/T-72M	700	700	1982	
• Assad Babil (T-72 M1)	+	+	1989	
Subtotal	~800	~800		
Medium and low quality				
• T-62	+	+	1973	
• T-55/Type 59/ Type 69/M-77	+	+	1962/1982	Some upgraded
Subtotal	~1,600	~1,200		
Total	~2,400	~2,000		

APCs/AFVs

Model	Quantity	In service	Since	Notes
APCs				
• YW-531	+	+	1990	
• MT-LB	+	+		
• M60P	+	+	1986	
• Engesa EE-11	+	+	1981	
• BTR-40/50/60	+	+	1974	
• FUG-70/PSZH-IV	+	+	1981	
• M-3 (Panhard)	+	+	1981	
• OT-62/OT-64	+	+	1977	
IFVs				
• BMP-1	900	900	1977	
• BMP-2			1990	
• BMD	+	+	1978	
Reconnaissance				
• Engesa EE-9	+	+	1981	
• AML-90/60	+	+	1969	
• BRDM-2	+	+	1982	
Total	2,900	2,000		

Artillery

Model	Quantity	In service	Since	Notes
Self-propelled guns and howitzers				
• 155mm M109	+	+	1984	
• 155mm GCT	+	+	1985	
• 155mm Majnoon	+	+	1982	
• 152mm M-1973	+	+	1975	
• 122mm M-1974	+	+	1977	
Subtotal	150	150		

Artillery (continued)

Model	Quantity	In service	Since	Notes
Towed guns and howitzers				
• 180mm S-23	+	+	1974	
• 155mm G-5	+	+	1986	
• 155mm GHN-45	+	+	1984	
• 155mm M114 A1	+	+	1983	
• 152mm D-20	+	+	1977	
• 152mm M-1976 (2A36)	+	+	1986	
• 152mm M-1943 (D-1)	+	+	1974	
• 130mm M-46/ Type 59	+	+	1962	
• 122mm D-30/Saddam	+	+	1984	
• 122mm M-1938	+	+	1977	
• 105mm M56	+	+	1982	
• 105mm M102	+	+	1984	
• 85mm field/AT	+	+	1974	
Subtotal	1,800	1,800		
Mortars, over 160mm				
• 160mm mortar	+	+	1975	
Mortars, under 160mm				
• 120mmx4 SP	+	+		
• 120mm M-43	+	+	1975	
Rockets				
• FROG - 7	29	29		
• Laith 90	+	+	1988	
Subtotal	~30	~30		
MRLs				
• Ababil	+	+	1988	262mm Ababil-50, 400mm Ababil-100
• Astros II	+	+	1986	127mm SS-30, 180mm SS-40, 300mm SS-60
• 132mm BM-13	+	+	1986	
• 130mm	+	+		
• 128mm M-63	+	+		
• 122mm BM-21/BM-11	+	+	1977	
• 122mm Firos-25	+	+		
• 107mm	+	+	1986	
Subtotal	130	130		
Total	~2,100	~2,100		

Ground Radars

Model	Quantity	In service	Since	Notes
Artillery/mortar locating radars				
• Cymbeline	+	+		
• Rasit	+	+		

Logistics and Engineering Equipment

BLG-60, MTU-55 bridging tanks, GSP self-propelled ferries, mine-clearing rollers, minefield crossing system, PMP pontoon bridges, TPP pontoon bridges, Soviet-model tank-towed bridges, AFV transporters (1,500-2,000).

Anti-Tank Weapons

Missiles
AT-3 (Sagger), AT-4 (Spigot), BGM-71A TOW, MILAN, AT-5 (Spandrel) mounted on BMP-2, BRDM-2 (carrying AT-3) SP, M-3 (carrying HOT) SP, VCR/TH (carrying HOT) SP, M901 ITV

Total	1,500

Guns
• 107mm B-11	+

Air Force

Order-of-Battle

Category	Quantity	In service	Notes
Combat	~333	~215	119 additional planes flown to Iran during the Gulf War (1991)
Transport	+	+	
Helicopters	460	360	

Combat Aircraft

Model	Quantity	In service	Since	Notes
Interceptors				
• MiG-25 (Foxbat)	15	8 – 10	1982	Additional 4 in Iran
• MiG-29 (Fulcrum)	15	8 – 10	1988	Additional 4 in Iran
• MiG-23 MF/ML	30	~20	1976	
Subtotal	60	~40		
Multi-role				
• Mirage F-1B/EQ5/ EQ2/EQ4	30	30	1980	Additional 24 in Iran

Combat Aircraft *(continued)*

Model	Quantity	In service	Since	Notes
Ground attack				
• Su-24 (Fencer C)	6	0	1989	Additional 24 in Iran
• MiG-23 B (Flogger)/ MiG-27	30	25	1976	Additional 12 in Iran
• Su-20/22 (Fitter C/H)	45	30	1974	Additional 24 in Iran
• Su-25 (Frogfoot)	25	~15	1985	Additional 7 in Iran
Subtotal	106	~70		
Obsolete				
• MiG-21 MF/ BIS/U (Fishbed)/F-7	130	~70	1974	
• Su-7B (Fitter A)	*	*	1969	Possibly phased out
Subtotal	130	~70		
Bombers				
• Tu-22 (Blinder)	6	~4	1973	Additional 20 in Iran
• Tu-16 (Badger)/ An-6 (B-6D)	1	1	1987	
Subtotal	7	5		
Total	~333	~215		

Transport Aircraft

Model	Quantity	In service	Since	Notes
• An-12 (Cub)	5	5	1966	
• An-24 (Coke)	+	+	1967	
• An-26 (Curl)	+	+	1977	
• Il-76 (Candid)	+	+	1989	Including some tankers
• Mystère-Falcon 20/ Falcon 50	+	+		
• Tu-124A/Tu-134 (Crusty)	+	+	1962	
Total	small number	small number		

Note: Additional 15 aircraft in Iran, 6 in Kuwait and 8 in Jordan.

Training and Liaison Aircraft

Model	Quantity	In service	Since	Notes
Jet trainers				
• L-29 (Delfin)	~20	~20	1974	
• L-39 (Albatross)	~30	~30	1975	
• Embraer EMB-312 (Tucano)	~60	~60	1985	
Subtotal	~110	~110		
Piston/Turbo-prop				
• MBB-223 Flamingo/ AS 202 Braud/Zlin 326	~35	~35	1979	
• Pilatus PC-7	25	25	1980	
• Pilatus PC-9	30	30	1987	
Subtotal	~90	~90		
Total	~200	~200		

Helicopters

Model	Quantity	In service	Since	Notes
Attack helicopters				
• Alouette III (armed)	30	30	1971	
• Mi-24/Mi-25 (Hind)	30	30	1982	
• SA-342 Gazelle	50	50	1977	
• MBB BO-105	40	40	1979	Number unconfirmed
Subtotal	150	150		
Heavy transport				
• Mi-6 (Hook)	15	~10	1974	
Medium transport				
• AS-332 Super Puma	+	+		
• AS-61	5	3	1982	
• Mi-8/Mi-17 (Hip)	100	100	1974	
• SA-330 Puma	20	10	1977	
• Bell 214	40	10 – 20	1985	
• Mi-2 (Hoplite)	+	+		
• SA-321 Super Frelon	10	10	1976	Also employed in naval combat role
Subtotal	~180	~150		
Light transport				
• BK-117	20 – 25	10 – 20	1988	
• Hughes 500D	30	10	1983	
• Hughes 300C	30	10	1983	
• Hughes 530F	25	16	1985	
Subtotal	~110	~50		
Total	~460	~360		

Miscellaneous Aircraft

Model	Quantity	In service	Notes
AEW/AWACS			
Adnan-1/Adnan-2 AEW	2	1–2	2 Adnan-2 flown to Iran
UAVs and mini-UAVs			
Mirach 100	+	+	

Advanced Armament

Air-to-air-missiles
AA-2 (840), AA-6, AA-7 (96), AA-8 (304), R-530 (267), R-550 Magic (680), Super 530D/F.

Air-to-ground-missiles
AM-39 Exocet (750), Armat (750), AS-2 (Kipper), AS-4 (Kitchen), AS-5 (Kelt), AS-6 (Kingfish), AS-7 (Kerry), AS-9 (Kyle), AS-10, AS-12, AS-14 (40), AS-15TT (50), AS-20, AS-30L (180), AT-2 (Swatter), C-601, HOT, LX, X-23.

Bombs
Belouga CBU, Cardoen CBU, fuel-air explosive (FAE)

Note: Number in parentheses refers to quantity of missiles purchased.

Air Force Infrastructure

Aircraft shelters
For all combat aircraft (some damaged)

Military airfields: 28
Abu-Ajal, al-Assad, al-Bakr, Balad, Basra, H-2, H-3, Habbaniyah, Irbil, Jalibah, Khalid, Kirkuk, Kut al-Amarah, Kut al-Amarah new field, Mosul, Mudaysis, Muthanah, al-Nasiriyah, al-Qadisiyah, al-Rashid, al-Rumaylah, Saddam, Salman, al-Shuaiba, al-Tallil, al-Taqaddum, al-Tuz, Wadi al-Khir.

Air Defense Forces

Surface-to-Air Missiles

Model	Batteries	Launchers	Since	Notes
Heavy missiles				
• SA-2 (Guideline)/ SA-3 (Goa)	60		1972	
Total	60			
Medium missiles				
• SA-6 (Gainful)	+		1974	
• SA-8 (Gecko)		20	1987	
Total		20		

Surface-to-Air Missiles (continued)

Model	Batteries	Launchers	Since	Notes
Light missiles				
• Roland I/II		100	1981	
• SA-9 (Gaskin)		+	1981	
• SA-13 (Gopher)		30	1989	
Total		130		
Shoulder-launched missiles				
• SA-7 (Grail)		400	1975	
• SA-14 (Gremlin)		+	1989	
• SA-16 (Gimlet)		+	1992	
Total		~400		

Note: Serviceability of missile batteries is uncertain due to American bombing (40% were damaged).

Other Air Defense Systems

Model	Quantity	In service	Since	Notes
Short-range guns				
• 57mm ZSU 57x2 SP	+	+	1977	
• 57mm S-60	+	+	1972	
• 37mm M-1939	+	+	1972	
• 23mm ZSU 23x4 SP (Gun Dish)	+	+	1977	
• 23mm ZU 23x2	+	+	1972	
Total		2,000 – 3,000		
Radars				
• P-35/37 Barlock	+	+		
• P-15/P-18 Flat Face	+	+		
• P-15M Squat Eye	+	+		
• P-14 Tall King	+	+		
• P-12 Spoon Rest	+	+		
• TRS-2215	+	+		
• TRS-2230	+	+		

Navy

Combat Vessels

Type	Original class name	Quantity	Length (m.)/ displacement (t.)	Notes/ armament
The following vessels are currently non-operational: 2 Assad corvettes, 20 Sawari PBs, 2 Vosper PBRs, 2 PB-90, 1 Bogomol, 2 Zhuk, 1 Osa-I, 3 SRN-6				

Naval Infrastructure

Naval bases: Basra, Umm Qasr, Faw, al-Zubayir	4
Ship maintenance and repair facilities: 6,000-ton capacity floating dock, held in Egypt	1

Major Non-Governmental Paramilitary Forces

Personnel

	Active	Reserves	Total
• Kurdish Democratic Party (KDP)	25,000	30,000	55,000
• Kurdish Workers Party (PKK)	20,000		20,000
• Patriotic Union of Kurdistan (PUK)	18,000		18,000
• Supreme Assembly of the Islamic Revolution (SAIRI)	2,000		2,000
• National Liberation Army (NLA - Mujahedin Khalq)	15,000		15,000
Total	80,000	30,000	110,000

Equipment

Organization	Category	System	Quantity	Notes
NLA	Helicopters	• MI-17		
		• MD-530		
	Tanks	• Chieftain		
PUK	Tanks	• T-54/55		

6. ISRAEL

General Data

Official Name of the State: State of Israel
Head of State: President Moshe Katsav
Prime Minister: Ehud Barak
Minister of Defense: Ehud Barak
Chief of General Staff: Lieutenant General Shaul Mofaz
Commander of the Air Force: Major General Dan Halutz
Commander of Army HQ: Major General Moshe Ivri-Sukenik
Commander of the Navy: Rear Admiral Yedidia Ya'ari

Area: 22,145 sq. km, including East Jerusalem and its vicinity, and the Golan Heights.
Population: 6,120,000

Demography

Ethnic groups		
Jews	4,982,000	81.4%
Arabs, Druze, and others	1,138,000	18.6%
Religious groups		
Jews	4,982,000	81.4%
Muslims	863,000	14.1%
Christians	171,000	2.8%
Druze and others	104,000	1.7%

Economic Data

		1995	1996	1997	1998	1999
GDP (current price)	$ bn	86.9	95.5	98.6	97.5	98.9
GDP per capita	$	15,685	16,754	16,912	16,331	16,160
Real GDP growth (at 1995 prices)	%	6.8	4.6	2.9	2.2	2.2
Consumer price index	%	10.0	11.3	9.0	5.4	5.2
External debt	$ bn	29.718	31.972	33.919	35.893	36.248
Balance of payments						
• Exports fob	$ bn	19.268	21.241	22.650	22.972	25.386
• Imports fob	$ bn	26.834	28.426	27.824	26.197	29.927
• Current account balance (including services and income)	$ bn	-5.196	-5.316	-3.399	-0.667	-2.602

Economic Data *(continued)*

		1995	1996	1997	1998	1999
Government expenditure						
• Total expenditure	$ bn	39.514	44.802	44.407	38.437	40.032
• Defense expenditure	$ bn	7.075	8.150	8.264	7.836	8.777
• Real change in defense expenditure	%	7.71	15.19	1.39	-5.17	12.00
• Defense expenditure/GDP	%	8.14	8.53	8.38	8.03	8.87
Population	m	5.54	5.70	5.83	5.97	6.12
Official exchange rate	NIS: $1	3.14	3.25	3.54	4.16	4.15

Sources: EIU Quarterly Report, EIU Country Profile, IMF International Financial Statistical Yearbook, SIPRI Yearbook

Arms Procurement and Security Assistance Received

Country	Type	Details
France	• Arms transfers	Spare parts, Socata training aircraft (1998), CW detectors (1998)
Germany	• Arms transfers	NBC detection vehicles, CW personal protection gear (1998), 3 Dolphin submarines (1999), Seahake heavy torpedoes (1999)
	• Assistance	Partial financial support for 3 submarines constructed in Germany
Netherlands	• Arms transfers	CW personal protection gear (1998)
	• Cooperation in arms production, assembly, R&D	Cooperation in building patrol boats (1998)
South Africa	• Arms transfers	Patrol boats (1997)
Turkey	• Arms transfers	Akrep reconnaissance vehicle (1998)
US	• Arms transfers	F-15I combat a/c (1999), F-16I (1999), helicopters (1998), upgrading of AH-64A (2000), missile corvettes, SP artillery, naval SSMs (1998), SAMs, MLRS (1998), upgrading of MLRS (1998), tank transporters (1997), heavy trucks (1999), ATGMs, MIM-120 AAMs (1999), JDAMs guided bombs (2000)

Arms Procurement and Security Assistance Received *(continued)*

Country	Type	Details
	• Assistance	$1.92 bn grant (2000), will be gradually increased up to $2.4 bn in 2008; additional $1.2 bn between 1999 – 2001 within the framework of Wye River Memorandum
	• Cooperation in arms production, assembly, R&D	Finance and assistance for Arrow ATBM, THEL defense system (Nautilus) and other projects
	• Military training	Trainees abroad

Arms Sales and Security Assistance Extended

Country	Type	Details
Argentina*	• Arms transfers	Upgrading Boeing 707 transport a/c (1995), HUD for Pampas trainers (1997), radars and electronic reconnaissance systems for naval surveillance a/c (1998)
Australia	• Arms transfers	Radars for upgraded P-3C (1995), jointly with a US company; ESM for Australian C-130 a/c, Popeye AGMs (1999), ESM for helicopters (1998), night vision equipment for helicopters (1999), ESM for frigates (1999)
Austria	• Arms transfers	Command and control systems (2000)
Belgium	• Arms transfers	Hunter UAVs (2000)
Brazil*	• Arms transfers	HUD and avionics for trainer a/c (1997), avionics suit for ALX attack a/c and upgrading of F-5 fighter (1998)
Cambodia	• Arms transfers	Upgrading of MiG-21 a/c (1997); avionics for L-39 trainer a/c
Chile*	• Arms transfers	Sa'ar 4 missile patrol boats (1997), Patrol boats (1996), AAMs, AAGs (1998), artillery, Barak shipborne anti-missile missile, mini-UAVs, components for upgrading of F-5 combat a/c (1998), AEW a/c (1995), tanker a/c (1996)
Colombia*	• Cooperation in arms production	Co-production of Galil assault rifle
Croatia	• Arms transfers	Upgrading of MiG-21 aircraft (1999)
Cyprus	• Arms transfers	Torpedo boats (1997), electronic communication systems (1999), flak jackets (1999)

* According to foreign publications, as cited by Israeli publications.

Arms Sales and Security Assistance Extended *(continued)*

Country	Type	Details
Czech Republic	• Arms transfers	Ground forces radar, jointly produced (1995)
	• Cooperation in arms production, assembly, R&D	Cooperation in upgrading T-72 tanks (1997)
Ecuador*	• Arms transfers	Kfir combat aircraft (1999)
Eritrea*	• Arms transfers	Fast patrol boats (1997), landing craft (1993)
Ethiopia	• Arms transfers	Upgrading MiG-21 combat a/c (temporarily suspended - 1999)
Finland	• Arms transfers	AD command and control system (1996), Ranger UAVs (1999), Spike ATGMs (2000)
France	• Arms transfers	Hunter UAVs (1996), hand-held SAR systems (1997)
	• Cooperation in arms production, assembly, R&D	Cooperation with ALCATEL in military communications (1997), Litening designators for combat a/c (1999)
Germany	• Arms transfers	Litening designators for combat a/c (1997), EHUD air combat debriefing system (1996), upgrading of CH-53 helicopters (1998)
	• Cooperation in arms production, assembly, R&D	Joint production of EW systems for Tornado a/c (1998), joint production of Litening pods for NATO (1998), joint production of Panzerfaust 3LR light ATRL (1995), joint development of a satellite (1996), joint production of NT series ATGMs (1999)
India*	• Arms transfers	Aerial early warning technology (2000), Harpy anti-radar drone,* executive jets (1996), EL/M-2032 radar for Jaguar a/c (1997), Litening pods (1997), communication equipment (1998), ballistic missile detection radar (2000), Super-Dvora patrol boats (1998), upgrading of tanks (1995), upgrading of guns (2000), avionics for upgrade of fighter aircraft (1999)
	• Cooperation in arms production, assembly, R&D	Battlefield surveillance radar (2000)
Indonesia	• Arms transfers	Mini-UAVs (1996)

---

* According to foreign publications, as cited by Israeli publications.

Arms Sales and Security Assistance Extended *(continued)*

Country	Type	Details
Italy	• Arms transfers	Enhanced add-on armor kit for some Italian M113 family APCs (1995), Opher guiding kit for bombs (1997), airborne SAR system (1997), Litening designators (2000)
Myanmar (Burma)	• Arms transfers	Upgrading of F-7 fighter a/c (1998), AA missiles (1998)
Nepal	• Arms transfers	Galil assault rifles (1997)
Netherlands	• Arms transfers	Ranger mini-UAVs, under negotiation, artillery C^2 systems (1998), aircraft debriefing system (1997)
	• Cooperation in arms production, assembly, R&D	Training simulators (1996)
Nicaragua	• Arms transfers	Dabur patrol boats (1997)
Poland	• Cooperation in arms production, assembly, R&D	Upgrading Huzar attack helicopters and supply of ATGMs (1999-cancelled)
Portugal	• Arms transfers	EHUD air combat debriefing systems (1998)
PRC*	• Arms transfers	Python-3 AAMs, a/c radars (1995); thermal imaging tank-sights, IL-76 Phalcon AEW aircraft with Russia (2000 suspended)
	• Military training	Advisers/instructors/technicians
	• Cooperation in arms production, assembly, R&D*	Contribution to Chinese combat a/c avionics (1995), joint development of an AGM/cruise missile (1995); thermal imaging tank sights
Romania	• Arms transfers	OWS-25 weapon system for APCs (1997), ground radar system (2000), upgrading of tanks (2000)
	• Cooperation in arms production, assembly, R&D	Joint production of night vision equipment for Romanian IAR-330 Puma helicopters (1999), upgrading Dracula attack helicopters (1999), cooperation in upgrading 100 MiG-21s in Romania (2000), cooperation in upgrading IAR-99/109 trainer a/c (2000), cooperation in production of avionics (2000)
Russia	• Cooperation in arms production, assembly, R&D	Joint development and marketing of KA 50/52 attack helicopter (1998)

---

* According to foreign publications, as cited by Israeli publications.

Arms Sales and Security Assistance Extended *(continued)*

Country	Type	Details
Singapore*	• Arms transfers	Electronic components for F-5 combat a/c (1998), Barak shipborne anti-missile missile, AAMs, air combat debriefing system (1998), NT-S ATGMs (1999)
	• Military training	Advisers/instructors/technicians
	• Cooperation in arms production, assembly, R&D	Cooperation in upgrading Turkish F-5 combat a/c (2000)
Slovakia	• Cooperation in arms production, assembly, R&D	Upgrading T-72 tanks (1995), developing Strop light air defense system (1995)
Slovenia	• Arms transfers	155mm canons (1997), 120 mm mortars (1997), upgrading of PC-9 training a/c (1999)
South Africa	• Arms transfers	Upgrading Boeing 707 to SIGINT configuration (1996)
South Korea*	• Arms transfers	Popeye-2 AGM (2000), Harpy anti-radar drones (1997), night vision systems (1996), EHUD debriefing systems for air combat training (2000)
Spain*	• Arms transfers	Upgrading Boeing 707 to SIGINT configuration (1995), Litening designators (2000), UAVs (1995), military communications (1997)
Sri Lanka	• Arms transfers	Kfir aircraft (2000), Sa'ar 4.5 MFPBs (2000) Superhawk UAVs (1997), mine detection radar (1997), ESM systems (1998)
Sweden	• Arms transfers	120mm ammunition for tanks (1996), ground penetrating radar (1997)
	• Cooperation in arms production, assembly, R&D	Joint development of NBC protection for civilians (1997), joint development of explosives detection system (1999)
Switzerland	• Arms transfers	Communication intelligence systems (1999)
	• Cooperation in arms production, assembly, R&D*	Ranger UAVs and ADS-95 systems (1998 2000), C³I simulators (1999)
Thailand	• Arms transfers	Searcher mini-UAVs (1998), Popeye AGM (1999-temporarily suspended), upgrading F-5 a/c (2000), upgrading L-39 training a/c (2000), conversion of transport a/c to tanker (1999-temporarily suspended), ARS-700 search and rescue systems (1999)

---

* According to foreign publications, as cited by Israeli publications.

Arms Sales and Security Assistance Extended *(continued)*

Country	Type	Details
Turkey	• Arms transfers	Upgrading F-4 and F-5 a/c (2000), upgrading of M60 tanks (2000), Popeye AGMs (1998), EHUD debriefing system for air combat training (1998), aerial reconnaissance systems (2000), ARS-700 airborne search and rescue systems for Cougar helicopters (1998), mine detection and ground penetrating radar (1997)
	• Cooperation in arms production, assembly, R&D	Joint production of Popeye AGMs (2000), production of Delila anti-radar air-launched drone (2000)
Uganda	• Arms transfers	Upgrading of MiG-21 a/c (temporarily suspended-1999)
UK	• Arms transfers	Artillery and infantry ammunition (1996), CATS and ACE simulators, ESM for Nimrod 2000 (1998), EHUD air combat debriefing systems (1998)
Ukraine	• Cooperation in arms production, assembly, R&D	Joint upgrading of MiG-21 a/c for Ethiopia (temporarily suspended-1999)
US	• Arms transfers and cooperation in arms production	**Air Force equipment:** Python 4 AAMs (1998), Popeye AGMs (2000), F-15I fuselage parts (1999), engine parts for F-15/F-16 a/c (2000), digital mapping systems for V-22 a/c (1998), Helmet Mounted Cueing-system for US Air Force (1998), Litening pods for F-16 a/c (2000), laser designators for the Comanche helicopter (1998), upgrading UH-1 helicopters, ARS-700 airborne search and rescue systems (1998), Pioneer and Hunter UAVs, tactical air-launched decoys (1999), terminal guidance bombs, image processing technology (1998), joint research on Arrow ATBM (2000), joint research on THEL laser weapon (2000), BPI ATBM systems (2000), upgrading of T-38 a/c (2000), crashworthy troop seats for helicopters (1999), Astra SPX a/c, production and marketing of satellite launchers (2000), remote sensing satellites **Ground Forces equipment:** central computer for Bradley AFVs, 120mm mortars, tactical communication, Enhanced Applique Armor kits for APCs (1999), upgrading MLRS (2000)

---

* According to foreign publications, as cited by Israeli publications.

Arms Sales and Security Assistance Extended *(continued)*

Country	Type	Details
Venezuela	• Arms transfers	EW radars and command and control systems for frigates (2000), Litening pods (1998), Barak SAMs (ground based version-2000)
Zambia	• Military training	Advisers/instructors/technicians, foreign trainees (1995)
	• Arms transfers	Upgrading MiG-21 a/c (temporarily suspended - 1999)

* According to foreign publications, as cited by Israeli publications.

Foreign Military Cooperation

Type	Details
• Pre-positioning of equipment	$200 million worth of stockpile of US military equipment
• Cooperation in military training	US and Turkish use of Israeli airfields and airspace for training (2000); Israeli use of Turkish airspace and airfields for training
• Joint maneuvers	Jordan (SAR-1998), Turkey (SAR-1999), US

Defense Production

	M	P	A
Ground Forces equipment			
Tanks	√		
Overhead weapon systems for IFVs	√		
Artillery pieces	√		
ATGMs: NT-G, NT-S, NT-D, Lahat (barrel-launched ATGM)	√		
ATRLs	√		
Artillery, mortar and small arms ammunition	√		
Mines	√		
Mine-clearing rollers	√		
Tank guns	√		
Tread-width mine plows for tanks (TWMP)	√		
SP AAGs (Soviet gun, US carrier)			√
Tank-towed bridges (TAB)	√		
Upgrading of tanks	√		
Small arms	√		

Defense Production *(continued)*

	M	P	A
Airforce equipment (some joint ventures with US companies)			
Arrow ATBM	√		
AAMs	√		
Upgrading of combat aircraft	√		
AGMs	√		
CBUs	√		
TV- and laser-terminal guidance bombs	√		
UAVs and mini-UAVs	√		
Operational flight trainer systems	√		
Radars	√		
Refueling system for aircraft	√		
Helicopter parts		√	
Combat aircraft parts		√	
Navy equipment			
LCTs	√		
MFPBs	√	√	
PBs	√		
SSMs	√		
Torpedo components		√	
Electronics			
Radars	√		
Direction finders	√		
Pilot rescue radio sets	√		
ELINT equipment	√		
EW jammers	√		
Radio transceivers	√		
Audio/video microwave transceivers	√		
Radio voice scramblers and encryption units	√		
Air-launched decoys	√		
AEW aircraft conversion	√		
Aircraft warning systems	√		
Optronics			
Night vision devices	√		
Laser rangefinders and target designators	√		
Space			
Military satellites including launching capability	√		
Amos communications satellite (launched in May 1996)	√		

Note: M - manufacture (indigenously developed)
P - production under license
A - assembly

Weapons of Mass Destruction

NBC Capabilities

Nuclear capabilities
Two nuclear research reactors; alleged stockpile of nuclear weapons.* Not a party to the NPT.

CW capabilities and protective equipment
Personal protective equipment; unit decontamination equipment. Fuchs (Fox) NBC detection vehicles (8 vehicles); SPW-40 P2Ch NBC detection vehicles (50 vehicles); AP-2C CW detectors. Signed but not yet ratified the CWC. Not a party to BWC.

* According to foreign publications, as cited by Israeli publications.

Ballistic Missiles

Model	Launchers	Missiles	Since	Notes
• MGM-52C (Lance)	12	+	1976	
• Jericho Mk 1/2/3* SSM*	+	+		
Total	+			

* According to foreign publications, as cited by Israeli publications.

Armed Forces

Major Changes: Israeli forces withdrew from south Lebanon in May 2000. US military aid to Israel increased and is $1.92 bn for 2000. The Air Force ordered 50 new F-16I combat aircraft, which will be delivered starting 2003. The Air Force will upgrade 12 of its AH-64 Apache attack helicopters to the AH-64D Longbow standard. The Navy received its third Dolphin submarine.

Order-of-Battle

Year	1995	1996	1997	1999	2000
General data					
• Personnel (regular)	177,500	187,000	187,000	186,500	186,500
• SSM launchers	+	+	+	+	+
Ground Forces					
• Divisions	16	16	16	16	16
• Total number of brigades	77	77	77	77	76
• Tanks	3,845	3,870	3,900	3,895	3,930
• APCs/AFVs	8,000	8,010	8,010	8,040	8,040
• Artillery (including MRLs)	1,300	1,292	1,312	1,348	1,348
			(1,912)	(1,948)	(1,948)

Order-of-Battle (continued)

Year	1995	1996	1997	1999	2000
Air Force					
• Combat aircraft	677	640	613 (780)	624(801)	628(800)
• Transport aircraft	83	83	83 (93)	77(87)	77(87)
• Helicopters	269	285	278 (288)	289(299)	287(297)
Air Defense Forces					
• Heavy SAM batteries	4+	4+	21*	22	22
• Light SAM launchers	50	50	50	~70	~70
Navy					
• Submarines	3	3	4	4	6
• Combat vessels	22	22	21	21	20
• Patrol crafts	36	36	35	35	32

Note: Beginning with 1997, data refers to quantities in active service. The number in parentheses refers to the total inventory.
* Due to change in estimate.

Personnel

	Regular	Reserves	Total
Ground Forces	141,000	380,000	521,000
Air Force	36,000	55,000	91,000
Navy	9,500	10,000	19,500
Total	**186,500**	**445,000**	**631,500**
Paramilitary			
• Border Police	7,650		7,650

Ground Forces

Formations

	Corps/HQ	Divisions	Independent brigades/groups	Brigades in divisions
• All arms	3*			
• Armored		12		2 – 3 armd., 1 mech., 1 aty. each
• Mechanized/ Infantry/ Territorial		4	8	
• Airborne			4	
Total		16	12	

Formations (continued)

Anti-guerrilla HQ: 3 divisional HQ for control of units engaged in anti-guerrilla activities in Judea, Samaria and Gaza (after May 1994, Gaza HQ stationed in Jewish settlements) and on the Lebanese border. In emergency, the HQ will be reinforced by armor, infantry, helicopters, engineering and anti-tank forces.

* According to foreign publications, as cited by Israeli publications.

Tanks

Model	Quantity	In service	Since	Notes
MBTs				
High quality				
• Merkava Mk I/ Mk II/Mk III	1,280	1,280	1979/ 1983/1989	
Medium and low quality				
• Centurion/ upgraded Centurion	1,000	1,000	1965	
• M60 A3/ upgraded M60/ Magach 7	1,040	1,040	1980	
• M60/M60 A1	360	360	1970	
• M48 A5	200	200		
• T-62	50	50	1974	
Subtotal	2,650	2,650		
Total	**3,930**	**3,930**		
Future procurement				
• Merkava Mk III/Mk IV				

APCs/AFVs

Model	Quantity	In service	Since	Notes
• Achzarit	+	+	1994	
• M113 (various marks)	+	+		
• Nagmashot*	100	100	1989	
• Nagmachon	+	+		
• Nakpadon	15	15		
• M-2 and M-3 halftrack	2,685	2,685		Some phased out
• Akrep	30	30	1998	
• RBY	+	+		
Total	**8,040**	**8,040**		

* According to foreign publications, as cited by Israeli publications.

Artillery

Model	Quantity	In service	Since	Notes
Self-propelled guns and howitzers				
• 203mm M110	+	+	1975	
• 175mm M107	+	+	1974	
• 155mm M109 A1/A2 }				
• 155mm M109 Doher }	600	600		
• 155mm M-50	+	+		
• 155mm L-33	+	+		
Subtotal	900	900		
Towed guns and howitzers				
• 155mm M-71	+	+		
• 130mm M-46	+	+		
• 122mm D-30	+	+		
Mortars, over 160mm				
• 160mm SP	+	+		
Mortars, under 160mm				
• 120mm	250	250		
MRLs				
• 240mm	+	+	1974	
• 140mm	+	+		
• 122mm BM-21	+	+		
• 227mm MLRS	48	48		
Rockets				
• 290mm MAR 290	+	+		
• Keres anti-radar missile	+	+		
• Kachlilit anti-radar missile	+	+		
Total	1,948	1,348		

Ground Radars

Model	Quantity	In service	Since	Notes
Artillery/mortar-locating radars				
• AN/TPQ-37	+	+		
• AN/PPS-15	+	+		
• Shilem	+	+		

Logistics and Engineering Equipment

Gilois motorized bridges, M-123 Viper minefield crossing system, M60 AVLB, mine-clearing rollers, mine layers, Pomins II portable mine neutralization system,* Puma ECVs, TAB (towed assault bridge, towed by tanks), TLB (trailer-launched bridge), TWMP (tread width mine ploughs), M-1000 heavy equipment transporters

* According to foreign publications as cited by Israeli publications.

Anti-Tank Weapons

Missiles
Spike, Gil and Dandy* AT missiles (NT-S, NT-G, NT-D), BGM-71A TOW and BGM-71C Improved TOW, Mapats SP, Nimrod, Israeli BGM-71C Improved TOW SP, M47 Dragon, AT-3 (Sagger)

Future procurement
BGM-71E (TOW 2A)

* According to foreign publications, as cited by Israeli publications.

Air Force

Order-of-Battle

Category	Quantity	In service	Notes
• Combat	800	628	Including aircraft in operational storage
• Transport	87	77	
• Helicopters	297	287	

Combat Aircraft

Model	Quantity	In service	Since	Notes
Advanced multi-role				
• F-15I	25	25	1998	
• F-15 A/B	72	72	1976	
• F-16 A/B	110	110	1980/1986	
• F-16 C/D	138	138		
Subtotal	345	345		
Multi-role				
• F-4E/RF-4E Phantom and Phantom 2000	140	140	1969	
• A-4 Skyhawk	175	118	1967	57 in operational storage, for sale/emergency use
• Kfir C-2/TC-2/C-7/TC-7	140	25	1976	120 in operational storage, for sale/emergency use
Subtotal	455	283		
Total	**800**	**628**		
Future procurement				
• F-16I	50			Delivery 2003

Transport Aircraft

Model	Quantity	In service	Since	Notes
• Arava	10	10	1984	
• Beechcraft Queen Air	6	6	1990	
• Boeing 707	10	10	1973	Some in EW role
• Boeing 707 tanker	3	3		
• C-130H Hercules	22	22	1970	
• DC-3 Dakota (C-47)	18	8	1948	10 in storage, for sale
• Dornier Do-28	15	15	1971	
• KC-130 tanker (refueling)	3	3	1976	
Total	87	77		

Training and Liaison Aircraft

Model	Quantity	In service	Since	Notes
Jet trainers				
• CM-170 Fouga Magister/Tzukit	80	80	1960	Some in storage
Piston/Turbo-prop				
• Socata Trinidad TB-21	22	22	1995	
• Cessna U-206 (Stationair-6)	21	0		In storage, for sale
• Piper Cub	35	35		
Subtotal	78	57		
Total	**158**	**137**		

Helicopters

Model	Quantity	In service	Since	Notes
Attack				
• AH-64A Apache	41	41	1990	
• AH-1G/1S Cobra	64	64	1981	
• 500MD Defender	30	30	1979	
Subtotal	135	135		
Heavy transport				
• CH-53	39	39	1970	Including CH-53-2000
Medium transport				
• Bell 212	55	45		10 in storage, for sale
• UH-60L Black Hawk	15	15	1998	
• UH-60A Black Hawk	10	10	1994	
Subtotal	80	70		

Helicopters *(continued)*

Model	Quantity	In service	Since	Notes
Light transport				
• AB-206 JetRanger/Bell 206L	38	38		
Naval combat				
• AS 536 Panther	5	5	1995	
Total	297	287		
Future procurement				
• AH-64D Apache	12			Upgrading of former models; delivery 2003

Miscellaneous Aircraft

Model	Quantity	In service	Since	Notes
AEW/AWACS				
• E-2C Hawkeye	4	4	1978	
• Boeing 707 AEW*	+	+		Also listed under Transport Aircraft
ELINT and EW				
• Boeing 707 ELINT*	+	+		
• Boeing 707 EW*	+	+		
• Beechcraft King Air EW	6	6	1990	
Maritime surveillance aircraft				
• Seascan (Westwind 1124N)	3	3		
UAVs and mini-UAVs				
• Hermes 450S, Hermes 450 High Altitude,* Mastif, Pioneer, Scout, Searcher				
Target drones				
• Beech AQM-37A; Beech BQM107B, MQM-74C Chuckar II, Teledyne Ryan 1241				
Future procurement				
• Beechcraft King Air				Delivery 2000
• Hunter UAV; Heron UAV				

* According to foreign publications, as cited by Israeli publications.

Advanced Armament

Air-to-air missiles
AIM-9 Sidewinder, AIM-9L, AIM-7 Sparrow, Python 3, Python 4, Shafrir, AMRAAM AIM-120

Air-to-ground missiles
AGM-78D Standard ARM, AGM-65 Maverick, AGM-62A Walleye, AGM-45 A/B Shrike, Hellfire, Hellfire II, Delilah, Popeye (equivalent to AGM-142),* NT-D ATGM*

Bombs
CBU (including Tal-1, ATA-1000, ATA-500), runway-penetration bombs, Pyramid, Griffin, Harpy anti-radar drone,* Guillotine, Opher

EW and CEW
Chaff and flare dispensers for combat aircraft, Samson AN/ADM-141 TALD, EL/L 8202 ECM pod, EL/L-8230 ECM system, EL/L-8231 ECM system, EL/L-8240 ECM system, EL/M-2160 warning system, LWS-20 system, SRS-25 airborne receiver, SPS-20 self-protection system, SPS-65 self-protection system, SPS-200 airborne self-protection system, SPS-1000 EW system, SPS-2000 self-protection system, Sky-Jam 200 jammer, AN/ALQ 131 electronic countermeasure systems (20)

Future procurement
AIM-9M AAM, Hellfire 2, Star-1 AGM/cruise missile (under development), AMRAAM AIM-120B (42), JDAMs guided bombs (700)

* According to foreign publications, as cited by Israeli publications.

Air Force Infrastructure

Aircraft shelters
In all operational airfields, for combat aircraft

Military airfields: 11
Haifa, Hatzerim, Hatzor, Lod, Nevatim, Palmachim, Ramat David, Ramon, Tel Aviv, Tel Nof, Uvda

Aircraft maintenance and repair capability
Maintenance on all models in service, partly in airfields, partly at Israel Aircraft Industries facilities

Air Defense Forces

Surface-to-Air Missiles

Model	Batteries	Launchers	Since	Notes
Heavy missiles				
• MIM-23B Improved HAWK	17		1965	
• MIM-104 Patriot	4		1991	
• Arrow	1		1998	Including Green Pine radar and Citrus Tree command post
Total	22			
Light missiles				
• MIM-72A Chaparral		~50		
• Mahbet SP		~20		M163 Vulcan with Stinger SAMs
Total		~70		
Shoulder-launched missiles				
• FIM-92C Stinger		500 missiles		
• MIM-43A Redeye		+	1975	
Future procurement				
• MIM-104 Patriot	3			Under negotiation
• Arrow ATBMs	2			Total order - 3

Other Air Defense Systems

Model	Quantity	In service	Since	Notes
Short-range guns				
• 40mm Bofors L70	+	+		
• 23mm ZU 23x2	+	+		
• 20mm M163 A1 Vulcan SP	20	20		Being converted to Mahbet
• 20mm TCM-20 Hispano Suiza SP	+	+		
• 20mm Hispano Suiza	+	+		
Total	~900	~900		

Radars
• Ramit, FPS-100, AN/TPS-43, Green Pine, Alufa-3

Aerostats with airborne radars
• Status

Navy

Submarines

Type	Original class name	Quantity	Length (m.)/ displacement (t.)	Notes/ armament
Submarines				
• GAL	IKL/Vickers Type 540	3	45/600	Sub-Harpoon SSMs 8x533mm torpedoes (to be sold)
• Dolphin	(Thyssen)	3	57.3/1,900	Sub-Harpoon SSMs 6x533mm torpedoes
Total		6		

Combat Vessels

Type	Original class name	Quantity	Length (m.)/ displacement (t.)	Notes/ armament
Missile corvettes				
• Eilat class	Sa'ar 5	3	86.4/1,075	1xSA-536 helicopter 8xHarpoon SSMs 8xGabriel II SSMs 64xBarak-1 SAM 1x76mm gun 2x25mm Sea Vulcans 6x324mm torpedoes
MFPBs				
• Aliya class	Sa'ar 4.5	5	61.7/498	1xSA 536 helicopter 8xHarpoon SSMs 4xGabriel II SSMs 2x20mm guns 1xVulcan Phalanx 2x12.7mm MGs
• Hetz class	Sa'ar 4.5	6	61.7/488	8xHarpoon SSMs 6xGabriel II SSMs 32xBarak I SAMs 1x76mm gun 1xVulcan Phalanx 2x12.7mm MGs

Combat Vessels *(continued)*

Type	Original class name	Quantity	Length (m.)/ displacement (t.)	Notes/ armament
• Reshef class	Sa'ar 4	5	58/415	4xHarpoon SSMs 4-6xGabriel II SSMs 1-2x76mm guns 1xVulcan Phalanx 2x20mm guns 2x12.7mm MGs used for ASW with 2-3x324 torpedoes with sonar
• Mivtach class	Sa'ar 2	1	45/250	5xGabriel II SSMs 2-3x324 torpedoes sonar used for ASW
Subtotal		17		
Total		20		
Future procurement				
• Hetz class				Upgrading of Sa'ar 4 class to improved Sa'ar 4.5/Nirit level

Patrol Craft

Type	Original class name	Quantity	Length (m.)/ displacement (t.)	Notes/ armament
• Super Dvora		14	21.6/54	2x20mm guns or 2x25mm guns 2x12.7mm MGs 1x84mm MRL depth charges
• Dabur		15	19.8/39	2x20mm guns 2x12.7mm MGs 2x324mm torpedoes 1x84mm MRL depth charges
• Nahshol	Bobcat	3	22/36.5	1x20mm gun
Total		32		
Future procurement				
• Super Dvora		2		

Landing Craft

Type	Original class name	Quantity	Length (m.)/ displacement (t.)	Notes/ armament
• Ashdod class LCT		3	62.7/400	In reserve
• LCM		2		
Total		5		
Future procurement				
• Newport LST		1		

Auxiliary Vessels

Type	Original class name	Quantity	Length (m.)/ displacement (t.)	Notes/ armament
• Ro-Ro		1		
• Bat Sheva support ship		1	95.1/1,150	4x20mm guns 4x12.7 MGs

Special Maritime Forces

Midget submarines; Zaharon fast boats

Naval Infrastructure

Naval bases: 3
Ashdod, Eilat, Haifa

Ship maintenance and repair facilities
Repair and maintenance of all naval vessels at Haifa, partly in conjunction with Israel Dockyards

7. JORDAN

General Data

Official Name of the State: The Hashemite Kingdom of Jordan
Head of State: King Abdullah bin Hussein al-Hashimi
Prime Minister: Ali Abu al-Ragheb
Minister of Defense: Ali Abu al-Ragheb
Inspector General of the Armed Forces: Major General Abd Khalaf al-Najada
Chief of the Joint Staff of the Armed Forces: Major General Mohammad Malkawi
Commander of the Air Force: Major General Muhammad Khair al-Ababna
Commander of the Navy: Commodore Ali Mahmoud al-Khasawna

Area: 90,700 sq. km.
Population: 5,960,000

Demography

Ethnic groups		
Arabs	5,840,800	98.0%
Circassians and Armenians	119,200	2.0%
Religious groups		
Sunni Muslims	5,721,600	96.0%
Greek Orthodox and other Christians	238,400	4.0%

Economic Data

		1994	1995	1996	1997	1998
GDP (current prices)	$ bn	6.1	6.51	6.64	6.98	7.38
GDP per capita	$	1,173	1,202	1,190	1,210	1,238
Real GDP growth	%	8.5	5.5	0.6	1.3	-1.0
Consumer price index	%	3.5	2.4	6.5	3.0	4.5
External debt	$ bn	7.7	8.11	8.07	8.23	8.43
Balance of payments						
• Exports fob	$ bn	1.43	1.77	1.82	1.83	1.8
• Imports fob	$ bn	3.0	3.29	3.82	3.65	3.4
• Current account balance (including services and income)	$ bn	-0.4	-0.26	-0.22	0.03	0.01
Government expenditure						
• Total expenditure	$ bn	2.09	2.23	2.47	2.61	2.48
• Defense expenditure	$ bn	0.5	0.55	0.56	0.58	0.59

Economic Data (continued)

		1994	1995	1996	1997	1998
• Real change in defense expenditure	%	11.1	10.0	1.8	3.6	1.7
• Defense expenditure/GDP	%	8.2	8.44	8.43	8.3	8.0
Population	m	5.2	5.44	5.58	5.77	5.96
Official exchange rate	JD: $1	0.699	0.700	0.709	0.709	0.709

Sources: EIU Quarterly Report, EIU Country Profile, IMF International Financial Statistical Yearbook, SIPRI Yearbook

Arms Procurement and Security Assistance Received

Country	Type	Details
Canada	• Arms transfers	Avionics upgrade for C-130 (1998)
Taiwan	• Military training	Trainees abroad (1999)
Turkey	• Arms transfers	CN-235 a/c (1998)
	• Military training	Flight simulation (1998), training of helicopter pilots (1999)
UK	• Arms transfers	Challenger MBTs (1999)
	• Military training	Trainees abroad (1999)
Ukraine	• Arms transfers	BTR-94 APCs (1999)
US	• Arms transfers	F-16 combat aircraft (1997), M60 MBTs (1998), helicopters (1996), M110 SP guns (1998), aircraft simulators (1999), Mk 3 patrol boats (1999)
	• Assistance	$126.5 million in military aid out of $276 million total aid (1999)
	• Military training	Advisers, training exercises

Arms Sales and Security Assistance Extended

Country	Type	Details
Bahrain	• Military training	Training of fighter pilots (1999)
Philippines	• Arms transfers	F-5 a/c (1997)
Oman	• Military training	Training of infantry soldiers (1999)
Qatar	• Military training	Training of Special Forces (1999)
Singapore	• Arms transfers	F-5 a/c (1994)
US	• Facilities	Use of airfields by combat a/c

Foreign Military Cooperation

Type	Details
• Cooperation in military training	Turkey (use of facilities and airspace for training of pilots) (1998)

Foreign Military Cooperation *(continued)*

Type	Details
• Forces deployed abroad	Small contingency force in Bosnia, Croatia and Sierra Leone (UNAMSIL); observers in Georgia and Tajikistan
• Joint maneuvers	Egypt, Israel (SAR), France, Oman, Qatar, Turkey, UAE, UK, US
• Security agreements	Turkey, US

Defense Production

	M	P	A
Army equipment			
• Upgrading of M60 MBTs	√	√	
• Upgrading of Scorpion light tanks	√		
• Conversion of M47 tanks to ARVs	√		
• Badia's APCs and Sangyong vehicles	√		
• High explosives (with assistance from India)	√		
Electronics			
• Upgrading of avionics (joint venture)	√		
Optronics			
• Night vision equipment			√

Note: M - manufacture (indigenously developed)
P - production under license
A - assembly

Weapons of Mass Destruction

NBC Capabilities

Nuclear capability
No known capability. Party to the NPT.

Chemical weapons and protective equipment
No known CW activities. Personal protective and decontamination equipment. Party to the CWC.

Biological weapons
No known capability. Party to the BWC.

Armed Forces

Major Changes: The Jordanian Army received first Challenger I MBT, out of an order of 228 tanks from the UK. The Navy received three patrol boats from the US

Order-of-Battle

Year	1995	1996	1997	1999	2000
General data					
• Personnel (regular)	94,000	94,000	94,200	94,200	94,200
Ground Forces					
• Divisions	4	4	4	4	4
• Total number of brigades	15	15	14	14	14
• Tanks	765	815	834 (1,226)	~900 (~1,200)	~900 (~1,200)
• APCs/AFVs	1,480	1,480	1,475 (1,575)	1,475 (1,575)	1,500 (1,600)
• Artillery (including MRLs)	450	450	770* (795)	788 (813)	788 (813)
Air Force					
• Combat aircraft	85	85	91	101	100
• Transport aircraft	12	12	11 (13)	12 (14)	14 (16)
• Helicopters	70	60	68	68	68
Air Defense Forces					
• Heavy SAM batteries	14	14	14	14	14
• Medium SAM batteries	50	50	50	50	50
• Light SAM launchers	+	+	50*	50	50
Navy					
• Patrol crafts	12	12	10	10	13

Note: Beginning with 1997, data refers to quantities in active service. The number in parentheses refers to the total inventory.
* Due to change in estimate.

Personnel

	Regular	Reserves	Total
Ground Forces	85,000	60,000	145,000
Air Force	8,500		8,500
Navy	700		700
Total	94,200	60,000	154,200
Paramilitary			
• General Security Forces (including Desert Patrol)	25,000		
• Popular Army		200,000 – 250,000	

Note: The Popular Army is not regarded as a fighting force.

Ground Forces

Formations

	Divisions	Independent brigades/groups	Brigades in divisions
Armored	2		3 armd., 1 aty., 1 AD each
Mechanized	2		1 inf., 2 mech., 1 arty., 1 AD each
Infantry/Royal Guard		1	
Special forces		1	
Artillery		5	
Total	4	7	

Tanks

Model	Quantity	In service	Since	Notes
MBTs				
High quality				
• Challenger I	+	+	1999	Out of 228 ordered
• Khalid	275	275	1984	Improved Chieftain
Subtotal	~300	~300		
Medium and low quality				
• Tariq	290	290	1995	Improved Centurion
• M60 A1/A3	288	288	1980	
• Chieftain	90	0		From Iran, captured by Iraq, in storage.
• M48 A1	212	0	1966	
Subtotal	880	578		
Light Tanks				
• Scorpion	19	19		With Desert Patrol
Total	~1,200	~900		
Future procurement				
• Challenger I	228			Some already delivered

APCs/AFVs

Model	Quantity	In service	Since	Notes
APCs				
• M113 A1/A2	1,240	1,240	1968	
• Engesa EE-11	100	100	1987	With General Security Forces

APCs/AFVs (continued)

Model	Quantity	In service	Since	Notes
• Saracen	+	0	1963	Included under Saladin
Subtotal	1,340	1,340		
IFVs				
• BMP-2	35	35	1989	
• BTR-94	24	24	1999	Out of 50 ordered
Total	~60	~60		
Reconnaissance				
• Saladin	60	0	1963	Quantity includes both Saracen and Saladin
• Ferret	140	~100	1955	
• Subtotal	200	100		
Total	~1,600	~1,500		
Future procurement				
• BTR 94	50			Some already delivered

Artillery

Model	Quantity	In service	Since	Notes
Self-propelled guns and howitzers				
• 203mm M110 A2	128	128	1980	
• 155mm M109 A2	220	220	1980	
Subtotal	348	348		
Towed guns and howitzers				
• 203mm (8") M-115	25	0	1965	
• 155mm M-59 (Long Tom)	10	10	1965	
• 155mm M114	30	30	1970	
• 105mm M102 A1	50	50	1970	
Subtotal	115	90		
Mortars, under 160mm				
• 120mm	300	300	1975	
• 107mm	50	50	1975	
Subtotal	350	350		
Total	813	788		

Ground Radars

Model	Quantity	In service	Since	Notes
Artillery/mortar locating radars				
• AN/TPQ-36/37	7	7	1990	

Logistics and Engineering Equipment

Mk 2 (D) flail, bridges, mine-clearing plows and bulldozers, UDK-1, AFV transporters (200), M578 recovery vehicles (30)

Anti-Tank Weapons

Model	Quantity	In service	Since	Notes
Missiles				
• BGM-71A TOW/ BGM-71C improved TOW	260	260	1974	
• M47 Dragon	310	310	1976	
• M901 ITV	70	70	1988	
Total	**640**	**640**		
Guns				
• 106mm M40	330	330	1987	
PGMs				
• 155mm Copperhead projectiles (CLGP)	100	100		

Air Force

Order-of-Battle

Category	Quantity	In service	Notes
• Combat	100	100	
• Transport	16	14	
• Helicopters	68	68	

Combat Aircraft

Model	Quantity	In service	Since	Notes
Advanced multi-role				
• F-16 (A/B)	16	16	1997	
Multi-role				
• Mirage F-1 C/E	29	29	1981	
• F-5 E/F	55	55	1975	To be upgraded for training purposes
Subtotal	84	84		
Total	**100**	**100**		
Future procurement				
• F-16 A/B	8			Under negotiation
• A-10				Under negotiation

Transport Aircraft

Model	Quantity	In service	Since	Notes
• C-130 Hercules	7	5	1972	
• CASA C-212	2	2	1975	
• Dove	1	1	1965	
• CN-235	2	2	1998	
• Gulfstream III/IV	3	3	1986	
• L-1011-500	1	1	1984	
Total	16	14		
Future procurement				
• Challenger 604	2			Delivery in 2001

Training and Liaison Aircraft

Model	Quantity	In service	Since	Notes
Jet trainers				
• CASA C-101	13	13	1987	
• Cessna 318 (T-37)	10	10	1975	
Subtotal	23	23		
Piston/Turbo-prop				
• AS-202 Bravo	20	20		
• BAe-SA-3-125 Bulldog	15	15	1978	
Subtotal	35	35		
Total	58	58		

Helicopters

Model	Quantity	In service	Since	Notes
Attack helicopters				
• AH-1G/1S Cobra	22	22	1985	
Medium transport				
• UH-60A Black Hawk	3	3	1987	
• AS-332 Super Puma	10	10	1986	
• Bell 205/UH-1H	18	18	1995	
Subtotal	31	31		
Light transport				
• Alouette III	1	1	1977	
• MD 500D	8	8	1980	
• MBB BO-105	3	3		With General Security Forces
• BK-117	3	3		
Subtotal	15	15		
Total	68	68		
Future procurement				
• UH-60A Black Hawk	4			Under negotiation

Miscellaneous Aircraft

Future procurement
TTL BTT-3 Banshee target drones (82), 2 launchers

Advanced Armament

Air-to-air-missiles
AIM-9J/M/P Sidewinder (750), AIM-7M Sparrow (96), R-550 Magic

Air-to-ground-missiles
AS-30L (10), AGM-65C Maverick (60)

Bombs
Belouga CBU, Durandal anti-runway bombs

Note: Number in parentheses refers to the quantity of missiles purchased.

Air Force Infrastructure

Aircraft shelters
For all combat aircraft

Military airfields: 6
Amman (Marka), Azrak, H-4, H-5, Jaafar, Mafraq

Air Defense Forces

Surface-to-Air Missiles

Model	Batteries	Launchers	Since	Notes
Heavy missiles				
• MIM-23B Improved HAWK	14		1978	
Total	14			
Medium missiles				
• SA-8 (Gecko)		50	1982	
Total		50		
Light missiles				
• SA-13 (Gopher)		50	1986	
Total		50		
Shoulder-launched missiles				
• Javelin		+		
• MIM-43A Redeye		250	1977	
• SA-14 (Gremlin)		300	1987	
• SA-16 (Igla)		240	1991	
Total		~800		

Other Air Defense Systems

Model	Quantity	In service	Since	Notes
Short-range guns				
• 40mm M42 SP	218	0	1966	To be phased out
• 23mm ZSU 23x4 SP (Gun Dish)	45	45	1983	
• 20mm M163 A1 Vulcan SP	100	100	1976	
Total	363	145		
Radars				
• AN/TPS-43	2	2		
• AN/TPS-63	5	5		
• S-711	5	5		

Navy

Patrol Craft

Type	Original class name	Quantity	Length (m.)/ displacement (t.)	Notes/ armament
• Feysal class	Bertram	4	11.6/ 8	1x12.7mm MGs
• al-Hussein class	VT Hawk	3	30.5/124	2x30mm guns 1x20mm gun 2x12.7mm MGs
• al-Hashim class	Rotork type 412	3	12.7/9	In Dead Sea 1x12.7mm MG
• MK-3		3	19.8/41.6	1x 20mm gun 1x 12.7 MG
Total		13		

Naval Infrastructure

Naval bases: 2
Aqaba, Hingat al-Ramat

8. KUWAIT

General Data

Official Name of the State: State of Kuwait
Head of State: Jabir al-Ahmad al-Jabir al-Sabah
Prime Minister: Saad Abdallah al-Salim al-Sabah
Minister of Defense: Salim al-Sabah al-Salim al-Sabah
Chief of General Staff: Major General Ali al-Mumin
Commander of the Air Force and Air Defense Forces: Brigadier General Sabir al-Suwaidan
Commander of the Navy: Commodore Ahmad Yousuf al-Mualla

Area: 17,820 sq. km. (including 2,590 sq. km. of the Neutral Zone)
Population: 2,030,000

Demography

Ethnic groups		
Kuwaitis	914,000	45.0%
Other Arabs	710,000	35.0%
Southeast Asians	183,000	9.0%
Persians/Iranians	81,000	4.0%
Others	142,000	7.0%
Religious groups		
Sunni Muslims	914,000	45.0%
Shi'ite Muslims	812,000	40.0%
Christians, Parsis, Hindus, and others	304,000	15.0%

Economic Data

		1994	1995	1996	1997	1998
GDP (current price)	$ bn	24.765	26.610	30.702	30.231	25.147
GDP per capita	$	15,287	14,783	16,244	15,268	12,387
Real GDP growth (1984 prices)	%	8.4	1.0	3.3	2.8	-2.5
Consumer price index	%	2.5	2.7	3.6	0.6	0.2
External debt	$ bn	9.92	9.99	7.54	9.41	9.37
Balance of payments						
• Exports fob	$ bn	11.23	12.78	14.89	14.22	9.61
• Imports cif	$ bn	6.68	7.78	8.37	8.25	8.62
• Current account balance (including services and income)	$ bn	3.23	5.02	7.11	7.94	2.53

Economic Data *(continued)*

		1994	1995	1996	1997	1998
Government expenditure						
• Total expenditure	$ bn	14.070	13.848	13.006	13.128	10.865
• Defense expenditure	$ bn	3.285	3.697	3.705	3.422	3.344
• Real change in defense expenditure	%	10.23	12.54	0.21	-7.63	-2.27
• Defense expenditure/GDP	%	13.26	13.89	12.06	11.31	13.29
Population	m	1.62	1.80	1.89	1.98	2.03
Official exchange rate	KD: $1	0.298	0.298	0.299	0.303	0.305

Sources: EIU Quarterly Report, EIU Country Profile, IMF International Financial Statistical Yearbook, SIPRI Yearbook

Arms Procurement and Security Assistance Received

Country	Type	Details
Belgium	• Arms transfers	90mm ammunition (1998)
Finland	• Arms transfers	CW protective equipment (1998)
France	• Arms transfers	Radars (1996), SAMs, MFPBs (1999), MM-40 anti-ship missiles (1999)
	• Military training	Trainees abroad (1999)
PRC	• Arms transfers	PLZ-45 SP artillery (1998)
Russia	• Arms transfers	Smerch MRLs (1995), BMP-3 AIFVs (1995), AT-4 ATGMs (1995)
Singapore	• Arms transfers	Two landing craft (1995)
South Africa	• Arms transfers	Mortars, laser range-finders, light armament (1997)
UK	• Arms transfers	APCs (1997), Starburst shoulder-launched SAMs (1997), Sea-skua anti-ship missiles (1999)
	• Military training	Foreign advisers/instructors, trainees abroad (1999)
US	• Arms transfers	M1A2 tanks (1995), ARVs (1995), TOW-2B ATGMs (1999)
	• Maintenance aid	M-88 ARVs (1998), M1A2 tanks (1998), M113 APCs (1998)
	• Infrastructure	Upgrading of 2 air bases and construction of one brigade HQ

Arms Sales and Security Assistance Extended

Country	Type	Details
Brazil	• Arms transfers	A-4 combat aircraft (1998)
UN	• Assistance	$35 million for UNIKOM force (2000)
US	• Assistance	Annual grant for US force in Kuwait
	• Facilities	Facilities for US forces

Foreign Military Cooperation

Type	Details
• Foreign forces	Some 3,700 US soldiers, including some 2,300 air force personnel, 150 army and navy personnel, and some 1,250 marine personnel. 2 batteries of MIM-104 Patriot SAMs, pre-positioning of US tanks (110), APCs (110) and artillery pieces (equipment for one brigade); 24 US A-10 attack a/c stationed in Kuwait; 12 UK Tornado GR1/1A a/c; 900 UNIKOM troops and 200 observers
• Joint maneuvers	US (amphibious, command post and naval exercises) (1998); UK (marines); GCC countries; France; Egypt; Syria (1996); Iran (1998)
• Security agreements	GCC countries, US, UK, France, Russia, PRC, Italy

Weapons of Mass Destruction

NBC Capabilities

Nuclear capability
No known nuclear activity. Party to the NPT.

Chemical weapons and protective equipment
No known CW activities. Personal protective equipment; unit decontamination equipment. Party to the CWC.

Biological weapons
No known BW activities. Party to the BWC.

Armed Forces

Major Changes: No major change was recorded in the Kuwaiti order-of-battle.

Order-of-Battle

Year	1995	1996	1997	1999	2000
General data					
• Personnel (regular)	32,500	32,500	15,500*	19,500	19,500

Order-of-Battle (continued)

Year	1995	1996	1997	1999	2000
Ground Forces					
• Number of brigades	6	6	6	6	6
• Number of battalions	1	1	1	1	1
• Tanks	472	700	318 (455)*	318 (483)	318 (483)
• APCs/AFVs	50	50	455 (515)*	436 (715)	490 (755)
• Artillery (including MRLs)	24	24	75 (128)*	75 (128)	~70 (~125)
Air Force					
• Combat aircraft	78	59	40 (59)	40 (59)	40 (59)
• Transport aircraft	4	6	5	5	5
• Helicopters	22	18 – 21	24 – 27	24 – 27	~25
Air Defense Forces					
• Heavy SAM batteries	12	12	12	12	12
Navy					
• Combat vessels	2	2	4	6	10
• Patrol craft	33	33	54*	51	69

Note: Beginning with 1997, data refers to quantities in active service. The number in parentheses refers to the total inventory.
* Due to change in estimate.

Personnel

	Regular	Reserves	Total
Ground Forces	15,000	24,000	39,000
Air Force	2,500		2,500
Navy	2,000		2,000
Total	**19,500**	**24,000**	**43,500**
Paramilitary			
• National Guard	5,000		5,000
• Civil Defense	2,000		2,000

Ground Forces

Formations

	Independent brigades/groups	Independent battalions
Armored	2	
Mechanized	2	
Artillery	1	
Border Defense	1	
Royal Guard	1	
Commando		1
Total	7	1

Tanks

Model	Quantity	In service	Since	Notes
MBTs				
High quality				
• M1A2 Abrams	218	218	1994	
• M-84	200	100	1990	
Subtotal	418	318		
Medium and low quality				
• Chieftain	45	0	1977	
• Vickers Mk 1	20	0	1970	
Subtotal	65	0		
Total	483	318		

APCs/AFVs

Model	Quantity	In service	Since	Notes
APCs				
• M113	230	60	1981	8 M901 ITV
• Fahd	60	+	1994	
Subtotal	290	~65		
IFVs				
• BMP-3	55	20	1995	
• BMP-2	46	40	1988	
• Pandur	70	70	1998	Various models
• Desert Warrior	254	254	1994	
• M577	40	40	1995	Artillery command post vehicle
Subtotal	465	424		
Total	755	~490		
Future procurement				
• Pandur				Option for up to 200 vehicles

Artillery

Model	Quantity	In service	Since	Notes
Self-propelled guns and howitzers				
• 155mm M109 A3	24	24		
• 155mm M109 A2	23	0	1986	Damaged during the Gulf War, being overhauled
• 155mm AMX-13 F-3	18	0		In storage, offered for sale
• 155mm GCT AuF-1	12	0	1992	In storage, offered for sale
Subtotal	77	24		
Mortars, under 160mm				
• 120mm RTF-1	~15	~15		
• 107mm	6	6		
Subtotal	~20	~20		
Rockets				
• 300mm Smerch (BM9A52-2)	27	27	1995	
Total	~125	~70		
Future procurement				
• 155mm Norinco PLZ-45	27			Ordered 1997, total requirement for 75
• 120mm SP mortars	30 – 100			
• M109 A6 Paladin	48			Under negotiation

Logistics and Engineering Equipment

Model	Quantity	In service	Since	Notes
• Mk 3 (D) flail	+	+	+	Anti-mine vehicle
• M88 ARVs	14	14	1996	

Anti-Tank Weapons

Model	Launchers	Missiles	Since	Notes
Missiles				
• AT-4 Spigot	+	80	1994	
• AT-5 Spandrel	+	240	1994	
• AT-10 Bastion	+	600	1995	
• BGM-71A/B TOW	82	+	1977	
• BGM-71C	*	*		Status unknown
• M901 ITV	8	+		
• M47 Dragon	+	+		
Future procurement				
• BGM-71F (TOW 2B)		728		

Air Force

Order-of-Battle

Category	Quantity	In service	Notes
• Combat	59	40	
• Transport	5	5	
• Helicopters	~25	~25	

Combat Aircraft

Model	Quantity	In service	Since	Notes
Advanced multi-role				
• F/A-18C/D	40	40	1992	Fewer pilots than a/c
Multi-role				
• Mirage F1-B/C	19	0	1976	Not in service
Total	59	40		

Transport Aircraft

Model	Quantity	In service	Since	Notes
• Boeing 737-200	1	1		
• C-130-30 Hercules/ L-100-30	3	3	1971	
• DC-9	1	1	1976	
Total	5	5		
Future procurement				
• C-130J	4			

Training and Liaison Aircraft

Model	Quantity	In service	Since	Notes
Jet trainers				
• BAC-167	8	0	1969	
• Hawk	12	0	1985	
Subtotal	20	0		
Piston/Turbo-prop				
• S-312 (Shorts Tucano)	18	18	1995	
Total	38	18		

Helicopters

Model	Quantity	In service	Since	Notes
Attack				
• SA-342K Gazelle	16	16	1974	
Medium transport				
• SA-330 Puma	~7	~7	1975	

Helicopters (continued)

Model	Quantity	In service	Since	Notes
Naval combat				
• AS-332 Super Puma	3	3	1985	
Total	~26	~26		

Miscellaneous Aircraft

Model	Quantity	In service	Since	Notes
Future procurement				
• Skyeye UAVs				3 systems, 12 UAVs under negotiation

Advanced Armament

Air-to-air-missiles
AIM-9M Sidewinder, AIM-7F Sparrow (200)

Air-to-ground-missiles
AGM-65G Maverick (300), AGM-84 Harpoon (40), AS-11, AS-12, HOT

Bombs
Paveway II laser-guided

Note: Numbers in parentheses refer to number of units purchased.

Air Force Infrastructure

Aircraft shelters
In airfields; for combat aircraft; under reconstruction

Military airfields: 3
Al-Ahmadi, al-Jahra (Ali al-Salam), Kuwait International Airport

Air Defense Forces

Surface-to-Air Missiles

Model	Batteries	Launchers	Since	Notes
Heavy missiles				
• MIM-23B Improved HAWK	6		1977	
• Aspide	6			Part of Skyguard
Total	12			
Shoulder-launched missiles				
• FIM-92A Stinger		+		
• Starburst		48	1997	Approx. 250 missiles
Total		48+		

Other Air Defense Systems

Model	Quantity	In service	Since	Notes
Air defense systems (missiles, radars and guns)				
• Skyguard AD system	6	6		Each battery with 2xAspide launchers, 2xOerlikon 35mm
Short-range guns				
• 40mm Bofors L-70/L-60	+	+		Unconfirmed
• Oerlikon-Buhrle 2x35 GDF-002	+	+		Part of Skyguard AD system
• 23mm ZSU 23x4 SP (Shilka)	+	+		
• 20mm Oerlikon GAI	+	+		
Radars				
• AN/FPS-117 (Seek Igloo)	1	1		
• AN/TPS-32	1	1		
• Tiger (TRS-2100)	1	1		
• AD command and control unit (ADGE)	1	1		

Navy

Combat Vessels

Type	Original class name	Quantity	Length (m.)/ displacement (t.)	Notes/ armament
MFPBs				
• Istiklal	Lurssen FPB-57	1	58.1/410	4xExocet MM 40 SSMs 1x76mm gun 2x40mm guns mines
• Sanbouk	Lurssen TNC-45	1	44.9/255	4xExocet MM 40 SSMs 1x76mm gun 2x40mm guns
• Um almaradim	P-37 BRL	8	42/245	4xSea Skua SSMs 1x40mm gun 1x20mm gun
Total		10		

203

Patrol Craft

Type	Original class name	Quantity	Length (m.)/ displacement (t.)	Notes/ armament
• Inttisar	OPV-310	4	31.5/150	1x22mm gun 1x12.7mm MG
• Manta		12	14/10	3x12.7mm MGs
• Shaheed	100K FPB	2	33.3/104	1x20mm gun 2x12.7mm MGs
• Various small patrol boats		51	10-12m	Cougar and al-Shaali class PBs carrying 12.7mm MGs
Total		69		
Future procurement				
• Magnum Sedan PBs		20		
• 2,000 ton OMV corvettes		4		

Landing Craft

Type	Original class name	Quantity	Length (m.)/ displacement (t.)	Notes/ armament
• al-Tahaddy Landing Craft		2	45/215	80 tons
• RTK Sea Truck		1	12.7/9	
Total		3		

Auxiliary Vessels

Type	Original class name	Quantity	Length (m.)/ displacement (t.)	Notes/ armament
• Logistic support ship		2	32.3/320	170 tons
• Logistic support ship		1	27/170	40 tons equip.
• Support ship		1	55.4/545	2x12.7mm MGs

Naval Infrastructure

Naval bases (including Coast Guard): 6
Kuwait City (Shuwaikh), al-Qulaya (Ras al-Qalaya), Umm al-Hainam, al-Bida, Verba, al-Harian

Ship maintenance and repair facilities:
190 meter floating dock at Kuwait City, repair capacity 35,000 dwt

9. LEBANON

General Data

Official Name of the State: Republic of Lebanon
Head of State: President Emile Lahoud
Prime Minister: Salim al-Huss
Minister of Defense: Ghazi Zaitar
Commander-in-Chief of the Armed Forces: Lieutenant General Michel Sulayman
Chief of General Staff: Brigadier General Samir al-Kadi
Commander of the Air Force: Brigadier General George Shaàban
Commander of the Navy: Rear Admiral George Maàlouf

Area: 10,452 sq. km.
Population: 3,300,000

Demography

Ethnic groups		
Arabs	3,135,000	95.0%
Armenians	132,000	4.0%
Others	33,000	1.0%
Religious groups		
Shi'ite Muslims	1,056,000	32.0%
Sunni Muslims	693,000	21.0%
Druze	198,000	6.0%
Alawis	33,000	1.0%
Christians:		
Maronites	693,000	21.0%
Greek Orthodox	264,000	8.0%
Greek Catholic	165,000	5.0%
Armenians (Orthodox and Catholic)	132,000	4.0%
Others	66,000	2.0%

Economic Data

		1994	1995	1996	1997	1998
GDP (current prices)	$ bn	9.11	11.12	13.00	14.96	16.71
GDP per capita	$	3,131	3,694	4,221	4,764	5,189
Real GDP growth	%	8.0	6.5	4.0	4.0	2.0
Consumer price index	%	12.0	13.0	8.9	5.2	3.8
External debt	$ bn	2.12	2.96	4.0	5.04	6.6
Balance of payments						
• Exports fob	$ bn	0.54	0.82	1.02	0.63	0.72
• Imports fob	$ bn	5.54	6.72	6.99	6.87	6.52

Economic Data (continued)

		1994	1995	1996	1997	1998
• Current account balance (including services and income)	$ bn	-3.28	-3.59	-3.4	-3.24	-2.75
Government expenditure						
• Total expenditure	$ bn	3.1	3.61	4.61	5.95	5.15
• Defense expenditure	$ bn	0.48	0.49	0.43	0.37	0.41
• Real change in defense expenditure	%	26.3	2.1	-10.4	-14.0	7.9
• Defense expenditure/GDP	%	5.3	4.4	3.3	2.5	2.4
Population	m	2.91	3.01	3.08	3.14	3.3
Official exchange rate	L£: $1	1,680	1,621	1,571	1,539	1,516

Sources: EIU Quarterly Report, EIU Country Profile, IMF International Financial Statistical Yearbook, SIPRI Yearbook

Arms Procurement and Security Assistance Received

Country	Type	Details
Syria	• Military training	Advisers; approx. 50 trainees in Syria annually (1997)
US	• Arms transfers	Jeeps, trucks, M113 APCs (1996), helicopters (1996)
	• Assistance	Approx. $550,000 for training in 2000
	• Military training	Advisers; few dozen trainees in US (1998)

Foreign Military Cooperation

Type	Details
• Foreign forces in country	Syria (25,000 in Beka', Tripoli area, and Beirut); Palestinian organizations; 300 Iranian Islamic Revolution Guards Corps (IRGC), several instructors with Hizbullah non-government militia in the Syrian-held Beka', UNIFIL force in south Lebanon (4,900 from Fiji, Finland, France, Ghana, Ireland, Italy, India, Nepal, and Poland)

Weapons of Mass Destruction

NBC Capabilities

Nuclear capability
No nuclear capability. Party to the NPT.
CW capabilities and protective equipment
No known CW activity. Not a party to the CWC.
Biological weapons
No known BW activities. Party to the BWC.

Armed Forces

Major Changes: No major change was recorded in the Lebanese order-of-battle. The Israeli supported South Lebanese Army ceased to exist after Israel's withdrawal from Lebanon.

Order-of-Battle

Year	1995	1996	1997	1999	2000
General data					
• Personnel (regular)	52,000	52,000	51,400	51,400	51,400
Ground Forces					
• Number of brigades	17	17	17	13*	13
• Tanks	350	350	320 (350)	280* (350)	280 (350)
• APCs/AFVs	670	670	730 (875)*	730 (875)	1,235* (1,380)
• Artillery (including MRLs)	190	190	328* (331)	~330	~330
Air Force					
• Combat aircraft	16	16	(16)	(16)	(16)
• Transport aircraft	1	1	(2)	(2)	(1)
• Helicopters	40	40	16 (34)*	16 (34)	16 (38)
Navy					
• Patrol crafts	36	36	39 (43)	39 (41)	32 (35)

Note: Beginning with 1997, data refers to quantities in active service. The number in parentheses refers to the total inventory.
* Due to change in estimate.

Personnel

	Regular	Total
Ground Forces	50,000	50,000
Air Force	1,000	1,000
Navy	400	400
Total	51,400	51,400

Personnel *(continued)*

	Regular	Total
Paramilitary		
• Gendarmerie/ internal security	13,000	

Ground Forces

Formations

	Independent brigades/groups	Independent battalions
Mechanized/Infantry	11	
Presidential guard	1	
Special forces/ Airborne/Intervention	1	6
Artillery	2	
Support/Logistics/Medical	3	
Total	18	6

Tanks

Model	Quantity	In service	Since	Notes
MBTs				
Medium and low quality				
• M48 A1/A5	130	60	1983	
• T-55/upgraded T-54	180	180	1985	
Subtotal	310	240		
Light tanks				
• AMX-13/105mm gun	20	20	1982	
• AMX-13/75mm gun	20	20	1981	
Subtotal	40	40		
Total	350	280		

APCs/AFVs

Model	Quantity	In service	Since	Notes
APCs				
• M113 A1/A2	1,100	1,100	1970	
• M-3 (Panhard VIT)	15	15	1976	
Subtotal	1,115	1,115		
IFVs				
• V-150 Commando	50	0	1981	
• VAB - VCI/VTT	75	75	1984	
Subtotal	125	75		

APCs/AFVs (continued)

Model	Quantity	In service	Since	Notes
Reconnaissance				
• Saracen/Saladin	60	0	1979	Possibly phased out
• AML-90	80	45	1993	
Subtotal	140	45		
Total	**1,380**	**1,235**		
Future procurement				
• M113 A1/A3	500			

Artillery

Model	Quantity	In service	Since	Notes
Towed guns and howitzers				
• 155mm M198	36	36	1984	
• 155mm M114	20	20	1980	
• 155mm M-50	12	12	1970	
• 130mm M-46	20	20	1986	
• 122mm D-30	24	24	1985	
• 122mm M-1938	36	36	1973	
• 105mm M 101A1	15	15	1982	
• 105mm M 102	10	10	1983	
Subtotal	173	173		
Mortars, under 160mm				
• 120mm Brandt M-50 and M-60	130	130	1973	
MRLs				
• 122mm BM-21/BM-11	30	~30	1993	
Total	**333**	**~330**		

Logistics and Engineering Equipment

• M578 recovery vehicles (25)

Anti-Tank Weapons

Model	Quantity	In service	Since	Notes
Missiles				
• BGM-71A TOW	24	24	1975	
• MILAN	+	+	1979	
Total	~80	~80		
Guns				
• 106mm M-40 A2 recoilless rifle	+	+	1977	
• 85mm M-1945/D-44	+	+	1984	

Air Force

Order-of-Battle

Category	Quantity	In service	Notes
• Combat	16	0	
• Transport	1	0	
• Helicopters	38	16	

Combat Aircraft

Model	Quantity	In service	Since	Notes
Obsolete				
• Mirage III BL/EL	10	0	1963	
• Hawker Hunter F-70/T-66	6	0	1965	
Total	16	0		

Transport Aircraft

Model	Quantity	In service	Since	Notes
• Dove	1	0		
Total	1	0		

Training and Liaison Aircraft

Model	Quantity	In service	Since	Notes
Jet trainers				
• CM-170 Fouga Magister	5	0	1966	
Piston/Turbo-prop				
• BAe SA-3-120/126 Bulldog	5	0	1975	
Total	10	0		

Helicopters

Model	Quantity	In service	Since	Notes
Attack				
• SA-342 Gazelle	5	0	1980	
Medium transport				
• AB-212	5	0	1973	
• SA-330 Puma (possibly IAR-330)	5	0	1980	
• UH-1H (Bell 205)	16	16	1995	
Subtotal	26	16		
Light transport				
• Alouette II/III	7	0	1960	
Total	38	16		
Future procurement				
• UH-1H	8			

Advanced Armament

Air-to-ground-missiles
- SS-11/12 (96)

Note: Number in parentheses refers to the quantity of missiles purchased.

Air Force Infrastructure

Military airfields: 3
Rayaq, Kleiat, Beirut

Air Defense Forces

Surface-to-Air Missiles

Model	Launchers	Since	Notes
Shoulder-launched missiles			
• SA-7 (Grail)	+		

Other Air Defense Systems

Model	Quantity	In service	Since	Notes
Short-range guns				
• 40mm M42 SP	10 – 12	10 – 12	1966	Probably in storage
• 23mm ZU 23x2	+	+	1981	
• 23mm ZU 23x2 SP	+	+	1985	On M113
• 20mm	+	+	1984	Probably in storage
Total	~75	~75		

Navy

Patrol Craft

Type	Original class name	Quantity	Length (m.)/ displacement (t.)	Notes/ armament
• Tracker II class		0	19.3/31	2x23mm guns 2 unserviceable
• Attacker		5	20/38	2x23mm guns
• Fairey Marine small patrol craft		27	8.2/6	
Total		32		

Landing Craft

Type	Original class name	Quantity	Length (m.)/ displacement (t.)	Notes/ armament
• EDIC class LCT		2	59/ 670	33 Troops 8 APCs 1x81mm MRL 2x20mm guns 2x12.7mm MGs

Naval Infrastructure

Naval bases: 5
Beirut, Junieh, Sidon, Tripoli, Tyre
Ship maintenance and repair facilities
55 meter slipway for light craft repairs in Junieh

Major Non-Governmental Paramilitary Forces

Personnel

	Active	Reserves	Total
• Hizbullah	600 – 800	3,000 – 5,000	5,800
• Popular Liberation Army (Druze)		10,000	10,000
• Amal		10,000	10,000

Equipment

Organization	Category	System	Quantity	Notes
Hizbullah	APCs	• M113	several	
	Aircraft	• Ultra-light aircraft		
	Air Defense	• SA-7		
		• SA-18		
		• Stinger		
		• ZU-23x2		
		• 57mm		
	ATGMs	• AT-3 Sagger		
		• AT-4 Fagot		
		• TOW		
	Artillery guns	• 106mm		
	Mortars	• 81mm		
		• 120mm		
	MRLs	• 122mm BM-21		
	Artillery rockets	• 240mm Fajr-3		Alleged
		• 333mm Fajr-5		Alleged

10. LIBYA

General Data

Official Name of the State: The Great Socialist People's Libyan Arab Jamahiriya
Head of State: Colonel Muammar al-Qaddafi
Prime Minister: Mohammad Ahmad al-Manqush
Inspector General of the Armed Forces: Colonel Mustapha al-Kharrubi
Commander-in-Chief of the Armed Forces: Colonel Abu-Bakr Yunis Jaber
Commander of the Air Force and Air Defense Forces: Brigadier General Ali Riffi al-Sharif

Area: 1,759,540 sq. km.
Population: 5,990,000

Demography

Ethnic groups			
Arabs and Berbers		5,810,000	97.0%
Others:			
Greeks, Maltese, Italians, Egyptians, Pakistanis, Indians, Tunisians, Turks		180,000	3.0%
Religious groups			
Sunni Muslims		5,810,000	97.0%
Christians and others		180,000	3.0%

Economic Data

		1994	1995	1996	1997	1998
GDP (current price)	$ bn	22.11	29.47	32.87	34.81	41.53
GDP per capita	$	4,512	5,447	5,880	6,022	6,933
Real GDP growth	%	-4.5	2.0	1.1	0.5	-2.0
Consumer price index	%	50.0	26.7	38.9	25.0	24.2
External debt	$ bn	3.336	3.381	3.319	3.363	3.800
Balance of payments						
• Exports fob	$ bn	7.805	8.484	10.115	9.716	7.175
• Imports fob	$ bn	7.356	6.210	6.645	6.445	6.059
• Current account balance (including services and income)	$ bn	-1.397	0.192	1.253	0.459	-1.111
Government expenditure						
• Total expenditure	$ bn	NA	15.236	12.480	14.086	13.617
• Defense expenditure	$ bn	NA	NA	NA	NA	NA

Economic Data (continued)

		1994	1995	1996	1997	1998
• Real change in defense expenditure	%	NA	NA	NA	NA	NA
• Defense expenditure/GDP	%	NA	NA	NA	NA	NA
Population	m	4.90	5.41	5.59	5.78	5.99
Official exchange rate	LD : $1	0.321	0.346	0.362	0.382	0.390

Sources: EIU Quarterly Report, EIU Country Profile, IMF International Financial Statistical Yearbook, SIPRI Yearbook

Arms Procurement and Security Assistance Received

Country	Type	Details
Iran	• Cooperation in arms production	SSMs production (1999)
North Korea	• Arms transfers	Alleged sales of SSMs (1999)
PRC	• Arms transfers	Alleged sale of SSMs technology (1998)
Ukraine	• Arms transfers	Alleged sale of SSMs (1997)

Note: Foreign advisers/instructors/serving personnel: 300 – 500 on individual contracts

Arms Sales and Security Assistance Extended

Country	Type	Details
Niger	• Arms transfers	Antonov cargo aircraft (1997)

Defense Production

	M	P	A
Weapons of mass destruction			
• Toxic chemical agents	√		
• Plans to upgrade SSMs, with assistance by foreign experts, and efforts to produce an indigenous SSM (al-Fatah), not yet operational	√		
Army equipment			
• Tank upgrading facility, with assistance of Czech Republic		√	

Note: M - manufacture (indigenously developed)
P - production under license
A - assembly

Weapons of Mass Destruction

NBC Capabilities

Nuclear capabilities
5 Mw Soviet-made research reactor at Tadjoura; basic R&D; Party to the NPT. Safeguards agreement with the IAEA in force. Signed but not ratified the African Nuclear Weapon Free Zone (Treaty of Pelindaba).

Chemical weapons and protective equipment
CW production facilities, stockpile of chemical agents, nerve gas and mustard gas. Personal protective equipment; Soviet type decontamination units. Not a party to the CWC.

Biological weapons
Alleged production of toxins and other biological weapons (unconfirmed). Party to the BWC.

Ballistic Missiles

Model	Launchers	Missiles	Since	Notes
• Scud B/C	80	500	1976/1999	In storage
Total	80			
Future procurement				
• Nodong				Alleged

Note: See also under Rockets

Armed Forces

Major Changes: No major change was recorded in the Libyan order-of-battle.

Order-of-Battle

Year	1995	1996	1997	1999	2000
General data					
• Personnel	76,000	76,000	76,000	76,000	76,000
• SSM launchers	110	110	110	128	80*
Ground Forces					
• Number of brigades	+	+	5	1*	1
• Number of battalions	+	+	46	46	46
• Tanks	2,700	2,700	950 (2,700)	600 – 700* (2,210)	~650 (2,210)
• APCs/AFVs	3,000	3,000	2,750 (2,970)	~2,750 (2,970)	~2,750 (2,970)
• Artillery (including MRLs)	2,600 – 3,000	2,600 – 3,000	2,245 (2,325)	2,220 (2,300)	~2,270 (~2,350)

Order-of-Battle (continued)

Year	1995	1996	1997	1999	2000
Air Force					
• Combat aircraft	483	483	~360 (483)	~360 (443)	~360 (443)
• Transport aircraft	106	106	85 (90)	85 (90)	85 (90)
• Helicopters	210	210	164 (212)	127 (204)	127 (204)
Air Defense Forces					
• Heavy SAM batteries	90	90	~30*	~30	~30
• Medium SAM batteries	35	35	~10*	~10	~10
• Light SAM launchers	55	55	55	55	55
Navy					
• Submarines	6	6	4	0 (4)	0 (4)
• Combat vessels	43	43	34	34	24
• Patrol craft	9	9	2	2	0

Note: Beginning with 1997, data refers to quantities in active service. The number in parentheses refers to the total inventory.
* Due to change in estimate.

Personnel

	Regular	Reserves	Total
Ground Forces	50,000		50,000
Air Force and Air Defense	18,000		18,000
Navy	8,000		8,000
Total	76,000		76,000
Paramilitary			
• People's Militia		40,000	40,000
• Revolutionary Guards (part of the People's Militia)	3,000		3,000
• Islamic Pan African Legion (part of the People's Militia)	2,500		2,500

Ground Forces

Formations

	Independent brigades/groups	Independent battalions
Presidential Security Force	1	
Armored		10
Mechanized/Infantry		21
Artillery		22

Formations (continued)

	Independent brigades/groups	Independent battalions
Paratroops		15
Air Defense		8
SSM	5	
Total	6	76

Tanks

Model	Quantity	In service	Since	Notes
MBTs				
High quality				
• T-72/T-72M	360	150	1979	
Medium and low quality				
• T-62	600	+	1975	
• T-55	1,250	+	1974	
Subtotal	1,850	~500		
Total	2,210	~650		

APCs/AFVs

Model	Quantity	In service	Since	Notes
APC				
• BTR-50/60	750	750	1970	
• Engesa EE-9/11	300	200	1975/1977	
• M113 A1	50	~30	1972	
• OT-62/OT-64	200	100	1975	
• Oto-Breda 6614/6616	400	400	1980	
Subtotal	1,700	~1,480		
IFV				
• BMP-1/BMP-2	1,050	1,050	1972	
Reconnaissance				
• BRDM-2	220	220		
• Oto-Breda 6616			1980	Also listed under APCs
• Engesa EE-9			1975	Also listed under APCs
Total	2,970	~2,750		

Artillery

Model	Quantity	In service	Since	Notes
Self-propelled guns and howitzers				
• 155mm M109	20	0	1973	
• 155mm Palmaria	160	160	1983	
• 152mm M-1973	60	60	1982	

Artillery *(continued)*

Model	Quantity	In service	Since	Notes
• 152mm ZTS Dana	80	80	1986	
• 122mm M-1974	130	130	1980	
Subtotal	450	430		
Towed guns and howitzers				
• 130mm M-46	330	330	1978	
• 122mm D-30	245	245		
• 122mm M-1974	60	60		
• 105mm M-101	60	0	1970	
Subtotal	695	635		
Mortars, over 160mm				
• 240mm	120	120		
• 160mm	24	24		
Subtotal	144	144		
Mortars, under 160mm				
• 120mm	48	48		
• 107mm	64	64		
Subtotal	112	112		
MRLs				
• 140mm	+	+		
• 130mm M-51	+	+	1980	
• 122mm BM-21/ RM-70/BM-11	600	600	1980	
• 107mm Type 63	300	300	1979	
Subtotal	~900	~900		
Rockets				
• FROG-7	48	48		
Total	~2,350	~2,270		

Anti-Tank Missiles

Model	Launchers	Missiles	Since	Notes
• AT-3 (Sagger)	+	620	1977	
• AT-4 (Spigot)	+	+	1990	
• AT-5 (Spandrel)	+	+		
• BRDM-2	40			carrying AT-3 (Sagger) SP
• MILAN	+	400	1981	
Total	+	3,000		

Anti-Tank Guns

Model	Quantity	In service	Since	Notes
• 106mm recoilless rifle	220	220		
• 84mm Carl Gustav	400	400		

Air Force

Order-of-Battle

Category	Quantity	In service	Notes
• Combat	443	~360	
• Transport	90	85	
• Helicopters	204	127	

Combat Aircraft

Model	Quantity	In service	Since	Notes
Interceptors				
• MiG-25 and MiG-25R (Foxbat)	80	~70	1980	
• MiG-23	170	~125	1976	Also listed under Ground attack a/c
Subtotal	250	~195		
Multi-role				
• Mirage F-1	30	30	1979	
Ground attack				
• Su-24 (Fencer C)	6	6	1989	
• Su-20/22 (Fitter C)	40	40		
• MiG-23/27 (Flogger)				Also listed under Interceptors a/c
Subtotal	46	46		
Bombers				
• Tu-22 (Blinder)	7	5	1974	
Obsolete				
• MiG-21 bis (Fishbed)	70	45		
• Mirage V	40	40	1971	
Subtotal	110	85		
Total	**443**	**~360**		

Transport Aircraft

Model	Quantity	In service	Since	Notes
• An-26 (Curl)	15	10	1983	
• C-130H Hercules/ L-100-20/L-100-30	10	10	1970	
• C-140 Jetstar	1	1		
• Fokker F-27-400/600	9	9	1981	
• G-222L	19	19	1980	
• IL-76 (Candid)	19	19	1979	Including about 4 tankers

Transport Aircraft *(continued)*

Model	Quantity	In service	Since	Notes
• L-410 UVP	15	15		
• Mystère-Falcon 20/50	2	2	1981	
Total	90	85		

Training and Liaison Aircraft

Model	Quantity	In service	Since	Notes
Jet trainers				
• G-2AE Galeb/J-1E Jastreb	120	80	1975	
• L-39 Albatross	177	110	1978	
Subtotal	297	190		
Piston/Turbo-prop				
• SF-260 M/L/W	70	20	1977	
• Fouga Magister	12	0	1971	
Subtotal	82	20		
Total	379	210		

Helicopters

Model	Quantity	In service	Since	Notes
Attack				
• Mi-24/Mi-25	56	30	1978	Number unconfirmed
• Mi-35	13	13	1990	
Subtotal	69	43		
Heavy transport				
• CH-47C Chinook	15	15	1976	
Medium transport				
• AB-212/205	2	2	1974	
• Mi-8/Mi-17 (Hip)	25	25	1975	
• SA-321 Super Frelon	10	10	1971	Also employed in naval combat role
Subtotal	37	37		
Light transport				
• Alouette III	14	14	1971	Possibly with police
• Mi-2 (Hoplite)	35	0		
• AB-206	4	4	1970	
• A-109	2	2		
Subtotal	55	20		
Naval combat				
• Mi-14 (Haze)	28	12	1983	
Total	204	127		

Advanced Armament

Air-to-air-missiles
AA-2 (Atoll), AA-6 (Acrid), AA-7 (Apex), AA-8 (Aphid), AA-11 (Archer), R-530 (75), R-550 Magic (130), Super 530D/F

Air-to-ground missiles
AS-9 (Kyle), AS-10 (Karen), AS-14 (Kedge), AT-2 (Swatter), AT-6 (Spiral) (unconfirmed)

Note: The number in parenthesis refers to the quantity of missiles purchased.

Air Force Infrastructure

Military airfields: 13

Al-Adem (Tobruk), Benghazi (Baninah), Beni Walid, al-Bumbah, Ghurdabiyah (Surt), Jufra, Kufra, Maatan al-Sarra, Misratha, Ouqba ben Nafi (Al-Watiya), Sabhah, Tripoli International (Idriss), Umm al-Tika.

Air Defense Forces

Surface-to-Air Missiles

Model	Batteries	Launchers	Since	Notes
Heavy missiles				
• SA-2 (Guideline)	~15		1975	
• SA-3 (Goa)	~10		1975	
• SA-5 (Gammon)	4		1985	
Total	~30			
Medium missiles				
• Crotale	+		1974	
• SA-6 (Gainful)	6		1975	
• SA-8 (Gecko)		20		
Total	~10			
Light missiles				
• SA-9 (Gaskin)/ SA-13 (Gopher)		55	1981	
Shoulder-launched missiles				
• SA-7 (Grail)		400	1979	
• SA-14 (Gremlin)		+		
Total		~400		

Note: Serviceability of air defense systems is unclear.

Other Air Defense Systems

Model	Quantity	In service	Since	Notes
Short-range guns				
• 57mm S-60	90	90		
• 40mm Bofors L-70	50	0		
• 30mm 30x2 M-53/59 SP	240	0		
• 23mm ZSU 23x4 SP (Shilka)	250	250		
• 23mm ZU 23x2	100	100		
Total	730	440		

Navy

Submarines

Type	Original class name	Quantity	Length (m.)/ displacement (t.)	Notes/ armament
• F class (Foxtrot)	Type 641	0	91/2,475	4 non-operational 10x533mm torpedoes 44 mines
Total		0		

Combat Vessels

Type	Original class name	Quantity	Length (m.)/ displacement (t.)	Notes/ armament
Missile frigates				
• Koni class	Type 1159	2	96.4/1,440	4xSS-N-2C Styx SSMs 2xSA-N-4 SAMs 4x76mm guns 4x30mm guns 4x406mm torpedoes 1xRBU 6000 A/S mortar 20 mines
Missile corvettes				
• Nanuchka class		3	59.3/660	4xSS-N-2C Styx SSMs 2xSA-N-4 SAMs 2x57mm guns

Combat Vessels (continued)

Type	Original class name	Quantity	Length (m.)/ displacement (t.)	Notes/ armament
MFPBs				
• Combattante II		5	49.0/311	4xOtomat SSMs 1x76mm gun 2x40mm guns 4 non-operational
• Ossa II		6	38.6/245	4xSS-N-2C Styx SSMs 4x30mm guns 6 non-operational
Subtotal		11		
Mine warfare vessels				
• Natya class minesweepers	Type 266ME	8	61.0/804	4x30mm guns 4x25mm guns 2xRBU 1200 A/S mortars 10 mines Acoustic & Magnetic sweep
Total		24		

Landing Craft

Type	Original class name	Quantity	Length (m.)/ displacement (t.)	Notes/ armament
• Turkish type		3	56.0/280	100 troops; 350 tons
• PS-700 class LST		2	99.5/2,800	240 troops; 11 tanks; 6x40mm guns helicopter platform
• Polnochny class LCT	Type 773U	2	83.9/1,305	4x30mm guns 2x140mm MRLs 100 mines 1 non-operational
Total		7		

Auxiliary Vessels

Type	Original class name	Quantity	Length (m.)/ displacement (t.)	Notes/ armament
• Vosper (Tobruk)		1	54.0/500	1x102mm gun 2x40mm guns used for training
• Zeltin	LSD type	1	98.8/2,200	2x40mm guns Maintenance and repair craft
• Yelva		1	40.9/300	Diving-support ship
• Spasilac class		1	55.5/1,590	Yugoslav salvage ship 4x12.7mm MGs
• Transporters (Ro-Ro)		10	166.5/2,412	

Coastal Defense

Type	Quantity	Notes
SS-2C Styx	3	

Naval Infrastructure

Naval bases: 6
Al-Khums, Benghazi, Misratah, Tobruk, Tripoli, Derna

Ship maintenance and repair facilities
Facilities at Tripoli with foreign technicians for repair of vessels of up to 6,000 dwt; a 3,200-ton lift floating dock; floating docks at Benghazi and Tobruk

11. MOROCCO

General Data

Official Name of the State: Kingdom of Morocco
Head of State: King Mohammed VI
Prime Minister: Abd al-Rahmane Youssoufi
Minister of Defense: King Mohammed VI
Secretary General of National Defense Administration: Abdel Rahaman Sbai
Commander-in-Chief of the Armed Forces: King Mohammed VI
Inspector General of the Armed Forces: General Abd al-Kader Loubarisi
Commander of the Air Force: Ali Abd al-Aziz al-Omrani
Commander of the Navy: Captain Muhammad al-Tariqi

Area: 622,012 sq. km., including the former Spanish Sahara
Population: 27,800,000

Demography

Ethnic groups		
Arabs	16,569,000	59.6%
Berbers	10,981,000	39.5%
Europeans and others	250,000	0.9%
Religious groups		
Sunni Muslims	27,438,600	98.7%
Christians	305,800	1.1%
Jews	55,600	0.2%

Economic Data

		1994	1995	1996	1997	1998
GDP (current prices)	$ bn	30.34	32.98	36.66	33.52	35.55
GDP per capita	$	1,162	1,249	1,363	1,227	1,279
Real GDP growth	%	10.4	-6.6	12.1	-2.0	6.5
Consumer price index	%	5.1	6.2	3.0	0.9	2.9
External debt	$ bn	22.2	22.7	21.7	19.3	19.3
Balance of payments						
• Exports fob	$ bn	4.13	6.87	6.89	7.04	7.14
• Imports cif	$ bn	7.17	9.35	9.08	8.9	9.46
• Current account balance (including services and income)	$ bn	-0.72	-1.3	0.06	-0.17	-0.24

Economic Data (continued)

		1994	1995	1996	1997	1998
Government expenditure						
• Total expenditure	$ bn	8.53	9.63	9.9	9.03	9.8
• Defense expenditure	$ bn	1.68	1.55	1.43	NA	NA
• Real change in defense expenditure	%	15.8	-7.8	-7.8	NA	NA
• Defense expenditure/GDP	%	5.5	4.7	3.9	NA	NA
Population	m	26.1	26.4	26.9	27.3	27.8
Official exchange rate	Dh: $1	9.203	8.54	8.716	9.527	9.604

Sources: EIU Quarterly Report, EIU Country Profile, IMF International Financial Statistical Yearbook, SIPRI Yearbook

Arms Procurement and Security Assistance Received

Country	Type	Details
Denmark	• Arms transfers	Patrol craft (1995)
France	• Arms transfers	OPV 64 patrol ships (1997)
US	• Arms transfers	T-37 aircraft (1996)
	• Assistance	$2.9 million grant in 1999, $3.125 million grant for 2000

Arms Sales and Security Assistance Extended

Country	Type	Details
US	• Facilities	Use of Sidi Slimane, Marrakech and Casablanca airfields in emergencies; permission for space shuttle to land at Marrakech AFB; use of communications center at Kenitra; storage and use of naval facilities at Mohammedia

Foreign Military Cooperation

Type	Details
• Forces deployed abroad	Small contingency force in Bosnia and Croatia (1998)
• Joint maneuvers	France, US

Defense Production

Army equipment	M	P	A
• Small arms ammunition	√		
• Assembly of trucks			√

Note: M - manufacture (indigenously developed)
P - production under license
A - assembly

Weapons of Mass Destruction

NBC Capabilities

Nuclear capability
No nuclear capability. Party to the NPT.
CW capabilities and protective equipment
No known CW activity. Party to the CWC.
Biological weapons
No known BW activities. Signed but not ratified the BWC.

Armed Forces

Major Changes: No major change was recorded in the Moroccan order-of-battle in 1999.

Order-of-Battle

Year	1995	1996	1997	1999	2000
General data					
• Personnel (regular)	141,000	141,000	196,500	145,500	145,500
Ground Forces					
• Number of brigades	12	12	7*	6	6
• Tanks	415	415	364*	379	540*
• APCs/AFVs	1,500	1,500	1,200*	1,074	1,120*
			(1,537)	(1,374)	(1,420)
• Artillery	386	386	970*	967	1,027*
(including MRLs)			(1,020)	(1,017)	
Air Force					
• Combat aircraft	74	74	72	72	72
• Transport aircraft	48	48	45	43	43
• Helicopters	127	127	129	130	130
Air Defense Forces					
• Light SAM launchers	+	+	37*	37	37

Order-of-Battle *(continued)*

Year	1995	1996	1997	1999	2000
Navy					
• Combat vessels	14	13	13	13	13
• Patrol crafts	32	52	49	48	52

Note: Beginning with 1997, data refers to quantities in active service. The number in parentheses refers to the total inventory.
* Due to change in estimate.

Personnel

	Regular	Reserves	Total
Ground Forces	125,000	150,000	275,000
Air Force	13,500		13,500
Navy and Marines	7,000		7,000
Total	**145,500**	**150,000**	**295,500**
Paramilitary			
• Gendarmérie Royale	10,000		10,000
• Force Auxiliere	25,000		25,000
• Mobile Intervention Corps	5,000		5,000

Ground Forces

Formations

	Independent brigades/groups	Independent battalions
Armored		10
Mechanized	3	19
Infantry		35
Light Security	1	
Camel Corps		5
Paratroops	2	
Airborne/Commando		2+4
Artillery		12
Air Defense		1
Total	**6**	**88**

Tanks

Model	Quantity	In service	Since	Notes
MBTs				
Medium and low quality				
• M60 A1/A3	250	250	1981/93	
• M48 A5	185	185	1974	
Subtotal	435	435		
Light tanks				
• SK-105 (Kürassier)	105	105	1985	
Total	**540**	**540**		

APCs/AFVs

Model	Quantity	In service	Since	Notes
APCs				
• M113 A1/A2	383	383	1979	Including 23 M901. Also listed under Anti-Tank Weapons
• OT-62	150	0	1968	
• M-3 half-track	50	0	1966	
• M-3 (Panhard)	30	30	1981	Unconfirmed
• UR-416	55	55	1977	Also listed under Anti-Tank Weapons
Subtotal	668	468		
IFVs				
• Ratel 20/90	60	60	1981	
• VAB -VCI/VTT	290	290	1979	
• Engesa EE-11	+	0	1981	Included with Engesa EE-9
Subtotal	350	350		
Reconnaissance				
• AMX-10 R/CM	110	110	1981	
• Engesa EE-9	50	0	1981	Quantity includes Engesa EE-11
• BRDM-2	50	0	1992	36 carrying AT-3. Also listed under Anti-Tank Weapons
• EBR-75	16	16	1970	
• AML-90/AML-60	175	175	1966	
Subtotal	401	301		
Total	**1,419**	**1,119**		

Artillery

Model	Quantity	In service	Since	Notes
Self-propelled guns and howitzers				
• 203mm M110 A2	60	60	1996	
• 155mm M109 A1	40	40	1978	
• 155mm Mk F-3 (AMX)	100	100	1980	
• 105mm Mk 61	5	5	1963	
Subtotal	205	205		
Towed guns and howitzers				
• 155mm M114	20	20	1976	
• 155mm M198	35	35		
• 155mm FH-70	30	30	1993	
• 130mm M-46	18	18	1981	
• 105mm L-118 light gun	30	30	1980	
• 105mm M-1950	35	35	1972	
• 105mm M101/M101A1	18	18	1970	
Subtotal	186	186		
Mortars, under 160mm				
• 120mm	600	600	1972	20 SP mounted on VAB
MRLs				
• 122mm BM-21	36	36	1980	
Total	1,027	1,027		

Logistics and Engineering Equipment

- M578 recovery vehicles (60)

Anti-Tank Weapons

Model	Quantity	In service	Since	Notes
Missiles				
• BGM-71A TOW	150	150	1978	
• Cobra SP	42	42	1979	Mounted on UR-416
• M901 ITV	23	23	1999	Also listed under APCs
• AT-3 (Sagger) SP	36	0	1992	Mounted on BRDM-2
• M47 Dragon	480	480	1978	
• MILAN	80	80	1982	
Total	811	775		
Guns				
• 106mm M-40 A2	350	350	1977	
• 90mm M56	28	28	1975	
Total	378	378		

Air Force

Order-of-Battle

Category	Quantity	In service	Notes
• Combat	72	72	
• Transport	43	43	
• Helicopters	130	130	

Combat Aircraft

Model	Quantity	In service	Since	Notes
Multi-role				
• F-5E/F	22	22	1981	
• Mirage F1	34	34	1979	
Subtotal	56	56		
Ground attack				
• OV-10 Bronco	3	3	1981	
Obsolete				
• F-5A/B	13	13	1967	
Total	72	72		

Transport Aircraft

Model	Quantity	In service	Since	Notes
• Beechcraft King Air 100	5	5	1975	
• Beechcraft Super King Air 200	5	5	1983	
• Beechcraft Super King Air 300	1	1	1991	
• Boeing 707	2	2	1982	
• C-130H Hercules	15	15	1974	Including 2 employed in electronic surveillance and 2 tankers
• CN-235	7	7	1990	
• Dornier DO-28 D-2	3	3	1981	
• Gulfstream II/III	2	2	1976	
• Mystère-Falcon 50	1	1	1980	
• Mystère-Falcon 20	2	2	1968	Electronic countermeasures
Total	43	43		

Training and Liaison Aircraft

Model	Quantity	In service	Since	Notes
Jet trainers				
• Cessna 318 (T-37)	14	14	1996	
• Alpha jet	22	22	1979	
• Beechcraft T-34C	12	10	1977	
• CM-170 Fouga Magister	22	22	1964	
Subtotal	70	68		
Piston/Turbo-prop				
• AS-202/18A Bravo	10	10	1978	
• CAP 10/232	9	9	1983	Aerobatic team
Subtotal	19	19		
Total	89	87		

Helicopters

Model	Quantity	In service	Since	Notes
Attack helicopters				
• SA-342 Gazelle	22	22	1976	Of which 6 with gendarmerie
Heavy transport				
• CH-47C Chinook	7	7	1979	
Medium transport				
• AB-212	5	5	1973	
• AB-205	32	32	1969	
• AS-365 Dauphin II	2	2	1983	With gendarmerie
• SA-330 Puma	28	28	1976	Of which 6 with gendarmerie
Subtotal	67	67		
Light transport				
• Alouette II/III	5	5	1981	With gendarmerie
• AB-206 JetRanger	26	26	1975	
• SA-315B Lama	3	3		With gendarmerie
Subtotal	34	34		
Total	130	130		

Miscellaneous Aircraft

Model	Quantity	In service	Since	Notes
Reconnaissance				
• RF-5	2	2	1981	Also listed under Combat Aircraft
• C-130H	2	2	1974	Also listed under Transport Aircraft

Miscellaneous Aircraft *(continued)*

Model	Quantity	In service	Since	Notes
Tanker				
• KC-130	2	2	1974	Also listed under Transport Aircraft
Electronic warfare				
• Mystère 20F	2	2	1968	Also listed under Transport Aircraft
Maritime surveillance				
• BN-2T Defender	7	7	1993	Possibly used for fishery protection
UAVs and mini-UAVs				
• Skyeye R4E-50	+	+	1990	

Advanced Armament

Air-to-air-missiles
AIM-9J Sidewinder (320), R-530, R-550 Magic (300), Super 530D

Air-to-ground-missiles
AGM-65 Maverick (380), HOT

Note: Number in parentheses refers to the quantity of missiles purchased.

Air Force Infrastructure

Military airfields: 10
Agadir, Casablanca (Nouasseur), Fez, Kenitra, Larache, L'Ayoun, Marrakech, Meknes, Rabat, Sidi Slimane

Air Defense Forces

Surface-to-Air Missiles

Model	Batteries	Launchers	Since	Notes
Light missiles				
• MIM-72A Chaparral		37	1977	
Shoulder-launched missiles				
• SA-7 (Grail)		70	1978	

Other Air Defense Systems

Model	Quantity	In service	Since	Notes
Short-range guns				
• 37mm M-1939	100	14	1972	
• 23mm ZU 23x2	90	30	1986	

Other Air Defense Systems (continued)

Model	Quantity	In service	Since	Notes
• 20mm M163 Vulcan SP	115	115	1983	
• 20mm M167 SP	40	40	1993	
Total	345	199		
Radars				
• AN/TPS-43	8	8		
• AN/TPS-63	8	8		Upgraded

Navy

Combat Vessels

Type	Original class name	Quantity	Length (m.)/ displacement (t.)	Notes/ armament
Missile frigates				
• Descubierta		1	88.8/1,233	4xMM38 Exocet SSMs 1x8 Aspide SAMs 6x324mm torpedoes 1xSR 375 ASW mortar 1x76mm gun 1x40mm gun
MFPBs				
• Lazaga		4	58.1/524	4xMM38 Exocet SSMs 1x76mm gun 1x40mm gun 2x20mm guns
Gunboats				
• Okba class	PR-72	2	57.5/375	1x76mm gun 1x40mm gun
• Cormoran class	P-200D Vigilance	6	58.1/425	1x40mm gun
Subtotal		8		
Total		13		
Future procurement				
• Floreal frigates		2	93.5/2,950	To be delivered in 2001

Patrol Craft

Type	Original class name	Quantity	Length (m.)/ displacement (t.)	Notes/ armament
• El Wacil/Erraid	P-32 class	10	32/74	6 Elwacil class, 4 Erraid clas, 4 with customs/Coast Guard 1x20mm gun
• Rais Bargech class	OPV 64	5	64/580	1x40mm gun 1x20mm gun 4x14.5mm MGs
• Osprey mk II		4	54.8/475	2x20mm guns
• Arcor 46		18	14.5/15	With customs/Coast Guard 2x12.7mm MGs
• Arcor 53		15	16/17	With customs/Coast Guard 1x12.7mm MG
Total		52		

Landing Craft

Type	Original class name	Quantity	Length (m.)/ displacement (t.)	Notes/ armament
• Batral LSL		3	80/750	140 troops, 12 vehicles Helicopter pod 2x81mm mortars 4x40mm guns
• EDIC LCT		1	59/250	11 vehicles 1x120mm mortar 2x20mm guns
• Newport class LST		1	159.2/8,450	400 troops, 500-ton vehicles 4xLCVP/LCPL boats 1x20mm Phalanx gun
Total		5		

Auxiliary Vessels

Type	Original class name	Quantity	Length (m.)/ displacement (t.)	Notes/ armament
• Cargo ship		1	77/1,500	2x14.5mm MGs
• Agor survey ship	Robert D. Conrad class	1	67.3/1,370	
• Dakhla support ship		1	69/800	
• SAR craft		3	19.4/40	With Coast Guard
Total		6		

Naval Infrastructure

Naval bases: 7
Agadir, al-Hoceima, Casablanca, Kenitra, Dakhla, Safi, Tangier

Ship maintenance and repair facilities
156-meter dry-dock at Casablanca, repair ships of up to 10,000 dwt; facility for minor repairs at Agadir

12. OMAN

General Data

Official Name of the State: Sultanate of Oman
Head of State: Sultan Qabus ibn Said al-Said
Prime Minister: Sultan Qabus ibn Said al-Said
Minister of Defense: Sultan Qabus ibn Said al-Said
Minister of Defense Affairs: Badr bin Saud bin Harib al-Busaidi
Chief of General Staff: General Khamis al-Kalabani
Commander of the Ground Forces: Major General Ali ibn Rashid al-Kalabani
Commander of the Air Force: Major General Mohammad Ibn Mahfoodh al-Ardhi
Commander of the Navy: Rear Admiral Shihab al-Said

Area: 212,000 sq. km.
Population: 2,290,000

Demography

Ethnic groups		
Arabs	2,075,000	90.6%
Others (Africans, Persians, Southeast Asians)	215,000	9.4%
Religious groups		
Ibadi Muslims	1,717,000	75.0%
Sunni Muslims	431,000	18.8%
Shi'ite Muslims, Hindus	142,000	6.2%

Economic Data

		1994	1995	1996	1997	1998
GDP (current price)	$ bn	11.612	13.784	15.257	15.779	14.174
GDP per capita	$	5,555	6,381	6,903	6,981	6,189
Real GDP growth	%	3.8	4.8	2.9	6.4	2.9
Consumer price index	%	-0.7	-1.1	0.3	-0.4	-0.5
External debt	$ bn	3.085	3.181	3.415	3.655	4.119
Balance of payments						
• Exports fob	$ bn	5.54	6.07	7.34	7.63	5.51
• Imports fob	$ bn	3.69	4.05	4.39	4.65	5.83
• Current account balance (including services and income)	$ bn	-0.805	-0.801	0.180	-0.057	-2.949

Economic Data *(continued)*

		1994	1995	1996	1997	1998
Government expenditure						
• Total expenditure	$ bn	5.849	6.054	5.851	5.992	5.753
• Defense expenditure	$ bn	2.02	2.01	1.91	1.81	1.81
• Real change in defense expenditure	%	5.75	-0.49	-4.97	-5.23	0.00
• Defense expenditure/GDP	%	17.39	14.58	12.51	11.47	12.76
Population	m	2.09	2.16	2.21	2.26	2.29
Official exchange rate	OR:$1	0.385	0.385	0.385	0.385	0.385

Sources: EIU Quarterly Report, EIU Country Profile, IMF International Financial Statistical Yearbook, SIPRI Yearbook

Arms Procurement and Security Assistance Received

Country	Type	Details
France	• Arms transfers	Patrol craft (1995)
Jordan	• Military training	Trainees abroad
Netherlands	• Arms transfer	Surveillance radar (1997), fire control radar (1997)
South Africa	• Arms transfers	G-6 guns (1995)
Switzerland	• Arms transfers	AA guns (1995), Skyguard fire control radar (1995), Pilatus PC-9 trainer a/c (1999)
UK	• Arms transfers	Challenger tanks (1995), Piranha APCs (1998), upgrade kits for Rapier SAMs (1995), missile corvettes (1997), upgrading Jaguar a/c (1999), early warning system (2000), early warning simulators (2000)
US	• Arms transfers • Military training	Tank ammunition (1999) Foreign advisers/instructors/serving personnel

Arms Sales and Security Assistance Extended

Country	Type	Details
UK	• Facilities	Use of airfields
US	• Facilities	Airfields at Masira, Seeb, al-Khasb, Thamarit; storage facilities and pre-positioning of US Army and Air Force support equipment; naval facilities at Masira and Ghanam Peninsula; communications center

Foreign Military Cooperation

Type	Details
• Foreign forces	Some 180 US soldiers
• Joint maneuvers	Egypt, GCC countries, UK, US
• Security agreement	GCC countries, Iran, US

Weapons of Mass Destruction

NBC Capabilities

Nuclear capability
No known nuclear activity. Signatory to the NPT.

Chemical weapons and protective equipment
No known CW activities. Party to the CWC.

Biological weapons
No known BW activities. Party to the BWC.

Armed Forces

Major Changes: No major change was recorded in the Omani order-of-battle.

Order-of-Battle

Year	1995	1996	1997	1999	2000
General data					
• Personnel (regular)	29,600	29,600	34,000*	34,000	34,000
Ground Forces					
• Number of brigades	4	4	4	4	4
• Total number of battalions	22	22	18*	18	18
• Tanks	106	156	178	131 (181)	131 (181)
• APCs/AFVs	62	142	135 (166)	135 (166)	~135 (~165)
• Artillery	177	177	148 (154)*	148 (154)	148 (154)
Air Force					
• Combat aircraft	37	37	31 (47)	31 (47)	31
• Transport aircraft	44	44	38 (42)	38 (42)	38 (42)
• Helicopters	37	37	37	37	35
Air Defense Forces					
• Light SAM launchers	54	54	58	58	58

Order-of-Battle *(continued)*

Year	1995	1996	1997	1999	2000
Navy					
• Combat vessels	8	14	9	9	9
• Patrol craft	18	18	23	23	22

Note: Beginning with 1997, data refers to quantities in active service. The number in parentheses refers to the total inventory.
* Due to change in estimate.

Personnel

	Regular	Reserves	Total
Ground Forces	25,000		25,000
Air Force	5,000		5,000
Navy	4,000		4,000
Total	**34,000**		**34,000**
Paramilitary			
• Tribal force (Firqat)	3,500		3,500
• Police/border police (operating aircraft, helicopters and PBs)			7,000
• Royal Household (including Royal Guard, Royal Yachts and Royal Flight)			6,500

Ground Forces

Formations

	Independent brigade/group	Independent battalion/regiment
Royal Guard	1 HQ	
Armored	1 HQ	2+1 royal guard
Infantry (Partly Mechanized)	2 HQ	8+2 royal guard
Reconnaissance		2 (1 inf.+1 armd.)
Paratroops/Special Forces		1+2 royal guard
Artillery		4
Air Defense		1
Total	**4**	**23**

Tanks

Model	Quantity	In service	Since	Notes
MBTs				
High quality				
• Challenger 2	18	18	1995	
Medium and low quality				
• M60 A3	93	43	1990	
• M60 A1	6	6	1980	
• Chieftain	27	27	1982	
• Scorpion	37	37	1980	
Subtotal	163	113		
Total	**181**	**131**		
Future procurement				
• Challenger 2	20			

APCs/AFVs

Model	Quantity	In service	Since	Notes
APCs				
• GKN-Defense Piranha	80	80	1995	
• BTR-80	+	+	1994	Small number
• AT-105 Saxon	15	15	1986	
• Fahd	31	+		Unconfirmed
• VAB	14	14	1986	Number unconfirmed
Subtotal	~140	~110		
IFVs				
• V-150 Commando	20	20	1982	
Reconnaissance				
• VBC-90	6	6	1986	
Total	**~165**	**~135**		
Future procurement				
• Piranha	46			Optional

Artillery

Model	Quantity	In service	Since	Notes
Self-propelled guns and howitzers				
• 155mm M109 A2	15	15	1986	
• 155mm G-6	24	24	1995	
Subtotal	39	39		
Towed guns and howitzers				
• 155mm FH-70	12	12	1986	
• 130mm Type 59	12	12	1981	

Artillery (continued)

Model	Quantity	In service	Since	Notes
• 122mm D-30	25	25		
• 105mm light gun	12	36	1976	
Subtotal	91	85		
Mortars, under 160mm				
• 120mm	12	12	1976	
• 107mm (4.2") M-30 SP	12	12	1986	
Subtotal	24	24		
Total	**154**	**148**		

Logistics and Engineering Equipment
• Challenger ARV (4); tank transporters (9)

Anti-Tank Missiles

Model	Launchers	Missiles	Since	Notes
• BGM-71A TOW	18	+		
• MILAN	32	+	1984	

Air Force

Order-of-Battle

Category	Quantity	In service	Notes
• Combat	31	31	
• Transport	42	38	
• Helicopters	35	35	

Combat Aircraft

Model	Quantity	In service	Since	Notes
Multi-role				
• SEPECAT Jaguar S(O) Mk 1/Mk 2/T2	19	19	1977	To be upgraded to Jaguar 97 standard
• HAWK Mk-203	12	12	1994	
Total	31	31		

Transport Aircraft

Model	Quantity	In service	Since	Notes
• BAe-111	3	3	1974	
• Britten-Norman BN-2 Defender/Islander	4	0	1974	
• C-130H Hercules	3	3	1981	

Transport Aircraft (continued)

Model	Quantity	In service	Since	Notes
• CN-235	3	3	1993	With police
• DC-8	1	1	1982	
• DC-10	1	1		
• DHC-5D Buffalo	4	4	1982	
• Dornier Do-228-100	2	2	1984	Used by police air wing for maritime surveillance and border patrol
• Gulfstream	1	1	1992	
• Learjet	1	1	1981	With police service
• Mystère-Falcon 20	1	1	1983	
• Mystère-Falcon 10	1	1	1980	
• Mystère-Falcon 900	2	2		
• Short Skyvan Srs 3M	15	15	1970	7 employed in maritime patrol role
Total	42	38		

Training and Liaison Aircraft

Model	Quantity	In service	Since	Notes
Jet trainers				
• BAC-167 Strikemaster Mk 82	12	12	1967	
• Hawk Mk-103	4	4	1993	
Subtotal	16	16		
Piston/Turbo-prop				
• AS-202 Bravo	4	4	1976	
• Mushshak	3	3	1994	
Subtotal	7	7		
Total	23	23		
Future procurement				
• PC-9	12			

Helicopters

Model	Quantity	In service	Since	Notes
Medium transport				
• AB-205	18	18	1970	
• AB-212B/Bell 212	2	2	1976	
• AB-214	10	10	1974	
• AS-332 Super Puma/ SA-330 Puma	2	2	1982	
Subtotal	32	32		

Helicopters (continued)

Model	Quantity	In service	Since	Notes
Light transport				
• AB-206 JetRanger	3	3	1970	
Total	**35**	**35**		

Miscellaneous Aircraft

Model	Quantity	In service	Since	Notes
Maritime surveillance				
• Short Skyvan Srs 3M	7	7	1970	Also listed under Transport Aircraft
• Dorniem Do-288-100	2	2	1984	Also listed under Transport Aircraft
Target drones				
• TTL BTT-3 Banshee	53	+		Original number supplied (53)

Advanced Armament

Air-to-air-missiles
R-550 Magic (70), AIM-9P/J Sidewinder (330)
Bombs
BL-755 CBU

Note: Numbers in parentheses refer to number of units purchased.

Air Force Infrastructure

Aircraft shelters
For all combat aircraft, at Masira and Thamarit
Military airfields: 6
Bureimi, Dukha, Masira, Muscat (Seeb), Salala, Thamarit

Air Defense Forces

Surface-to-Air Missiles

Model	Batteries	Launchers	Since	Notes
Light missiles				
• Rapier, upgraded to Mk 2/Jernas		28		
• Javelin		30	1989	
• Tigercat		*		
Total		**58**		

Surface-to-Air Missiles (continued)

Model	Batteries	Launchers	Since	Notes
Shoulder-launched missiles				
• Blowpipe		+	1982	
• SA-7 (Grail)		34	1988	

Other Air Defense Systems

Model	Quantity	In service	Since	Notes
Air defense systems (missiles, radars and guns)				
• Skyguard AD system	+	+	1995	With 35mm guns
Short-range guns				
• 40mm Bofors L-60	12	12	1987	
• 35mm Oerlikon Contraves	+	+	1995	With Skyguard AD system
• 23mm ZU 23x2	4	4	1980	
• 20mm 20x2 VDAA SP	9	9		
Total	25	25		
Radars				
• AR-15	+	+		
• S-713 Martello 3D	2	2		
• S-600	+	+		
• Watchman	+	+		

Navy

Combat Vessels

Type	Original class name	Quantity	Length (m.)/ displacement (t.)	Notes/ armament
Missile corvettes				
• Qahir class	Vosper Thornycroft	2	83.7/1,450	1xhelicopter 8xExocet MM-40 SSMs 1x8 Crotale-NG 1x76mm gun 2x20mm guns 6x324mm torpedoes
MFPBs				
• Dhofar class	Province class	4	56.7/394	6-8 Exocet MM 40 SSMs 1x76mm gun 2x40mm guns 2x12.7mm MGs

Combat Vessels *(continued)*

Type	Original class name	Quantity	Length (m.)/ displacement (t.)	Notes/ armament
Gunboats				
• al-Bushra	P-400	3	54.5/475	1x76mm gun 1x40mm gun 2x20mm guns 2x12.7mm MGs 4x406mm torpedoes to be upgraded to MFPB by addition of MM-38 missiles (unconfirmed)
Total		9		

Patrol Craft

Type	Original class name	Quantity	Length (m.)/ displacement (t.)	Notes/ armament
• CG-29		3	28.9/84	2x20mm guns with police
• CG-27		1	24/53	1x20mm gun with police
• Seeb	Vosper Thornycroft	4	25/60.7	1x20mm gun 2x7.62mm MGs
• Zahra	Emsworth type	2	16.0/18	2x7.62mm MGs with police
• Zahra	Watercraft type	3	13.9/16	2x7.62mm MG with police
• P-2000		1	20.8/80	1x12.7mm MG with police
• P-1903		1	19.2/26	2x12.7mm MGs with police
• Vosper Thornycroft		5	22.9/50	1x20mm gun with police
• Dheeb al-Bahar	D-59116	2	23/65	1x12.7mm MG with police
Total		22		

Landing Craft

Type	Original class name	Quantity	Length (m.)/ displacement (t.)	Notes/ armament
• Nasr al-Bahar	Brooke Marine LST	1	93/2,500	Helicopter deck 4x40mm guns 2x20mm guns 2x12.7mm MGs 8 tanks or 400 tons; 240 troops; 2 LCVP
• Neemran	LCU	1	25.5/30	
• Vosper LCM		3	33.0/230	100 tons
Total		5		

Auxiliary Vessels

Type	Original class name	Quantity	Length (m.)/ displacement (t.)	Notes/ armament
• Mabrukah	Brooke Marine training ship	1	62/900	1x40mm gun 2x20mm guns helicopter deck ex-royal yacht
• Conoship, Groningen		1	65.7m/ 1,380dwt	
• Coastal freighter		1		
• Survey craft		1	15.5/23.6	
• Diving craft		1		
• Harbor craft		2	15m	

Naval Infrastructure

Naval bases: 4
Mina Raysut (Salala), al-Khasb, Muscat, Wuddam

Ship maintenance and repair facilities
Muscat

13. PALESTINIAN AUTHORITY

General Data

This section includes information on the Palestinian Authority and Palestinian security organizations inside the Palestinian Authority. It does not cover Palestinians living elsewhere.

Official Name: Palestinian Authority (PA)
Chairman: Yasser Arafat
Chief of Security Forces: General Abd al-Rizak al-Majaida

Area: 400 sq. km. (Gaza), 5,800 sq. km. (West Bank). By the terms of the Interim Agreement, the West Bank is divided into three areas, designated A, B, and C. The PA has civilian responsibility for Palestinians in all three areas, exclusive internal security responsibility for Area A (18.2%), and shared security responsibility for Area B (24.8%). Israel maintains full responsibility for the remaining 57% (Area C).
Population: Gaza 1,020,000 (estimate); West Bank 1,900,000 (estimate).

Demography

Religious group		
Sunni Muslims	2,628,000	90%
Christians	292,000	10%

Economic Data

		1994	1995	1996	1997	1998
GDP (current price)	$ bn	3.336	3.574	3.897	3.951	4.030
GDP per capita	$	1,419	1,429	1,470	1,406	1,380
Real GDP growth (at 1986 prices)	%	10.8	-5.6	-1.7	-0.8	3.0
Consumer price index	%	14.0	10.8	7.7	6.1	10.2
External debt	$ bn	NA	NA	NA	NA	NA
Balance of payments						
• Exports fob	$ bn	0.423	0.467	0.511	0.476	NA
• Imports cif	$ bn	2.017	2.232	2.534	2.252	NA
• Current account balance	$ bn	-0.614	-0.704	-0.897	-0.955	NA

Economic Data *(continued)*

		1994	1995	1996	1997	1998
Government expenditure						
• Total expenditure	$ bn	0.334	0.578	0.780	0.863	0.960
• Security expenditure	$ bn	NA	0.170	0.248	0.250	0.300
• Real change in security expenditure	%	NA	NA	45.9	0.8	20.0
• Security expenditure/GDP	%	NA	4.75	6.36	6.32	7.44
Population	m	2.35	2.50	2.65	2.81	2.92
Official exchange rate (Israeli currency)	NIS:$1	3.011	3.011	3.192	3.449	3.800

Sources: EIU Quarterly Report, EIU Country Profile, IMF International Financial Statistical Yearbook, SIPRI Yearbook

Arms Procurement and Security Assistance Received

Country	Type	Details
Egypt	• Military training	Trainees abroad, police, and civil defense (1997)
Netherlands	• Arms transfers	Light arms (1998)
Russia	• Arms transfers	BRDM - 2 Scout cars (1995)

Security Forces

Major Changes: No major change was recorded in the Palestinian security forces.

Order-of-Battle

Year	1995	1996	1997	1999	2000
General data					
• Personnel (regular)	~24,000	~30,000	~34,000	~34,000	~36,000
Ground Forces					
• APCs/AFVs	45	45	45	45	45
Aerial Police					
• Helicopters	2	2	2 (4)	2 (4)	2 (4)
Coastal Police					
• Patrol craft	-	-	7	13	10

Note: Beginning with 1997, data refers to quantities in active service. The number in parentheses refers to the total inventory.

Personnel

	Gaza	West Bank	Total	Notes
General Security Service branches				
• Public Security	+	+	14,000	Also referred to as the "National Security Force"
• Coastal Police	+	+	1,000	
• Aerial Police	+	+	+	Rudimentary unit operating the VIP helicopters
• Civil Police	+	+	10,000	The "Blue Police" - a law enforcement agency; operates the 700-strong "rapid deployment special police"
• Preventive Security Force	+	+	5,000	Plainclothes internal security force
• General Intelligence	+	+	3,000	Intelligence gathering organization
• Military Intelligence	+	+	+	Unrecognized preventive security force; includes the Military Police
• Civil Defense	+	+	+	Emergency and rescue service
Additional security forces				
• Presidential Security	+	+	3,000	Elite unit responsible for Arafat's security
• Special Security Force	+	+	+	Unrecognized intelligence organization
Total	20,000	16,000	~36,000	

Note: The Palestinian security services include several organizations under the "Palestinian Directorate of Police Force" recognized in the Cairo and Washington agreements. In addition, there are some organizations that report directly to Arafat. Some of the security organizations (particularly the "Blue Police") have little or no military significance. They are mentioned here because of the unusual organizational structure, and because it is difficult to estimate the size of the total forces that do have military significance.

APCs/AFVs

Model	Quantity	In service	Since	Notes
Reconnaissance				
• BRDM-2	45	45	1995	

Aerial Police

Helicopters

Model	Quantity	In service	Since	Notes
Medium transport				
• Mi-8/Mi-17	4	2	1996	

Air Defense Forces

Air Defense Systems

Model	Quantity	In service	Since	Notes
Short-range guns				
• 23mm AA guns	+	+		Alleged

Coastal Police

Patrol Craft

Type	Original class name	Quantity	Length (m.)/ displacement (t.)	Notes/ armament
• Gindallah		1		
• P-76		1		
• Volvo		2	8.0/5	7.62mm MG 2 non-operational
• Zodiak Mk 3		0		3 non-operational
• Zodiak Mk 5		4	5.8m	7.62mm MG 6 non-operational
• Zodiak Mk 7		2		
Total		10		

Major Non-Governmental Paramilitary Forces

- Hamas - several hundred members
- Islamic Jihad - several hundred members

14. QATAR

General Data

Official Name of the State: State of Qatar
Head of State: Shaykh Hamad ibn Khalifa al-Thani
Prime Minister: Abdallah Ibn Khalifa al-Thani
Minister of Defense: Shaykh Hamad ibn Khalifa al-Thani
Commander in Chief of the Armed Forces: Shaykh Hamad ibn Khalifa al-Thani
Chief of General Staff: Brigadier General Hamad bin Ali al-Attiyah
Commander of the Ground Forces: Colonel Saif Ali al-Hajiri
Commander of the Air Force: General Ali Saeed al-Hawal al-Marri
Commander of the Navy: Captain Said al-Suwaydi

Area: 11,437 sq. km.
Population: 600,000

Demography

Ethnic groups		
Arabs	240,000	40.0%
Pakistanis	108,000	18.0%
Indians	108,000	18.0%
Persians	60,000	10.0%
Others (mostly Southeast Asians)	84,000	14.0%
Religious groups		
Sunni Muslims	421,800	70.3%
Shi'ite Muslims	145,800	24.3%
Others	32,400	5.4%

Economic Data

		1994	1995	1996	1997	1998
GDP (current prices)	$ bn	7.4	7.5	9.1	11.3	10.5
GDP per capita	$	12,333	12,600	15,167	18,833	17,500
Real GDP growth	%	2.4	1.6	5.0	10.0	2.0
Consumer price index	%	1.3	3.0	7.4	2.8	2.9
External debt	$ bn	2.2	4.5	7.2	9.0	9.8
Balance of payments						
• Exports fob	$ bn	2.98	3.1	3.83	4.47	4.35
• Imports fob	$ bn	3.12	3.31	3.91	2.99	3.33
• Current account balance (including services and income)	$ bn	-1.26	-2.32	-2.67	-1.06	-1.67

Economic Data (continued)

		1994	1995	1996	1997	1998
Government expenditure						
• Total expenditure	$ bn	3.2	3.7	4.38	4.73	3.78
• Defense expenditure	$ bn	0.3	0.33	NA	NA	NA
• Real change in defense expenditure	%	-8.4	10.0	NA	NA	NA
• Defense expenditure/GDP	%	4.0	4.4	NA	NA	NA
Population	m	0.6	0.6	0.6	0.6	0.6
Official exchange rate	QR: $1	3.64	3.64	3.64	3.64	3.64

Sources: EIU Quarterly Report, EIU Country Profile, IMF International Financial Statistical Yearbook, SIPRI Yearbook.

Arms Procurement and Security Assistance Received

Country	Type	Details
France	• Military training	Advisers (1999)
	• Arms transfer	APCs (1996), combat a/c (1997), AMX-30 MBTs (1998), Crotale SAMs (1996), Mica and Magic II AAMs (1997)
UK	• Arms transfer	Rapier SAMs (1996), combat vessels (1996), a/c (1996), APCs (1996)
US	• Military training	Advisers, trainees abroad
	• Facilities	Construction and upgrading of air base (2000)

Arms Sales and Security Assistance Extended

Country	Type	Details
France	• Facilities	Training facilities, deployment of equipment (1999)
Spain	• Arms transfer	F-5 a/c (1996)
US	• Facilities	Transportation equipment, deployment of maritime patrol aircraft (1998), pre-positioning for an armored brigade (1999)

Foreign Military Cooperation

Type	Details
• Forces deployed abroad	Troops part of GCC "Peninsula Shield" rapid deployment force in Saudi Arabia
• Joint maneuvers	France, GCC countries, UK, US, Yemen

Weapons of Mass Destruction

NBC Capabilities

Nuclear capability
No known nuclear activity. Party to the NPT.
Chemical weapons and protective equipment
No known CW activities. Party to the CWC.
Biological weapons
No known BW activities. Party to the BWC.

Armed Forces

Major Changes: The Qatari Army received all of its 40 Piranha IFVs. No other major change was recorded in the Qatari order-of-battle in 1999.

Order-of-Battle

Year	1995	1996	1997	1999	2000
General data					
• Personnel (regular)	10,300	10,300	11,800	11,800	11,800
Ground Forces					
• Number of brigades			1*	1	2
• Number of regiments	1	1	1	1	0
• Total number of battalions	7	7	10*	10	11
• Tanks	24	24	24	44	44
• APCs/AFVs	310	310	230* (310)	222 (302)	260 (338)
• Artillery (including MRLs)	37	37	56*	56	56
Air Force					
• Combat aircraft	14	14	9	14	18
• Transport aircraft	7	7	8	8	8
• Helicopters	41	41	32*	31	31
Air Defense Forces					
• Light SAM launchers	32	29	48*	48	48
Navy					
• Combat vessels	3	5	7	7	7
• Patrol crafts	50	48	44	36	26

Note: Beginning with 1997, data refers to quantities in active service. The number in parentheses refers to the total inventory.
* Due to change in estimate.

Personnel

	Regular	Total
Ground Forces	8,500	8,500
Air Force	1,500	1,500
Navy (including Marine Police)	1,800	1,800
Total	**11,800**	**11,800**
Paramilitary		
• Armed Police	8,000	

Ground Forces

Formations

	Independent brigades/groups	Independent battalions	Battalions in brigades
Armored	1		1 armd., 1 mech., 1 aty.
Mechanized		4	
Royal Guard	1		3 inf.
Special forces		1	
Artillery		2	
Total	2	7	

Tanks

Model	Quantity	In service	Since	Notes
MBTs				
Medium and low quality				
• AMX-30	44	44	1978/1996	
Total	44	44		
Future procurement				
• Challenger	50			Under negotiation
• Leclerc	50 – 100			Under negotiation

APCs/AFVs

Model	Quantity	In service	Since	Notes
APCs				
• VAB	134	134	1978	4 mortar carriers, 24 mounted with HOT ATGM
• Fahd	10	6 – 10		
• Saracen	25	6	1970	
Subtotal	169	~150		

APCs/AFVs *(continued)*

Model	Quantity	In service	Since	Notes
IFVs				
• V-150 Commando	8	8	1986	
• AMX-10P/VCI	45	45	1978	
• Piranha II	40	40	1998	36 with LAV 90mm guns, 2 CMP and 2 ARV
Subtotal	93	93		
Reconnaissance				
• VBL	16	16	1994	
• AMX 10RC			1981	Included with other models of AMX-10
• Engesa EE-9	20	0	1978	
• Saladin	30	0	1970	
• Ferret	10	0	1968	
Subtotal	76	16		
Total	338	~260		

Artillery

Model	Quantity	In service	Since	Notes
Self-propelled guns and howitzers				
• 155mm Mk F-3 (AMX)	22	22	1984	
Towed guns and howitzers				
• 155mm G-5	12	12	1991	
Mortars, under 160mm				
• 120mm Brandt	15	15	1993	
• VPM 81mm SP	4	4	1977	Mounted on VAB APCs
Subtotal	19	19		
MRLs				
• 122mm BM-21	+	+		
• Astros II	3	3	1992	127mm SS-30 or 180mm SS-40
Total	56	56		
Future procurement				
• 155mm Mk F-3 SP howitzers				Undergoing upgrading

Anti-Tank Weapons

Model	Launchers	Missiles	Since	Notes
Missiles				
• HOT	48	+	1978	24 are mounted on VAB
• MILAN	60 – 100	+	1987	
Guns				
• 84mm Carl Gustav light recoilless rifle	+	+	1978	

Air Force

Order-of-Battle

Category	Quantity	In service	Notes
• Combat	18	18	
• Transport	8	8	
• Helicopters	31	31	

Combat Aircraft

Model	Quantity	In service	Since	Notes
Advanced multi-role				
• Mirage 2000	12	12	1997	
Multi-role				
• Mirage F1-E/B	6	6	1984	To be sold; 7 planes already sold to Spain
Total	18	18		

Transport Aircraft

Model	Quantity	In service	Since	Notes
• Boeing 707	2	2	1977	
• Airbus 340	1	1	1993	
• Boeing 727	1	1	1979	
• Britten-Norman BN-2 Islander	1	1	1986	
• Mystère-Falcon 900	3	3	1991	
Total	8	8		

Qatar

Training and Liaison Aircraft

Model	Quantity	In service	Since	Notes
Jet trainers				
• Alpha jet	6	6	1980	
Total	6	6		
Future procurement				
• Hawk 100	15 – 18		1996	Not finalized

Helicopters

Model	Quantity	In service	Since	Notes
Attack helicopters				
• SA-342 Gazelle	13	13	1983	2 employed as light helicopters with police
Medium transport				
• AS-332 Super Puma/ AS 532 Cougar	6	6	1987	
• Westland Commando Mk 2/Mk 3	4	4	1982	4 out of 12 used for VIP transport
Subtotal	10	10		
Naval combat				
• Westland Commando Mk 2/Mk 3	8	8	1982	
Total	31	31		
Future procurement				
• Naval combat helicopter				

Miscellaneous Aircraft

Model	Quantity	In service	Since	Notes
Target drones				
• TTL BTT-3 Banshee				Unconfirmed

Advanced Armament

Air-to-air-missiles
Mica (144), R-550 Magic II (272), R-530 (128)

Air-to-ground-missiles
AM-39 Exocet, AS-30L (128)

Note: Number in parentheses refers to the quantity of missiles purchased.

Air Force Infrastructure

Military airfields: 2
Doha; Al Ghariyeh

Air Defense Forces

Surface-to-Air Missiles

Model	Launchers	Since	Notes
Light missiles			
• Rapier	15	1984	
• Roland 2	9	1988	Number unconfirmed
• Mistral	24	1995	
Total	48		
Shoulder-launched missiles			
• Blowpipe	6	1986	
• FIM-92A Stinger	12	1989	
Total	18		
Future procurement			
• Shorts Starburst			

Navy

Combat Vessels

Type	Original class name	Quantity	Length (m.)/ displacement (t.)	Notes/ armament
MFPBs				
• Barzan (new)	Vita Vosper Thornycroft	4	56.3/376	8xMM 40 Exocet SSMs 8xMistral SAMs 1x76mm gun 1x30mm gun
• Damsah class	Combattante III	3	56/345	8xMM 40 Exocet SSMs 1x76mm gun 2x40mm guns 4x30mm guns
Total		7		
Future procurement				
• Vosper Thornycroft PBs		2		

Patrol Craft

Type	Original class name	Quantity	Length (m.)/ displacement (t.)	Notes/ armament
• Helmatic	M-160	3	16/20	
• Damen	Polycat 1450	3	14.5/18	1x20mm gun
• Crestitalia	MV-45	4	14.5/17	1x20mm gun with police
• Spear class		12	9.1/4.3	
• P-1200		4	11.9/4.3	With police
Total		26		

Coastal Defense

Type	Batteries	Notes
• MM-40 Exocet	3-4	

Naval Infrastructure

Naval bases: 2
Doha, Halul Island

15. SAUDI ARABIA

General Data

Official Name of the State: The Kingdom of Saudi Arabia
Head of State: King Fahd ibn Abd al-Aziz al-Saud
Prime Minister: King Fahd ibn Abd al-Aziz al-Saud
First Deputy Prime Minister and Heir Apparent: Crown Prince Abdullah ibn Abd al-Aziz al-Saud
Defense and Aviation Minister: Prince Sultan ibn Abd al-Aziz al-Saud
Chief of General Staff: General Salih ibn Ali al-Muhaya
Commander of the Ground Forces: Lieutenant General Sultan ibn Ali al-Mutayri
Commander of the National Guard: Crown Prince Abdallah ibn Abd al-Aziz al-Saud
Commander of the Air Force: Lieutenant General Abd al-Aziz ibn Muhammad Hunaydi
Commander of the Air Defense Forces: Lieutenant General Majid ibn Talhab al-Qutaibi
Commander of the Navy: Vice Admiral Talal ibn Salem al-Mufadhi

Area: 2,331,000 sq. km.
Population: 20,150,000

Demography

Ethnic groups		
Arabs	18,417,000	91.4%
Afro-Arabs	1,008,000	5.0%
Others	725,000	3.6%
Religious groups		
Sunni Muslims	18,558,000	92.1%
Shi'ite Muslims	1,008,000	5.0%
Others (mainly Christians)	584,000	2.9%
Nationality		
Saudis	14,649,000	72.7%
Others	5,501,000	27.3%

Economic Data

		1994	1995	1996	1997	1998
GDP (current price)	$ bn	120.16	127.82	141.33	146.51	128.89
GDP per capita	$	6,765	7,003	7,501	7,517	6,396
Real GDP growth	%	0.5	0.5	1.4	1.9	1.6
Consumer price index	%	0.6	4.9	1.2	0.0	-0.3
External debt	$ bn	NA	NA	NA	NA	NA

Economic Data (continued)

		1994	1995	1996	1997	1998
Balance of payments						
• Exports fob	$ bn	42.6	50.0	60.7	60.7	39.8
• Imports fob	$ bn	21.3	25.7	25.4	26.4	27.5
• Current account balance (including services and income)	$ bn	-10.5	-5.3	0.7	0.3	-12.9
Government expenditure						
• Total expenditure	$ bn	42.723	40.053	40.053	48.331	52.336
• Defense expenditure	$ bn	14.298	13.217	13.357	18.150	17.356
• Real change in defense expenditure	%	-13.12	-7.56	1.05	35.88	-4.37
• Defense expenditure/GDP	%	11.89	10.34	9.45	12.38	13.46
Population	m	17.76	18.25	18.84	19.49	20.15
Official exchange rate	SR:$1	3.745	3.745	3.745	3.745	3.745

Sources: EIU Quarterly Report, EIU Country Profile, IMF International Financial Statistical Yearbook, SIPRI Yearbook

Arms Procurement and Security Assistance Received

Country	Type	Details
Belgium	• Arms transfers	Turrets for LAV IFVs (1997)
Canada	• Arms transfers	LAV APCs/IFVs (1999), naval simulators (1999)
France	• Arms transfers	Upgrading SAMs (1999), upgrading F-2000 missile frigates (1999), La Fayette missile frigates (1999)
	• Military training	Foreign advisers/instructors/serving personnel (1999); trainees abroad for Cougars helicopters (1998)
	• Maintenance aid	Naval vessels (1999)
Germany	• Arms transfers	Cougar helicopters (1998)
PRC	• Military training	Foreign advisers/instructors/serving personnel for CSS-2 missiles (unconfirmed)
Sweden	• Arms transfers	Early warning system for GCC countries (1997)
UK	• Arms transfers	Combat aircraft (1999), mortars (1997), ARM missiles (1997)
	• Military training	Foreign advisers/instructors/serving personnel (1999); trainees abroad

Arms Procurement and Security Assistance Received *(continued)*

Country	Type	Details
US	• Arms transfers	F-15 combat aircraft (1999), AIM-120 AAMs (1999), AGMs, SAMs, M1A2 tanks (1996), surveillance radars (1997), integration of air defense system (1999), upgrading of AIM-9L and AIM-7M AAMs (1999), upgrading of GBU-10 bombs (1999) medium-caliber ammunition (1999), radio systems (1995)
	• Military training	Foreign advisers/instructors/serving personnel; trainees abroad

Arms Sales and Security Assistance Extended

Country	Type	Details
Bosnia	• Arms transfers	Chinese-made small arms (1995), 26 Russian Mi-8 helicopters; French-made Crotale/Shahine SAMs (1995), Rapier SAMs, Stinger SAMs (1995)
GCC	• Facilities	For "Peninsula Shield" forces
USA	• Facilities	HQ at Riyadh, AWACS a/c, U-2 a/c at Taij, 48 F-16 and F-15 at Dhahran with C-130, F-111 EW a/c and KC-135

Foreign Military Cooperation

Type	Details
• Joint maneuvers	UK, Egypt (1999), France, GCC countries, Pakistan, US
• Foreign forces	GCC "Peninsula Shield" rapid deployment force: 7,000 – 10,000 men at Hafr al-Batin; mostly Saudis and from other GCC countries; As of June 1999, there are some 6,200 US soldiers stationed in Saudi Arabia.

Defense Production

	M	P	A
Army equipment			
• al-Fahd 8x8 APC		√	
• Small arms ammunition, electronic components		√	
Air force equipment			
• Some accessories and components for foreign-made aircraft, flares and chaff			√

Defense Production (continued)

	M	P	A
Electronics			
• Radio transceivers, components of a/c radars, parts for EW equipment			√
• Hand-held thermal imager/binocular		√	

Note: M - manufacture (indigenously developed)
P - production under license
A - assembly

Weapons of Mass Destruction

NBC Capabilities

Nuclear capability
No known nuclear activity. Party to the NPT.

Chemical weapons and protective equipment
No known CW activities. Personal protective equipment; decontamination units; US-made CAM chemical detection systems; Fuchs (Fox) NBC detection vehicles. Party to the CWC.

Biological weapons
No known BW activities. Party to the BWC.

Ballistic Missiles

Model	Launchers	Missiles	Since	Notes
• CSS-2	8 – 12	30 – 50	1988	Number of launchers unconfirmed

Armed Forces

Major Changes: No major change was recorded in the Saudi order-of-battle.

Order-of-Battle

Year	1995	1996	1997	1999	2000
General data					
• Personnel (regular)	132,000	161,000	165,000	165,000	171,500
• SSM launchers	8 – 12	8 – 12	8 – 12	8 – 12	8 – 12
Ground Forces					
• Number of brigades	18	18	18	20	20
• Tanks	900	1,015	865 (1,015)	865 (1,015)	750 (1,015)

Order-of-Battle (continued)

Year	1995	1996	1997	1999	2000
• APCs/AFVs	4,040	~4,100	5,220*	~5,300 (5,540)	~5,300 (~5,440)
• Artillery (incl. MRLs)	770	770	~410 (~580)*	~410 (~780)	~410 (~780)
Air Force					
• Combat aircraft	250	249	321*	~345	~355
• Transport aircraft	77	76	61	61	61
• Helicopters	180	180	175	160	160
Air Defense Forces					
• Heavy SAM batteries	23	23	22	22	22
• Medium SAM batteries	16	16	16	16	16
Navy					
• Combat vessels	27	27	24	24	24
• Patrol craft	82	102	92*	80	74

Note: Beginning with 1997, data refers to quantities in active service. The number in parentheses refers to the total inventory.
* Due to change in estimate.

Personnel

	Regular	Reserves	Total
Ground Forces	75,000		75,000
Air Force	20,000		20,000
Air Defense	4,000		4,000
Navy (including a marine unit)	13,500		13,500
National Guard	57,000	20,000	77,000
Royal Guard	2,000		2,000
Total	**171,500**	**20,000**	**191,500**
Paramilitary			
• Mujahidun (affiliated with National Guard)			30,000
• Coast Guard	4,500		4,500
• Frontier Corps	10,500		10,500

Ground Forces

Formations

	Independent brigades/groups	Independent battalions
Armored (Ground Forces)	4	
Mechanized (5 Ground Forces, 3 National Guard)	8	
Infantry (Royal Guard)	1	
Infantry (National Guard)	6	19
Marines		2
Airborne/Special Forces (Ground Forces)	1	
Total	**20**	**21**

Note: Saudi Ground Forces comprise 10 brigades (5 mechanized, 4 armored, 1 airborne/infantry), plus 1 Royal Guard brigade; the National Guard has 9 brigades (3 mechanized, 6 infantry)

Tanks

Model	Quantity	In service	Since	Notes
MBTs				
High quality				
• M1A2	315	200	1993	115 in storage
Medium and low quality				
• AMX-30	300	150	1975	
• M60 A3	400	400	1985	
Subtotal	700	550		
Total	**1,015**	**750**		

APCs/AFVs

Model	Quantity	In service	Since	Notes
APCs				
• AMX-10/AMX-10P	500	500	1975	Of which 90 are carrying ATGMs
• BMR-600	140	140	1985	With marines
• Engesa EE-11 Urutu	+	+		
• M113 A1/A2	1,600	1,600	1976/1981	
• M-3 (Panhard)	150	150		
Subtotal	~2,390	~2,390		

APCs/AFVs *(continued)*

Model	Quantity	In service	Since	Notes
IFVs				
• AML-60/90	350	~225	1969	
• Fox/Ferret	200	200		Possibly phased out
• Piranha of various models	1,117	1,117	1992	Of which 73 are 120mm TDA rifled mortar carriers
• M-2/M-3 Bradley	400	400		
• V-150 Commando	980	980	1977	Number unconfirmed
Subtotal	3,047	~2,900		
Total	**5,440**	**~5,300**		
Future procurement				
• al-Fahd AD-40-8-1	100			

Artillery

Model	Quantity	In service	Since	Notes
Self-propelled guns and howitzers				
• 155mm M109 A2	280	110		
• 155mm GCT	51	51	1980	
Subtotal	331	161		
Towed guns and howitzers				
• 155mm FH-70	72	0		
• 155mm M198	90	60	1982	
• 155mm M114	50	50	1980	
• 105mm M102/M101	100	0	1975	
Subtotal	312	110		
Mortars, under 160mm				
• 120mm TDA, SP	73	73		On Piranha
• 107mm (4.2") M30	+	+	1981	
MRLs				
• 180mm SS-40 Astros II/ 127mm SS-30 Astros II	60	60		10 batteries
Total	**~780**	**~410**		
Artillery/mortar-locating radars				
• AN/TPQ-37	+	+		

Logistics and Engineering Equipment

M-123 Viper minefield crossing system, MK 3 (D) flail, M-69 A1 bridging tanks, bridging equipment, AFV transporters (600), LAV ARVs

Anti-Tank Missiles

Model	Launchers	Missiles	Since	Notes
• AMX-10P SP	90	+	1982	Also listed under APCs (carrying HOT)
• VCC-1	200	+		Carrying TOW
• BGM-71C Improved TOW/BGM-71D TOW II	750	+	1988	
• M47 Dragon	1,000	+	1977	
Total	2,040	+		

Anti-Tank Guns

Model	Quantity	In service	Since	Notes
• 106mm M-40 recoilless rifle	50	50		
• 84mm Carl Gustav light recoilless rifle	300	300		

Air Force

Order-of-Battle

Category	Quantity	In service	Notes
• Combat	~355	~355	
• Transport	61	61	
• Helicopters	160	160	

Combat Aircraft

Model	Quantity	In service	Since	Notes
Interceptors				
• F-15 C/D Eagle	91	91	1982	
• Tornado ADV (F Mk 3)	22	22	1989	
Subtotal	113	113		
Advanced multi-role				
• F-15S	72	72	1995	
Multi-role				
• Tornado IDS (GR Mk 1/GR-1A)	92	92	1986	12 of which are reconnaissance
• F-5E/F	~65	~65	1973	
Subtotal	~155	~155		
Obsolete				
• F-5A/B	15	15		Mostly employed as trainer a/c
Total	~355	~355		

Transport Aircraft

Model	Quantity	In service	Since	Notes
• C-130E/H Hercules	46	46	1970/1980	
• CN-235	4	4	1987	
• Gulfstream III	1	1	1983	
• Learjet 35	2	2	1981	Employed in target-towing role
• Mystère-Falcon 20	2	2		
• VC-140 Jetstar	2	2	1969	
• HS-125	4	4		
Total	61	61		

Training and Liaison Aircraft

Model	Quantity	In service	Since	Notes
Jet trainers				
• BAC-167 Strikemaster	30	0	1968	Possibly phased out
• Hawk Mk 65	29	29	1987	
Subtotal	59	29		
Piston/Turboprop				
• BAe Jetstream 31	2	2	1987	
• Cessna 172 G/H/L	17	17	1967	
• Pilatus PC-9	49	49	1987	
Subtotal	68	68		
Total	127	97		
Future procurement				
• Hawk 100/200	20			Under negotiation

Helicopters

Model	Quantity	In service	Since	Notes
Attack				
• Bell 406CS	15	15	1990	In army aviation
• AH-64A Apache	12	12	1993	In army aviation
Subtotal	27	27		
Naval combat				
• AS-365 Dauphin 2/ AS-565MA	27	27	1986	Including 6 in medical evacuation role
• AS-332 Super Puma	11	11	1992	
Subtotal	38	38		
Medium transport				
• SH-3 (AS-61A)	3	3	1978	
• KV-107/KV-107 IIA	17	17	1979	

Helicopters (continued)

Model	Quantity	In service	Since	Notes
• AB-212/Bell-205	25	25	1977	Number unconfirmed
• UH-60A Black Hawk/ Desert Hawk/Medevac	20	20	1990	In Army Aviation
Subtotal	65	65		
Light transport				
• AB-206 JetRanger	30	30	1967	
Total	**160**	**160**		
Future procurement				
• AS-532 Cougar	12			

Miscellaneous Aircraft

Model	Quantity	In service	Since	Notes
Reconnaissance				
• Tornado IDS	12	12	1986	Also listed under Combat Aircraft
• RF-5E	10	10	1973	
AEW/AWACS				
• E-3A AWACS	5	5	1986	
Tankers				
• KC-130H	7	7	1973	
• KE-3/Boeing 707	8	8	1986	
Target drones				
• TTL BTT-3 Banshee	+	+		
• MQM-74C Chukar II	+	+		

Advanced Armament

Air-to-air-missiles
AIM-7F Sparrow (1,100); AIM-7M (1,000); AIM-9J/P Sidewinder (1,800); AIM-9L/M Sidewinder (1,500); AIM-9S (150), Red Top; Sky Flash (550)

Air-to-ground-missiles
AGM-65A/D/G Maverick (1,700); ALARM (200); AM-39 Exocet; AS-15TT (220); Sea Eagle (350)

Bombs
CBU-86; CBU-87; BL-755 CBU; Paveway III laser-guided (100); GBU-10/12/15

Future procurement
AIM-120 AMRAAM

Note: Numbers in parentheses refer to number of units purchased.

Air Force Infrastructure

Aircraft shelters
For combat aircraft

Military airfields: 15
Abqaiq, al-Ahsa, Dhahran, Gizan, al-Hufuf, Jidda, Jubail, Khamis Mushayt, al-Kharj, Medina, Riyadh, Sharawra, al-Sulayyil, Tabuk, Taif

Air Defense Forces

Surface-to-Air Missiles

Model	Batteries	Launchers	Since	Notes
Heavy missiles				
• MIM-104 Patriot	5		1991	
• MIM-23B Improved HAWK	17		1982	One used for training
Total	22			
Medium missiles				
• Crotale	16			Some are sheltered mounted for fixed sites
• Shahine I/II	+		1981	To be upgraded
Total	16			
Shoulder-launched missiles				
• FIM-92A/C Stinger		400	1984	
• MIM-43A Redeye		500		
• Mistral		900		
Total		1,800		
Future procurement				
• FIM-92C Stinger		50		
• Crotale NG II				
• Mistral				

Other Air Defense Systems

Model	Quantity	In service	Since	Notes
Air defense systems (missiles, radars and guns)				
• 35mm Skyguard AD system	60	60		
Short-range guns				
• 35mm Oerlikon-Buhrle 35x2 GDF	150	150		Included in Skyguard AD system

Other Air Defense Systems (continued)

Model	Quantity	In service	Since	Notes
• 20mm M163 Vulcan SP	72	72		
• 30mm AMX-30 SA	52	52		
Total	274	274		
Radars				
• AN/FPS-117 (Seek Igloo)	17	17		
• AN/TPS-43G	28	28		
• AN/TPS-59	+	+		
• AN/TPS-63	35	35		
Command and control system				
• C³I Peace Shield System				Currently installed
Aerostat with airborne radars				
• LASS	+	+		

Navy

Combat Vessels

Type	Original class name	Quantity	Length (m.)/ displacement (t.)	Notes/ armament
Missile frigates				
• Madina class	F-2000	4	115.0/2,000	In process of upgrading (2 already upgraded) 1xSA-365 helicopter 8xOtomat SSMs 1x8 Crotale Naval 1x100mm gun 4x40mm guns 4x533mm torpedoes
Missile corvettes				
• Badr class	PCG-1 class	4	74.7/870	8xHarpoon SSMs 1x76mm gun 2x20mm AA guns 1x20mm Phalanx 6x324mm torpedoes

Combat Vessels *(continued)*

Type	Original class name	Quantity	Length (m.)/ displacement (t.)	Notes/ armament
MFPBs				
• al-Siddiq	PGG-1 class	9	58.1/425	4xHarpoon SSMs 1x76mm gun 2x20mm AA guns 1x20mm Phalanx gun
Mine warfare vessels				
• Addriyah	MSC-322 class minesweeper	4	46.6/320	1x20mm AA gun magnetic sweepers
• al-Jawf	Sandown class	3	52.7/450	2x30mm guns 2 PAP 104 Mk 5
Subtotal		7		
Total		24		
Future procurement				
• Lafayette class frigates	Type 3000	3	128/4,100	Delivery in 2001 and 2003 1xAS-365 helicopter 8xMM40 SSM 8xCrotale Naval 1x100mm gun 2x20mm guns 4x533mm torpedoes
• Sandown class minesweepers		3		

Patrol Craft

Type	Original class name	Quantity	Length (m.)/ displacement (t.)	Notes/ armament
• al-Jubatel	Abeking-Rasmussen	2	26.2/96	1x20mm gun (with Coast Guard)
• al-Jouf	Blohm & Voss	4	38.6/210	2x20mm guns (with Coast Guard)
• Halter type		17	23.8/56	2x25mm guns
• Sea Guard		2	22.5/56	2x20mm guns (with Coast Guard)
• Simonneau Type 51		39	15.8/22	1x20mm gun
• Skorpion class		10	17.0/33	Light armament (with Coast Guard)
Total		74		

Note: Coast Guard has some 650 small patrol craft.

Landing Craft

Type	Original class name	Quantity	Length (m.)/ displacement (t.)	Notes/ armament
• LCM-6 class		4	17.1/62	34 tons or 80 troops
• Slingsby SAH 2200 hovercraft		3	10.6/-	2.2 tons or 24 troops with coast guard
• US 1610 class LCU		4	41.1/375	170 tons or 120 troops
Total		11		
Future procurement				
• Slingsby SAH 2200 hovercraft		4		

Auxiliary Vessels

Type	Original class name	Quantity	Length (m.)/ displacement (t.)	Notes/ armament
• Tabouk training ship		1	60/585	1x20mm gun
• Dammam	Jaguar class	3	42.5/160	Ex-gunboat now used for training
• Royal yacht		1	1,450 dwt	
• Royal yacht		1	670 ton	
• Royal yacht al-Yamama		1		
• Royal yacht		1	112-ton	
• Royal yacht Pegasus		1		
• Durance class tanker		2	135.0/11,200	4x40mm guns 2 helicopter pads
• Ocean tugs		3	680 ton	
• Coastal tugs		13		
• Small tankers		3	28.7/233	
• Training ship		1	21.4/75	With Coast Guard
• Brooke marine fire-fighting craft		1	24.5/82	Fire-fighting with Coast Guard

Coastal Defense

Type	Quantity	Notes
Otomat	4	

Naval Infrastructure

Naval bases (including coast guard): 13
al-Dammam, Aziziya (coast guard), al-Haql (coast guard), Jidda, Jizan, Jubayl, Makna (coast guard), al-Qatif, Ras al-Mishaab, Ras Tanura, al-Sharma, al-Wajh, Yanbu

Ship maintenance and repair facilities
Repair of vessels, dependent on foreign experts; 22,000-ton and 62,000-ton floating docks at Dammam; 45,000-ton and 16,000-ton floating docks at Jidda

16. SUDAN

General Data

Official Name of the State: The Republic of Sudan
Head of State: President Omar Hassan Ahmad al-Bashir
Defense Minister: Abd al-Rahman Sir al-Khatim
Chief of General Staff: General Abbas Arabi
Commander of the Air Force: Major General Ali Mahjoub Mardi
Commander of the Navy: Commodore Abbas al-Said Othman

Area: 2,504,530 sq. km.
Population: 28,500,000

Demography

Ethnic groups		
Arabs	11,110,000	39%
Nilotics	14,820,000	52%
Beja	1,710,000	6%
Foreigners	570,000	2%
Others	285,000	1%
Religious groups		
Sunni Muslims	19,950,000	70%
Indigenous beliefs	7,125,000	25%
Christians (Coptic, Greek Orthodox, Catholic, Protestant)	1,425,000	5%

Economic Data

		1994	1995	1996	1997	1998
GDP (current price)	$ bn	7.078	6.211	7.042	8.485	7.835
GDP per capita	$	244.06	232.62	257.94	304.12	274.91
Real GDP growth	%	4.3	4.4	4.7	6.7	5.0
Consumer price index	%	115.4	68.4	132.8	46.7	17.1
External debt	$ bn	16.92	17.60	16.97	16.33	16.77
Balance of payments						
• Exports fob	$ bn	0.524	0.556	0.620	0.594	0.596
• Imports fob	$ bn	1.045	1.066	1.340	1.422	1.732
• Current account balance (including services and income)	$ bn	-0.602	-0.500	-0.827	-0.828	-0.957

Economic Data (continued)

		1994	1995	1996	1997	1998
Government expenditure						
• Total expenditure	$ bn	9.602	6.472	5.813	7.063	NA
• Defense expenditure	$ bn	1.723	1.387	1.664	NA	NA
• Real change in defense expenditure	%	-6.96	-19.50	19.97	NA	NA
• Defense expenditure/GDP	%	24.34	22.33	23.62	NA	NA
Population	m	29.0	26.7	27.3	27.9	28.5
Official exchange rate	SD: $1	28.96	58.09	125.08	157.57	200.80

Sources: EIU Quarterly Report, EIU Country Profile, IMF International Financial Statistical Yearbook, SIPRI Yearbook

Arms Procurement and Security Assistance Received

Country	Type	Details
Iran	• Arms transfers	Small arms, ammunition, EW equipment, vehicles, spare parts for Soviet and Chinese arms, tanks, aircraft, allegedly CW (1997)
	• Military training	Technicians and IRGC; trainees abroad
Belarus	• Arms transfers	Mi-24 Combat helicopters (1997)
Kyrgyzstan	• Arms transfers	Mi-24 Combat helicopter (1995)
Poland	• Arms transfers	T-55 tanks (1999) (via Yemen-unauthorized by Poland)
PRC	• Arms transfers	F-7 combat a/c (1996)

Arms Sales and Security Assistance Extended

Country	Type	Details
Iran	• Facilities	Iranian IRGC; facilities for Iranian ships at Port Sudan
Lebanon	• Facilities	Lebanese militia, camps with the popular defense forces

Weapons of Mass Destruction

NBC Capabilities

Nuclear capability
No known nuclear activity. Party to the NPT.

Chemical weapons and protective equipment
Alleged CW from Iran unsubstantiated. Alleged production of CW, unsubstantiated. Personal protective equipment; unit decontamination equipment. Party to the CWC.

Biological weapons
No known BW activities. Party to the BWC.

Armed Forces

Major Changes: No major change was recorded in the Sudanese order-of-battle.

Order-of-Battle

Year	1995	1996	1997	1999	2000
General data					
• Personnel (regular)	86,500	86,500	84,500	103,000*	103,000
Ground Forces					
• Divisions	10	10	9*	9	9
• Total number of brigades	+	+	58*	61	61
• Tanks	450	450	~320	~320	~350
• APCs/AFVs	950	950	~560 (~700)*	~560 (~700)	~560 (~700)
• Artillery (including MRLs)	360	360	753 (765)*	~760(~770)	~760 (~770)
Air Force					
• Combat aircraft	45	45	~35 (~55)*	~35 (~55)	~35 (~55)
• Transport aircraft	25	25	26	26	25
• Helicopters	53	53	~55 (67)	~60 (69)	~60 (69)
Air Defense Forces					
• Heavy SAM batteries	5	5	5	5	5
Navy					
• Patrol craft	10	23	22	22	18

Note: Beginning with 1997, data refers to quantities in active service. The number in parentheses refers to the total inventory.

* Due to change in estimate.

Personnel

	Regular	Reserves	Total
Ground Forces	100,000		100,000
Air Force	2,000		2,000
Navy	1,000		1,000
Total	**103,000**		**103,000**
Paramilitary			
• People's Defense Forces	15,000	85,000	100,000
• Border Guard	2,500		2,500

Ground Forces

Formations

	Divisions	Independent brigades/groups
Armored	1	
Mechanized/Infantry	7	24
Airborne	1	
Artillery		3
Reconnaissance		1
Engineering	1	
Total	**10**	**28**

Tanks

Model	Quantity	In service	Since	Notes
MBTs				
Medium and low quality				
• M60 A3	20	20	1981	
• T-54/T-55/Type 59	~250	~250	1969	Number unconfirmed
• Type 62	70	70	1972	
Total	**~350**	**~350**		

APCs/AFVs

Model	Quantity	In service	Since	Notes
APCs				
• al-Walid	150	100	1986	
• AMX-VCI	+	+		
• M113	80	36	1982	
• BTR-152	80	80	1960	
• BTR-50	20	20	1970	
• Fahd	*	*	1989	

APCs/AFVs (continued)

Model	Quantity	In service	Since	Notes
• M-3 (Panhard)	*	*	1983	
• OT-62	20	20		
• OT-64	55	55	1973	
Subtotal	~420	~320		
IFVs				
• BMP-2	6	6		
• V-150 Commando	100	55	1984	
Subtotal	106	61		
Reconnaissance				
• AML-90	5	5		
• BRDM 1/2	60	60		
• Ferret	60	60	1960	
• Saladin	50	50	1961	
Subtotal	175	175		
Total	~700	~560		

Artillery

Model	Quantity	In service	Since	Notes
Self-propelled guns and howitzers				
• 155mm Mk F-3 (AMX)	10	6	1984	
Towed guns and howitzers				
• 155mm M114	20	12	1981	
• 130mm Type 59/M-46	75	75		
• 105mm M101	20	20		
Subtotal	115	107		
Mortars, under 160mm				
• 120mm mortar	+	+	1970	
MRLs				
• 122mm BM-21	90	90	1989	
• 122mm Saqer	50	50	1986	
• 107mm Type 63	500	500		
Subtotal	640	640		
Total	~770	~750		

Anti-Tank Missiles

Model	Launchers	Missiles	Since	Notes
• BGM-71C improved TOW	+	+		Not all serviceable
• AT-3 (Sagger)	+	+		

Anti-Tank Guns

Model	Quantity	In service	Since	Notes
• 100mm M-1955 field/AT	+	+		
• 100mm M-1944	50	0	1975	
• 85mm M-1945/D-44 field/AT	100	0	1973	
• 76mm M-1942	+	0		

Air Force

Order-of-Battle

Category	Quantity	In service	Notes
• Combat	~55	~35	Low serviceability
• Transport	25	25	Low serviceability
• Helicopters	69	~60	Low serviceability

Combat Aircraft

Model	Quantity	In service	Since	Notes
Interceptors				
• MiG-23	~3	~3	1987	
Multi-role				
• F-5E/F	9	0	1984/1982	
Obsolete				
• A-5 (Fantan)/Q-5	10	10		
• F-6 Shenyang/J-6	11	11	1981	
• MiG-21 (Fishbed)/F-7	19	9	1970	
Subtotal	40	30		
Total	~55	~35		

Transport Aircraft

Model	Quantity	In service	Since	Notes
• An-24 (Coke)/An-26	5	5		
• C-130H Hercules	4	4	1978	
• DHC-5D Buffalo	3	3	1978	
• Fokker F-27	1	1	1974	
• Mystère-Falcon 50	1	1	1983	
• Mystère-Falcon 20	1	1	1978	
• C-212	4	4	1986	
• EMB-110P	6	6	1980	
Total	25	25		

Training and Liaison Aircraft

Model	Quantity	In service	Since	Notes
Jet trainers				
• BAC-145 Jet Provost	5	5	1969	
• BAC-167 Strikemaster	5	3	1984	
Total	10	8		

Helicopters

Model	Quantity	In service	Since	Notes
Attack				
• Mi-24	6	6	1991	
Medium transport				
• Mi-4 (Hound)	3	3	1974	Possibly phased out
• Mi-8 (Hip)	14	~7		
• SA-330/ IAR-330 Puma	10	10	1985	
• Bell 212/AB-212	5	5	1982	
• AB-412	10	10	1990	
Subtotal	42	~40		
Light transport				
• MBB BO-105	18	18	1980	Some serving with police
• Bell 206	3	3	1992	
Subtotal	21	21		
Total	69	~60		

Advanced Armament

Air-to-air-missiles
AA-2 (Atoll)

Air Force Infrastructure

Military airfields: 13
Atbara, al-Fasher, al-Geneina, Juba, Khartoum, Malakal, Merowe, al-Obeid, Port Sudan, Port Sudan (new), Wad Medani, Wadi Sayidina, Wau

Air Defense Forces

Surface-to-Air Missiles

Model	Batteries	Launchers	Since	Notes
Heavy missiles				
• SA-2 (Guideline)	5		1981	
Shoulder-launched missiles				
• SA-7 (Grail)		250	1980	
• MIM-43A Redeye		25	1984	
Total		275		

Other Air Defense Systems

Model	Quantity	In service	Since	Notes
Short-range guns				
• 57mm	+	+		
• 40mm	60	60		
• 37mm M-1939	110	110	1973	
• 23mm ZU 23x2	50	50	1984	
• 20mm M-3 VDA	12	12		
• 20mm M163 A-1 Vulcan SP	8	8	1986	
• 20mm M167 Vulcan	30	30	1986	
Total	~270	~270		

Navy

Patrol Craft

Type	Original class name	Quantity	Length (m.)/ displacement (t.)	Notes/ armament
• Kadir class	Abeking and Rasmussen	2	22.9/70	1x20mm gun YJ-1 SAM
• Ashoora I class		8	8.1/3	
• Sewart class		4	12.9/92	1x7.62mm MG
• Kurmuk	Yugoslav type 15	4	16.9/19.5	1x20mm gun
Total		18		

Auxiliary Vessels

Type	Original class name	Quantity	Length (m.)/ displacement (t.)	Notes/ armament
• Yugoslav supply ships		7	47.3/410	1x20mm gun

Naval Infrastructure

Naval bases: 3
Port Sudan, Flamingo Bay, Khartoum

Major Non-Governmental Paramilitary Forces

Personnel

	Regular	Reserves	Total	Notes
• National Democratic Alliance (NDA)				A coordinating organization of all active opposition organizations
• Sudan People's Liberation Army (SPLA)	30,000	100,000	130,000	The main non-governmental military organization active in southern Sudan
• South Sudan Independence Movement (SSIM)	10,000		10,000	Also known as SPLA United; in 1996 signed a truce with the government
• Sudan Alliance Forces	1,000 – 2,000		1,000 – 2,000	Active in eastern Sudan
• Beja Congress Forces	500		500	Active in eastern Sudan
• New Sudan Brigade	2,000		2,000	Recent activity unknown

Equipment

Organization	Category	System	Notes
SPLA	Tanks	• T-54/55	
	MRLs	• BM-21	
	Artillery guns	• +	
	Mortars	• 120mm	
		• 60mm	
	Air Defense	• SA-7 SAM	
		• 14.5mm AAG	

17. SYRIA

General Data

Official Name of the State: The Arab Republic of Syria
Head of State: President Bashar al-Assad
Prime Minister: Mohammed Mustafa Miro
Minister of Defense: Lieutenant General Mustafa al-Tlass
Chief of General Staff: General Ali Aslan
Commander of the Air Force: Major General Kamal Makhafut
Commander of the Navy: Vice Admiral Wa'il Nasser

Area: 185,180 sq. km.
Population: 15,580,000

Demography

Ethnic groups		
Arabs	14,068,700	90.3%
Kurds, Armenians and others	1,511,300	9.7%
Religious groups		
Sunni Muslims	11,529,000	74.0%
Alawis, Druze, and Shi'ite Muslims	2,493,000	16.0%
Christians (Greek Orthodox, Gregorian, Armenian, Catholics, Syrian Orthodox, Greek Catholics)	1,558,000	10.0%

Economic Data

		1994	1995	1996	1997	1998
GDP (current prices)	$ bn	12.05	13.6	15.91	16.5	17.1
GDP per capita	$	871	958	1,088	1,093	1,097
Real GDP growth	%	7.7	5.8	7.3	2.5	7.8
Consumer price index	%	15.3	8.0	8.3	2.3	-1.2
External debt	$ bn	20.6	21.3	21.4	20.9	22.4
Balance of payments						
• Exports fob	$ bn	3.33	3.86	4.18	4.06	3.13
• Imports fob	$ bn	4.6	4.0	4.52	3.6	3.3
• Current account balance (including services and income)	$ bn	-1.62	0.37	0.08	0.48	0.06
Government expenditure						
• Total expenditure	$ bn	3.47	3.86	4.42	4.77	5.24
• Defense expenditure	$ bn	0.9	0.96	0.98	0.88	0.87

Economic Data *(continued)*

		1994	1995	1996	1997	1998
• Real change in defense expenditure	%	20.0	6.6	2.1	-10.3	-1.2
• Defense expenditure/GDP	%	7.4	7.0	6.2	5.3	5.1
Population	m	13.84	14.19	14.62	15.1	15.58
Official exchange rate	S£: $1	41.5	42.0	42.5	44.2	45.3

Sources: EIU Quarterly Report, EIU Country Profile, IMF International Financial Statistical Yearbook, SIPRI Yearbook

Arms Procurement and Security Assistance Received

Country	Type	Details
Czech Republic	• Arms transfers	T-72 MBTs (1995)
India	• Arms transfers	Aircraft spare parts (1996); CW precursors (1996)
Iran	• Arms transfers	Assistance in MBT upgrade (1997)
	• Assistance	Promised guarantees for debts to Russia (1997)
	• Cooperation in arms production	Cooperation in production of SSMs (1999)
North Korea	• Arms transfers	Scud C SSMs (1996), including assistance in production
Russia	• Arms transfers	Kornet ATGMs (1998)
	• Facilities	Repairs of naval base (2000)
	• Military training	Approx. 50 advisers; 70 trainees in Russia (1998)
Ukraine	• Arms transfers	Upgraded T-55 MBTs (1997)

Arms Sales and Security Assistance Extended

Country	Type	Details
Lebanon	• Military training	Approx. 200 trainees annually, advisers
Palestinian organizations	• Facilities	Camps of the rejectionist front
	• Assistance	Grant for Fatah-Intifada, al-Saiqa, PPSF, PLF and PFLP-GC

Foreign Military Cooperation

Type	Details
• Forces deployed abroad	Lebanon-25,000 in Beka', northern Lebanon (Tripoli area) and Beirut

Defense Production

	M	P	A
Weapons of mass destruction			
• Production and upgrading of SSMs (in cooperation with North Korea and Iran)		√	√
• Production of chemical and biological agents, chemical warheads for SSMs	√		
Army equipment			
• Upgrading of tanks		√	
• Ammunition	√		

Note: M - manufacture (indigenously developed)
P - production under license
A - assembly

Weapons of Mass Destruction

NBC Capabilities

Nuclear capability
Basic research. Alleged deal with Russia for a 24 Mw reactor. Deals with China for a 27 kw reactor and with Argentina for a 3 Mw research reactor probably cancelled. Party to the NPT. Safeguards agreement with the IAEA in force.

Chemical weapons and protective equipment
Stockpiles of nerve gas, including sarin, mustard, and VX. Delivery vehicles include chemical warheads for SSMs and aerial bombs. Personal protective equipment; Soviet-type unit decontamination equipment. Not a party to the CWC.

Biological weapons
Biological weapons and toxins (unconfirmed). Signed but not ratified the BWC.

Ballistic Missiles

Model	Launchers	Missiles	Since	Notes
• SS-1 (Scud B)	18	200	1974	
• SS-1 (Scud C variant from North Korea)	8	60	1992	
• SS-21 (Scarab)	18		1983	
Total	44			
Future procurement				
• Scud D	+			Under development

Note: See also under Rockets

Armed Forces

Major Changes: No major change was recorded in the Syrian order-of-battle in 1999.

Order-of-Battle

Year	1995	1996	1997	1999	2000
General data					
• Personnel (regular)	390,000	390,000	380,000	380,000	380,000
• SSM launchers**	44	44	44	44	44
Ground Forces					
• Divisions	12	12	12	12	12
• Total number of brigades	59	59	67*	67	67
• Tanks	4,800	4,800	3,700*	3,700	3,700
			(4,800)	(4,800)	(4,800)
• APCs/AFVs	4,980	4,980	4,980	~5,000	~5,000
• Artillery (including MRLs)	2,500	2,500	2,575*	2,575	~2,600
			(2,975)	(2,975)	(~3,000)
Air Force					
• Combat aircraft	515	515	520	520	520
• Transport aircraft	23	23	23 (25)	23 (25)	23 (25)
• Helicopters	285	285	295*	295	295
Air Defense Forces					
• Heavy SAM batteries	108	108	108	108	108
• Medium SAM batteries	70	70	65	65	64
• Light SAM launchers	+	+	55*	55	55
Navy					
• Submarines	3	3	0 (3)*	0 (3)	0 (3)
• Combat vessels	32	32	25 (30)*	24 (27)	14*
• Patrol crafts	16	16	8*	8	8

Note: Beginning with 1997, data refers to quantities in active service. The number in parentheses refers to the total inventory.
* Due to change in estimate.
** Number does not include unguided rockets.

Personnel

	Regular	Reserves	Total
Ground Forces	306,000	100,000	406,000
Air Force	30,000	10,000	40,000
Air Defense	40,000	20,000	60,000
Navy	4,000	2,500	6,500
Total	**380,000**	**132,500**	**512,500**
Paramilitary			
• Gendarmerie	8,000		8,000
• Workers' Militia		400,000	400,000

Ground Forces

Formations

	Corps/armies	Divisions	Independent brigades/groups	Brigades in divisions
All arms	3			
Armored		7	1	3 armd., 1 mech., 1 aty. each
Mechanized		3	1	2 mech., 2 armd., 1 aty. each
Republican Guard		1		3 armd., 1 mech., 1 aty. each
Infantry/Special Forces		1	3	
Airborne/Special Forces			8 – 10	
Artillery			2	
SSM forces			3	
Anti-tank/Infantry			2	
Total	3	12	20 – 22	

Note: One armored division is a reserve unit.

Tanks

Model	Quantity	In service	Since	Notes
MBTs				
High quality				
• T-72/T-72M	1,600	1,600	1979/1993	
Medium and low quality				
• T-62	1,000	1,000	1974	
• T-55/T-54	~2,200	1,100	1957	Some upgraded to MV standard
Subtotal	~3,200	2,100		
Total	~4,800	3,700		

APCs/AFVs

Model	Quantity	In service	Since	Notes
APCs				
• BTR-152	560	560	1967	
• BTR-40/50/60	1,000	1,000	1956	
Subtotal	1,560	1,560		

APCs/AFVs *(continued)*

Model	Quantity	In service	Since	Notes
IFVs				
• BMP-1	2,450	2,450	1977	
• BMP-2	~70	~70	1988	
Subtotal	~2,520	~2,520		
Reconnaissance				
• BRDM-2	900	900	1978	Also listed under Anti-Tank Weapons
Total	~5,000	~5,000		

Artillery

Model	Quantity	In service	Since	Notes
Self-propelled guns and howitzers				
• 152mm 2S3	50	50	1984	
• 122mm 2S1	400	400	1982	
• 122mm D30	55	55	1986	Syrian-made
Subtotal	505	505		
Towed guns and howitzers				
• 180mm S-23	10	10	1975	
• 152mm M-1943	50	50	1987	
• 152mm D-20	20	20	1982	
• 130mm M-46	800	800	1970	
• 122mm D-30	500	500	1984	
• 122mm D-74	400	0		
• 122mm M-1938	150	150	1976	
Subtotal	1,930	1,530		
Mortars, over 160mm				
• 240mm	10	10	1986	
• 160mm	80	80	1976	
Subtotal	90	90		
Mortars, under 160mm				
• 120mm	+	+	1975	
Rockets				
• FROG-7	18	18	1971	
MRLs				
• 122mm BM-21	250	250	1979	
• 107mm Type 63	200	200	1994	
Subtotal	450	450		
Total	~3,000	~2,600		

Syria

Logistics and Engineering Equipment

MTU-67 bridging tanks, MT-55 bridging tanks (90), tank-towed bridges, mine-clearing rollers, AFV transporters (800)

Anti-Tank Missiles

Model	Quantity	In service	Since	Notes
• AT-14 (Kornet)	1,000	1,000	1998	Being delivered
• AT-4 (Spigot)	150	150	1980	
• AT-5 (Spandrel)	40	40	1995	
• AT-3 (Sagger) SP	3,000	3,000	1974	Mounted on BRDM-2 and BMP-1
• MILAN	200	200	1980	
Total	4,390	4,390		

Air Force

Order-of-Battle

Category	Quantity	In service	Notes
• Combat	520	520	
• Transport	25	23	
• Helicopters	295	295	

Combat Aircraft

Model	Quantity	In service	Since	Notes
Interceptors				
• MiG-25 (Foxbat)	35	35	1980	
• MiG-29 (Fulcrum)	20	20	1987	
• MiG-23 ML/MF	100	100	1974	
Subtotal	155	155		
Ground attack				
• Su-24 (Fencer)	20	20	1988	
• MiG-23 U/BN (Flogger)	35	35	1978	
• Su-20/22 (Fitter C/D)	100	100	1978	
Subtotal	155	155		
Obsolete				
• MiG-21 MF/BIS/U (Fishbed)	200 – 210	200 – 210	1966	Some possibly phased out
Total	520	520		

Combat Aircraft *(continued)*

Model	Quantity	In service	Since	Notes
Future procurement				
• Su-24 (Fencer)				Unconfirmed
• MiG-29 (Fulcrum)				Unconfirmed
• Su-27				Unconfirmed

Transport Aircraft

Model	Quantity	In service	Since	Notes
• An-24/26 (Coke/Curl)	6	6	1979	
• IL-76 (Candid)	4	4	1983	
• Tu-134	2	2	1985	
• Mystère-Falcon 20/900	5	3	1980	
• Piper Navajo	2	2		
• Yak-40 (Codling)	6	6	1989	
Total	25	23		

Training and Liaison Aircraft

Model	Quantity	In service	Since	Notes
Jet trainers				
• L-39 Albatross	90	90	1980	
Piston/Turbo-prop				
• MBB 223 Flamingo	40	40	1976	
• Mushshak	6	6	1994	
Subtotal	46	46		
Total	136	136		

Helicopters

Model	Quantity	In service	Since	Notes
Attack helicopters				
• Mi-25 (Hind)	55	55	1980	
• SA-342 Gazelle	45	45	1976	
Subtotal	100	100		
Medium transport				
• Mi-8/Mi-17 (Hip H)	160	160	1971	
• Mi-2	10	10	1975	
Subtotal	170	170		
Naval combat				
• Ka-28 (Helix)	5	5	1990	
• Mi-14 (Haze)	20	20	1984	
Subtotal	25	25		
Total	295	295		

Miscellaneous Aircraft

Model	Quantity	In service	Since	Notes
Reconnaissance				
• MiG-25 R	7	7	1985	
UAVs and mini-UAVs				
• Shmel/Malachit	+	+		

Advanced Armament

Air-to-air-missiles
AA-2 (610), AA-6 (150), AA-7 (470), AA-8 (1,120), AA-10, AA-11

Air-to-ground-missiles
AS-7, AS-9, AS-10, AS-11, AS-12, AS-14, AT-2, HOT

Note: Number in parentheses refers to the quantity of missiles purchased.

Air Force Infrastructure

Aircraft shelters
In all airfields, for combat aircraft

Military airfields: 21

Abu Duhur, Afis North, Aleppo, Damascus (international), Damascus (Meze), Dir ez-Zor, Dumayr, Hama, Jarah, Khalkhala, Latakia, Marj-royal (Bley), Nassiriyah, Tudmur, al-Qusayr, Rasm al-Aboud, Sayqal, Shayarat, al-Suweida, T-4, Tabaka

Air Defense Forces

Surface-to-Air Missiles

Model	Batteries	Launchers	Since	Notes
Heavy missiles				
• SA-2 (Guideline)/ SA-3 (Goa)	100		1971	
• SA-5 (Gammon)	8		1983	
Total	108			
Medium missiles				
• SA-8 (Gecko)		56	1982	
• SA-6 (Gainful)	50		1973	
Total	50	56		
Light missiles				
• SA-9 (Gaskin)		20	1975	
• SA-13 (Gopher)		35	1986	
Total		55		

Surface-to-Air Missiles (continued)

Model	Batteries	Launchers	Since	Notes
Shoulder-launched missiles				
• SA-7 (Grail)		+	1973	
• SA-14 (Gremlin)		+		
• SA-16		+		
Future procurement				
• SA-10 (Grumble)				

Other Air Defense Systems

Model	Quantity	In service	Since	Notes
Short-range guns				
• 57mm S-60	700	~400	1973	Partly phased out
• 37mm M-1939	300	0	1973	
• 23mm ZSU 23x4 SP	400	400	1977	
• 23mm ZU 23x2	600	~300	1986	
Total	2,000	~1,100		

Radars

Long Track, P-14 (Tall King), P-15 (Flat Face), P-12 (Spoon Rest), P-30, P-35, P-80, PRV-13, PRV-16.

Navy

Submarines

Type	Original class name	Quantity	Length (m.)/ displacement (t.)	Notes/ armament
• R class (Romeo)	Type 633	0	76.6/1,830	8x533mm torpedoes 28 mines 3 unserviceable

Combat Vessels

Type	Original class name	Quantity	Length (m.)/ displacement (t.)	Notes/ armament
MFPBs				
• Ossa II		8	38.6/245	4xSS-N-2C Styx SSM 4x30mm guns

Syria

Combat Vessels *(continued)*

Type	Original class name	Quantity	Length (m.)/ displacement (t.)	Notes/ armament
ASW vessels				
• Petya II submarine chaser frigate		2	81.8/950	5-16x400mm torpedoes 4xRBU 2500 ASW mortars 22 mines 4x76mm guns
Mine warfare vessels				
• Sonya class	Type 1265	1	48/450	2x30mm guns 2x25mm guns
• Yevgenia class		3	24.6/77	2x25mm guns 2x14.5mm MGs
Subtotal		4		
Total		**14**		

Patrol Craft

Type	Original class name	Quantity	Length (m.)/ displacement (t.)	Notes/ armament
• Zhuk class	Type 1400M	8	24/39	4x14.5mm MGs

Landing Craft

Type	Original class name	Quantity	Length (m.)/ displacement (t.)	Notes/ armament
• Polnochny B-class LCT	Type 771	3	75/760	180 troops or 350 tons 2x140mm MRLs 4x30mm guns

Auxiliary Vessels

Type	Original class name	Quantity	Length (m.)/ displacement (t.)	Notes/ armament
• al-Assad		1	105/3,500	Training ship
• Natya	Type 226	1	61/804	2xSA-N-5 (Grail) SAMs 4x30mm guns; formerly a minesweeper, now converted to oceanographic research

Auxiliary Vessels (continued)

Type	Original class name	Quantity	Length (m.)/ displacement (t.)	Notes/ armament
• T43 class		1	60/580	16 mines 4x37mm guns 4x14.5mm MGs
• Sekstan class		1	40.8/400	115 tons
• Poluchat		1	29.6/100	2x14.5mm MGs; formerly a torpedo recovery vessel
Total		5		

Coastal Defense

Type	Batteries	Missiles	Since	Notes
Missiles				
• SSC-1B Sepal	12			
• SSC-3	12		1966	Armed with SS-N-2C missiles
Guns				
• 130mm	36			

Naval Infrastructure

Naval bases: Latakia, Minat al-Baida, Tartus	3
Ship maintenance and repair facilities: Repairs at Latakia	1

18. TUNISIA

General Data

Official Name of the State: The Republic of Tunisia
Head of State: President Zayn al-Abedine Bin Ali
Prime Minister: Mohamed Ghannouchi
Minister of Defense: Mohamed Jegham
Secretary of State for Security: Mohamed Ali Ghenzoui
Commander of the Ground Forces: Lieutenant General Muhammad Hadi Bin Hassin
Commander of the Air Force: Major General Rida Hamuda Atar
Commander of the Navy: Commodore al-Shadli Sharif

Area: 164,206 sq. km.
Population: 9,500,000

Demography

Ethnic groups		
Arabs/Berbers	9,310,000	98.0%
Europeans	95,000	1.0%
Others	95,000	1.0%
Religious groups		
Sunni Muslims	9,310,000	98.0%
Christians	95,000	1.0%
Others	95,000	1.0%

Economic Data

		1994	1995	1996	1997	1998
GDP (current prices)	$ bn	15.62	18.03	19.59	18.90	19.94
GDP per capita	$	1,775	2,002	2,153	2,054	2,144
Real GDP growth	%	3.3	2.3	7.1	5.4	5.0
Consumer price index	%	4.7	6.3	3.8	3.7	3.2
External debt	$ bn	9.6	10.9	11.46	11.32	11.5
Balance of payments						
• Exports fob	$ bn	4.64	5.47	5.52	5.56	5.72
• Imports fob	$ bn	6.21	7.46	7.28	7.51	7.87
• Current account balance (including services and income)	$ bn	-0.53	-0.77	-0.48	-0.6	-0.67

Economic Data (continued)

		1994	1995	1996	1997	1998
Government expenditure						
• Total expenditure	$ bn	3.38	3.89	4.05	3.91	4.02
• Defense expenditure	$ bn	0.40	0.35	0.35	0.36	0.38
• Real change in defense expenditure	%	0.0	-12.5	0.0	2.8	5.5
• Defense expenditure/GDP	%	2.6	1.9	1.8	1.9	1.9
Population	m	8.8	9	9.1	9.2	9.5
Official exchange rate	TD: $1	1.012	0.946	0.973	1.106	1.187

Sources: EIU Quarterly Report, EIU Country Profile, IMF International Financial Statistical Yearbook, SIPRI Yearbook

Arms Procurement and Security Assistance Received

Country	Type	Details
Czech Republic	• Arms transfers	Trainer and transport a/c (1996)
US	• Assistance	$2.9 million grant 1999, $3.125 million in 2000

Foreign Military Cooperation

Type	Details
• Joint maneuvers	France, US, Spain (unconfirmed)

Defense Production

	M	P	A
Naval Craft			
• 20 meter patrol craft, with assistance from South Korea		√	

Note: M - manufacture (indigenously developed)
P - production under license
A - assembly

Weapons of Mass Destruction

NBC Capabilities

Nuclear capability
No known nuclear activity. Signatory to the NPT.

Chemical weapons and protective equipment
No known CW activities. Party to the CWC.

NBC Capabilities *(continued)*

Biological weapons
No known BW activities. Party to the BWC.

Armed Forces

Major Changes: No major change was recorded in the Tunisian order-of-battle in 1999.

Order-of-Battle

Year	1995	1996	1997	1999	2000
General data					
• Personnel (regular)	35,500	35,500	35,500	35,500	35,500
Ground Forces					
• Number of brigades	8	8	5	5	5
• Tanks	200	200	139 (144)*	139 (144)	139 (144)
• APCs/AFVs	316	316	316	316	316
• Artillery (including MRLs)	91	91	205 (215)*	205 (215)	205 (215)
Air Force					
• Combat aircraft	13	13	12	12	12
• Transport aircraft	11	11	10 (11)	10 (11)	10 (11)
• Helicopters	35	35	40	40	44
Air Defense Forces					
• Light SAM launchers	+	+	73*	73	83
Navy					
• Combat vessels	19	19	11*	11	9
• Patrol crafts	17	17	36*	36	37

Note: Beginning with 1997, data refers to quantities in active service. The number in parentheses refers to the total inventory.
* Due to change in estimate.

Personnel

	Regular	Total
Ground Forces	27,000	27,000
Air Force	4,000	4,000
Navy	4,500	4,500
Total	**35,500**	**35,500**
Paramilitary		
• Gendarmerie	2,000	2,000
• National Guard	7,000	7,000

Ground Forces

Formations

	Independent brigades/groups	Regiments in brigades
Mechanized/Infantry	3	1 armd., 2 mech., 1 aty. each
Commando/Paratroops	1	
Sahara brigade	1	
Total	5	

Tanks

Model	Quantity	In service	Since	Notes
MBTs				
Medium and low quality				
• M60 A1/A3	89	84	1984	
Light tanks				
• SK-105 (Kurassier)	55	55	1983	
Total	144	139		

APCs/AFVs

Model	Quantity	In service	Since	Notes
APCs				
• M113 A1/A2/ M-125/M-577	120	120	1980	35 M901 ITV listed under Anti-Tank Weapons
• Fiat Type 6614	110	110	1980	
Subtotal	230	230		
IFVs				
• Engesa EE-11	+	+	1982	Included with Engesa EE-9
Reconnaissance				
• Engesa EE-9	36	36	1982	
• Saladin	20	20	1962	
• AML-60/AML-90	30	30	1969	
Subtotal	86	86		
Total	316	316		

Artillery

Model	Quantity	In service	Since	Notes
Self-propelled guns and howitzers				
• 105mm M-108	10	0	1950	Possibly phased out

Artillery (continued)

Model	Quantity	In service	Since	Notes
Towed guns and howitzers				
• 155mm M198	48	48	1987	
• 155mm M114	18	18	1970	
• 105mm M101	45	45	1980	
Subtotal	111	111		
Mortars, under 160mm				
• 120mm Brandt	18	18	1987	
• 107mm	40	40	1980	
• 107mm SP	36	36	1987	
Subtotal	94	94		
Total	**215**	**205**		

Logistics and Engineering Equipment

- M-728 ECV (4)

Anti-Tank Weapons

Model	Quantity	In service	Since	Notes
Missiles				
• BGM-71A TOW	100	100	1982	
• M901 ITV SP	35	35	1987	Also listed under APCs
• MILAN	500	500	1982	
Total	**635**	**635**		
Guns				
• 106mm M40A1	70	70	1990	Recoilless rifle

Air Force

Order-of-Battle

Category	Quantity	In service	Notes
• Combat	12	12	
• Transport	11	10	
• Helicopters	44	44	

Combat Aircraft

Model	Quantity	In service	Since	Notes
Multi-role				
• F-5 E/F	12	12	1984	
Total	**12**	**12**		

Transport Aircraft

Model	Quantity	In service	Since	Notes
• C-130B Hercules	8	7	1985	
• L-410	3	3	1994	
Total	11	10		

Training and Liaison Aircraft

Model	Quantity	In service	Since	Notes
Jet trainers				
• Aermacchi MB-326 B/KT/LT	10	10	1974	
• L-59	12	12	1995	
Subtotal	22	22		
Piston/Turbo-prop				
• SF-260WT/C	18	18	1974	
• S 208A/M	2	2	1979	
• Piper Cub	10	10		
Subtotal	30	30		
Total	52	52		

Helicopters

Model	Quantity	In service	Since	Notes
Attack helicopters				
• SA-342 Gazelle	5	5	1991	
Medium transport				
• S-61R/HH-3E	4	4	1994	
• AB-205/Bell-205/UH-1H	19	19	1978	
• AS 365 Dauphin II	1	1	1986	
Subtotal	24	24		
Light transport				
• Alouette II/III	9	9	1964	
• AS-350 Ecureuil	6	6	1982	
Subtotal	15	15		
Total	44	44		

Advanced Armament

Air-to-air-missiles
AIM-9J Sidewinder

Air Force Infrastructure

Military airfields: 5
Bizerta (Sidi Ahmad), Gabes, Gafsa, Sfax, 1 additional

Air Defense Forces

Surface-to-Air Missiles

Model	Launchers	Since	Notes
Light missiles			
• MIM-72A Chaparral	35	1977	
• RBS-70	48	1982	
Total	83		
Shoulder-launched missiles			
• SA-7 (Grail)	+		

Other Air Defense Systems

Model	Quantity	In service	Since	Notes
Short-range guns				
• 40mm	12	12	1964	
• 37mm M-1939	15	15	1980	
• 20mm M-55	100	100	1990	
Total	127	127		
Radars				
• TRS-2100 Tiger S	6	6	1988	

Navy

Combat Vessels

Type	Original class name	Quantity	Length (m.)/ displacement (t.)	Notes/ armament
MFPBs				
• Combattante III		3	56/345	8xMM40 Exocet SSMs 1x76mm gun 2x40mm guns 4x30mm guns
• Bizerte class	P-48	3	48/250	8xSS-12M SSMs 4x37mm guns
Subtotal		6		
Gunboats				
• Modified Hinzhui class		3	35/120	4x25mm guns
Total		9		

Patrol Craft

Type	Original class name	Quantity	Length (m.)/ displacement (t.)	Notes/ armament
• Kondor I class		5	51.9/377	2x25mm guns formerly a minesweeper, now with Coast Guard
• Coastal patrol craft	Ch. Navals de l'Esterel	4	31.5/60	2x20mm guns
• Tazarka class	Vosper Thornycroft	2	31.4/125	With Coast Guard 2x20mm guns 2x14.5mm MGs
• Coastal patrol craft	Ch. Navals de l'Esterel	6	25/38	1x20mm gun
• Bremse class		5	22.6/42	2x14.5mm MGs with Coast Guard
• Coastal patrol craft	Socomena	11	20.5/32	1x12.7mm MG with Coast Guard
• Gabes class		4	12.9/18	2x12.7mm MGs with Coast Guard
Total		37		

Auxiliary Vessels

Type	Original class name	Quantity	Length (m.)/ displacement (t.)	Notes/ armament
• Robert Conrad class		1	63.7/1,370	Survey ship
• Wilkes	T-AGS-33	1	87/2,843	Survey ship
• White Sumac		2	40.5/485	
• Guesette class		2	11/8.5	Survey ship
Total		6		

Naval Infrastructure

Naval bases:	6

Bizerta, Kelibia, La Goulette, Sfax, Sousse, Tunis

Ship maintenance and repair facilities:	2

4 dry-docks and 1 slipway in Bizerta; 2 pontoons and 1 floating dock at Sfax. Capability for maintenance and repair of existing vessels.

19. TURKEY

General Data

Official Name of the State: Republic of Turkey
Head of State: President Ahmet Necdet Sezer
Prime Minister: Bülent Ecevit
Minister of National Defense: Sabahattin Çakmakoğlu
Chief of General Staff: General Huseyin Kivrikoğlu
Commander of the Ground Forces: General Hilmi Ozkok
Commander of the Air Force: General Ergin Celasin
Commander of the Navy: Admiral Ilhami Erdil

Area: 780,580 sq. km.
Population: 63,500,000

Demography

Ethnic group		
Turkish	50,800,000	80%
Kurdish	12,700,000	20%
Religious group		
Sunni Muslims	50,673,000	79.8%
Alevis (Shi'ite Muslims)	12,700,000	20.0%
Other (Christians and Jews)	127,000	0.2%

Economic Data

		1994	1995	1996	1997	1998
GDP (current prices)	$ bn	135.96	172.89	175.91	189.11	202.18
GDP per capita	$	2,277	2,853	2,860	3,026	3,184
Real GDP growth	%	-5.0	6.7	7.3	7.6	2.9
Consumer price index	%	105.2	89.1	80.4	85.7	84.6
External debt	$ bn	66.3	73.8	81.8	91.2	101.2
Balance of payments						
• Exports fob	$ bn	18.4	22.0	32.45	32.65	31.22
• Imports fob	$ bn	22.61	35.2	43.03	48.03	45.55
• Current account balance (including services and income)	$ bn	2.6	-2.34	-2.44	-2.64	1.87
Government expenditure						
• Total expenditure	$ bn	30.3	37.31	48.4	52.61	59.77
• Defense expenditure	$ bn	6.44	6.61	7.4	7.7	7.92
• Real change in defense expenditure	%	-2.0	2.6	11.9	4.0	2.8

Economic Data *(continued)*

		1994	1995	1996	1997	1998
• Defense expenditure/GDP	%	4.7	3.8	4.2	4.1	3.9
Population	m	59.7	60.6	61.5	62.5	63.5
Official exchange rate	TL: $1	29,609	45,845	81,405	151,865	260,724

Sources: EIU Quarterly Report, EIU Country Profile, IMF International Financial Statistical Yearbook, SIPRI Yearbook

Arms Procurement and Security Assistance Received

Country	Type	Details
France	• Arms transfers	Helicopters (1997), Circe minesweepers (1998)
	• Cooperation in arms production	Eryx ATGMs (1999)
Germany	• Arms transfers	Meko frigates (1996), Preveze submarine (1996), Frankenthal minehunters (1999)
Israel	• Arms transfers	Upgrade of F-4s and F-5s (1997), Popeye guided missiles (1998), radars (1998), missile warning systems (1999), LOROPS reconn. pods (2000)
Italy	• Arms transfers	AB-412 helicopters (1998), APCs (1995)
PRC	• Cooperation in assembly/R&D	WS-1 artillery rockets (1996)
Romania	• Arms transfers	Bombs (1998)
Russia	• Arms transfers	Mi-17 helicopters (1996)
Spain	• Cooperation in arms production	CN-235 a/c (1997)
UK	• Arms transfers	S-55 APCs (1995), satellite communications system (1999)
	• Cooperation in arms production	Upgrading Rapier SAMs (1999)
US	• Arms transfers	Knox frigates (1997), ATACM SSMs (1997), Blackhawk helicopters (1999), APCs (1997), Harpoon missiles (1998), AMRAAM missiles (2000), LANTIRN pods (1999), Maverick missiles (1999), TPQ-36 radars (1999), Hellfire II ATGMs (1999), CH-53E helicopters (1999), F-16 a/c (1999)
	• Assistance	$122 million US foreign aid terminated in FY99

Arms Sales and Security Assistance Extended

Country	Type	Details
Albania	• Assistance	$7 million for harbor reconstruction (1998)
	• Military training	Advisers, trainees in Turkey (1999)
Algeria	• Arms transfers	Armored Land Rovers (1996)
Azerbaijan	• Assistance	$3.45 million military aid (1999)
	• Military training	Trainees in Turkey (1999)
Bosnia	• Arms transfers	Artillery (1995)
	• Assistance	$10 million (1997)
	• Military training	Trainees in Turkey (1998)
Croatia	• Arms transfers	CN-235 aircraft (1998)
Egypt	• Arms transfers	F-16s (1996)
Georgia	• Arms transfers	Gunboats (1998)
	• Assistance	$9.3 million aid for military construction (1999)
	• Military training	Trainees in Turkey (1999)
Israel	• Cooperation in assembly/R&D	Joint development of ATBM project (1998)
	• Arms transfers	Armored Land Rovers (1998)
Jordan	• Arms transfers	CN-235 aircraft (on lease - 1998)
	• Military training	Flight simulation (1998), training of helicopter pilots (1999)
KDP (Kurds)	• Arms transfers	Tanks, small arms (1997)
	• Assistance	Financial aid
Malaysia	• Arms transfers	FNSS ACVs (1999)
Macedonia	• Arms transfers	F-5 aircraft (1998)
NATO	• Facilities	HQ LANDSOUTHEAST, HQ 6 ATAF
Pakistan	• Arms transfers	Armored Land Rovers (1996), tactical radio communications (1999)
Poland	• Military training	
UAE	• Arms transfers	FNSS AAPCs (1999)

Foreign Military Cooperation

Type	Details
• Cooperation in training	Albania, Azerbaijan, Israel (mutual use of airspace and training facilities), Jordan (mutual use of airspace and training facilities; joint training of infantry), Georgia, PRC
• Forces deployed abroad	Albania; Cyprus (30,000 troops); northern Iraq (1,000 troops); Adriatic Sea (Sharp Guard operation); Bosnia (UNPROFOR); Georgia (UNIMIG); Iraq/Kuwait (UNIKOM); Italy (F-16 in KFOR operation); Kosovo (150 troops in KFOR); Israel (TIPH)

Foreign Military Cooperation *(continued)*

Type	Details
• Foreign forces	Italy, UK, US (2,460 troops)
• Joint maneuvers	Albania (naval), Georgia (naval), Israel, Jordan, Pakistan, Poland, NATO member states, US
• Security agreements	France, Georgia, Latvia

Defense Production

	M	P	A
Army equipment			
• Land Rover APCs, FMC-Nurol AAPCs and AIFVs	√		
• Cobra reconnaissance AFVs	√		
• Chines WS-1 rockets	√	√	
• Toros 230mm and 260mm MRLs	√		
• 155mm SP guns	√		
• Upgrade of 105mm and 155mm SP guns	√		
• 120mm SP mortars	√		
• 107mm and 122mm MRLs	√		
• M48 tank guns	√		
• 35mm Oerlikon anti-aircraft guns		√	
• 25mm guns			√
• Trucks and wheeled tactical vehicles	√		
• Eryx ATGMs		√	
• Hellfire ATGM mounted on ACVs	√	√	
• Small arms	√		
• Explosives	√		
Air Force equipment			
• F-16s		√	
• UH-1H helicopters, under negotiations			√
• Cougar helicopters		√	
• SF-260D basic trainers		√	
• CN-235 light transport aircraft		√	
• Participation in production of MD Explorer helicopter		√	
• UAVs	√		
• Modification of S-2E maritime patrol aircraft	√		
• Bora, Atiligan and Zipkin air defense systems	√	√	
• Jet engines		√	
• Popeye air-to-air missiles		√	
• Paveway II laser-guided bombs		√	
• Rapier surface-to-air missiles		√	√
Naval equipment			
• Atilay class submarines			√
• Berk class missile frigates			√
• Yildiz class and Dogan class MFPBs			√

Defense Production *(continued)*

	M	P	A
• Minehunters		√	
• Yonca PBs	√		
• Osman Gazi landing craft			√
Electronics			
• Land-based and naval EW sets	√		
• Navigation systems	√		
• Ground surveillance radars	√		
• Tactical communication systems	√	√	
• Artillery fire-control systems	√		
• HF/SSB radios		√	
• ALQ-178 EW systems for F-4s and F-16s		√	
• TRS-22 air surveillance radars		√	
• C³I systems		√	
Optronics			
• Optical targeting devices/FLIR		√	
• Night-vision equipment	√	√	
• Laser range-finders	√		

Note: M - manufacture (indigenously developed)
P - production under license
A - assembly

Weapons of Mass Destruction

NBC Capabilities

Nuclear capability
TR-2 (5Mw) research reactor at Cekmerce and ITV-TRR (250kw) research reactor at Istanbul. Turkey intends to order a 1,000Mw power reactor. As a member of NATO, nuclear weapons were deployed in Turkey in the past, and might be deployed again. Party to the NPT. Safeguards agreement with the IAEA in force.

Chemical weapons and protective equipment
Personal protective suits, portable chemical detectors, Fox detection vehicles. Party to the CWC.

Biological weapons
No known BW activity. Party to the BWC.

Ballistic Missiles

Model	Launchers	Missiles	Since	Notes
• ATACMS	28	72	1997	Using MLRS launchers

Note: See also under Rockets.

Armed Forces

Major Changes: The Turkish Land Forces received all of its 1,700 indigenously produced armored combat vehicles of various types, but a decision on the acquisition of new MBTs has not yet been made. Delivery of an order of 80 F-16 has been concluded. The Air Force also received its first upgraded F-4 combat aircraft from Israel. Other deliveries include the first batch out of an order of 50 Blackhawk helicopters from the US, and the first helicopter of an order of 30 Cougar helicopters from France. The Navy received its fourth Preveze class submarine, its fourth Barbaros class frigate, as well as additional 2 Geziantep (ex – Oliver Hazard Perry) class frigates, and two Kiliç class MFPBs.

Order-of-Battle

Year	1995	1996	1997	1999	2000
General data					
• Personnel (regular)	507,800	515,800	639,000*	633,000	633,000
• SSM launchers			28	28	28
Ground Forces					
• Divisions	2 – 3	2 – 3	5	5	5
• Total number of brigades	60	63	67	67	67
• Tanks	4,300	4,280	4,115*	4,115	4,205
			(4,190)	(4,190)	(4,280)
• APCs/AFVs	4,711	4,046	4,743*	4,520	5,460
• Artillery (including MRLs)	4,341	4,128	4,113	4,312	~4,350
			(4,412)	(4,611)	~(4,650)
Air Force					
• Combat aircraft	374	434	461*	416	485
• Transport aircraft	70	62	87*	87	93
• Helicopters	305	304	381*	381	384
Air Defense Forces					
• Heavy SAM batteries	30	30	24*	24	24
• Light SAM launchers	24	24	86*	86	86
Navy					
• Combat vessels	61	63	75	51	64
• Patrol crafts	27	32	96*	88	108
• Submarines	16	16	17	16	15

Note: Beginning with 1997, data refers to quantities in active service. The number in parentheses refers to the total inventory.
* Due to change in estimate.

Personnel

	Regular	Reserves	Total
Ground Forces	525,000	259,000	784,000
Air Force	57,000	74,000	131,000
Navy	51,000	65,000	116,000
Total	633,000	398,000	1,031,000
Paramilitary			
• Coast Guard	2,200		2,200
• Gendarmerie/National Guard	180,000	50,000	230,000

Ground Forces

Formations

	Corps/armies	Divisions	Independent brigades/groups	Independent battalions	Brigades in divisions
All arms	4 armies 9 corps				
Armored			15		2 armd., 2 mech., 1 aty. each
Mechanized		2	18		1 armd., 2 mech., 1 aty. each
Infantry		3	9		4 inf., 1 aty. each
Commando			4		3 inf., 1 aty. each
Presidential Guard			1 (reg.)		
Border Defense			5 (reg.)	26	
Coastal Defense (reserve)			4		
Marines			1		3 inf., 1 aty. each
Total		5	57	26	

Tanks

Model	Quantity	In service	Since	Notes
MBTs				
Medium and low quality				
• Leopard A1/A3	397	397	1982	
• M60 A1/A3	932	932	1992	

Tanks *(continued)*

Model	Quantity	In service	Since	Notes
• M48T	2,876	2,876	1984	Possibly some in storage
• M47	75	0	1970	
Total	4,280	4,205		
Future procurement				
• Leopard 1	170			Upgrading program
• M60 A1	170			Upgrading program under negotiation

APCs/AFVs

Model	Quantity	In service	Since	Notes
APCs				
• FNSS AAPC	830	830	1997	
• M113 A1/A2	2,815	2,815	1975	
• BTR-80	240	240	1993	
• BTR-60	340	340	1991	
• S-55	40	40	1995	
Subtotal	4,265	4,265		
IFVs				
• Condor	25	25	1988	
• UR-416	35	35	1984	
• FNSS AIFV	868	868	1997	Including 170 AMVs and 48 ATVs
Subtotal	928	928		
Reconnaissance				
• Cobra	~5	~5	1999	
• Akrep	260	260	1994	
Subtotal	~265	~265		
Total	~5,460	~5,460		
Future procurement				
• AIFV	665			Under negotiation

Artillery

Model	Quantity	In service	Since	Notes
Self-propelled guns and howitzers				
• 203mm M110	219	219	1981	
• 203mm M55	9	9	1978	
• 175mm M107	36	36	1976	
• 155mm M44T	222	222	1992	

Artillery (continued)

Model	Quantity	In service	Since	Notes
• 155mm M52T	365	365	1995	
• 105mm M108	26	26	1982	
Subtotal	877	877		
Towed guns and howitzers				
• 203mm M115	162	162	1983	
• 155mm M114	517	517	1979	
• 155mm M59	171	0	1975	
• 150mm Skoda	128	0	1976	
• 105mm M101/M102	640	640	1974	
Subtotal	1,618	1,319		
Mortars, under 160mm				
• 120mm	578	578	1981	
• 107mm M30	1,265	1,265	1974	
• 107mm M106 SP	+	+	1984	
• FNSS AMV	170	170	1997	
Subtotal	~2,050	~2,050		
Rockets				
• WS-1	~30	~30	1997	
MRLs				
• 227mm MLRS	28	28	1988	
• 122mm T-122	+	+		
• 107mm	48	48	1975	
Subtotal	~80	~80		
Total	~4,650	~4,350		
Future procurement				
• Toros 230/260mm				
• 155mm SP2000	400			Under development
• 155mm towed				Under development

Ground Radars

Model	Quantity	In service	Since	Notes
Artillery/mortar locating radars				
• AN/TPQ-37	4	4	1997	
• AN/TPQ-36	7	7	1988	
• Blindfire	13	13	1996	
• ARS-2000	+	+	1996	

Logistics and Engineering Equipment

Mine laying and clearing, bar mine-clearing system, crossing equipment, M48 ECVs (20)

Anti-Tank Missiles

Model	Launchers	Missiles	Since	Notes
• Cobra	186	+	1977	
• MILAN	392	+	1984	
• TOW SP	365	+	1980	48 of which are on FNSS ATV
Total	943	+		
Future procurement				
• Eryx		10,000		Delivery until 2009

Anti-Tank Guns

Model	Quantity	In service	Since	Notes
Guns				
• 106mm M40 A1	2,330	2,330	1975	
• 75mm	620	620	1975	
• 57mm M-18	925	925	1976	
Total	3,875	3,875		

Air Force

Order-of-Battle

Category	Quantity	In service	Notes
• Combat	~485	~485	
• Transport	93	93	
• Helicopters	385	385	

Combat Aircraft

Model	Quantity	In service	Since	Notes
Advanced multi-role				
• F-16C/D	240	240	1987	
Multi-role				
• Phantom 2000	~10	~10	1999	Out of total of 54 on order; 1 plane per month
• F-4E	135	135	1973	
Obsolete				
• F-5A/B	106	106	1965	
Total	~485	~485		
Future procurement				
• F-15E				Under negotiation

Combat Aircraft (continued)

Model	Quantity	In service	Since	Notes
• F-16 C/D	32			Total order
• F-5	48			To be upgraded
• F-4E	54			Being upgraded to Phantom 2000 standard

Transport Aircraft

Model	Quantity	In service	Since	Notes
• C-160D	19	19	1971	
• KC-135R	9	9	1995	Tanker
• C-130E	6	6	1964	
• C-130B	7	7	1991	To be converted to EW role
• Citation (VIP)	2	2	1985	
• CN-235	50	50	1991	2 employed in EW role
Total	93	93		
Future procurement				
• CN-235	12			Being delivered; 9 for maritime patrol

Training and Liaison Aircraft

Model	Quantity	In service	Since	Notes
Jet trainers				
• T-33	34	34	1975	
• T-38 (F-5)	70	70	1965	
• Cessna 318 (T-37)	60	60	1960	
Subtotal	164	164		
Piston/Turbo-prop				
• SF-260D	39	39	1990	
• Cessna 172 (T-41)	51	51	1972	26 with Army Aviation
Subtotal	90	90		
Total	254	254		

Helicopters

Model	Quantity	In service	Since	Notes
Attack helicopters				
• AH-1W/P	37	37	1990	With Army Aviation
Medium transport				
• AB-212	15	15	1985	13 with the Navy, in ASW role and 3 with Army Aviation

Helicopters (continued)

Model	Quantity	In service	Since	Notes
• AS-532 Cougar	18	18	1995	With Army Aviation
• Mi-17	19	19	1995	With gendarmerie
• UH-60/S-70 Blackhawk	56	56	1992	35 with gendarmerie
• UH-1H/AB-204/ AB-205	188	188	1966	160 in Army Aviation and 3 in Navy
Subtotal	296	296		
Light transport				
• AB 206	20	20	1968	3 with Coast Guard
• H-300C	28	28	1982	With Army Aviation
• OH-58B	3	3	1994	With Army Aviation
Subtotal	51	51		
Total	**384**	**384**		
Future procurement				
• AB-412	9		1999	Delivery in 2001
• CH-53	8		1999	
• S-70 Blackhawk	50		1998	Total order, 20 already delivered
• S-70B Seahawk	30		1998	With Navy
• Cougar AS- 532	30		1997	Delivery up to 2005; additional 20 under negotiation for police

Miscellaneous Aircraft

Model	Quantity	In service	Since	Notes
Reconnaissance				
• RF-4E	39	39	1977	
• RF-5	11	11	1965	
ELINT/EW				
• CN 235	2	2	1991	Also listed under Transport Aircraft
Maritime surveillance				
• Maule MX 7	1	1	1993	With Coast Guard
• S-2A/E Tracker	9	0	1970	
UAVs and mini-UAVs				
• CL-89	+	+		
• Gnat 750	6	6		

Miscellaneous Aircraft (continued)

Model	Quantity	In service	Since	Notes
Future procurement				
• AEW aircraft	4 – 7			Tender has not been decided
• UAVs	19			Tender has not been decided
• CN-235	9			Maritime surveillance, also listed under Transport Aircraft

Advanced Armament

Air-to-air-missiles
AIM-120 AMRAAM (138), AIM-9E/F Sidewinder (210), AIM-9J/M/S/P Sidewinder (1,460), AIM-7E Sparrow (690)

Air-to-ground-missiles
AGM-88 HARM (100), AGM-65 A/G Maverick (300), AGM-142 Popeye (50), Sea Skua (36), BLU-107 Durandel (523)

Avionics
LANTIRN   24

Future procurement
LANTIRN (20), Hellfire II (84), AGM-65 G/F Maverick, Popeye II (Light), LOROPS

Note: Number in parentheses refers to the quantity of missiles purchased.

Air Force Infrastructure

Military airfields: 23
Adnan-menderes, Afyon, Akhisar, Akinci, Ankara-güvercinlik, Balikesit, Bandirma, Dalaman, Diyarbakir, Elazig, Erhac, Erkilet, Erzincan, Eskisehir, Istanbul-Sarigazi, Izmir-Kaklic, Kayseri, Konya, Malatya, Merzifon, Murted, Yalova, Yesilkoy

Air Defense Forces

Surface-to-Air Missiles

Model	Batteries	Launchers	Since	Notes
Heavy missiles				
• Nike Hercules	24		1970	8 squadrons, 24 batteries
Light missiles				
• Rapier B1X		78	1999	Upgraded
• Rapier		8	1984	
Total		86		
Shoulder-launched missiles				
• Stinger		108	1991	
• Red eye		790	1986	
Total		898		
Future procurement				
• Armored Stinger SP		300		Under development

Other Air Defense Systems

Model	Quantity	In service	Since	Notes
Short-range guns				
• 40mm L60/70	800	800	1970	
• 40mm T1	40	40		
• 40mm M42 A1 SP	260	260	1976	
• 35mm GDF-003	120	120	1984	
• 20mm GAI-DO1	440	440	1975	
Total	1,660	1,660		
Radars				
• AN/FPS 117	1	1	1993	
• HR-3000 (Hadr)	3	3	1990	
• Stentor	5	5	1988	
• TRS-2100 (Tiger)	2	2	1988	
• MPQ-64 Sentinel	4	4	1998	
• TRS-22XX	14	14	1993	
• TRS-2000	4	4	1999	
• AN/TPS-59	+	+		
Future procurement				
• MPQ-64 Sentinel	10	10		
• P-STAR				

Navy

Submarines

Type	Original class name	Quantity	Length (m.)/ displacement (t.)	Notes/ armament
• Atilay	Type 1200	6	61.2/1,185	8x533mm torpedoes
• Burakreist class	Guppy II A	3	93.2/2,440	10x533mm torpedoes 40 mines
• Hizzirreis	Tang	2	87.4/2,700	8x533mm torpedoes mines
• Preveze	Type 1400	4	62/1,586	2xSub Harpoon SSMs 8x533mm torpedoes mines
Total		15		
Future procurement				
• Gur class submarines		4		Delivery 2003-2006

Combat Vessels

Type	Original class name	Quantity	Length (m.)/ displacement (t.)	Notes/ armament
Destroyers				
• Yücetepe	Gearing class	1	119/2,425	Helicopter pad 1xHarpoon SSM ASROC Mk112 8 torpedo launcher 6x324mm torpedoes 4x127mm guns 2x35mm guns
Frigates				
• Barbaros	MEKO 200 track II-A/B	4	116.7/3,350	AB 212 ASW helicopter 8xHarpoon SSMs 2xSeasparrow 8 SAMs 6x324mm torpedoes 1x127mm gun 3xOerlicon 25mm AD guns

Combat Vessels *(continued)*

Type	Original class name	Quantity	Length (m.)/ displacement (t.)	Notes/ armament
• Berk		2	95/1,450	Helicopter pad 2xHedgehog Mk 11 24 ASW rocket launchers 6x324mm torpedoes 4x76mm guns
• Gaziantep	Oliver Perry class	5	135.6/3,638	2xAB-212 ASW helicopters 4xHarpoon SSMs 36xStandard SAMs 6x324mm torpedoes 1x76mm gun 1x20mm Phalanx AD gun
• Tepe	Knox class	8	134/3,011	1xAB-212 ASW helicopter 8xHarpoon SSMs ASROC Mk112 8 torpedo launcher 4x324mm torpedoes 1x20mm Vulcan Phalanx AD gun 1x127mm gun
• Yavuz	MEKO 200	4	115.5/2,414	1xAB-212 ASW helicopter 8xHarpoon SSMs 6x324mm Trpedoes 8xSeasparrow SAMs 1x127mm gun 3xOerlicon 25mm AD guns
Subtotal		23		
MFPBs				
• Doğan clas	Lürssen	8	58.1/436	8xHarpoon SSMs 1x76mm gun 2x35mm guns
• Kiliç class	Lürssen	3	57.8/433	8xHarpoon SSMs 1x76mm gun 1x40mm gun

Combat Vessels *(continued)*

Type	Original class name	Quantity	Length (m.)/ displacement (t.)	Notes/ armament
• Yildiz class		2	57.8/433	8xHarpoon SSMs 1x76mm gun 2x35mm guns
• Kartal	Jaguar class	8	42.5/160	2 – 4 Penguin SSMs 2x533mm torpedoes 2x40mm guns 4 mines
Subtotal		21		
Mine warfare vessels				
• Nusret		1	77/1,880	4x76mm guns 400 mines
• Mehmecik	YMP class	1	39.6/540	
• Adjutant	MSC 268/294	9	43/320	Sonar search 2x20mm guns
• Karamürsel	Vegasack class	3	47.3/362	Active mine detectors 2x20mm guns
• Edincik	Circé class	5	50.9/495	Robot seeker/ destroyer 1x20mm gun
Subtotal		19		
Total		**64**		
Future procurement				
• Oliver Hazard Perry		1		Awaiting US Congressional approval
• Frankenthal minehunters		6		Delivery in 2007

Patrol Craft

Type	Original class name	Quantity	Length (m.)/ displacement (t.)	Notes/ armament
• Girne class		1	58.1/341	2xMousetrap Mk 20 4 ASW rocket launchers 2x40mm guns 2x20mm guns
• Bora class	Ashville	1	50.1/225	1x76mm gun 1x40mm gun 4x12.7mm MGs

Patrol Craft *(continued)*

Type	Original class name	Quantity	Length (m.)/ displacement (t.)	Notes/ armament
• Hisar class	PC - 1638	6	53/325	1xHedgehog Mk 15 24xASW rocket launchers 1x40mm gun 4x20mm guns
• Trabzon class		3	50/370	1x40mm gun 2x12.7mm MGs
• Turk class		11	40.2/170	1xMousetrap Mk 20 4xASW rocket launchers 2x40mm guns 1x20mm gun 2x12.7mm MGs
• PGM -71 class		4	30.8/130	2xMousetrap Mk 22 8xASW rocket launchers 1x40mm gun 4x20mm guns
• Coast Guard type		4	25.3/63	2xMousetrap Mk 20 8xASW rocket launchers 2x20mm guns
• Large patrol craft	Taskiçak	12	40.7/195	1x40mm gun 2x12.7mm MGs
• Large patrol craft	Gölcük	14	40.2/180	1x40mm gun 2x12.7mm MGs
• SAR 33 Type		10	34.6/180	1x40mm gun 2x12.7mm MGs
• SAR 35 Type		4	36.6/210	1x40mm gun 2x12.7mm MGs
• KW 15 class		8	28.9/70	1x40mm gun 2x20mm guns
• Kaan	Yonca	14	15.1/19	2x12.7mm MGs
• Coastal patrol craft	US Mk 5	1	16.8/45	1x12.7mm MG
• Coastal patrol craft		12	14.6/29	1x25mm or 1x12.7mm MG
• Inshore patrol craft		1	11.6/10	1x12.7mm MG
• Harbor patrol craft		2	17/15	
Total		**108**		

Patrol Craft *(continued)*

Type	Original class name	Quantity	Length (m.)/ displacement (t.)	Notes/ armament
Future procurement				
• Seaguard		10	29.6/90	Delivery to commence in 2000

Landing Craft

Type	Original class name	Quantity	Length (m.)/ displacement (t.)	Notes/ armament
• Osman Gazi		1	105/3,773	900 troops, 15 tanks 4 LCVPs 3x40mm guns 2x35mm guns
• Sarucabey	LST	2	92/2,600	600 troops, 11 tanks 2 LCVPs 2x40mm guns 4x20mm guns
• Çakabey	LSM	1	77.3/1,600	400 troops, 9 tanks 2 LCVPs 4x40mm guns 4x20mm guns
• Ertugan LST	Terrebonne Parish class	2	117.1/5,800	395 troops, 2,200 tons 4 LCVPs 6x76mm guns
• LCM - 8		20	22/113	160 troops or 60 tons 2x12.7mm MGs
• LCT		28	59.6/600	100 troops, 5 tanks 2x20mm guns 2x12.7mm MGs
• Edic Type	LCT	6	57/580	100 troops, 5 tanks 2x20mm guns 2x12.7mm MGs
• Bayraktar	LST	2	100/1,653	6x40mm guns
Total		**62**		

Auxiliary Vessels

Type	Original class name	Quantity	Length (m.)/ displacement (t.)	Notes/ armament
• Tankers		4	1,440 – 19,000	2x20mm guns
• Water tankers		14	300 – 1,200 tons	
• Salvage/Rescue		3	1,200 – 1,600 tons	20mm guns 76mm guns 40mm guns
• Survey		3	680 tons	2x20mm guns
• Intelligence vessel		1	1,497 tons	
• Training ships		2	2,370 tons	2x100mm guns 4x40mm guns
• Transport		40	Various sizes	
• Tugs		12	750, 1,235 tons	
• Floating docks		10		400 – 16,000 tons. Lift
• Boom defense		2	560 – 780 tons	3 – 4 20mm, 76mm or 40mm guns

Naval Infrastructure

Naval bases: 18
Aksaz, Aksaz Bay, Ankara (HQ), Antalya, Bartin, Çanakkale, Erdek, Ereğli, Foça, Gölcük, Iskanderun, Istanbul, Izmir, Karamürsel (training), Marmaris, Mersin, Samsun, Trabzon

Naval aviation bases: 4
Antalia, Cigli, Topel, Trabzon

Ship maintenance and repair facilities: 3
Gölcük, Taşkizak, Pendik

Major Non-Governmental Paramilitary Forces

Personnel

	Active
• PKK	8,000

Equipment

Organization	Category	System	Quantity	Notes
PKK	Air defense	• SA - 7 (Garil)	+	

20. UNITED ARAB EMIRATES (UAE)

General Data

Official Name of the State: United Arab Emirates
Head of State: Shaykh Zayid ibn Sultan al-Nuhayan, Emir of Abu Dhabi
Prime Minister: Shaykh Maktum ibn Rashid al-Maktum, Emir of Dubai
Minister of Defense: Shaykh Muhammad ibn Rashid al-Maktum
Chief of General Staff: HRH Lieutenant General Muhammad ibn Zayid al-Nuhayan
Commander of the Air Force and Air Defense Forces: Brigadier General Atik Gum'a al-Hamli
Commander of the Navy: Captain Muhammad al-Muhairi

Area: 82,900 sq. km. (estimate)
Population: 2,760,000 (estimate)

Note: The UAE consists of seven principalities: Abu Dhabi, Dubai, Ras al-Khaima, Sharja, Umm al-Qaiwain, Fujaira, and Ajman.

Demography

Ethnic and national groups		
South Asians	1,380,000	50%
Other Arabs and Iranians	635,000	23%
Emiri	524,000	19%
Westerners and East Asians	221,000	8%
Religious groups		
Sunni Muslims	2,208,000	80%
Shi'ite Muslims	442,000	16%
Others	110,000	4%

Economic Data

		1994	1995	1996	1997	1998
GDP (current price)	$ bn	36.7	42.8	47.9	49.4	46.5
GDP per capita	$	16,457	18,528	19,631	18,854	16,847
Real GDP growth (at constant 1990 prices)	%	5.0	8.1	10.1	2.1	1.2
Consumer price index	%	5.0	4.4	3.2	3.3	3.0
External debt	$ bn	12.22	9.50	10.88	12.33	15.54

Economic Data (continued)

		1994	1995	1996	1997	1998
Balance of payments						
• Exports fob	$ bn	27.72	29.92	34.14	34.01	30.35
• Imports cif	$ bn	23.26	24.90	27.57	28.75	26.11
• Current account balance (including services and income)	$ bn	2.81	4.06	5.38	4.17	2.87
Government expenditure						
• Consolidated government expenditure	$ bn	15.784	17.282	20.879	17.540	19.501
• Defense expenditure	$ bn	2.0	1.950	2.015	NA	NA
• Real change in defense expenditure	%	-5.25	-2.5	3.33	NA	NA
• Defense expenditure/GDP	%	5.44	4.55	4.20	NA	NA
Population	m	2.23	2.31	2.44	2.62	2.76
Official exchange rate	Dh : $1	3.671	3.671	3.671	3.671	3.673

Sources: EIU Quarterly Report, EIU Country Profile, IMF International Financial Statistical Yearbook, SIPRI Yearbook
Note: Beginning in 2000, the consolidated government expenditure figures are being used.

Arms Procurement and Security Assistance Received

Country	Type	Details
France	• Arms transfers	Mirage 2000-9 combat a/c (1999), Panther helicopters (1999), AS-350B light helicopters (2000), Leclerc tanks (1998), CN-235 maritime patrol a/c (with Indonesia) (1998), radio sets (1996), thermal imaging night vision systems (1996), shoulder-launched SAMs (1997), ARVs (1997), torpedoes (1997), anti-ship missiles (1999), C³I systems (1998), upgrading naval navigation systems (1999)
	• Military training	Trainees abroad (1999)
Germany	• Arms transfers	Alpha jet/Mako trainer a/c (1999)
	• Military training	Trainees abroad (1997)
Indonesia	• Maintenance of equipment	CN-235 maritime patrol a/c (with France) (1998)

Arms Procurement and Security Assistance Received *(continued)*

Country	Type	Details
Netherlands	• Arms transfers	Kortenaer frigates (1997), artillery surveillance radar (1997), CIWS (1997), SP howitzers (1998)
	• Military training	Trainees abroad (1998)
Norway	• Arms transfers	Navy simulator (1997)
Russia	• Arms transfers	BMP-3 IFVs (1998), Smerch long-range MRLs (1998)
South Africa	• Arms transfers	Artillery (1995)
Sweden	• Arms transfers	Early warning system (1999)
Switzerland	• Arms transfers	Training simulators for BMP-3 IFVs (1999)
Turkey	• Arms transfers	Mobile optronic and radar surveillance system (1999), armored combat vehicles (1999)
UK	• Arms transfers	Sonar (1997), Black Shahin (1999)
US	• Military training	Foreign advisers/instructors/serving personnel (some civilians); trainees abroad
	• Arms transfers	F-16 Block 60 a/c (2000), AMRAAM (2000), missile frigates (1995), early warning system (1999), LANTIRN (1995), Sea Sparrow naval SAMs (1999)

Arms Sales and Security Assistance Extended

Country	Type	Details
Bosnia	• Arms transfers	AMX-30 MBTs (1997)
Netherlands	• Arms transfers	Artillery (1997)
UK	• Facilities	Logistical facilities
Unknown customer	• Arms transfers	Nibbio UAVs (1999)
US	• Facilities	Storage facilities for naval equipment at Jebel Ali and Fujaira, and pre-positioning of equipment for an armored brigade under negotiation

Foreign Military Cooperation

Type	Details
• Forces deployed abroad	In Saudi Arabia (part of GCC "Peninsula Shield" rapid deployment force); 1,200 soldiers with NATOs KFOR peacekeeping force in Kosovo (1999)
• Joint maneuvers	France, GCC countries, India (1996), US
• Security agreement	France, Germany, Slovak Republic

Defense Production

	M	P	A
Airforce equipment			
• Falco target drone	√		
• Nibbio mini-UAV	√		
Naval equipment			
• Construction of patrol boats at Ajman (with British cooperation)		√	
• Upgrading of TNC-45 Patrol Boats	√		

Note: M - manufacture (indigenously developed)
P - production under license
A - assembly

Weapons of Mass Destruction

NBC Capabilities

Nuclear capability
No known nuclear activity. Signatory to the NPT.

Chemical weapons and protective equipment
No known CW activities. Signed but not ratified the CWC. Personal protective equipment; unit decontamination equipment

Biological weapons
No known BW activities. Signed but not ratified the BWC.

Ballistic Missiles

Model	Launchers	Missiles	Since	Notes
• Scud B	6	+	1991	Owned by Dubai; unconfirmed

Armed Forces

Major Changes: The Emiri army continued the process of deploying its newly acquired Leclerc MBTs. The UAE decided to acquire 80 F-16 block 60 combat aircraft.

Order-of-Battle

Year	1995	1996	1997	1999	2000
General data					
• Personnel (regular)	46,500	46,500	46,500	46,500	46,500
• SSMs launchers	6	6	6	6	6

Order-of-Battle (continued)

Year	1995	1996	1997	1999	2000
Ground forces					
• Number of brigades	6	6	9*	8	8
• Tanks	212	216	~366*	~330	~430
			(~430)	(~430)	(~465)
• APCs/AFVs	1,100	1,100	~960	~960	~1,240
			(~1,120)	(~1,120)	(~1,400)
• Artillery (including MRLs)	264	264	411 (434)*	411 (434)	399 (422)
Air Force					
• Combat aircraft	65	66	54 (66)	54 (66)	54 (66)
• Transport aircraft	36	36	31 (34)	31 (34)	31 (34)
• Helicopters	85	85	93 (95)*	93 (95)	100 (102)
Air Defense Forces					
• Heavy SAM batteries	~7	~7	~7	~7	~7
• Medium SAM batteries	3	3	6*	6	6
• Light SAM launchers	+	+	113*	113	~115
Navy					
• Combat vessels	10	10	12	12	12
• Patrol craft	50	121	119	105	110

Note: Beginning with data for 1997, we refer to quantities in active service. The number in parentheses refers to the total inventory.
*Due to changes in estimate.

Personnel

	Regular	Reserves	Total
Ground Forces	40,000		40,000
Air Force	4,500		4,500
Navy	2,000		2,000
Total	**46,500**		**46,500**
Paramilitary			
• Coast Guard			+
• Frontier Corps			+

Ground Forces

Formations

	Independent brigades/groups
Armored	3
Mechanized	4
	(including two brigades under Dubai National Command)
Royal Guard	1
Artillery	1
Total	9

Tanks

Model	Quantity	In service	Since	Notes
MBTs				
High quality				
• Leclerc	~250	~250	1995	Estimated number supplied, out of total number of 436
Medium and low quality				
• AMX-30	100	64	1981	
• OF-40 Lion Mk 2	36	36	1982	
Subtotal	136	100		
Light tanks				
• Scorpion	80	80	1975	
Total	~470	~430		
Future procurement				
• Leclerc tanks	436			390 MBTs, 46 recovery vehicles and 2 training vehicles

APCs/AFVs

Model	Quantity	In service	Since	Notes
APCs				
• FNSS-AAPC	61	61	1999	Also listed under Logistics and Engineering Equipment
• AMX-VCI	10	10	1978	
• Engesa EE-11 Urutu	30	30	1985	
• Saracen	30	0	1977	
• VAB	20	20	1980	
• VCR	+	+		

APCs/AFVs (continued)

Model	Quantity	In service	Since	Notes
• M-3 (Panhard)	300	300	1977	
• Fahd	100	100		
• AT-105 Saxon	20	20		Possibly with police
Subtotal	~570	~540		
IFVs				
• AMX-10P	20	20	1980	
• BMP-3	400	400	1980	
Subtotal	420	420		
Reconnaissance				
• AML-60/AML-90	105	105	1980	
• Engessa EE-9 Cascavel	100	100		
• Ferret	60	0		
• FNSS-AAOV	75	75	1999	Being delivered
• Saladin	70	0		
• VBC-90	+	+		
Subtotal	~410	~280		
Total	**~1,400**	**~1,250**		
Future procurement				
• FNSS-AAPC	136			AAPC/AAOV being delivered (2000)

Artillery

Model	Quantity	In service	Since	Notes
Self-propelled guns and howitzers				
• 155mm Mk F3 (AMX-13)	20	20	1976	
• 155mm G-6	78	78		
• 155mm M109A3	85	85	1995	
Subtotal	183	183		
Towed guns and howitzers				
• 130mm Type 59	30	30		
• 105mm L-118 light gun	81	81		
• 105mm M102	50	50		
• 105mm M56 Pack	18	18		
Subtotal	179	179		
Mortars, under 160mm				
• 120mm	12	12		
MRLs				
• 122mm Firos-25/30	48	25		
Total	**422**	**399**		
Future procurement				
• 227mm MLRS				

Logistics and Engineering Equipment

Matenin automatic mine layers, Mk 3 (D) flail ; Leclerc ARVs (46), FNSS-AAPC-ENGs (53), FNSS-ARVs (8)

Anti-Tank Missiles

Model	Launchers	Missiles	Since	Notes
• BGM-71B TOW	24	+	1983	
• HOT	50	+		
• MILAN	230	+		
Total	~300	+		

Anti-Tank Guns

Model	Quantity	In service	Since	Notes
• 120mm BAT L-4 recoilless rifle	*	*		
• 84mm Carl Gustav M-2 light recoilless rifle	250	250		

Air Force

Order-of-Battle

Category	Quantity	In service	Notes
• Combat	66	54	
• Transport	34	31	
• Helicopters	102	100	

Combat Aircraft

Model	Quantity	In service	Since	Notes
Advanced multi-role				
• Mirage 2000-5	36	36	1989	8 are reconn.
Obsolete				
• Mirage V-AD/RAD/DAD	18	18	1974	
• Mirage III	12	0		
Subtotal	30	18		
Total	66	54		
Future procurement				
• Mirage 2000-9	30			
• F-16 Block 60	80			

Transport Aircraft

Model	Quantity	In service	Since	Notes
• BAe 125	1	1		
• Boeing 747	3	3	1985	
• Boeing 737	1	1	1976	
• Boeing 707	2	2	1976	
• Britten-Norman BN-2 Islander	1	1	1983	
• C-130H Hercules/L-100-30	6	6	1975/1981	
• CASA C-212	4	4	1982	Employed in EW role
• CN-235	7	7	1993	Some in maritime patrol role
• DHC-4 Caribou	3	0		Possibly phased out
• G-222	1	1		Number unconfirmed
• IL-76	4	4	1994	On lease
• Mystère-Falcon 20	1	1		
Total	34	31		

Training and Liaison Aircraft

Model	Quantity	In service	Since	Notes
Jet trainers				
• Aermacchi MB-326 KD/LD	8	8	1974	
• Aermacchi MB-339	5	5	1984	
• Hawk Mk 102	26	26	1993	
• Hawk Mk 61/63	22	22	1983/1984	
Subtotal	61	61		
Piston/Turbo-prop				
• Cessna 182 Skylane	1	1		
• Pilatus PC-7	23	23	1982	
• G-115T (Grob)	12	12	1997	
• SF-260 WD	5	5	1983	
Subtotal	41	41		
Total	102	102		
Future procurement				
• G-115T (Grob)				Option for additional 12
• Alpha jet	30			

Helicopters

Model	Quantity	In service	Since	Notes
Attack				
• AH-64A Apache	20	20	1993	
• SA-342K Gazelle	12	10	1980	
• Alouette III	7	7		
Subtotal	39	37		
Medium transport				
• AB-205/Bell 205	8	8	1969	
• AB-212	3	3	1977	
• AB-214	4	4	1981	
• AB-412	5	5	1994	Possibly with police
• SA-330 Puma/ possibly IAR-330	11	11	1972	
Subtotal	31	31		
Light transport				
• A-109	3	3	1995	Possibly with police
• AB-206 JetRanger/ Bell 206L	10	10	1984	
• BO-105	5	5	1992	Employed in liaison role; number unconfirmed
Subtotal	18	18		
Naval combat				
• AS-332/532 Super Puma/Cougar	7	7	1982	
• AS-565 Panther	7	7	1998	
Subtotal	14	14		
Total	**102**	**100**		
Future procurement				
• AS-350B	14			

Miscellaneous Aircraft

Model	Quantity	In service	Since	Notes
AEW aircraft				
• C-130 EW				Also listed under Transport Aircraft
• CASA C-212				Also listed under Transport Aircraft
Maritime surveillance aircraft				
• CN-235	5	5		Also listed under Transport Aircraft

Miscellaneous Aircraft *(continued)*

Model	Quantity	In service	Since	Notes
Target drones				
• TTL BTT-3 Banshee	+	+		
UAVs and mini-UAVs				
• Beech MQM-107A	20	20		
• Nibbio	+	+		
Future procurement				
• SAT 800 Falco				

Advanced Armament

Air-to-air-missiles
AIM-9L Sidewinder, R-550 Magic (108)

Air-to-ground-missiles
AS-11, AS-12, AS-30L, AM-39 Exocet, al-Hakim (PGM-1/2/3) (1,750)

Bombs
BAP-100 anti-runway

Future procurement
AS-15TT (56); AM-39, AIM-120 (491), Black Shahin, Harpoon, ASRAAM, Pave Way, AIM-9M1/2 (267), AGM-88 HARM (163), AGM-84 (52), AGM-65D/G (1,163), Mica EM, Mica IR

Note: Numbers in parentheses refer to number of units purchased.

Air Force Infrastructure

Aircraft shelters:
For combat aircraft at Abu Dhabi and Jabil (Jebel) Ali AF bases

Military airfields: 7
Abu Dhabi (international), al-Dhafra (Sharja), Bateen (Abu Dhabi), Dubai (international), Fujaira, Sharja, Mindhat

Air Defense Forces

Surface-to-Air Missiles

Model	Batteries	Launchers	Since	Notes
Heavy missiles				
• MIM-23B improved HAWK	~7		1989	
Medium missiles				
• Crotale	3		1978	
• Rapier	3		1976	
Total	6			

Surface-to-Air Missiles (continued)

Model	Batteries	Launchers	Since	Notes
Light missiles				
• RBS-70		13	1980	
• Mistral		100	1993	
• Javelin		+		
• Tigercat		+		Probably phased out
Total		~115		
Shoulder-launched missiles				
• Blowpipe		~20	1992	Probably phased out
• FIM-92A Stinger		+		
• SA-7 (Grail)		+		
• SA-14 (Gremlin)		+		
• SA-16 (Gimlet)		10	1992	
Total		~30		

Other Air Defense Systems

Model	Quantity	In service	Since	Notes
Air defense systems (missiles, radars, and guns)				
• Skyguard AD system	7	7		
Short-range guns				
• 2x30mm M-3 SP	+	+		
• 2x20mm GCF-BM2 SP	+	+	1986	
Radars				
• AN/TPS-70	3	3		
• Watchman	+	+		

Navy

Combat Vessels

Type	Original class name	Quantity	Length (m.)/ displacement (t.)	Notes/ armament
Missile frigates				
• Abu Dhabi	Kortenaer class	2	130.5/3,050	2xhelicopters 8xHarpoon SSM 4x324mm torpedoes 8xSea Sparrow SAM 1x76mm gun 1x30mm gun 2x20mm guns

Combat Vessels (continued)

Type	Original class name	Quantity	Length (m.)/ displacement (t.)	Notes/ armament
Missile corvettes				
• Muray-Jib	Lürssen 62	2	63/630	1xAlouette helicopter 8xExocet MM40 SSMs 8xCrotale Navale SAMs 1x76mm gun 1x30mm Goal-keeper
MFPBs				
• Ban-Yas	Lürssen TNC-45	6	44.9/260	4xExocet MM40 SSMs 1x76mm gun
• Mubarraz class	Lürssen	2	44.9/260	4xExocet MM40 SSMs 1x6 Mistral SAM 1x76mm gun
Subtotal		8		
Total		**12**		

Patrol Craft

Type	Original class name	Quantity	Length (m.)/ displacement (t.)	Notes/ armament
• Ardhana	Vosper Thornycroft	6	33.5/110	2x30mm guns 1x20mm gun
• Camcraft		5	23.4/70	2x20mm guns with Coast Guard
• Camcraft		16	19.8/50	1x20mm gun with Coast Guard
• Watercraft		6	13.7/25	
• Boghammar		3	13m	With police
• Baglietto GC-23		6	24/50.7	1x20mm gun with Coast Guard
• Baglietto		3	18.1/22	With Coast Guard
• Arctic 28/al-Shaali		20	8.5/4	
• Harbor patrol craft		35	6.6-10m	With Coast Guard
• Dhafeer/Spear (Coast Guard)		10	9-12m	With police
Total		**110**		
Future procurement				
• Oliver Hazard Perry missile frigates		2		From US Drawdown
• Protector patrol craft		2	33/180	1x20mm gun 2x12.7mm MGs

Landing Craft

Type	Original class name	Quantity	Length (m.)/ displacement (t.)	Notes/ armament
• al-Feyi	Siong Huat LSL	3	50/650	
• LCM		1	40/100	
• LCT		2		
• Serana class		2	26.3/105	45 tons or 100 troops
Total		8		
Future procurement				
• LCT		2		

Auxiliary Vessels

Type	Original class name	Quantity	Length (m.)/ displacement (t.)	Notes/ armament
• Arun pilot craft		2		
• Coastal tug		1	35.0/795	
• Diving tender		1	31.4/100	
• Diving tender		2		Coast Guard

Coastal Defense

Type	Quantity	Notes
• MM-40 Exocet		Unconfirmed

Naval Infrastructure

Naval bases (including Coast Guard): 11
Ajman, Dalma (Abu Dhabi), Fujaira, Mina Jabil (Jebel) Ali (Dubai), Mina Khalid (Sharja), Mina Khor Fakkan (Sharja), Mina Rashid (Dubai), Mina Saqr (Ras al-Khaima), Mina Sultan (Sharja), Taweela, Mina Zayd (Abu Dhabi)

Ship maintenance and repair facilities
Dubai wharf for maintenance and repair of merchant and naval vessels, 2 dry-docks available, ship building facility in Mussafah to be enlarged

21. YEMEN

General Data

Official Name of the State: Republic of Yemen
Head of State: President Ali Abdallah Salih
Prime Minister: Abd al-Karim al-Iryani
Minister of Defense: Major General Muhammad Dayfallah
Chief of General Staff: Major General Abdallah Ali Aliwah
Commander of the Air Force: Colonel Muhammad Salih al-Ahmar
Commander of the Navy: Admiral Abdel Karim Yahya Moharrem

Area: 527,970 sq. km.
Population: 17,060,000

Demography

Ethnic groups		
Arabs	15,644,000	91.7%
Afro-Arabs	1,075,000	6.3%
Others	341,000	2.0%
Religious Groups		
Sunni Muslims	10,577,000	62.0%
Shi'ite Zaydi Muslims	6,142,000	36.0%
Shi'ite Ismaili Muslims	85,000	0.5%
Others	256,000	1.5%

Economic Data

		1994	1995	1996	1997	1998
GDP (current price)	$ bn	3.328	3.679	5.111	5.727	5.160
GDP per capita	$	222	239	321	347	302
Real GDP growth	%	-0.8	8.6	5.6	5.2	4.8
Consumer price index	%	71.3	56.3	30.0	5.4	12.9
External debt	$ bn	6.121	6.217	6.362	3.856	4.226
Balance of payments						
• Exports fob	$ bn	1.82	1.937	2.263	2.264	1.501
• Imports fob	$ bn	2.17	1.948	2.294	2.407	2.223
• Current account balance (including services and income)	$ bn	0.366	0.183	0.106	0.052	-0.228

Economic Data (continued)

		1994	1995	1996	1997	1998
Government expenditure						
• Total expenditure	$ bn	1.048	1.041	2.203	2.266	1.884
• Defense expenditure	$ bn	0.374	0.294	0.350	0.410	0.396
• Real change in defense expenditure	%	-7.88	-21.39	19.04	17.14	-3.41
• Defense expenditure/GDP	%	11.23	7.99	6.85	7.16	7.67
Population	m	14.93	15.37	15.92	16.48	17.06
Official exchange rate	YR: $1	80.75	121.69	128.18	129.30	135.89

Sources: EIU Quarterly Report, EIU Country Profile, IMF International Financial Statistical Yearbook, SIPRI Yearbook

Arms Procurement and Security Assistance Received

Country	Type	Details
Bulgaria	• Arms transfers	T-62 tanks (1995), small arms (1995)
Czech Republic	• Arms transfers	L-39C jet trainers (1999), T-54/55 MBTs (1999)
France	• Military training	Trainees abroad
Moldova	• Arms transfers	MiG-29 of Russian origin (1995), MRLs (1997)
Poland	• Arms transfers	T-55 MBTs (suspended - 1999), trucks (1999)
Russia	• Arms transfers	T-72 MBTs (2000)
US	• Arms transfers	Spare parts for American-made systems (1996)

Arms Sales and Security Assistance Extended

Country	Type	Details
Iraq	• Facilities	Refuge to a few Iraqi aircraft (unconfirmed)
Sudan	• Arms transfers	T-55 MBTs (from Poland - 1999)

Weapons of Mass Destruction

NBC Capabilities

Nuclear capability
No known nuclear activity. Signatory to the NPT.

Chemical weapons and protective equipment
No known CW activities. Signed but not ratified the CWC.

Biological weapons
No known BW activities. Party to the BWC.

Ballistic Missiles

Model	Launchers	Missiles	Since	Notes
• SS-1 (Scud B)	6			
• SS-21 (Scarab)	4		1988	
Total	10			

Note: Serviceability of missiles and launchers unknown.

Armed Forces

Note: All figures are rough estimates, due to 1994 civil war.

Major Changes: 30 new T-72 MBTs arrived from Russia. No other major change was recorded in the Yemeni order-of-battle.

Order-of-Battle

Year	1995	1996	1997	1999	2000
General data					
• Personnel (regular)	~65,000	~65,000	~60,000	~60,000	~60,000
• SSM launchers	10	10	10	10	10
Ground Forces					
• Number of brigades	30	30	33	33	33
• Tanks	1,000	1,040	575 (1,040)	575 (1,040)	605 (1,070)
• APCs/AFVs	870	1,320	480 (1,165)	480 (1,170)	~480 (~1,180)
• Artillery (including MRLs)	1,020	1,020	~670 (~1,020)	~670 (~990)	~670 (~1,000)
Air Force					
• Combat aircraft	166	166	~55 (~150)	~50 (~150)	~50 (~150)
• Transport aircraft	23	23	18 (23)	18 (23)	18 (23)
• Helicopters	67	67	27 (67)	27 (67)	26 (66)
Air Defense Forces					
• Heavy SAM batteries	25	25	25	25	25
• Medium SAM batteries	+	+	+	+	+
• Light SAM launchers	+	+	120*	120	120
Navy					
• Combat vessels	12	13	11	11	10
• Patrol craft	11	7	7	3	9

Note: Beginning with 1997, data refers to quantities in active service. The number in parentheses refers to the total inventory.
* Due to change in estimate.

Personnel

	Regular	Reserves	Total
Ground Forces	~60,000	200,000	~260,000
Air Force	3,000		3,000
Navy	2,000		2,000
Total	~65,000	200,000	~265,000
Paramilitary			
• Central Security Force	50,000		50,000

Note: The military forces are a combination from the personnel of former Yemen Arab Republic and the People's Democratic Republic of Yemen; no information regarding reorganization is available.

Ground Forces

Formations

	Independent brigades/groups	Independent battalions
Armored	7	
Mechanized	5	
Infantry (mostly skeleton or undermanned units)	18	
Artillery	4	
SSM	1	
Air Defense		2
Commando/Paratroops	1	
Special Forces	1	
Central Guards	1	
Total	38	2

Tanks

Model	Quantity	In service	Since	Notes
MBTs				
High quality				
• T-72	30	30	2000	
Medium and low quality				
• T-62	200	75	1995	
• M60 A1	140	50	1979	
• T-54/55	700	450	1999	
Subtotal	1,040	575		
Total	1,070	605		

APCs/AFVs

Model	Quantity	In service	Since	Notes
APCs				
• al-Walid	+	+	1977	
• BTR-152	+	+	1977	
• BTR-40/50/60	650	180	1977	
• M113 A1	76	70	1979	Including several derivatives
Subtotal	~750	~250		
IFVs				
• BMP-1/BMP-2	150	100		
Reconnaissance				
• AML-90/AML-60	125	80	1975	
• BRDM-2	100	50		
• Ferret	10	*	1974	Possibly phased out
• Saladin	60	*	1974	Possibly phased out
Subtotal	295	130		
Total	~1,200	~480		

Artillery

Model	Quantity	In service	Since	Notes
Self-propelled guns and howitzers				
• 122mm M-1974	+	+		
• 100mm SU-100	30	0		Possibly phased out
Subtotal	~50	+		
Towed guns and howitzers				
• 155mm M114	12	12	1980	
• 152mm D-20	10	+		
• 130mm M-46	75	60	1976	
• 122mm D-30	150	130	1977	
• 122mm M-1938	100	40	1975	
• 122mm M-1931/7	30	30		
• 105mm M101	30	25		
Subtotal	407	~300		
Mortars, over 160mm				
• 160mm	100	100		
Mortars, under 160mm				
• 120mm	100	100	1978	
• 107mm	12	12		
Subtotal	112	112		
MRLs				
• 240mm BM-24	35	+	1991	Unconfirmed
• 140mm BM-14	14	+	1986	

Artillery (continued)

Model	Quantity	In service	Since	Notes
• 132mm BM-13	15	+		
• 122mm BM-21	280	150	1980	
Subtotal	344	~150		
Rockets				
• Frog-7	12	12		
Total	~1,000	~670		

Anti-Tank Missiles

Model	Launchers	Missiles	Since	Notes
• AT-3 (Sagger)	+	+		
• BGM-71A TOW	12	+	1979	
• M47 Dragon	24	+	1982	

Anti-Tank Guns

Model	Quantity	In service	Since	Notes
• 107mm B-11 recoilless rifle	+	+		
• 100mm M-1955 field/AT	20	+		
• 85mm M-1945/D-44 field/AT	100	90		
• 82mm recoilless rifle	+	+		
• 76mm M-1942	100	70		
• 75mm recoilless rifle	+	+	1975	
• 57mm	+	+		

Air Force

Order-of-Battle

Category	Quantity	In service	Notes
• Combat	~150	~50	Some in storage
• Transport	23	18	
• Helicopters	66	26	

Combat Aircraft

Model	Quantity	In service	Since	Notes
Interceptors				
• MiG-29 (Fulcrum)	~5	+	1995	
• MiG-23/27 (Flogger B/D)	15	0	1980	
Subtotal	~20	+		

Combat Aircraft *(continued)*

Model	Quantity	In service	Since	Notes
Multi-role				
• F-5E/B	10	10	1980	
Ground attack				
• Su-20/22 (Fitter C)	35	15	1980	
Obsolete				
• MiG-21 (Fishbed)	82	21	1979	
• MiG-17 (Fresco)/ MiG-15 (Faggot/Midget)	+	+		In training role, some not serviceable
Total	~150	~50		

Transport Aircraft

Model	Quantity	In service	Since	Notes
• An-24/An-26 (Coke/Curl)	15	10	1984/1985	
• C-130H Hercules	2	2	1979	
• IL-14 (Crate)	4	4		
• Short Skyvan Srs. 3	2	2		
Total	23	18		

Training and Liaison Aircraft

Model	Quantity	In service	Since	Notes
Jet trainers				
• L-39C	12	12	1999	

Helicopters

Model	Quantity	In service	Since	Notes
Attack				
• Mi-24 (Hind)	12	6	1980	
Medium transport				
• AB-212	5	3	1980	
• AB-204	2	2		
• AB-205	2	2	1976	
• Mi-8/Mi-17 (Hip)	39	9	1974	
Subtotal	48	16		
Light transport				
• AB-206 JetRanger	6	4	1980	
Total	66	26		

Advanced Armament

Air-to-air-missiles
AA-2 (Atoll)

Air-to-ground-missiles
AT-2 (Swatter)

Air Force Infrastructure

Military airfields: 15
Aden (Khormaksar), al-Anad, Ataq, Bayhan, Ghor Ubyad, al-Hudaydah, Ir-Fadhl, Kamaran Island, Lawdar, al-Mukalla, Nugaissa, al-Qasab, al Riyan (Rayane), San'a, Socotra

Air Defense Forces

Surface-to-Air Missiles

Model	Batteries	Launchers	Since	Notes
Heavy missiles				
• SA-2 (Guideline)	+			
• SA-3	+		1980	
Total	25			
Medium missiles				
• SA-6	+			
Light missiles				
• SA-9 (Gaskin)		120	1979	
Shoulder-launched missiles				
• SA-7 (Grail)		100 – 200	1975	

Other Air Defense Systems

Model	Quantity	In service	Since	Notes
Short-range guns				
• 57mm ZSU 57x2 SP	+	+	1978	
• 57mm S-60	150	100	1974	
• 37mm M-1939	150	150	1974	
• 23mm ZSU 23x4 SP (Shilka)	10	+	1978	
• 23mm ZU 23x2	30	30	1976	
• 20mm M163 Vulcan SP	20	20	1979	
• 20mm M167 Vulcan	52	20	1979	
Total	~415	~330		

Navy

Combat Vessels

Type	Original class name	Quantity	Length (m.)/ displacement (t.)	Notes/ armament
Gun corvettes				
• Tarantul-I	Type 1241	1	56.1/385	1x76mm gun 2x30mm guns possibly not operational
MFPBs				
• Huang-Feng		3	33.6/171	4xYJ-1 (C-801) SSMs 4x25mm guns
Mine warfare vessels				
• Yevgenia class	Type 1258	5	24.6/177	2x25mm guns
• Natya class	Type 266ME	1	61/804	Acoustic and magnetic sweeps 4x30mm guns 4x25mm guns 2xRBU 1200 A/S mortars 10 mines
Subtotal		6		
Total		10		

Patrol Craft

Type	Original class name	Quantity	Length (m.)/ displacement (t.)	Notes/ armament
• Baklan	CMN	6	15.5/12	2x12.7mm MGs
• Broadsword class (customs)		1	32/90.5	2x25mm guns 2x14.5mm MGs 2x12.7mm MGs
• Zhuk class	Type 1400M	2	24/39	4x14.5mm MGs
Total		9		

Landing Craft

Type	Original class name	Quantity	Length (m.)/ displacement (t.)	Notes/ armament
• Ondatra LCU	Type 1176	2	24/145	1 tank
• Ropucha LST	Type 775	1	112.5/4,080	4xSA-N-5 SAMs 4x57mm guns 2x122mm MRLs 92 mines 10 tanks and 190 troops
• T-4 LCM/LCU		1	19.9/93	
Total		4		

Auxiliary Vessels

Type	Original class name	Quantity	Length (m.)/ displacement (t.)	Notes/ armament
• Toplivo class		3	53.7/1,029	500 tons

Coastal Defense

Type	Quantity	Notes
• SS-N-2 Styx	8	

Naval Infrastructure

Naval bases: 6
Aden, al-Hudaydah, anchorage at Kamaran Island (unconfirmed), al-Mukalla, Perim Island, Socotra

Ship maintenance and repair facilities
National Dockyards, Aden; 4,500-ton floating dock and 1,500-ton slipway

Tables and Charts

The Middle East Military Balance at a glance

	Personnel			Ground Forces			Ballistic Missile Launchers
	Regular	Reserves	Total	Tanks	Fighting Vehicles	Artillery	
Eastern Mediterranean							
Egypt	450,000	254,000	704,000	~2,750	~3,400	~3,550	24
Israel	186,500	445,000	631,500	3,930	8,040	1,348	12
Jordan	94,200	60,000	154,200	~900	~1,500		788
Lebanon	51,400		51,400	280	1,235		~330
Palestinian Authority	34,000		34,000		45		
Syria	380,000	132,500	512,500	3,700	~5,000	~2,600	44
Turkey	633,000	398,000	1,031,000	4,205	~5,460	~4,350	28
Subtotal	1,829,100	1,289,500	3,118,600	~15,750	~24,700	~13,000	108
The Gulf							
Bahrain	7,400		7,400	180	277		48
Iran	~520,000	350,000	~870,000	~1,500	~1,240	~2,700	~30
Iraq	432,500	650,000	1,082,500	~2,000	~2,000	~2,100	5
Kuwait	19,500	24,000	43,500	318	~490		~70
Oman	34,000		34,000	131	~135		148
Qatar	11,800		11,800	44	~260		56
Saudi Arabia	171,500	20,000	191,500	750	~5,300	404	12
UAE	46,500		46,500	~430	~1,250	399	6
Subtotal	~1,250,000	1,044,000	~2,290,000	~5,350	~10,950	~5,900	~50
North Africa and others							
Algeria	127,000	150,000	277,000	860	1,930		~900
Libya	76,000		76,000	~650	~2,750	~2,270	80
Morocco	145,500	150,000	295,500	540	1,119		1,027
Sudan	103,000		103,000	~350	~560		~750
Tunisia	35,500		35,500	139	316		205
Yemen	~65,000	200,000	~265,000	605	~480	~670	10
Subtotal	~552,000	500,000	~1,052,000	~3,140	~7,160	~5,800	90

The Middle East Military Balance at a glance *(continued)*

	Air Force			Air Defense			Navy		
	Combat Aircraft	Transport Aircraft	Helicopters	Heavy Batteries	Medium Batteries	Light launchers	Sub-marines	Combat Vessels	Patrol craft
Eastern Mediterranean									
Egypt	481	44	~225	109	44	50	4	65	104
Israel	628	77	287	22		70	6	20	32
Jordan	100	14	68	14	12	50			13
Lebanon			16						32
Palestinian Authority			2						10
Syria	520	23	295	108	64	55		14	8
Turkey	~485	93	384	24		86	15	64	108
Subtotal	~2,215	251	~1,280	277	120	311	25	163	307
The Gulf									
Bahrain	24	2	41	1	2	40		11	22
Iran	205	92	~300	~35		95	6	29	~120
Iraq	215	10	360	60					130
Kuwait	40	5	~25	12				10	69
Oman	31	38	35			58		9	22
Qatar	18	8	31			48		7	26
Saudi Arabia	~355	61	160	22	16			24	74
UAE	54	31	100	7	6	~115		12	110
Subtotal	~940	247	~1,050	~135	24	~485	6	102	~440
North Africa and others									
Algeria	187	39	114	11	16	78	2	26	21
Libya	~360	85	127	~30	~10	55			24
Morocco	72	43	130			37		13	52
Sudan	~35	25	~60	5					18
Tunisia	12	10	44			83		9	37
Yemen	~50	18	26	25		120		10	9
Subtotal	~720	220	~500	~70	~25	373	2	82	137

The Eastern Mediterranean Military Forces

Personnel (In Thousands)

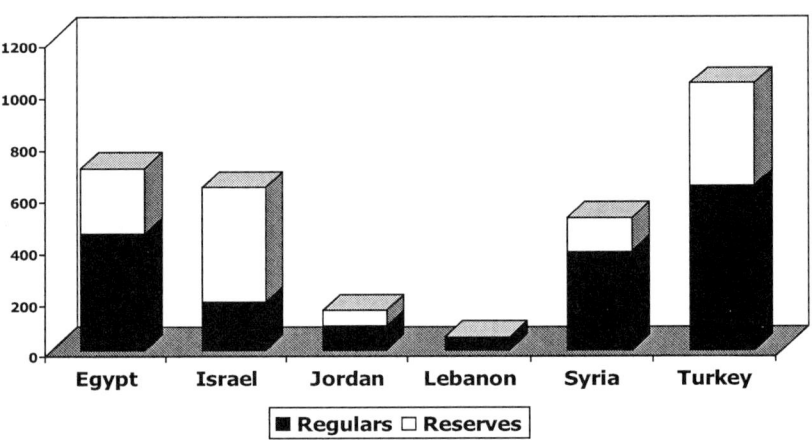

Tanks

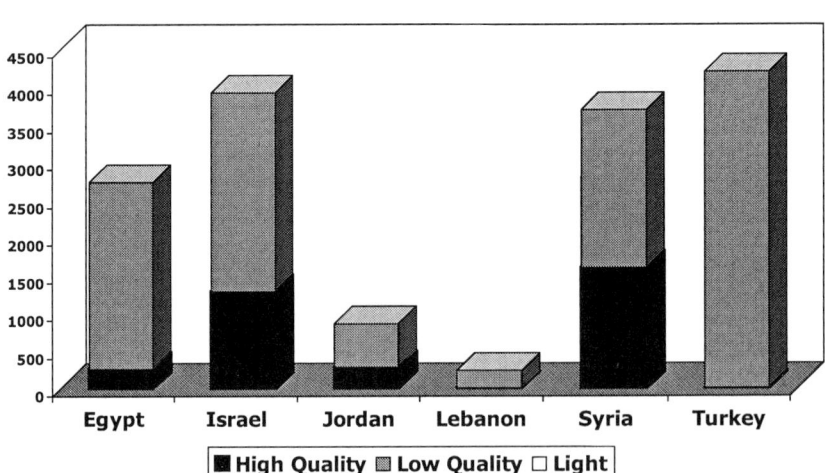

The Eastern Mediterranean Military Forces *(continued)*

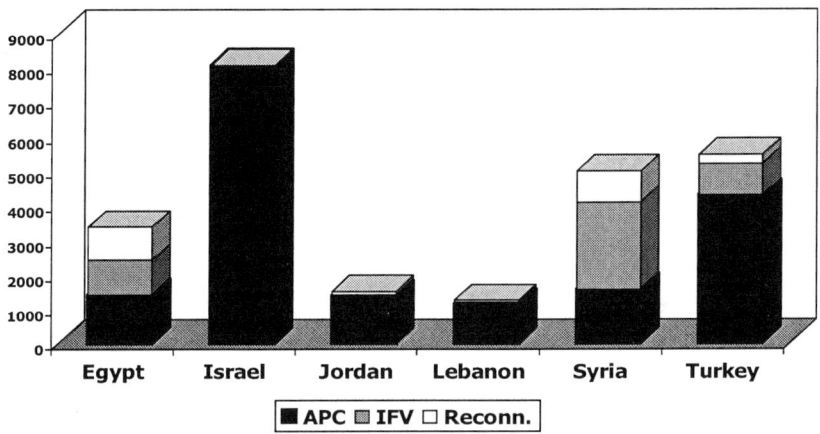

AFVs

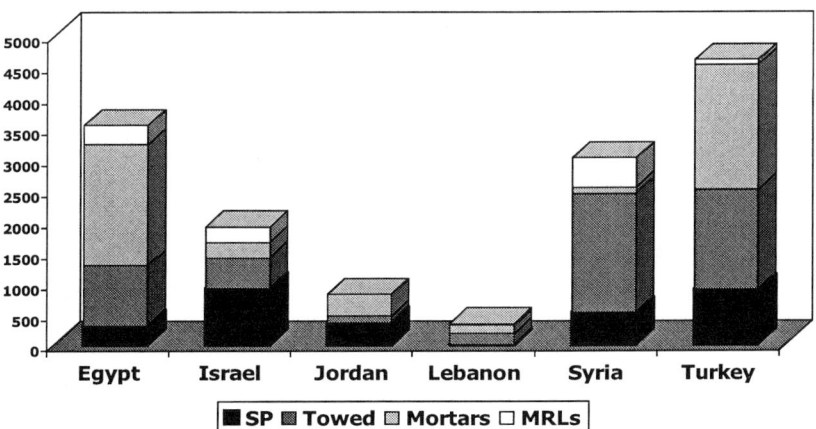

Artillery

The Eastern Mediterranean Military Forces *(continued)*

Air Defense

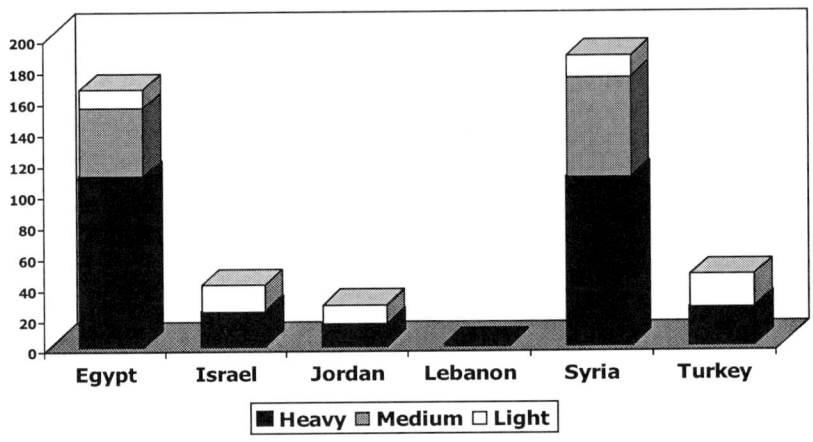

Combat Aircraft

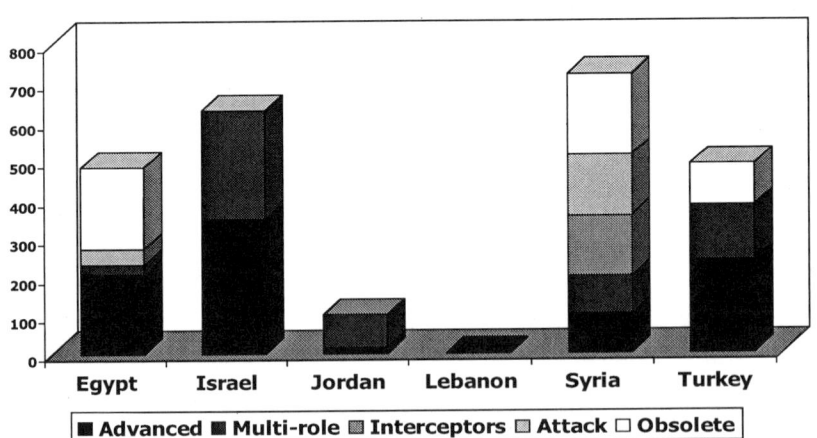

The Eastern Mediterranean Military Forces *(continued)*

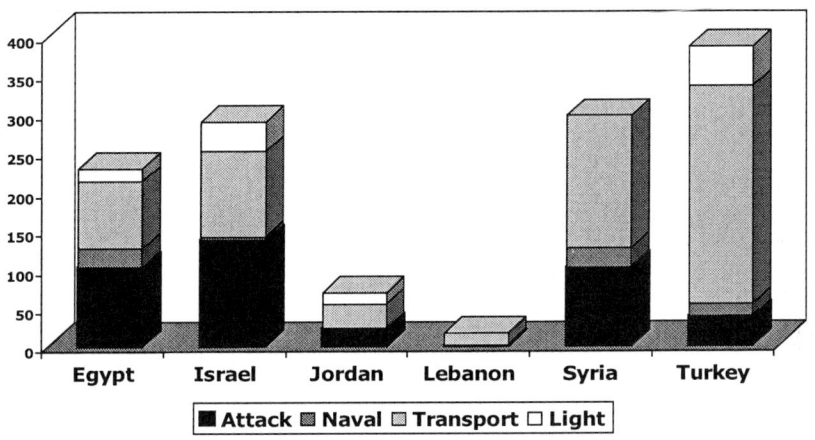

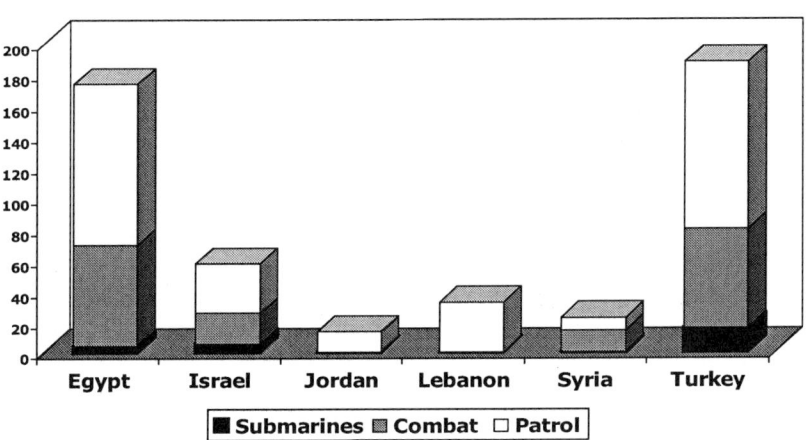

359

The Persian Gulf Military Forces

Personnel (In Thousands)

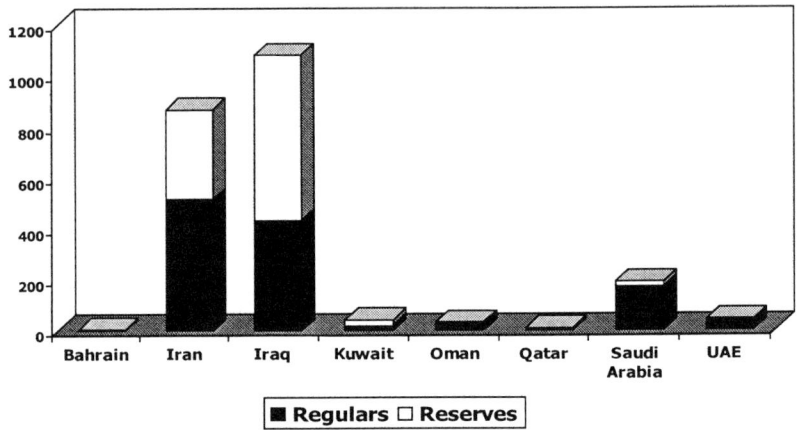

Tanks

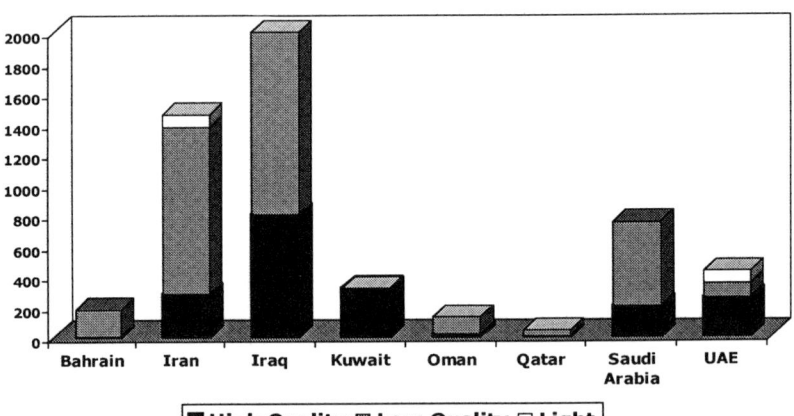

The Persian Gulf Military Forces *(continued)*

AFVs

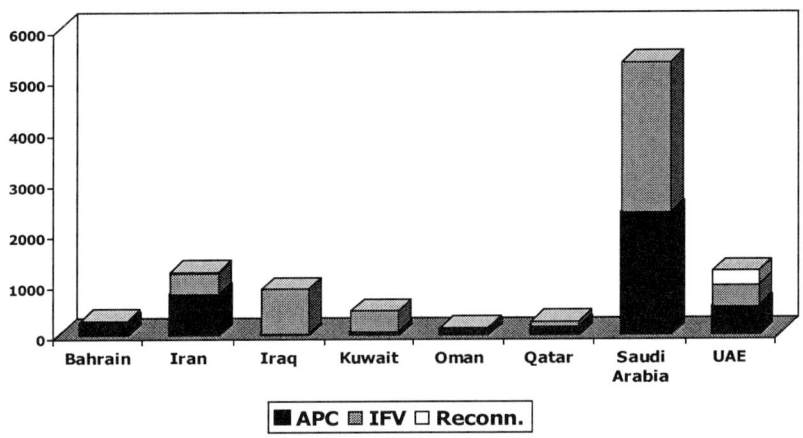

Artillery

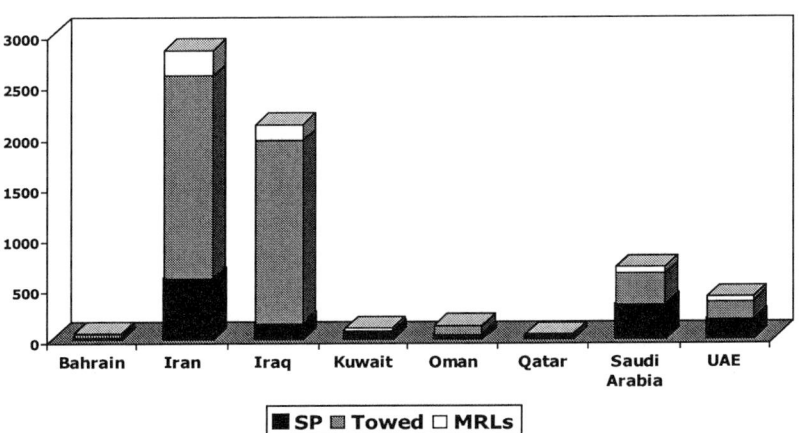

The Persian Gulf Military Forces *(continued)*

Air Defense

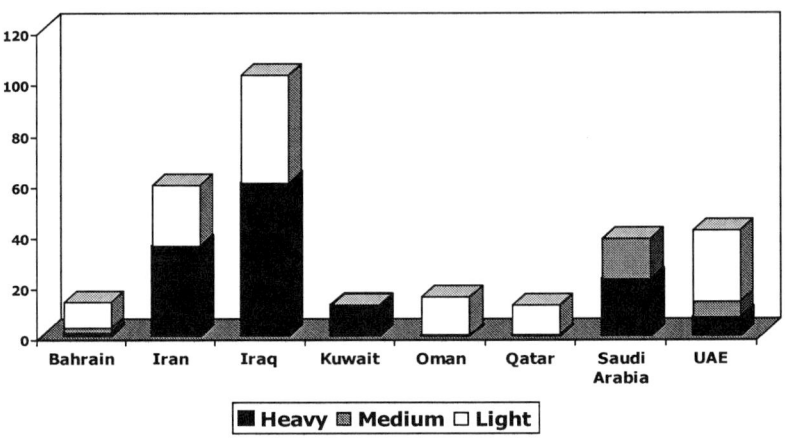

Combat Aircraft

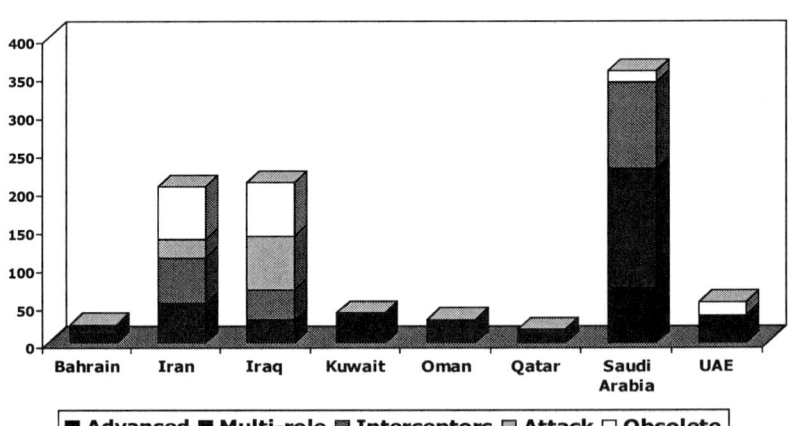

The Persian Gulf Military Forces *(continued)*

Helicopters

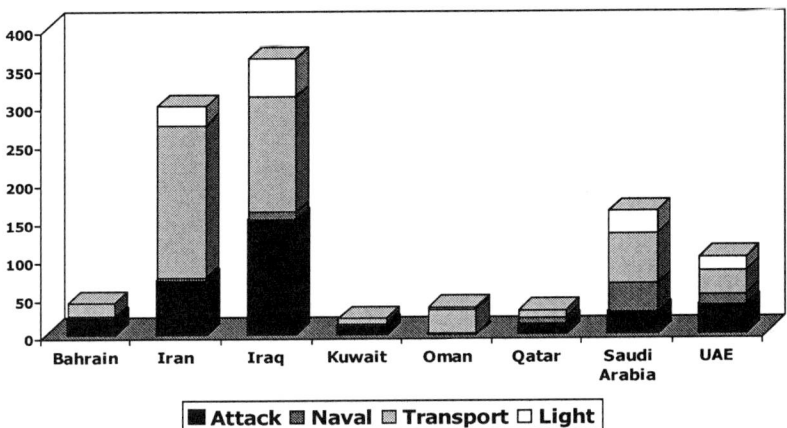

Combat Naval Vessels

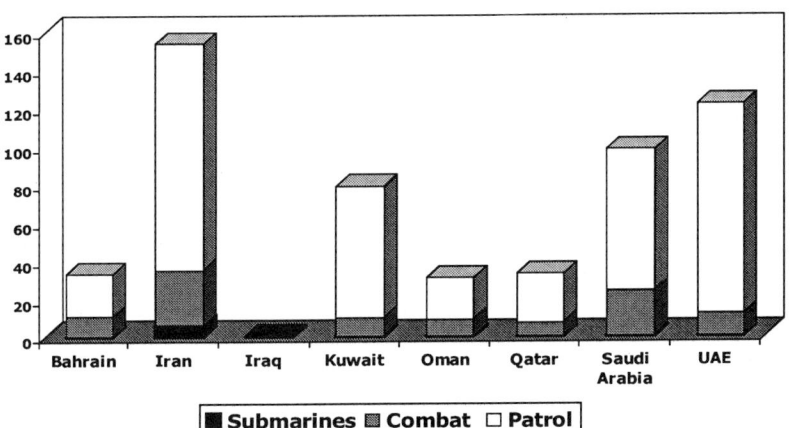

The North African Military Forces

Personnel (In Thousands)

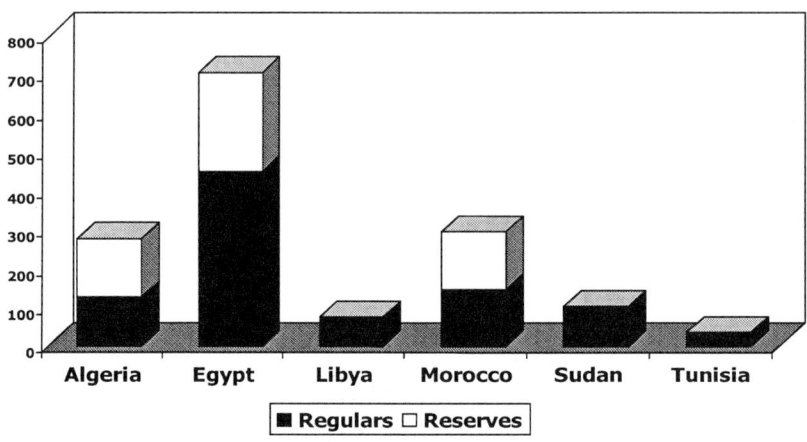

Tanks

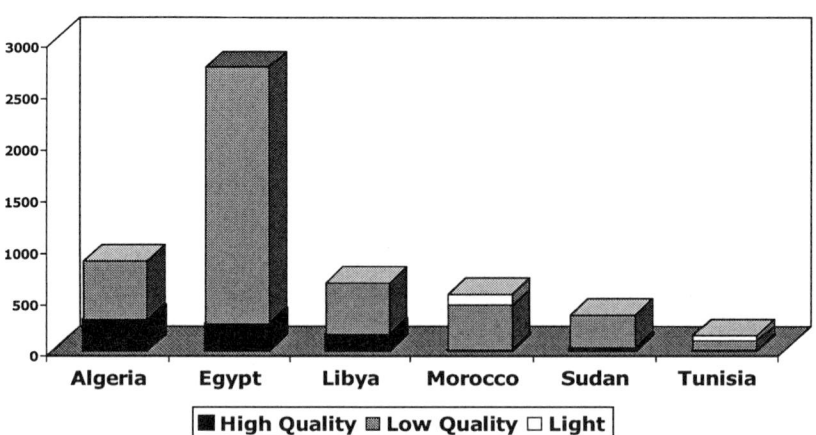

The North African Military Forces (continued)

AFVs

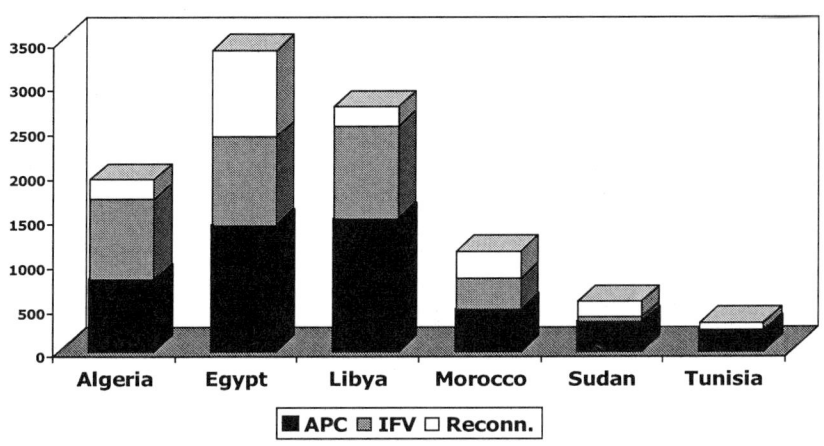

Artillery

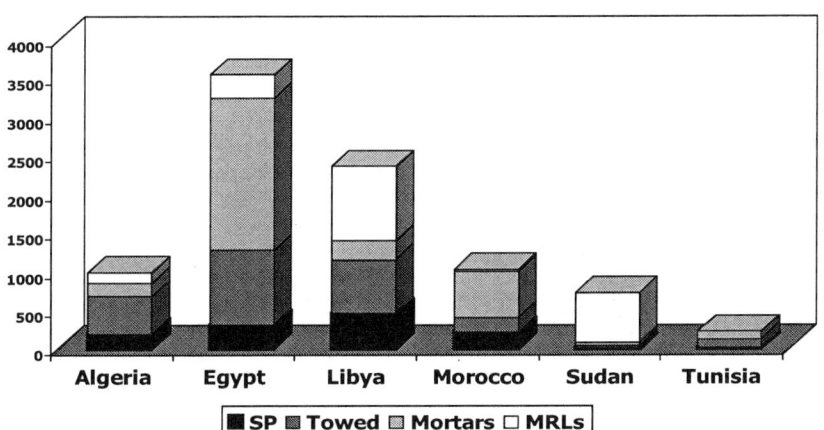

The North African Military Forces *(continued)*

Air Defense

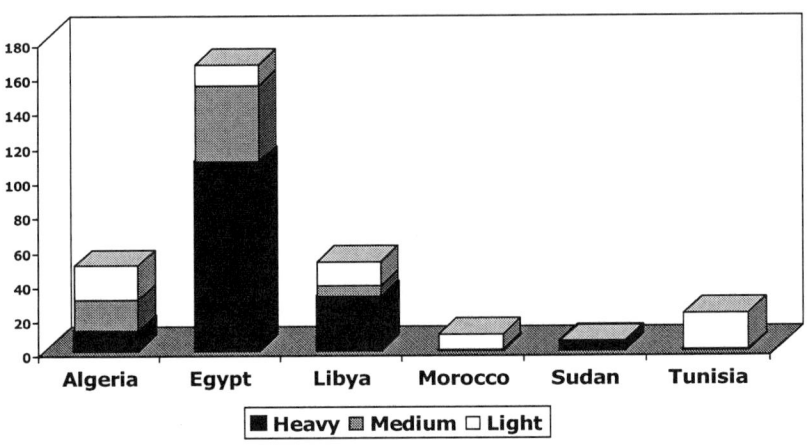

Combat Aircraft

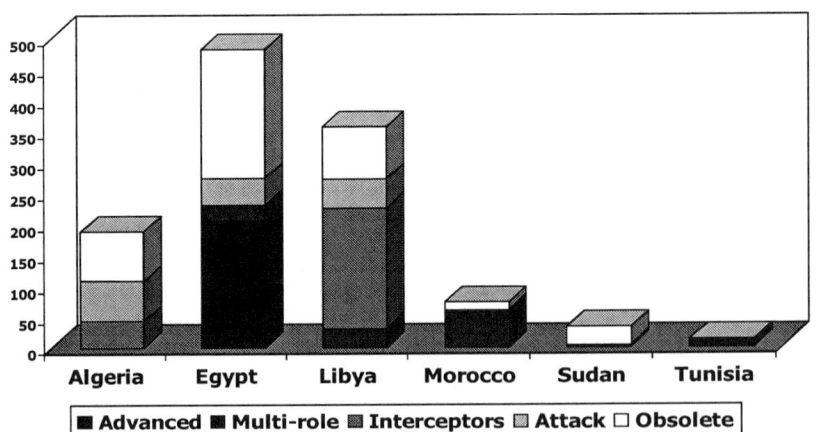

The North African Military Forces *(continued)*

Helicopters

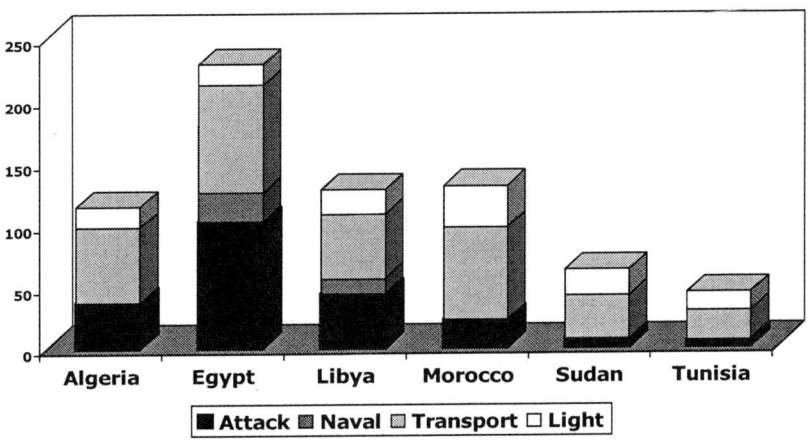

Combat Naval Vessels

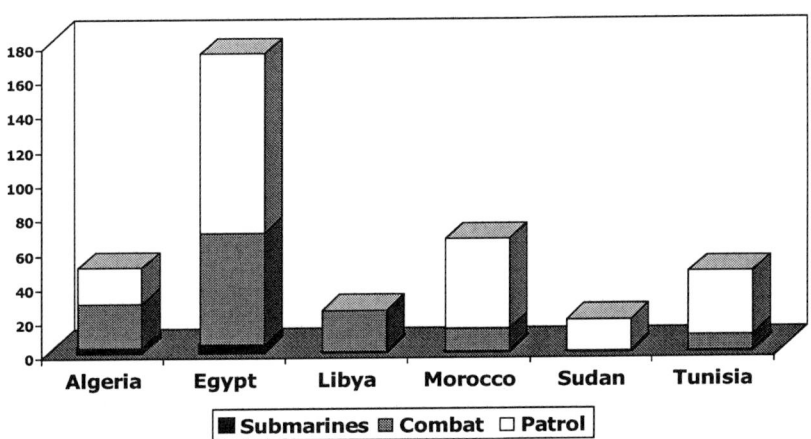

GLOSSARY OF WEAPONS SYSTEMS

GROUND FORCES EQUIPMENT

Armor

Tanks

MBTs
High quality

Type	Crew	Combat weight/ power-to-weight ratio (hp/t)	Gun	Ammunition	Max. op. range (km)	Country of origin	Notes
Challenger 1	4	62/19.35	120mm L11A5	64 Shells	450 road 250 cross country	UK	Incorporating Choblam armor and IFCS
Challenger 2	4	62.5/19.2	120mm L30	Up to 50 shells	450 road 250 cross country	UK	
Khalid	4	58/20.68	120mm L11A5	64 shells	550	Jordan	Improved Chieftain Mk 5 with Choblam armor
Leclerc	3	54.5/27.52	120mm	40 shells	550	France	
Leopard A1/A3	4	42.4/20.75	105mm L7A3	60 shells	600 road 450 cross country	Germany	
M1A1	4	57.15/26.24	105mm	40 shells	465	US	The Egyptian version is fitted with a 120mm gun
M1A2	4	54.54/27	120mm	55 shells	500	US	
M-84 A	3	42/23.8	125mm	42 shells		Yugoslavia	An improved T-72

371

Tanks (continued)

Type	Crew	Combat weight/ power-to-weight ratio (hp/t)	Gun	Ammunition	Max. op. range (km)	Country of origin	Notes
Merkava Mk I	4	60/15	105mm	62 shells	400	Israel	
Merkava Mk II	4	61/15	105mm, 60mm mortar	62 shells	400	Israel	
Merkava Mk III	4	61/19.67	120mm	50 shells	500	Israel	
Sabra	4	55/16.5	120mm, 60mm mortar	42 shells	450	Israel	Upgraded M60A3
T-72	3	44.5/18.9	125mm 2A46	45 shells (including 6 ATGW)	480	Russia	
Zulfikar		40/25	125mm			Iran	
Medium and low quality tanks							
AMX-30	4	37/20	105mm	47 shells	450	France	
Centurion	4	51.8/12.54	105mm	64 shells	190	UK	Upgraded version
Chieftain Mk 5	4	55/13.63	120mm L11A5	64 shells	400 – 500 road 200 – 300 cross country	UK	
Chieftain Mk 3	4	54.1/13.49	120mm	53 shells	400 – 500 road 200 – 300 cross country	UK	

Tanks (continued)

Type	Crew	Combat weight/ power-to-weight ratio (hp/t)	Gun	Ammunition	Max. op. range (km)	Country of origin	Notes
M47	5	46.17/17.54	90mm	71 shells	130	US	
M47M	4	46.8/16.1	90mm	79 shells	600	US	
M48 A1	4	47.173/17.17	90mm M41	60 shells	113	US	
M48 A5	4	48.98/15.89	105mm M68	54 shells	500	US	
M60 A1	4	52.61/14.24	105mm M68	63 shells	500	US	
M60 A3	4	52.61/14.24	105mm M68	63 shells	480	US	
Magach-7	4	53.6/16.97	105mm M68	63 shells	480	Israel	Upgraded M60, including passive armor and FCS
OF-40 Mk 2	4	45.5/18.24	105mm	57 shells	600	Italy	
Qayd Ard	4	55/13.63	120mm L11A5	64 shells	400 – 500 road 200 – 300 cross country	Oman	Improved Chieftain Mk 5
PT-76	3	14.6/16.4	76.2mm	40 shells	400	Russia	
Shot Kal	4	51.8/12.54	105mm	72 shells	190	Israel	Upgraded Centurion
SK-105	3	17.7/18.1	105mm 105G1	41 shells	500	Austria	
T-54	4	36/14.44	100mm D-10	35 shells	510	Russia	

Tanks (continued)

Type	Crew	Combat weight/ power-to-weight ratio (hp/t)	Gun	Ammunition	Max. op. range (km)	Country of origin	Notes
T-55	4	36.5/16.3	100mm D-10 T2S	43 shells	460	Russia	
Tariq	4	51.8/12.54	105mm	64 shells	190	Jordan	Upgraded Centurion
Type 72Z/ Safir-74		36/21.66	105mm	50 Shells		Iran	Upgrade of T-55 incorporates Fontana EFCS-3 and ERA
T-62	4	40/14.5	115mm 2A20	40 shells	450 road 320 cross country	Russia	
Type 59	4	36/14.44	100mm	34 shells	420 – 440	PRC	(Chinese T-54) The same designation also used for a 130mm gun
Type 69	4	36.5/15.9	100mm	34 shells		PRC	
T-55/Type-69	3		125mm				Iraqi upgrade
Vickers Mk 1	4	38.6/16.8	105mm L7	44 shells	480	UK	
Light tanks							
AMX-13	3	15/16.6	90mm	32 shells	350 – 400	France	There are versions with 75mm and 105mm guns
Scorpion	3	8/23.5	76mm	40 shells	644 road	UK	Alvis Scorpion reconnaissance vehicle

Armored Personnel Carriers

Type	Crew	Configuration	Combat weight/ power-to-weight ratio (hp/ton)	Country of origin	Notes
Achzarit	3+7	Tracked		Israel	Based on T-55 MBT hull
AT-105	2+8	4x4	11.66/14.06	UK	
BMR-600	2+10	6x6	14/22	Spain	
BTR-152	2+17	6x6	9/12.29	Russia	
BTR-40	2+8	4x4	5.3/15	Russia	
BTR-50	2+20	Tracked	14.2/16.9	Russia	
BTR-60PA	2+16	8x8	10/18.03	Russia	
BTR-80	3+7	8x8	13.6/19.11	Russia	
Boragh	12	Tracked	13/25.4	Iran	Iranian version of BMP-1
Cobra	11	4x4	6/31	Turkey	
Engesa EE-11	13	6x6	14/18.6	Brazil	
al-Fahd	2+10	4x4	10.9/15.4	Egypt	
al-Fahd 240	2+10	4x4	10.9/22	Egypt	
al-Fahd	2+12	8x8		Saudi Arabia	Also known as AD-40-8-1
FIAT OtoBreda 6614	1+10	4x4	8.5/18.82	Italy	
FNSS-AAPC	13	Tracked	12.94/23.16	Turkey	
FUG-70/PSZH-IV	3+6	Wheeled	7.6/13.15	Hungary	
GKN-Defence Piranha	15	8x8	12.3/24.4	UK	

Armored Personnel Carriers *(continued)*

Type	Crew	Configuration	Combat weight/ power-to-weight ratio (hp/ton)	Country of origin	Notes
M113 A1	2+11	Tracked	11.07/19.27	US	
M113 A2	2+11	Tracked	11.25/18.51	US	
M125 A1	6	Tracked	11.26/19.09	US	
M-2 halftrack	10	Halftrack	8.89/14.39	US	
M-3 halftrack	13	Halftrack	8.89/14.39	US	
M-3 Panhard	2+10	4x4	6.1/14.75	France	
M-60P	3+10	Tracked	11/12.73	Slovenia	
MT-LB	2+11	Tracked	11.9/20.16	Russia	
Nagmachon	8	Tracked		Israel	Based on MBT hull
Nagmashot	8	Tracked		Israel	Based on Centurion MBT hull
Nakpadon		Tracked		Israel	
OT-62B	2+18	Tracked	15/20	Czech Republic/ Poland	Czech/Polish BTR-50
OT-64C(1) SKOT-2A	2+10	8x8	14.5/12.41	Czech Republic/ Poland	
Peninsula Shield	9	6x6	16/22.8	Saudi Arabia	See also Armored Reconn. Vehicles
RBY	2+6	4x4	4/30	Israel	
S-55	2+6	4x4	3.6/31.2	UK	

Armored Personnel Carriers (continued)

Type	Crew	Configuration	Combat weight/ power-to-weight ratio (hp/ton)	Country of origin	Notes
Saracen FV603 (C)	2+10	6x6	10.17/15.73	UK	
UR-416	2+8	4x4	7.6/16.5	Germany	
VAB-VTT	2+10	4x4	13/16.92	France	
VAB-VTT	2+10	6x6	14.2/16.54	France	
VCR	3+9	6x6	7.9/18.35	France	
al-Walid	2+8-10	4x4		Egypt	
YW-531	2+13	Tracked	12.6/25.39	PRC	

Infantry Fighting Vehicles

Type	Crew	Configuration	Combat weight/ power-to-weight ratio (hp/ton)	Armament	Country of origin
AMX-10P	3+8	Tracked	14.5/17.93	1x20mm cannon	France
AMX-VCI	3+10	Tracked	15/16.67	1x20mm cannon	France
BMD-1	3+4	Tracked	7.5/32	1x73mm 2A28 gun AT-3 Sagger ATGW	Russia
BMP-1	3+8	Tracked	13.5/22.22	73mm 2A28 gun 1 launcher rail for Sagger ATGW	Russia
BMP-2	3+7	Tracked	14.3/20.30	30mm 2A42 cannon 1 launcher for AT-5 Spandrel or AT-4 Spigot ATGW	Russia

Infantry Fighting Vehicles (continued)

Type	Crew	Configuration	Combat weight/power-to-weight ratio (hp/ton)	Armament	Country of origin
BMP-3	3+7	Tracked	18.7/26.73	1x100mm 2A70 gun 1x30mm 2A72 cannon	Russia
BTR-94	2+8	8x8		1x 23mm ZU 23x2 canon	Ukraine
Condor	2+12	4x4	12.4/13.54	1x20mm cannon	Germany
Desert Warrior	3+7	Tracked	25.7/21.4	1x25mm cannon 2xTOW ATGW launchers	UK
Engesa EE-11	3+5	6x6	14/18.6	1x90mm gun	Brazil
al-Fahd 240-30	2+10	4x4	12.5/19.2	1x30mm 2A42 cannon 1x AT-5 Spandrel ATGW	Egypt
FNSS-AIFV	13	Tracked	13.68/21.92	1x25mm cannon	Turkey
LAV-25	3+6	8x8	12.79/21.49	1x25mm cannon	Canada
M2 Bradley	3+6	Tracked	22.94/20.38	1x25mm cannon 2-tube TOW launcher	US
M3 Bradley CFV	3+2	Tracked	22.44/20.51	1x25mm cannon 2-tube TOW launcher	US
Pandur	2+8	6x6	13/25.3	1x30mm cannon	Austria
Ratel 20	11	6x6	18.5/15.24	1x20mm cannon	South Africa
Ratel 90	10	6x6	19/14.84	1x90mm gun	South Africa
V-150	3+2	4x4	9.88/20.42	1x20mm cannon	US
V-150 S	3+2	4x4	10.88/22.96	1x20mm cannon	US

Glossary

Infantry Fighting Vehicles (continued)

Type	Crew	Configuration	Combat weight/ power-to-weight ratio (hp/ton)	Armament	Country of origin
V-300	3+9	6x6	14.96/18.94	90mm or 76mm or 25mm or 20mm gun	US
VAB-VCI	2+10	4x4	13/16.92	1x20mm cannon	France
VAB-VCI	2+10	6x6	14.2/15.49	1x20mm cannon	France
YPR-765	3+7	Tracked	13.68/19.29	1x25mm cannon	Netherlands

Armored Reconnaissance Vehicles

Type	Crew	Configuration	Combat weight/ power-to-weight ratio (hp/ton)	Armament	Country of origin	Notes
Akrep (Scorpion)	4	4x4	3.6/37		Turkey	
AML-60	3	4x4	5.5/16.36	60mm mortar	France	
AML-90	3	4x4	5.5/16.36	1x90mm gun	France	
AMX-10RC	4	6x6	15.88/16.45	1x105mm gun	France	
BRDM-1	5	4x4	5.6/16.07		Russia	
BRDM-2	4	4x4	7/20	14.5mm KPVT MG or 1x23mm cannon AT-3 (Sagger) ATGW	Russia	
Cobra	4	4x4	6/31	1x25mm gun	Turkey	See Armored Personnel Carriers
EBR-75	4	8x8	13.5/14.81	1x75mm gun	France	
Engesa EE-9	3	6x6	13.4/15.82	1x90mm gun	Brazil	

379

Armored Reconnaissance Vehicles (continued)

Type	Crew	Configuration	Combat weight/ power-to-weight ratio (hp/ton)	Armament	Country of origin	Notes
al-Fahd	3	8x8		Various turrets can be fitted, up to a three-man model with a 105mm gun	Saudi Arabia	Also known as AD-40-8-2
Ferret	2	4x4	4.4/29.35	2xVigilance ATGWs	UK	
Ferret Mk 1/2	3	4x4	4.37/29.51		UK	
FIAT OtoBreda 6616	3	4x4	8/20.2	1x20mm cannon	Italy	
Fox	3	4x4	6.12/30.04		UK	
M-3 (Panhard)		4x4	6.1/14.75	HOT ATGW	France	Also listed under Armored Personnel Carriers
M901 ITV	4	Tracked	11.8/18	TOW ATGW	US	
Peninsula Shield	3	6x6	18.5/22.8	1x90mm gun	Saudi Arabia	Also listed under Armored Personnel Carriers
Saladin	3	6x6	11.6/14.66		UK	
VBC-90	3	6x6	13.5/16	1x90mm gun	France	
VCR/TH		6x6		HOT ATGW	France	

Artillery

Guns, Howitzers and Mortars

Caliber	Designation	Type	Range (km)	Country of origin	Notes
240mm	M-240	Towed mortar	9.7	Russia	
210mm	al-Faw	SP gun	57	Iraq	With assistance from Belgium and UK companies
203mm/8"	M110 A1	SP howitzer	16.8	US	
203mm/8"	M115	Towed howitzer	16.8	US	
180mm	S-23	Towed gun	32	Russia	
175mm	M107	SP gun	32.7	US	
170mm	M-1978 (Koksan)	SP gun	40	North Korea	
160mm	M-43/53	Towed mortar	5.1	Russia	
160mm	M-66	SP mortar	9.3	Israel	
155mm	FH-70	Towed howitzer	24	Germany	
155mm	FH2000	Towed howitzer	40	Turkey	Variant of Singaporean 155mm gun
155mm	G-5	Towed howitzer	30	South Africa	
155mm	G-6	SP howitzer	30	South Africa	
155mm	GCT	SP howitzer	23.5	France	
155mm	GHN-45	Towed howitzer	17.8	Austria	
155mm	L-33 (Sherman/Soltam)	SP howitzer	21	Israel	Gun-Israel; chassis - obsolete US-made tanks

Guns, Howitzers and Mortars (continued)

Caliber	Designation	Type	Range (km)	Country of origin	Notes
155mm	M109 A1/A2/A6	SP howitzer	21	US	
155mm	M109 Doher	SP howitzer		Israel	Upgrading of M109
155mm	M114 A2	Towed howitzer	14.6	US	
155mm	M-1950	Towed howitzer	17.5	France	
155mm	M198 A1	Towed howitzer	18.1	US	
155mm	M-41	Towed gun	30	Iraq/Austria	Combination of the 130mm gun and Austrian 155mm tubes
155mm	M44	SP howitzer	14.6	US	
155mm	M-50 (Sherman)	SP howitzer	17.5	Israel	Gun-France; chassis-US tank
155mm	M52T/M44T	SP howitzer	18/30	Turkey	Upgrading of former US M52 and M44
155mm	M59 (Long Tom)	Towed gun	22	US	
155mm	M-71	Towed howitzer	24	Israel	
155mm	Majnoon	SP howitzer	30.2	Iraq	With assistance from a Belgian company
155mm	Mk F-3 (AMX)	SP howitzer	18	France	
155mm	Palmaria	SP howitzer	24	Italy	
155mm	SP2000	SP howitzer	30	Turkey	
155mm	Thunder-2	SP gun		Iran	
152mm	D-20	Towed howitzer	18	Russia	

Guns, Howitzers and Mortars (continued)

Caliber	Designation	Type	Range (km)	Country of origin	Notes
152mm	ZTS DANA	SP howitzer	20	Czech Republic	
152mm	M-1943 (D-1)	Towed howitzer	12.4	Russia	
152mm	M-1946 2A36	Towed howitzer	27	Russia	
152mm	M-1973	SP howitzer	18	Russia	
130mm	M-46	Towed gun	27.1	Russia	
130mm	Type 59	Towed gun	27.4	PRC	Copy of Soviet 130mm M-46; the same designation is also used for a Chinese MBT
122mm	SP-122	SP howitzer	15.4	Russia/Egypt	Conversion to SP with US aid
122mm	D-30	Towed howitzer	16	Russia	
122mm	D-74	Towed gun	24	Russia	
122mm	ISU	SP gun	16	Russia	
122mm	M-1938	Towed howitzer	11.8	Russia	
122mm	M-1974	SP howitzer	15.3	Russia	
122mm	Saddam	Towed howitzer	16	Iraq/Russia	Russian 122mm D-30, produced in Iraq, with assistance from Yugoslavia
122mm	Thunder-1	SP gun		Iran	Based on Russian 12mm D-30
120mm		SP mortar	11.5	Iraq	Mounted on Russian-made MT-LB carrier

Guns, Howitzers and Mortars (continued)

Caliber	Designation	Type	Range (km)	Country of origin	Notes
120mm	Brandt	SP mortar		France/Canada	Mounted on LAV chassis
120mm	Brandt M-50/M-60	Towed mortar	6.6	France	
120mm	M-43	Towed mortar	5.7	Russia	
120mm	M-65	Towed mortar	6.3	Israel	Also available as SP, mounted on US made M-2 halftrack
120mm	TDA	SP rifled mortar	13	France	Mounted on Mowag Piranha 8x8 APC
107mm (4.2')	M30	SP/towed mortar	5.6	US	Mounted on M106 A2 carrier, a derivative of M113 APC
105mm	L-118	Towed light gun	17.2	UK	
105mm	M101 A1	Towed howitzer	11.3	US	
105mm	M102 A1	Towed howitzer	11.5	US	
105mm	M108	SP howitzer	11.5	US	
105mm	M52	SP howitzer	11.3	US	
105mm	M-56	Towed pack howitzer	10.6	Italy	
105mm	Mk 61	SP howitzer	15	France	
100mm	M-1955	Towed field/AT gun	21	Russia	
100mm	SU-100	SP gun		Russia	
87mm (25lb.)		Towed howitzer	12.2	UK	
85mm	M-1945/D-44	Towed field/AT gun	15.8	Russia	
76mm	M-1942 (ZIS-3)	Towed divisional gun	13.3	Russia	

Artillery/Mortar-Locating Radars

Designation	Detection range (km)	Frequency band	Country of origin
AN/TPQ-37	50	I/J-band	US
AN/PPS-15A	3	J-band	US
ARS 2000			Turkey
RATAC-S	30	I-band	Germany
Cymbeline	30	I-band	UK
Rasit	50	I-band	France
Shilem			Israel

Artillery Ammunition Carriers

Designation	Configuration	Country of origin	Notes
M-992	Tracked	US	
MT-LB	Tracked	Russia	Also serves as prime mover for towed artillery and APC

Surface-to-Surface Missiles

Designation	Range (km)/ CEP	Propulsion	Payload (kg)	Country of origin	Notes
al-Hussein	~600/~3 km	Single stage, liquid	300	Iraq	Extended range Scuds
CSS-2 (East Wind)	2,700/~4 km	Single stage, liquid	2,045	PRC	
Condor 2/Vector	800	Two stage, solid/liquid	450	Egypt/Iraq	Operational status unconfirmed
M-7 (CSS-8)	150	Single stage, liquid	190	PRC	This is derived from HQ-2 SAM for export
GHAURI-I	1,300–1,500		750	Pakistan	Possibly based on the No-Dong
GHAURI-II	2,000–2,300		1,000	Pakistan	
Jericho I	450	Single stage, liquid	500	Israel	According to foreign publications

Surface-to-Surface Missiles (continued)

Designation	Range (km)/ CEP	Propulsion	Payload (kg)	Country of origin	Notes
Jericho II	800		500	Israel	According to foreign publications
Jericho II B	1,500			Israel	According to foreign publications
M-9	600/600m	Solid	500	PRC	
M-11	250/250m	Solid	500	PRC	
MGM-52C Lance	75/150m	Liquid	225	US	
MGM-140 ATACMS	135	Solid	450	US	
No-Dong/Scud-D	1,000	Single stage, liquid	1,000	North Korea	
Shehab-3	1,300/~4 km	Single stage, liquid	1,000	Iran	Possibly based on No-Dong
Shehab-4	2,000			Iran	
SS-1 (Scud B, R-17 or 9K72)	280/1 km	Single stage, liquid	800 – 1,000	Russia	
Scud C	550/~2 km	Single stage, liquid	500 – 700	North Korea	Upgrading of Russian SS-1 Scud B
SS-21 (Scarab, OTR-21 or Tochka)	70/150m	Single stage, solid	120	Russia	Tochka-U has a range of 120km
Shaheen	750	Single stage, solid	1,000	Pakistan	Possibly based on Chinese M-9
Soumoud	150	Single stage, liquid	N/A	Iraq	Formally developed within the restrictions of the UNSC resolutions, but probably exceeds the limitations considerably
Taepo-Dong 1	1,700 – 2,200	Two stage, liquid	700 – 1,000	North Korea	
Taepo-Dong 2	4,000 – 6,000	Two stage, liquid	700 – 1,000	North Korea	
Tamuz 1	2,000	Two stage, liquid		Iraq	Not operational

Surface-to-Surface Strategic Rockets

Caliber	Designation	Number of rails/tubes	Range (km)	Payload (kg)	Country of origin	Notes
610mm	Zelzal 2	1	200	600	Iran	
540mm	FROG-7 (Luna-M or 9K52)	1	70	450	Russia	
540mm	Laith 90	1	90	450	Iraq	Extended range version of the Russian FROG-7
400mm	Ababil-100	4	100		Iraq	Improved version of Yugoslavia's 262mm LRSV M-87
355mm	Nazeat	1	90	150	Iran	
333mm	Fajer 5	4	70	110	Iran	
320mm	WS-1	4	80	150	Iran	
300mm	BM-9A52-2 Smerch	12	70 – 90	100	Russia	
300mm	Sajeel 60	4	60		Iraq	Copy of Brazilian 300mm SS-60
300mm	SS-60	4	60		Brazil	
260mm	Toros-260	2	100	144	Turkey	
230mm	Oghab	3	80	70	Iran	Improved version of Chinese Type 8 273mm rocket

Surface-to-Surface Strategic Rockets (continued)

Caliber	Designation	Number of rails/tubes	Range (km)	Payload (kg)	Country of origin	Notes
230mm	Toros-230	2	65	121	Turkey	
210mm	Saqr-80	1	80	200	Egypt	Launched from FROG 7 launchers

Multiple Rocket Launchers

Caliber	Designation	Number of rails/tubes	Range (km)	Country of origin	Notes
350mm	Kachlilit	4	40	Israel	Anti-radar missile
333mm	Shahin 2	2	20	Iran	190 kg warhead
290mm	MAR 290	4	25	Israel	
262mm	Ababil-50	12	50	Iraq	Copy or production under license of Yugoslavia's 262mm LRSV M-87
240mm	BM-24	12	10.2	Russia	
240mm	Fajer 3	12	43	Iran	
227mm	MLRS	12	30	US	
180mm	Sajeel 40	16	35	Iraq	Copy of Brazilian 180mm SS-40
180mm	SS-40 Astros II	16	35	Brazil	
160mm	Keres/LAR-160	18	25	Israel	Anti-radar missile; a derivative of USRGM-66D
140mm	BM-14-16	16	9.8	Russia	
140mm	RPU-14	16	9.8	Russia	
140mm	Teruel	40	18.2	Spain	
132mm	BM-13-16	16	9	Russia	
130mm	M-51 (RM-130)	32	8.2	Romania/Russia	

Multiple Rocket Launchers *(continued)*

Caliber	Designation	Number of rails/tubes	Range (km)	Country of origin	Notes
130mm	M-51	32	8.2	Czech Republic	
130mm	Type 63	19	10.4	PRC	
128mm	M-63	32	8.5	Yugoslavia	
127mm	Sajeel 30	32	30	Iraq	Copy of Brazilian 127mm SS-30
127mm	SS-30 Astros II	32	30	Brazil	
122mm	Azrash	40	21.5	Iran	
122mm	BM-11	30		North Korea	Variant of Russian BM-21
122mm	BM-21	40	20.8	Russia	
122mm	Firos-25	40	25	Italy	
122mm	Hadid	40	20.4	Iran	
122mm	Nur	40	18	Iran	
122mm	RM-70	40	20.4	Czech Republic	Similar to Russian BM-21
122mm	Saqr 10 and Saqr 18		18	Egypt	
122mm	Saqr 30	30	22.5	Egypt	
122mm	Saqr 36	30	20.4	Egypt	
122mm	TR-122	40	30	Turkey	
107mm		12	8	Iraq	Copy of 107mm from PRC or RM-11 from North Korea
107mm	RM-11		8.1	North Korea	
107mm	Type 63	12	8.5	PRC	

389

Engineering and Anti-Tank Equipment

Anti-Tank Guns

Caliber	Designation and Type	Country of origin	Notes
120mm	BAT L-4 recoilless rifle	UK	
107mm	B-11 recoilless rifle	Russia	
106mm	M40 A1C/A2 recoilless rifle	US/Israel	
100mm	M-1955 gun field/AT gun	Russia	Also listed under Guns and Howitzers
90mm	Light gun, low recoil Belgium	Used on AFVs	
85mm	M-1945/D-44 field/AT gun	Russia	Also listed under Guns and Howitzers
84mm	Carl Gustav light recoilless rifle	Sweden	
82mm	B-10 recoilless rifle	Russia	
76mm	M-1942 (ZIS-3) field/AT gun	Russia	Also listed under Guns and Howitzers
75mm	M20 recoilless rifle	US	
57mm	AT gun	Czech Republic	

Anti-Tank Guided Missiles

Designation	Range (m)	Guidance	Country of origin	Notes
AT-1 (Snapper)	2,300	Wire	Russia	
AT-2 (Swatter)	2,500	Radio	Russia	
AT-3 (Sagger)	3,000	Wire	Russia	
AT-4 (Spigot)	2,500	Wire	Russia	
AT-5 (Spandrel)	3,600	Wire	Russia	

Anti-Tank Guided Missiles (continued)

Designation	Range (m)	Guidance	Country of origin	Notes
AT-6 (Spiral)	5,000	Radio	Russia	
AT-14 (Kornet)	5,500	Laser	Russia	
Dandy (NT-D)	6,000	TV/IIR	Israel	
Dragon I/II	1,000	Wire	US	
Dragon II+/III (Superdragon)	2,000	Wire	US	
Eryx	600	Wire	France/Canada	
I-Raad	3,000	Wire	Iran	Licensed production of Russian AT-3
Gill (NT-G)	2,500	CCD/IIR	Israel	
Hellfire	8,000	Laser	US	
HOT	4,000	Wire	France/Germany	
Mapats	5,000	Laser	Israel	
MILAN	2,000	Wire	France/Germany	
Nimrod	26,000	Laser	Israel	Land-based variant of Nimrod AGM
SS-11	3,000	Wire	France	
SS-12	5,000	Wire	France	Can be employed as ATGM or as anti-ship missile launched from ground, helicopter, or ship
Spike (NT-S)	4,000	Fiber optics/IIR	Israel	
Swingfire	4,000	Wire	UK/Egypt	
TOW (BGM 71A/C/D)	3,750	Wire	US	
Towsan-1	4,000	Wire	Iran	Licensed production of Russian AT-5
BGM-71E TOW IIA	3,750	Wire	US	Tandem warhead
BGM-71F TOW IIB	3,750	Wire	US	Tandem warhead programmed for top attack
TRIGAT	2,000	Laser	France	

Engineering Equipment

Designation	Country of Origin	Notes
Bar mine-lying system	UK	
EWK pontoon bridge (Faltschwimmbrucke)	Germany	
FNSS-ENG	Turkey	Engineering combat vehicle
Gilois motorized bridge	France	Bridge and ferry system
GSP	Russia	Heavy amphibious self-propelled ferry
M60 AVLB	US	Bridging tank
M69 A1	US	Bridging tank
M123 Viper	US	Minefield-crossing system
M728	US	Engineering combat vehicle based on M60 tank chassis
Matenin SA	France	Automatic mine layers
Mk 3(D) flail	France	Anti-mine vehicle
MT-55	Russia	Bridging tank
MTU-55	Russia	Bridging tank
MTU-67	Russia	Bridging tank
PMP pontoon bridge	Russia	Heavy folding pontoon bridge
Pomins II	Israel	Portable (infantry) mine neutralization system
PRP motorized bridge	Russia	
Puma	Israel	Combat vehicle carrying a squad of combat engineers and some equipment (an improvement of existing foreign tank chassis)
TAB, tactical assault bridge	Israel	
TLB, trailer-launched bridge	Israel	
TPP, pontoon bridge	Russia	Can be used as a pontoon bridge or a raft
TWMP, tread-width mine ploughs	Israel	
UDK-1, bridge	UK	

Recovery Vehicles

Designation	Type	Combat weight (ton)	Lifting/towing capability	Country of origin	Notes
Leclerc	Armored recovery vehicle	54	Crane maximum capacity of 30 tons; main winch pull capacity of 35 tons	France	
Challenger	Armored recovery vehicle	62	Winch-52 tons capacity-direct pull; crane lift-6.5 tons-max	UK	
M88 A1	Armored recovery vehicle	50.8	Up to 22 tons when using a stabilizing blade; 2 winches: max. capacity of 40.8 ton at 6 m/min	US	Based on the M48 MBT
M578	Light armored recovery vehicle	24.3	Crane maximum lift capability: 6.7 tons, 2 winches with max. capacity of 27 tons on a bare drum	US	Hull is similar to that of the 175mm M107 and 203mm M110 SPGs
T-55	Armored recovery vehicle	34	Lifting capability of between 10 to 20 tons	Russia	Additional models were developed by the Czech Republic, Poland and Germany
T-62	Armored recovery vehicle	38		Russia	

AIR DEFENSE EQUIPMENT

Anti-Aircraft Guns

Caliber	Designation	SP, tracked or wheeled (where relevant)	Country of origin	Notes
57mm	ZSU 57x2	SP, tracked	Russia	
57mm	S-60		Russia	
40mm	M42 (twin 40mm)	SP, tracked	US	
40mm	Bofors L-70		Sweden	
40mm	Bofors L-60		Sweden	
37mm	M-1939		Russia	
35mm	Contraves Skyguard			Also listed under Air Defense Systems
35mm	Gepard	SP	Germany	
35mm	Oerlikon-Buhrle 35x2 GDF-002		Switzerland	May be part of 35mm Skyguard system
30mm	AMX DCA 30 (twin 30mm)	SP, tracked	France	
30mm	30x2 M-53/59	SP, wheeled	Czech Republic	
30mm	Oerlikon		Switzerland	
30mm	30x2 Wildcat	SP, wheeled	Germany	
30mm	30x2 M-3	SP	France	
23mm	ZSU 23x4	SP, tracked	Russia	Russian designation: Shilka
23mm	ZU 23x2		Russia	
20mm	20x2 VDAA	SP	France	Mounted on VAB APC

Anti Aircraft Guns *(continued)*

Caliber	Designation	SP, tracked or wheeled (where relevant)	Country of origin	Notes
20mm	TCM-20x2	SP	Israel	Mounting of French gun on US-made M-3 halftrack
20mm	Oerlikon GAI		Switzerland	
20mm	M163 A1 Vulcan	SP	US	
20mm	M167 Vulcan		US	
20mm	20x2	SP	France	Mounted on Panhard VCR 6x6
20mm	20x3 M-55 A4		Slovenia	
20mm	VDAA	SP	France	Mounted on VAB 6x6

Air Defense Systems

Caliber	Designation	Missiles	Country of origin	Notes
12.7mm	Zipkin	Stinger	Turkey	Based on Land Rover chassis, passive tracking system
20mm	Mahbet	Stinger	Israel	Based on M163 Vulcan
35mm	Skyguard (Contraves Skyguard) 2x35	Aspide or RIM-7M Sparrow	Italy	Gun-Switzerland, SAM-Italy, or US; chassis and radar-Italy or Austria; Egyptian designation: Amoun
23mm	Sinai 23 23x2	4xSA-7	Egypt	Gun and SAM-Russia or Egypt; chassis-US

Air Defense Missiles

Model	Range (km)	Guidance	Configuration	Country of origin
Heavy missiles				
HAWK	35	Semi-active radar	Towed	US
Improved HAWK (MIM-23B)	40	Semi-active radar	Towed	US
HQ-2J	34	Command	Towed	China
Nike Hercules	155	Command	Towed	US
Patriot (MIM-104)	160	Command, semi-active radar	Trucked	US
SA-10 (S-300P/300V)	70/150	Command, active radar	Trucked	Russia
SA-2	35	Command	Towed	Russia
SA-3	22	Command	Towed	Russia
SA-5	250	Command, active radar	Static	Russia
Medium missiles				
ADAMS	12	Command	SP	Israel
Crotale	9	Command	SP	France
Crotale NG	11	Command, IR, optical	SP	France
SA-11	28	Semi-active radar	SP	Russia
SA-6 (Kub)	24	Semi-active radar	Trucked	Russia
Roland I/II	6.3	Command	SP	France
SA-8 (Osa romb)	9.9	Command	SP	Russia
Shahine I/II	8-11	Command, IR or optical	SP	France
Light missiles				
ADATS	8	Laser	SP	Switzerland
Atiligan	5	Optical, IR	SP	Turkey
Avenger	4.5	IR	SP	US
Chaparral (MIM-72A)	8	Active, IR	SP	US

Air Defense Missiles *(continued)*

Model	Range (km)	Guidance	Configuration	Country of origin
Mistral	6	Optical, IR	Portable	France
Rapier	7	Command, optical command	Towed	UK
RBS-70	6	Laser	Portable	Sweden
SA-9	8	Optical, IR	SP	Russia
SA-13 (Strella 10)	5	Optical, IR	SP	Russia
Tigercat	5.5	Optical command	Towed	UK
Shoulder-launched missiles				
Ain al-Saqer	4.4	Optical, IR	Portable	Egypt
Blowpipe	3.5	Optical command	Portable	UK
HN-5	4	Optical, IR	Portable	China
Javelin	5	Optical command	Portable	UK
Redeye (MIM-43A)	5.5	Optical, IR	Portable	US
SA-7 (Strella)	3.5	Optical, IR	Portable	Russia
SA-4 (Strella 3)	6	Optical, IR	Portable	Russia
SA-16 (Igla)	5	Optical, IR	Portable	Russia
Starburst	4	Laser	Portable	UK
Stinger (FIM-92A)	4.5	Optical, IR	Portable	US

AIR FORCE EQUIPMENT

Fighter Aircraft

Model	Radius of action (km)	Radar	Air-to-air missiles	Air-to-ground missiles	Navigation and fire-control instrumentation	Country of origin
Interceptors						
F-14		AVG-12 (315 km)	Sparrow, Phoenix		IR seeker	US
F-15C/D		APG-63 look-down and shoot-down capability	Sidewinder, Sparrow, AMRAAM		ATLIS II laser illumination pod	US
MiG-25	1,130	Fox Fire (85km) limited look-down and shoot-down	AA-6, AA-7 (R-23), AA-8 (R-60)		ECCM pods	Russia
Tornado ADV Mk 3	740	Foxhunter multi-mode, ground mapping (185 km)	Sky Flash, Sidewinder		Internal ECM/ ECCM, TI FL radar	UK, Germany
MiG-23 MF/ML	1,150 (AA) 700 (AG)	High Lark look-down (85km)	AA-7 (R-23), AA-8 (R-60)		IR seeker	Russia
MiG-29		RLS RP-29 Slot Back (100km) look-down and shoot-down	AA-8 (R-60), AA-10 (R-27), AA-11 (R-73)		IR seeker	Russia

Fighter Aircraft (continued)

Model	Radius of action (km)	Radar	Air-to-air missiles	Air-to-ground missiles	Navigation and fire-control instrumentation	Country of origin
Advanced multi-role						
F-15E	1,270	APG-70 look-down and shoot-down capability	Sidewinder, Sparrow, AMRAAM	Maverick, Paveway	FLIR, LANTIRN targeting pod, SAR	US
F-16 A/B	925	APG-66 (74 km) look-down and shoot-down capability	Sidewinder, AMRAAM	Maverick, HARM/Shrike	FLIR, ALQ-119/131 ECM, Pave Penny laser pod	US
F-16 C/D	925	APG-68V air-to-air and air-to-ground	Sidewinder, AMRAAM, Sparrow, Python 4	Maverick, Paveway, HARM/Shrike, Harpoon, Popeye II	FLIR ALQ-131/187 ECM, Pave Penny laser pod, LANTIRN, Orphus (reconn.), Atils laser pod	US
F-18 C/D		APG-65, air-to-air and air-to-ground	Sidewinder, AMRAAM, Sparrow	Maverick, Paveway, HARM/Shrike, Harpoon	AAS-38 FLIR, ALQ-126/165 ECM, ASQ-173 laser pod	US
Phantom 2000		APG-76	Python 3, Sidewinder	Griffin, Popeye, Paveway, Maverick, GBU-15	INS, WDNS weapon and nav. computer, internal ECM, SAR	Israel

Glossary

Fighter Aircraft (continued)

Model	Radius of action (km)	Radar	Air-to-air missiles	Air-to-ground missiles	Navigation and fire-control instrumentation	Country of origin
Mirage 2000	1,200 (hi-lo-hi), 925 (lo-lo-lo)	RDM/RDY multi-mode (100 km)	R 530/550 Magic, Mica	ARMAT, Exocet, AS-30L, laser-guided bombs	Atlis laser pod, SLAR, reconn. pods, ECM pods, Astac ELINT pod	France
Multi-role						
Mirage F1	425 (hi-lo-hi)	Cyrano IV, Doppler nav. radar	R 530/550 Magic, Sidewinder	ARMAT, Exocet, AS-30L, laser-guided bombs	Nav./bombing computer, Atlis laser pod, SLAR, reconn. pods, ECM pods	France
Tornado IDS Mk 1	1,390 (hi-lo-lo-hi)	TI FL radar, Decca Doppler terrain-following radar	Sidewinder	AS-30L, Maverick, Paveway, Sea Eagle, munitions dispenser	Digital attack/nav. system, Ferranti laser pod, internal ECM	UK, Germany
Jaguar	1,400 (hi-lo-hi), 917 (lo-lo-lo)	Agave	R 550 Magic, Sidewinder	AS 37	HUDWAC weapons computer, reconn. pod, TV night sensors	UK
F-4E		APQ-72	Sparrow III, Sidewinder	Bullpop, Maverick, Standard/Shrike, Paveway, GBU-15, C-801	ASQ-19 navigation package, AJB-3 bombing system laser pod	US

Fighter Aircraft (continued)

Model	Radius of action (km)	Radar	Air-to-air missiles	Air-to-ground missiles	Navigation and fire-control instrumentation	Country of origin
F-5 E/F	222 (lo-lo-lo), 890 (hi-lo-hi)	APQ-159 (37km)	Sidewinder	Paveway	Laser pod	US
Hawk 200	945 (hi-lo-hi)	APG-66H multi-mode	Sky Flash, Sidewinder	Sea Eagle, Maverick	HUDWAC weapons computer, FLIR, reconn. pod	UK
Obsolete						
F-5 A/B	350		Sidewinder			US
Mirage III-E	1,200	Cyrano II	R 530 Magic	AS-30 IR/com	Nav./bombing computer	France
Mirage V	1,300 (hi-lo-hi), 650 (lo-lo-lo)	Agave	R 530/550 Magic Sidewinder	AS-30 IR/com	Laser range finder, refuel pod	France
MiG-21 MF/BIS	740 (hi-lo-hi)	Jay Bird (20km)	AA-2 C/D (K-13)			Russia
F-6	685	Izumrud	PL-2, PL-5			China
F-7	600 (hi-lo-hi), 370 (lo-lo-lo)	Ranging radar	PL-2, PL-5, PL-7, R 550 Magic		HUDWAC weapons computer	China
Ground attack						
OV-10	367	Doppler nav. radar	Sidewinder	Paveway	TV/laser designation pod	US
Su-20/22	2,300 (hi-hi-hi), 1,400 (lo-lo-lo)	SRD-5M ranging radar	AA-8 (R-60)	AS-7, AS-9, AS-10	ASP-5ND fire control system, laser pod, reconn. pod, ECM pod	Russia

Fighter Aircraft (continued)

Model	Radius of action (km)	Radar	Air-to-air missiles	Air-to-ground missiles	Navigation and fire-control instrumentation	Country of origin
Su-24	322 (lo-lo-lo) 950 (lo-lo-hi) 1,050 (hi-lo-hi)	PNS-24M terrain-following/ nav. system	AA-8 (R-60)	AS-10, AS-11, AS-12, AS-14	Kaira-24 laser/ TV guidance system, laser pod, internal ECM	Russia
Su-25	400 (lo-lo-lo) 630 (hi-hi-hi)	Kinzhal ground radar doppler nav. system	AA-8 (R-60)	AS-10, AS-11, AS-14, laser-guided bombs	Voskhod nav./attack system, internal TV/ laser guidance system, internal ECM, IIR pod	Russia
MiG-23BN	700	Doppler nav. radar	AA-8 (R-60)	AS-7	Laser range finder	Russia
Bombers						
Tu-16	3,150			AS-5, AS-6		Russia
Tu-22	2,200 (hi-hi-hi) 1,500 (lo-lo-lo)	Down Beat nav. radar		AS-4		Russia

Helicopters

Model	Number of passengers	External payload (kg)	Max range (km)	Armament	Avionics	Country of origin
Light transport						
300C	1+2		370			US
500D	6	408	482 (S/L); 531 (5,000 ft)			US
530F	6	907	371 (S/L); 429 (5,000 ft)		FLIR	US

Helicopters (continued)

Model	Number of passengers	External payload (kg)	Max range (km)	Armament	Avionics	Country of origin
AS-350 Ecureuil	6	907	720	Machine guns, 20mm guns, rockets		France
Bell 206B	3 – 4		645			US
Bell 406 (OH-58B) Kiowa	2+2		556		Doppler nav. system, night vision	US
BK-117	7		500		Laser-1 Doppler nav. system	Japan
Mi-2	8	800	440			Russia
SA-315 Lama	1+4	1,135	515			France
SA-318C Alouette II	1+4	600	300			France
SA-316 Alouette III	6	750	290			France
UH-12	1+2	454	346			US
Medium transport						
AS-330 Puma	16	3,200	572	Machine guns, 20mm gun, rockets	Doppler nav. radar, Decca nav. system, rolling map	France
AS-61/SH-3D	31	3,630	582		Doppler nav. system	US
AS-332 Super Puma/AS-532 Cougar	21 – 25	4,500	870	Machine guns, 20mm gun, rockets	Doppler nav. radar, Decca nav. system, rolling map	France
AS-365 Dauphin II	10	1,600	250		Digital nav. system	France

Helicopters (continued)

Model	Number of passengers	External payload (kg)	Max range (km)	Armament	Avionics	Country of origin
Bell 204	7 – 8	1,360	615	Machine-guns, rocket launchers		US
UH-1H (Bell 205, 212)	11 – 14	1,760	511	Machine-guns, rocket launchers		US
Bell 214	18		678			Italy
Bell 412	14	1,814	656 (S/L) 804 (5,000 ft)		Doppler nav. radar	Italy
KV-107	26	3,000	175	Machine guns, rockets, bombs	Doppler nav. radar	Japan
Mi-8/17	24		500		Doppler nav. radar	Russia
S-61R/HH-3E	25	3,620	748		Doppler nav. radar, night vision, ALQ-144 ECM	US
S-70/UH-60A Black Hawk	11	3,630	600	Machine guns		US
SA-321 Super Ferlon	27	4,500	630		Doppler radar, INS	France
Westland Commando	28	2,720	445		Doppler nav. radar	UK
Heavy transport						
CH-47D Chinook	44	12,700	185		Doppler nav. radar	US
CH-53D	64	14,515	413			US
Mi-6	70	8,000	620	Machine guns, rockets		Russia

Glossary

Helicopters *(continued)*

Model	Number of passengers	External payload (kg)	Max range (km)	Armament	Avionics	Country of origin
Ground attack						
500MD			389 (S/L), 428 (5,000 ft)	TOW missiles, Stinger missiles	TV/FLIR targeting system	US
A-109A Mk II	7	907	550	Machine guns, rocket launchers, TOW missiles	Doppler nav. radar, TV targeting system	Italy
AH-1 G/J/P			574	Minigun, TOW missiles	Optical targeting system	US
AH-1W			635	20mm gun, TOW missiles, Hellfire missiles	Optical targeting system, laser designator	US
AH-64A		771	482	30mm gun, Hellfire missiles, rockets, Stinger missiles	Doppler nav. system, ALQ-136/144 ECM, TV/FLIR targeting system, laser designator	US
BO-105	1+4		575 (S/L), 657 (5,000 ft)	HOT missiles, TOW missiles	Doppler nav. system, optical targeting system	Germany
Mi-24	8		450	AT-2 missiles, machine guns, rockets, bombs	Doppler nav. system, optical targeting system, internal ECM	Russia
OH-58D Kiowa Warrior (Bell 406)			556	Machine guns, TOW missiles, Stinger missiles	Doppler nav system, TV/IIR targeting system, laser designator, night vision system	US

405

Helicopters (continued)

Model	Number of passengers	External payload (kg)	Max range (km)	Armament	Avionics	Country of origin
SA-316 Alouette III	6	750	290	Machine guns, 20mm gun, AS-11/12 missiles	Optical targeting system	France
SA-342 Gazelle	1+4	700	670	AS-12 missiles, HOT missiles, rockets, machine guns	Optical targeting system, laser designator (342 L)	France
Naval combat						
AS-332 Super Puma / AS-532 Cougar		4,500	870	Exocet missiles, AS-15TT missiles, torpedoes	Doppler nav. radar, Decca nav. system, RDR 1400/1500 search radar or Varan ASW radar Sonar, magnetic sweep, Sonobuoys	France
AS-365 Dauphin II	10	1,600	250	AS-15TT, torpedoes	Agrion 15 plan position radar or Omera ORB 32 search radar, Croyzet magnetic sweep, HS 12 sonar, digital nav. system	France
AS-61/SH-3D	31	3,630	582	Torpedoes, depth charges	Doppler ASW nav. system, APS-707 radar, AQS-13/18 sonar	US
Bell 204		1,360	615	Torpedoes	Sonar	US

Helicopters (continued)

Model	Number of passengers	External payload (kg)	Max range (km)	Armament	Avionics	Country of origin
Bell 212		1,760	511	Torpedoes	Doppler ASW nav. system, AQS-13 B/F sonar	US
Bell 412		1,814	656 (S/L) 804 (5,000 ft)	25mm cannon, Sea Skua missiles	Doppler radar, TV/FLIR targeting system, ALQ-144 ECM	Italy
Kamov 28			200	Torpedoes, depth charges	Doppler nav. radar, radar, magnetic sweep, OKA-2 sonar, sonobuoys	Russia
Mi-14 PL			1,135	Torpedoes, depth charges	Doppler nav. radar, 12M radar, magnetic sweep, OKA-2 sonar, sonobuoys	Russia
SA-321 Super Ferlon		4,500	630	Torpedoes	Doppler radar or Sylphe ASW radar, INS, sonar	France
SH-2G Sea Sprite	4	1,814	885	Torpedoes	LN-66HP radar, magnetic and acoustic sweeps, 15 sonobuoys, FLIR	US
Westland Sea King Mk 47			1,230	Torpedoes, depth charges	AD 580 Doppler nav. system, AW 391 radar, AQS-13B Plessey sonar, sonobuoys	UK

Training Aircraft

Model	Range (km)	External weight (kg)	Armament	Avionics	Country of origin
Jet engines					
Alpha Jet	555	2,500	30mm gun, rockets, bombs, Magic AAM	Weapon aiming computer, camera reconn. pod	France, Germany
BAC 167	900	1,360	Machine guns, bombs, rockets		UK
C-101	964	2,250	30mm gun, rockets, bombs	INS, optical sight, laser designator, reconn. pod, ECM pod	Spain
Cessna 318/T-37B	1,400		Machine gun, rockets, bombs	INS, computing gun-sight, gun camera, camera reconn. pod	US
CM 170 Fuga Magister	910	500	Machine guns, rockets	Gyro gunsight	France
G2-A Galeb		700	Machine guns, bombs, rockets	Fixed gunsight	Yugoslavia
Hawk Mk 60	998	3,084	30mm gun, rockets, bombs, Magic/Sidewinder AAM, Maverick AGM, Sea Eagle AGM	INS, gunsight/camera, camera reconn. pod	UK
Hawk Mk 100	998	3,084	30mm gun, rockets, bombs, Magic/Sidewinder AAM, Maverick AGM, Sea Eagle AGM	INS, gunsight/camera, HUDWAC weapon system, FLIR, camera reconn. pod, ECM pod	UK

Training Aircraft (continued)

Model	Range (km)	External weight (kg)	Armament	Avionics	Country of origin
L-29 Delfin	397		Machine guns, rockets, bombs	Gyro gun sight or gun camera	Czech Republic
L-39 Albatros		1,100	23mm gun, rockets, bombs, IR missiles	Camera reconn. pod, gyro gun sight	Czech Republic
L-59	1,210	1,700	23mm gun, bombs, rockets, machine guns, rockets, bombs, AS-12 AGM	HUD mission computer	Czech Republic
MB 326	648	1,814		INS, fixed/gyro gunsight, gunsight camera, camera reconn. pod	Italy
MB 339	593	1,815	30mm guns, bombs, rockets, Magic/Sidewinder AAM	INS, fixed/gyro gunsight, camera reconn. pod, ECM pod	Italy
T-33			machine gun		US
T-38 Talon				INS	US
Piston/Turbo-prop					
AS-202 Bravo	965				Switzerland
Bonanza F 33C	1,326				US
CAP 10	1,000				France
Cessna 150	909				US
Cessna 172/T-41	963			INS	US
MBB 223 Flamingo	500				Germany, Spain
Mushshak		300	Machine guns, rockets, Bantam AGM		India
Sierra 200	1,270				US

409

Training Aircraft (continued)

Model	Range (km)	External weight (kg)	Armament	Avionics	Country of origin
TB 20/21/200	1,170				France
Zlin 142	525				Czech Republic
Cessna 180/185	1,100			INS	US
Cessna 182	1,380			INS	US
Cessna U-206	1,045		Minigun, bombs		US
EMB-312	1,844	625	Machine gun, rockets, bombs	Fixed gun-sight	Brazil
G-115T Acro	1,310				Germany
PC-7/9	1,200			Computer nav. system (PC-9)	Switzerland
PC-6	1,050				Switzerland
BAe SA-3-120 Bulldog	1,000	290	Machine guns, bombs		UK
SF 260 Warrior	556	300	Machine guns, bombs, rockets	Camera reconn. pod	US
T-34C	555	544	Machine guns, bombs, rockets, Walleye AGM		US

Transport Aircraft

Model	Passengers	Range (km)	Payload (kg)	Country of origin
Airbus A340	295	12,416	47,127	France
An-12	90	Max. load: 3,600, max. fuel: 5,700	20,000	Russia
An-24	44–50	Max. load: 550, max. fuel: 2,400	5,500	Russia
An-26	40	Max. load: 1,100, max. fuel: 2,550	5,500	Russia
An-74TK	20	Max. load: 1,350, max. fuel: 4,300	10,000	Ukraine

Transport Aircraft (continued)

Model	Passengers	Range (km)	Payload (kg)	Country of origin
An-140	52	2,500	6,000	Ukraine/Iran
Arava	20	Max. load: 486, max. fuel: 1,400	2,350	Israel
BAe 125/HS 125	8/12	3,120	857	UK
BN-2B Islander	10	Max. load: 672, max. fuel: 2,027	1,200	UK
Boeing 707	181	4,235	24,950	US
Boeing 727	145	4,390	18,144	US
Boeing 737	130	4,180	17,223	US
Boeing 747-200	452	10,562		US
Boeing 747-200F		8,060	109,315	US
C-130H	92	Max. load: 3,790, max. fuel: 7,876	19,356	US
C-140 Jetstar	10	Max. load: 3,410, max. fuel: 3,595	1,327	US
C-160	93	Max. load: 1,853, max. fuel: 5,095	16,000	Germany
CASA C-212	16	Max. load: 720, max. fuel: 1,920	2,000	Spain
Citation III	11	4,815		US
CN-235	48	4,350	6,000	Spain
Commander 690	8	2,116		Britain
DC-3 Dakota	38	1,853	2,500	US
DC-8	189	11,410	30,240	US
DC-9	105	3,100	12,743	US
DC-10	380	7,400	43,300	US
DHC-4	32	Max. load: 390, max. fuel: 2,100	3,965	Canada
DHC-5	41	Max. load: 815, max. fuel: 3,490	6,280	Canada
Dornier Do 228	15/20	1,740	2,200	Germany
Dove	11	620	670	Canada

Transport Aircraft (continued)

Model	Passengers	Range (km)	Payload (kg)	Country of origin
EMB 110P	18	2,000	1,681	Brazil
Falcon 10	7	3,370	603	France
Falcon 20	8/14	3,540	1,380	France
Falcon 50	8	6,480	1,570	France
Falcon 900	8	7,229	2,185	France
Fokker F-27	44	2,213	6,438	Netherlands
G222L	53	Max. load: 1,890, max. fuel: 5,100	9,000	Italy
Gulfstream II/III	19	7,590	907	US
Gulfstream V	19	12,038	2,948	US
IL-14	18	2,600	5,300	Russia
IL-76	120	6,700	48,000	Russia
IL-78 Tanker		2,500	60,000 fuel	Russia
KC-130 Tanker		1,850	23,587 fuel	US
KC-135 Tanker		4,630	92,210 fuel	US
King Air B100/ B200/200T	8/14	2,456		US
L-100-30	128	Max. load: 2,585, max. fuel: 10,000	23,679	US
L-1011-500	246	Max. load: 9,900, max. fuel: 11,286	42,000	US
L-410 UVP	15	Max. load: 390, max. fuel: 1,140	1,310	Czech Republic
Learjet 25	8	2,650		US
Maule MX-7	4	845	317	US
Piper Navajo	6	1,800		US
Skyvan Srs 3M	22	Max. load: 386, max. fuel: 1,075	2,358	UK
Tu-124	44	Max. load: 1,220, max. fuel: 3,500	6,000	Russia
Tu-134	80	Max. load: 2,400, max. fuel: 3,500	8,165	Russia
Yak-40	27	Max. load: 1,000, max. fuel: 1,480	2,300	Russia

Miscellaneous Aircraft

Model	Crew	Mission	Systems	Endurance (h)	Range (km)	In service	Country of origin
Adnan-1/2	8–10	AEW	Tiger TRS-2100 radar, ESM		5,000	Iraq	Iraq
Beechcraft 1900C	6	Maritime surveillance	Litton APS-504 radar, SLAM-MR, Singer S-3075 ESM		2,900	Egypt	US
Beechcraft 1900C	2	EW	ECM, comm. Relay, USD-9 Guardrail		2,900	Egypt	US
BN-2T Maritime Defender	4	Maritime surveillance	Bendix RDR-1400 radar, torpedoes		800	Morocco, Oman	UK
Boeing 707 AEW		AEW	Phalcon radar, ECM, ESM			Israel	Israel
Boeing 707 EW		EW	Elta EL-8300 SIGINT system, ESM	6		Israel	Israel
C-130		EW	COMINT, ELINT, EW systems			Israel	Israel
C-130H MP		Maritime surveillance	Search radar, IRDS, SLAR-PI, TV sensor	16	3,300	Egypt, Morocco	US
Casa C-212	4	ASW/ Maritime surveillance	APS-128 radar, ESM, MAD, sonobuoys, torpedoes		1,700	Sudan	UK
CN 235 MP	5	Maritime surveillance	Liton APS-504 radar, ALR-85 ESM, FLIR-2000HP, torpedoes		1,500	Turkey	Spain/ Indonesia

413

Miscellaneous Aircraft (continued)

Model	Crew	Mission	Systems	Endurance (h)	Range (km)	In service	Country of origin
CN-235 MPA	6	Maritime surveillance	Thomson-CSF Ocean Master 100 radar, AMASCOS 300 with FLIR and ESM systems	8	1,400	UAE, Tunisia	Spain/ Indonesia
E-2C Hawkeye	5	AEW	APS-138/139 radar (480 km), ALR-73 passive detection	6	2,500	Egypt, Israel	US
E-3A Sentry	20	AWACS	APY-1 radar, ECM, ESM, CC-1 mission computer	12		Saudi Arabia	US
Fokker F-27 MP	6	Maritime surveillance	Liton APS-504 radar	12	5,000	Algeria	Netherlands
Mystère - Falcon 20F	6	EW	ELINT, SIGINT and ECM systems		4,400	Morocco	France
P-3C Orion	10	ASW/ Maritime surveillance	APS-115 radar, ARR-72 sonar, ASQ-114 mission computer, magnetic and maritime anomaly detectors, sonobuoys, ESM, mines and torpedoes		3,800	Iran	US
Sea Scan 1124N	8	Maritime surveillance	Liton APS-504 radar	8	2,800	Israel	Israel
Super King Air 200CT	2	EW	ECM, comm. Relay, USD-9 Guardrail			Israel	US
Super King Air B-200T	8	Maritime surveillance	Search radar, FLIR, Seehawk ESM, sonobuoys	6.5	3,300	Algeria	US

UAVs and Mini-UAVs

Model	Length (m)	Wing span (m)	Endurance (h)	Range (km)	Payload (kg)	Payload type	Country of origin
Ababil-S	2.8	3.3	3	150		TV	Iran
Ababil-T				50 – 150		Strike drone	Iran
AQM-37	3.8	1	2.3	185		Target drone	US
Banshee BTT 342	2.9	2.46	1.5			Target drone	US
BQM-34	6.87	3.87				Target drone	US
BQM-74C Chukar II	3.87	1.68	1.7	450		Target drone	US
CL-89	2.5	0.9		135	20	TV, IR	Canada
Falco	3.5	2.7	1	150	20	Target drone	UAE
Gnat 750	5.4	10.5	40			TV, FLIR	US
Hermes 1500	8.4	10	24			TV, SAR	Israel
Hermes 450S	6	10	20		150	TV, SAR	Israel
Heron	8.4	16.4	50	140		Multipurpose reconn.	Israel
Hunter	6.9	8.7	12	140		TV, FLIR, laser	Israel
Mastiff	3.3	4.3	6	200	30	TV, FLIR, ECM, laser designator	Israel
Mirach 100	3.9	1.8	1.1		30	Target drone	Italy
Mohajer II			2	50		TV, EW	Iran
Mohajer III (Dorna)			3	100		TV, EW	Iran
Mohajer IV (Hodhod)			3	150		TV, IR, EW	Iran
MQM -107	5.5	3	2.5			Target drone	US
Nibbio	5.1	5.6	10	200	55	TV, ECM	UAE

UAVs and Mini-UAVs (continued)

Model	Length (m)	Wing span (m)	Endurance (h)	Range (km)	Payload (kg)	Payload type	Country of origin
Pioneer	4.2	5	6.5	210		TV, FLIR	US
Saeqeh I/II	6	3.3		50		Target drone	Iran
Scarab 324						TV	US
Scout	3.7	3.6	7	100	30	TV, IIR, laser designator	Israel
Searcher	5	7.1	12			TV, FLIR	Israel
Seeker			9	200	40	TV, IIR	South Africa
Shmel (Yak-61)	2.7	3.2	2			TV, IR	Russia
Skyeye R4E-50	4	7.2	12	430		TV, IR, FLIR, EW, IRLS	US
Teledyne Ryan model 124 Firebee	7	3.9	1.25	1,200		Target drone	US

Advanced Armament

Air-to-Air missiles

Type	Guidance	Range (km)	Counter measures	Country of origin
AA-2C/D	Semi-active radar/IR	8/3		Russia
AA-6	Semi-active radar/IR	30		Russia
AA-7	Semi-active radar/IR	25/15	IRCM	Russia
AA-8	IR	3-5		Russia
AA-10	Semi-active radar/IR	50/40	IRCM	Russia
AA-11	IR	30	Improved IRCM	Russia

Air-to-Air missiles (continued)

Type	Guidance	Range (km)	Counter measures	Country of origin
AIM-120 AMRAAM	Active radar	50		US
Mica	Active radar/imaging IR	50	Enhanced IRCM	France
Phoenix	Active radar	150	ECCM	US
PL-2	IR	3		PRC
PL-5	IR	3		PRC
PL-7	IR	3		PRC
Python 3	IR	5	IRCM	Israel
Python 4	IR	8	IRCM	Israel
R530	Semi-active radar/IR	15/3		France
Super 530F/D	Semi-active radar	30/40	Improved ECCM	France
R 550 Magic II	IR	5	Improved IRCM	France
Shafrir 2	IR	3		Israel
Sidewinder	IR	8	Improved IRCM	US
Sky Flash	Semi-active radar	40	Improved ECCM	UK
Sparrow	Semi-active radar	45	Improved ECCM	US

Air-to-Surface Missiles

Type	Purpose	Guidance	Range (km)	Country of origin
ALARM	Anti-radiation	Passive radar homing	45	UK
ARMAT	Anti-radiation	Passive radar homing	90	France
AS-4	Anti-radiation	Passive radar homing	400	Russia
AS-9	Anti-radiation	Passive radar homing	90	Russia
AS-11	Anti-radiation	Passive radar homing	50	Russia
AS-12	Anti-radiation	Passive radar homing	35	Russia
HARM	Anti-radiation	Passive radar homing	25	US
Shrike	Anti-radiation	Passive radar homing	12	US

Air-to-Surface Missiles (continued)

Type	Purpose	Guidance	Range (km)	Country of origin
Standard	Anti-radiation	Passive radar homing	55	US
AM 39 Exocet	Anti-ship	Active radar	50	France
AS 15TT	Anti-ship	Radar command	15	France
AS-5	Anti-ship	Active radar	180	Russia
C-801	Anti-ship	Active radar	40	China
Gabriel	Anti-ship	Active radar	35	Israel
Harpoon	Anti-ship	Active radar	120	US
Penguin	Anti-ship	IR	30	Norway
Sea Eagle	Anti-ship	Active radar	110	UK
Sea Skua	Anti-ship	Semi-active radar	18	UK
AS-11	Anti-tank	Manual wire	3	France
AS-12	Anti-tank	Manual wire	5	France
AT-2	Anti-tank	Radio command	4	Russia
AT-6	Anti-tank	Radio command	5	Russia
Hellfire	Anti-tank	Laser/IIR	8	US
HOT	Anti-tank	Auto wire	4	France
TOW	Anti-tank	Auto wire	4	US
Trigat 3LR	Anti-tank	IIR	4.5	France
AS 6	Ground attack	Internal/passive radar	400	Russia
AS 7	Ground attack	Radio command	5	Russia
AS 10	Ground attack	Laser	10	Russia
AS 14	Ground attack	Laser/TV	12	Russia
AS 30	Ground attack	Radio command/laser	10	France
Bullpop	Ground attack	Radio command	10	US

Glossary

Air-to-Surface Missiles (continued)

Type	Purpose	Guidance	Range (km)	Country of origin
Durandal	Ground attack	Internal navigation	7	France
Excalibur	Ground attack	Internal navigation	10	France
GBU-15	Ground attack	TV/IIR-guided bomb	80	US
Griffin	Ground attack	Laser-guided bombs	10	Israel
JDAM	Ground attack	INS/GPS-guided bomb	25	US
AGM-65 Maverick	Ground attack	TV/IIR/laser	8/25/20	US
Opher	Ground attack	IR-guided bombs		Israel
Paveway GBU-10/12/16	Ground attack	Laser-guided bombs	7	US
PGM 1/2/3	Ground attack	Laser/IR	20	UK
Popeye	Ground attack	TV/IIR	80	Israel
Pyramid	Ground attack	TV-guided bombs		Israel
Sattar-1/2	Ground attack	Laser	20/30	Iran
Skipper	Ground attack	Laser-guided bombs	7	US
Walleye	Ground attack	TV-guided bomb	20	US

Optical Systems

Type	Mission	Systems description	Range (km)	Country of origin
Atlis	Target acquisition	TV, laser designator	12	France
Iris	Target acquisition	FLIR		US
Lantirn/Sharpshooter	Target acquisition/navigation	TV, FLIR, laser, terrain-following radar		US
Litening	Target acquisition/navigation	TV, FLIR, laser, CCD		Israel
Lorops	Reconnaissance pod	TV, IIR, oblique cameras		Israel
Pave Penny	Target acquisition	Laser designator and tracer		US
Tiald	Target acquisition	IIR, laser designator		UK

419

NAVY EQUIPMENT

Sea-to-Sea missiles

Type	Guidance	Range (km)	Payload (kg)	Warhead	Country of origin
Barak 1	Command to line of sight	12	22	HE fragmentation	Israel
C-801/YJ-1	Inertial and active radar	40	165	HE	PRC
C-802/YJ-2	Inertial and active radar	120	165	HE	PRC
Gabriel Mk 2/3	Internal and semi-active radar	35	180	HE SAP	Israel
Hai Ying II/SY-1	Internal with active radar or IR	95	513	HE	PRC
Harpoon	Inertial and active radar	130	222	HE blast penetration	US
MM 40 Exocet	Inertial with active radar	70	165	HE fragmentation	France
Otomat Mk 1	Inertial, command and active radar	60	210	HE SAP	International
Penguin Mk 2	Inertial and passive IR	30	120	HE SAP	Norway
Sea Killer II	Command	25	70	HE SAP	Italy
Sea Skua SL	Semi-active radar	15	30	HE SAP	UK
SS-N-2A/B Styx	Internal with active radar/or IR	35/40	350/450	HE	Russia
SS-N-12	Internal, command and active radar	550	1,000	HE	Russia
Standard SM-1	Command and semi-active radar	40	115	HE fragmentation	US

Sea-to-Air Missiles

Type	Guidance	Range (km)	Country of origin	Notes
Aspide Mk 1	Semi-active radar	15	Italy	Based on the US AIM-7 Sparrow
Bora	Optical IR	5	Turkey	Based on Stinger SAMs and 12.7mm gun
Crotale-NG	Command	11	France	Naval version of Crotale
Mistral	Optical, IR	6	France	

Sea-to-Air Missiles *(continued)*

Type	Guidance	Range (km)	Country of origin	Notes
SA-N-4	Semi-active radar	14.8	Russia	Naval version of the SA-8
SA-N-5	IR homing	10	Russia	Naval version of the SA-7
Sea Sparrow	Semi-active radar	15	US	
Standard RIM-66A/C	Semi-active radar	40/70	US	

Coastal Defense

Type	Guidance	Range (km)	Payload (kg)	Warhead	Country of origin
Hai Ying II (Silkworm)	Autopilot with active radar or IR	95	513	HE	PRC
C-802	Inertial and active radar	120	165	HE	PRC
SS-N-22 (Sunburn)	Inertial with updates and active/passive radar	90	300	HE	Russia
SSC-1B (Sepal)	Inertial with commands and IR or active radar	300	1,000	HE	Russia
SSC-3 (Styx)/ SS-N-2 A/B	Autopilot with active radar or IR	80	513	HE	Russia

ABBREVIATIONS

a/c	aircraft
AA	air-to-air; anti-aircraft
AAG	anti-aircraft gun
AAM	air-to-air missile
AD	air defense
AEW	airborne early warning
AFB	airforce base
AFV	armored fighting vehicle
AGM	air-to-ground missile
APC	armored personnel carrier
APFSDS	armour-piercing fin-stabilized discarding-sabot
armd.	armored
ARV	armored recovery vehicle
AS	air-to-surface
ASW	anti-submarine warfare
AT	anti-tank
ATGM	anti-tank guided missile
aty.	artillery
AWACS	airborne warning and control system
batt.	battalion
bn	billion
BW	biological warfare
BWC	Biological Weapons Convention
CAS	close air support
CBU	cluster bomb unit
CBW	chemical and biological weapons, chemical and biological warfare
cif	cost insurance and freight
CW	chemical warfare, chemical weapons
CWC	Chemical Weapons Convention
dwt	deadweight tons
ECCM	electronic counter-countermeasures
ECM	electronic countermeasures
ELINT	electronic intelligence gathering
ERA	explosive reactive armor
ESM	electronic surveillance measures
EW	electronic warfare
FCS	fire control system
FLIR	forward looking infra-red
FMS	foreign military sales
fob	free on board
ft	feet

ABBREVIATIONS (*CONTINUED*)

GBU	glide bomb unit
GCC	Gulf Cooperation Council
GDP	gross domestic product
h	hours
HAWK	homing all way killer
HE	high explosive
HEAT	high explosive anti-tank
HUD	head up display (in combat aircraft)
IFV	infantry fighting vehicle
IIR	imaging infra-red
Inf.	infantry
IR	infra-red
IRCM	infra-red counter measures
IRLS	infra-red linescan
ITV	improved TOW vehicle
KDP	Kurdistan Democratic Party
KFOR	Kosovo Force (NATO)
kg	kilogram
km	kilometer
kw	kilowatt
Laser	light amplification by stimulated emission of radiation
LAW	light anti-tank weapon
LCM	landing craft, mechanized
LCT	landing craft, tank
LCU	landing craft, utility
LCVP	landing craft vehicle/personnel
LSM	landing ship, mechanized
LST	landing ship, tank
m	million; meter
max	maximum
MBT	main battle tank
mech.	mechanized
MFPB	missile fast patrol boat
MG	machine gun
Mk	mark
MLRS	multiple-launch rocket system
mm	millimeter
MRL	multiple-rocket launcher
MTI	moving target indication radar
Mw	megawatt
NATO	North Atlantic Treaty Organization

ABBREVIATIONS (*CONTINUED*)

nav	navigation
Naval SSM	sea-to-sea missile
NPT	Non-Proliferation Treaty
op	operational
PGM	precision-guided munition
PKK	Kurdish Workers' Party
PLO	Palestine Liberation Organization
PRC	People's Republic of China
PUK	People's Union of Kurdistan
R&D	research and development
reconn.	reconnaissance
SAM	surface-to-air missile
SAP	semi-armor piercing
SAR	search and rescue; synthetic aperture radar
SIGINT	signal intelligence
SLAR	sideways-looking airborne radar
SP	self-propelled
sq	square
SSM	surface-to-surface missile
TAB	towed assault bridge
TEL	transporter erector launcher
TLB	trailer launched bridge
TOW	tube-launched optically-tracked wire-guided
TV	television
TWMP	track-width mine plough
UAE	United Arab Emirates
UAV	unmanned aerial vehicle
UFO	unidentified flying object
UK	United Kingdom
UN	United Nations
UNAMSIL	United Nations Mission in Sierra Leone
UNDOF	United Nations Disengagement Observer Force (Golan Heights)
UNIFIL	United Nations Interim Force in Lebanon
UNIKOM	United Nations Iraq-Kuwait Observation Mission
UNMOVIC	United Nations Monitoring, Verification and Inspection Commission (in Iraq)
UNSC	United Nations Security Council
UNSCOM	United Nations Special Commission (in Iraq)
UNTSO	United Nations Truce Supervision Organization
US	United States
WAC	weapon aiming computer

Contributors

Shai Feldman

Head of Jaffee Center for Strategic Studies

Professor Feldman is the Head of the Jaffee Center for Strategic Studies at Tel Aviv University. He was a senior research associate at the Center since its establishment in 1978. During 1994 – 95, he was a visiting fellow at the Washington Institute for Near East Policy, and during 1995 – 97 he was a Senior Research Fellow at the Belfer Center for Science and International Affairs (BCSIA) at Harvard University's John F. Kennedy School of Government. In 1984 – 87 he was director of the Jaffee Center's Project on US Foreign and Defense Policies in the Middle East, and in 1989 – 94 he directed the Center's Project on Regional Security and Arms Control in the Middle East.

Educated at the Hebrew University in Jerusalem, Professor Feldman holds a Ph.D. from the University of California at Berkeley. He is a member of the Board of Directors of BCSIA at Harvard University, the Scientific Advisory Committee of the Stockholm International Peace Research Institute (SIPRI), and the International Institute for Strategic Studies (IISS) in London.

Professor Feldman is the author of numerous publications, including *Israeli Nuclear Deterrence: Strategy for the 1980s* (New York: Columbia University Press, 1982); *The Future of US-Israeli Strategic Cooperation* (Washington, D.C.: The Washington Institute for Near East Policy, 1996); *Nuclear Weapons and Arms Control in the Middle East* (Cambridge: MIT Press, 1997); and, with Abdullah Toukan (Jordan), *Bridging the Gap: A Future Security Architecture for the Middle East* (Lanham, md.: Rowman & Littlefield, 1997). He co-edited, with Ariel Levite, *Arms Control and the New Middle East Security Environment* (Study No. 23, Tel Aviv University, Jaffee Center for Strategic Studies, 1994), and edited *Confidence Building and Verification: Prospects in the Middle East* (Study No. 24, Tel Aviv: Tel Aviv University, Jaffee Center for Strategic Studies, 1994).

Yiftah Shapir

Yiftah Shapir joined the Jaffee Center in 1993 as an associate of the Center's Project on Security and Arms Control in the Middle East, where he followed proliferation of weapons of mass destruction (WMD) in the Middle East. Since 1996, he has been responsible for the quantitative section of *The Middle East Military Balance*. Before joining the center, Shapir served as an officer in the Israeli Air Force. He holds a B.Sc. degree in physics and chemistry from the Hebrew University of Jerusalem, and an MBA from the Recanati School of Business Administration at Tel Aviv University.

BCSIA Studies in International Security
Published by The MIT Press

Sean M. Lynn-Jones and Steven E. Miller, series editors
Karen Motley, executive editor
Belfer Center for Science and International Affairs (BCSIA)
John F. Kennedy School of Government, Harvard University

Allison, Graham T., Owen R. Coté, Jr., Richard A. Falkenrath, and Steven E. Miller, *Avoiding Nuclear Anarchy: Containing the Threat of Loose Russian Nuclear Weapons and Fissile Material* (1996)

Allison, Graham T., and Kalypso Nicolaïdis, eds., *The Greek Paradox: Promise vs. Performance* (1996)

Arbatov, Alexei, Abram Chayes, Antonia Handler Chayes, and Lara Olson, eds., *Managing Conflict in the Former Soviet Union: Russian and American Perspectives* (1997)

Bennett, Andrew, *Condemned to Repetition? The Rise, Fall, and Reprise of Soviet-Russian Military Interventionism, 1973–1996* (1999)

Blackwill, Robert D., and Michael Stürmer, eds., *Allies Divided: Transatlantic Policies for the Greater Middle East* (1997)

Blackwill, Robert D., and Paul Dibb, eds., *America's Asian Allies* (2000)

Brom, Shlomo, and Yiftah Shapir, eds., *The Middle East Military Balance 1999–2000* (1999)

Brown, Michael E., ed., *The International Dimensions of Internal Conflict* (1996)

Brown, Michael E., and Sumit Ganguly, eds., *Government Policies and Ethnic Relations in Asia and the Pacific* (1997)

Carter, Ashton B., and John P. White, eds., *Keeping the Edge: Managing Defense for the Future* (2001)

Elman, Colin, and Miriam Fendius Elman, eds., *Bridges and Boundaries: Historians, Political Scientists, and the Study of International Relations* (2001)

Elman, Miriam Fendius, ed., *Paths to Peace: Is Democracy the Answer?* (1997)

Falkenrath, Richard A., *Shaping Europe's Military Order: The Origins and Consequences of the CFE Treaty* (1994)

Falkenrath, Richard A., Robert D. Newman, and Bradley A. Thayer, *America's Achilles' Heel: Nuclear, Biological, and Chemical Terrorism and Covert Attack* (1998)

Feldman, Shai, *Nuclear Weapons and Arms Control in the Middle East* (1996)

Feldman, Shai, and Yiftah Shapir, eds., *The Middle East Military Balance 2000–2001* (2001)

Forsberg, Randall, ed., *The Arms Production Dilemma: Contraction and Restraint in the World Combat Aircraft Industry* (1994)

Hagerty, Devin T., *The Consequences of Nuclear Proliferation: Lessons from South Asia* (1998)

Heymann, Philip B., *Terrorism and America: A Commonsense Strategy for a Democratic Society* (1998)

Kokoshin, Andrei A., *Soviet Strategic Thought, 1917–91* (1998)

Lederberg, Joshua, *Biological Weapons: Limiting the Threat* (1999)

Shields, John M., and William C. Potter, eds., *Dismantling the Cold War: U.S. and NIS Perspectives on the Nunn-Lugar Cooperative Threat Reduction Program* (1997)

Tucker, Jonathan B., ed., *Toxic Terror: Assessing Terrorist Use of Chemical and Biological Weapons* (2000)

Utgoff, Victor A., ed., *The Coming Crisis: Nuclear Proliferation, U.S. Interests, and World Order* (2000)

Williams, Cindy, ed., *Holding the Line: U.S. Defense Alternatives for the Early 21st Century* (2001)

The Robert and Renée Belfer Center for Science and International Affairs

Graham T. Allison, Director
John F. Kennedy School of Government
Harvard University
79 JFK Street, Cambridge, MA 02138
(617) 495-1400

The Belfer Center for Science and International Affairs (BCSIA) is the hub of research, teaching, and training in international security affairs, environmental and resource issues, and science and technology policy at Harvard's John F. Kennedy School of Government. The Center's mission is to provide leadership in advancing policy-relevant knowledge about the most important challenges of international security and other critical issues where science, technology, and international affairs intersect.

BCSIA's leadership begins with the recognition of science and technology as driving forces transforming international affairs. The Center integrates insights of social scientists, natural scientists, technologists, and practitioners with experience in government, diplomacy, the military, and business to address these challenges. The Center pursues its mission in four complementary research programs:

- The International Security Program (ISP) addresses the most pressing threats to U.S. national interests and international security.

- The Environment and Natural Resources Program (ENRP) is the locus of Harvard's interdisciplinary research on resource and environmental problems and policy responses.

- The Science, Technology, and Public Policy (STPP) program analyzes ways in which science and technology policy influence international security, resources, environment, and development, and such cross-cutting issues as technological innovation and information infrastructure.

- The Strengthening Democratic Institutions (SDI) project catalyzes support for three great transformations in Russia, Ukraine, and the other republics of the former Soviet Union—to sustainable democracies, free market economies, and cooperative international relations.

The heart of the Center is its resident research community of more than one hundred scholars: Harvard faculty, analysts, practitioners, and each year a new, interdisciplinary group of research fellows. BCSIA sponsors frequent seminars, workshops, and conferences, many open to the public; maintains a substantial specialized library; and publishes books, monographs, and discussion papers. The Center's International Security Program, directed by Steven E. Miller, publishes the BCSIA Studies in International Security, and sponsors and edits the quarterly journal *International Security*.

The Center is supported by an endowment established with funds from Robert and Renée Belfer, the Ford Foundation, and Harvard University, by foundation grants, by individual gifts, and by occasional government contracts.